Letters

FROM

Death Row

An Inmate's Search for Peace

Erin Taylor Daniels

ISBN 978-1-64349-908-6 (paperback)
ISBN 978-1-64349-909-3 (digital)

Christian Faith Publishing, Inc.
832 Park Avenue
Meadville, PA 16335
www.christianfaithpublishing.com

Printed in the United States of America

Many times, one needs a "push" to get started on a writing project. I am dedicating this book to my son, Gregg, who gave me the push to start by encouraging me to write the first paragraph that culminated in this book that has been on my heart to write for twenty-two years. Thanks, Gregg, for your encouragement to fulfill God's calling. Much love!

Acknowledgments

Many family members and friends have taken an interest throughout the writing of this book and have played various encouraging roles— to my husband, thanks for reading each chapter and for your patience as I spent *many* hours on the computer during the last year; to my daughter, who spent many hours as my proofreader and "critic"; to my son, who gave input on the end-of-chapter topics; to my mother, who greatly encouraged me along the process with her prayers and constant interest; to Pastor Brian Spencer, who gave his godly advice both during the time I wrote to Larry and after the book was written; and to my many friends who read my "work in progress" and were so encouraging yet honest in their opinions, Wanda, Tresa, Susan, Jim, Marlene, and Patty. Most importantly, I give great thanks to my Lord and Savior who put on my heart the burden to minister to my cousin and write his story.

If the Good News we preach is hidden behind a veil, it is hidden only from people who are perishing. Satan, who is the god of this world, has blinded the minds of those who don't believe. They are unable to see the glorious light of the Good News. They don't understand this message about the glory of Christ, who is the exact likeness of God.

—2 Corinthians 4:3–4 (NLT)

The names of family members have been changed to protect their privacy.

Prologue

November 13, 1996, began almost like any other night. Yet as 7 p.m. approached, one question spread itself over the prison complex. Would it really happen tonight? Would the execution take place? As the hands of the clock methodically crawled toward midnight and ushered in a new day, it appeared not.

Then at 12:35 a.m., the lights dimmed for a few seconds as power was sucked from them. Seconds later, the lights dimmed again. One more death-row inmate had paid for his crime by electrocution.

The inmate was my cousin, Larry Lonchar, and this is his story. His hope in dying was to finally find peace. But did he find that peace in death?

Chapter 1

Have you ever read something that you had previously read about, but this time, the words leap off the page? Have you experienced a feeling that resonates deep within your heart and mind, and you really "see" the person being written about for the first time? On February 9, 1993, as I was reading a very short article in my local newspaper, this was my experience.

Although I had not seen him in many years, the man mentioned in the article was part of my family. Suddenly, I saw him as a *real* person with *real* needs who had only a short time left to live. No longer was he just a name in an article. Larry needed to know that he could experience peace, hope, and forgiveness despite his past life of crime. But I did not know if anyone had shared with him about the only source of peace and forgiveness and knew I had to share that hope.

The words below that appeared in the February 9 edition of the *Battle Creek Enquirer* started me on what I believed to be a one-letter journey with Larry. Never did I think that I would be writing to a convicted murderer who was on death row.

Execution date scheduled for man with ties to BC

ATLANTA — The State Department of Corrections said Monday that Larry Lonchar, convicted in the 1986 slaying of three people in DeKalb County, will be executed February 24.

Lonchar was on parole for armed robbery when Charles Wayne Smith, 54; his son, Steven

Wayne Smith; and the older man's girlfriend, Margaret Sweat, 45, were killed.

Lonchar's sister, Tina Lonchar Jones of Battle Creek, appealed his death sentence, saying that her brother is mentally ill.

The U.S. 11th Circuit Court of Appeals ruled in November that Lonchar is competent enough to decide his fate.[1]

Before I share the letter I wrote, I want you to know more about the Larry Lonchar who I felt compelled to write and about the road he traveled that eventually led him to death row.

Early Background and Criminal Beginnings

Larry Grant Lonchar was born on September 3, 1951, in Battle Creek, Michigan, the third of five children. Larry said, "I was a good student, little leaguer, and newspaper boy. I never used drugs or was never drunk."

In a letter to my daughter, Michelle, he said,

> I don't just like dogs. I love them! I don't really have a favorite breed of dog. I love them all. When I was young, we always had a beagle as our pet. All boys want a dog! When I was a kid, I stopped by the dog pound a lot to see the dogs and cats. To pet them. My grandma use to live two blocks from it. I would also go fishing a lot with my brother at the river that was by her house. Another favorite activity was catching fireflies and putting them in a jar to watch them light up.

In another letter, he asked, "Do they still have the yearly city children's play? I was in the play *Pinocchio* one year. I had two parts in it. I opened the show [my line was the opening line] and also played a character part." He also had a love for bowling, "I love bowling.

I remember when I was real young that I would sometimes get my name in the paper for having the highest score in our league. I would take the bus to Spring Lake Lanes. In our league, it cost us a dollar to play our three games." "Halloween was one of my favorite times when I was a kid, going 'trick or treating' and getting big pillowcases full [of candy]. Math was my favorite subject in school. I went to church when I was real young. It was required of all of us kids by my mother. At that age, I didn't grasp what it all meant though."

Although he had a loving mother, his father was abusive to the children and her. Imagine seeing your mother being chased down the street by your father who is aiming a gun at her. What a scar that memory would forever leave imprinted on a child's mind. Gambling and alcoholism also played a part in Larry's home life as a child.

At the age of eleven after his parents divorced, he was deeply affected psychologically and began getting into trouble. He was quoted in an interview as saying, "When my family fell apart, I fell apart and began committing crimes. I started small, damaging property with a BB gun, moved to breakings and enterings, then finally to committing armed robberies. I just did things to make sure I got caught so I could be punished."[2] Perhaps you or someone you know has experienced growing up in a family split by divorce and know that life as you once knew it is forever changed.

One of his brothers described him to a reporter in the February 21, 1993, *Battle Creek Enquirer* as follows:

> He was just real smart. I thought he was going to
> be like a genius . . . He could have been a doctor
> or lawyer, but he took his smartness and went a
> different way . . . He has a sheet [of corrections]
> that is real long. They probably have some full
> file cabinets just on him.[3]

Before being incarcerated in the Calhoun County jail in 1968, he completed the tenth grade at Battle Creek Central High School. Later, Larry was transferred to a facility in upper Michigan where he obtained his GED through the Michigan prison system.

While not being diagnosed with bipolar disorder until he was in the prison system, Larry definitely showed symptoms of it growing up. One source that I read pointed out that a traumatic event, such as a divorce, could act as a trigger for the illness to start manifesting itself. According to one of his uncles, who was his caretaker when his mother was not available, Larry was very hard to deal with because he was so unpredictable. He never knew what to expect from one day to the next.

He also acted very impulsively, another symptom of being bipolar. On one occasion that a relative relayed to me, he robbed a store during the winter. While most people who commit a crime try very hard to not get caught, Larry purposely left footprints in the snow that would lead the police to him. In one letter to me, he told me that at the murder scene, he knew that he had left his glasses behind and purposely did not go back to get them. He had the desire to be caught. Why as a teen did he want to lead the police to himself? Why would anyone, especially someone living in a state with the death penalty, *want* to be identified as being at the scene of a murder? Was he seeking attention, even if it was negative attention? Did he have self-hatred? As a young man, had he become so accustomed to prison life that he wanted to be in a more controlled, predictable environment that he was "used" to? Was living in the outside world too hard? Since I never got to ask him why, these are only my guesses. Perhaps, you can think of another reason that may be plausible. Whatever the reason, it was not a normal response.

Two days after being paroled from a Michigan prison in 1985 after serving a sentence for armed robbery, he moved to the Atlanta, Georgia, area where his mother and two of his brothers lived. He never married and had no children.

Think About It: Divorce

Were you or someone close to you the victim of a divorce when growing up as Larry was at the age of eleven? You read how divorce impacted his life. Divorce in general affects the child(ren) psychologically.

While I was personally fortunate to grow up in a two-parent home, many children do not have that luxury in today's society. The divorce rate is currently near the 50 percent mark in the United States. The changes divorce brings with it are sad for the child or children involved.

"As a rule, the first reaction of children to the news about the divorce is confusion, denial, and fear, which can be followed by aggression, anger, depression, suicidal thoughts, panic attacks, etc."[4] If I were in that child's place, I would feel that my life was totally out of control.

While my immediate family stayed intact, I witnessed other families whose children experienced the psychological trauma of divorce. It tugged at my heartstrings to know that a preschool child kept staring intently out the window all evening hoping his daddy would pull in the driveway that night after he abruptly left, but he did not see his daddy for several weeks and could not understand why his daddy left him. How about young women who have no male role model or father to love? Statistics prove that they seek that missing love in the arms of a boyfriend and are very likely to be an unwed mother at a young age.

Can you think of other life struggles that might become emotional hindrances to children of divorce?

What messages do parents who divorce send to their children? I feel one of the biggest messages sent is that the marriage vow "until death do us part" does not apply to all. If things get tough in a marriage, divorce is often considered an "easy" way out. Others impacted by divorce may feel that since marriage is not always permanent, why even bother to get married? The couple who merely lives together may theorize that should they decide to split, then there are no potentially ugly divorce proceedings to go through. Are there other messages that might also be sent through divorce?

Because God is all-wise, He knew how destructive divorce would be on both the couple and the family. For this reason, Jesus reiterated God's command in Matthew 19:3–6 (NCV) when asked by the Pharisees, "Is it right for a man to divorce his wife for any reason he chooses?" Jesus answered, "Surely you have read in the

Scriptures: When God made the world, 'he made them male and female.' And God said, 'So a man will leave his father and mother and be united with his wife, and the two will become one body.' So there are not two, but one. God has joined the two together, so no one should separate them." He added in verse 9 that the only justifiable cause for divorce was sexual infidelity.

Husbands are commanded in Ephesians 5:25 (NCV) to "love your wives, as Christ loved the church and gave himself for it." In today's society, however, this type of love between a husband and wife is frequently not displayed in a marriage. Domestic violence and abuse are becoming more widely reported. According to statistics published by the National Coalition against Domestic Violence (ncadv.org), "Domestic violence is the willful intimidation, physical assault, battery, sexual assault, and/or other abusive behavior as part of a systematic pattern of power and control perpetrated by one intimate partner against another. It includes physical violence, sexual violence, threats, and emotional/psychological abuse." The NCADV also reports, "On a typical day, domestic violence hotlines nationwide receive approximately 20,800 calls." The Center for Disease Control reports that every minute twenty people are victims of domestic violence.[5] Other research indicates that women are the main targets of the violence, but violence against men is also on the rise but is less reported.

Do you think that a husband or wife that is constantly a victim of domestic violence should continue subjecting herself/himself to his/her abusive spouse who is willingly breaking God's command to "love your wives [husbands] as Christ loved the church"? Do you think such abusive, often life-threatening, behavior would be grounds for a divorce? Why or why not?

If you are currently a victim of domestic abuse or know someone who is a victim, there is help through the National Domestic Violence Hotline at 1-800-799-SAFE (7233) or www.TheHotline.org.

Chapter 2

By late 1986, Larry had become several thousand dollars in debt to a bookmaking operation.

Rather than give you my explanation of the events that led to his death sentence conviction, the actual 911 call and excerpts from his trial (Lonchar v. The State, 258 Ga. 447 (1988), 369 S.E.2d 749 45437 State of Georgia Supreme Court Record, dated July 29, 1988) will speak for themselves.

911 Call

The following was made by Susan Sweat, one of the victims on October 18, 1986:

911:	DeKalb Emergency 911.
Caller:	Police.
911:	What address?
Caller:	[. . .]
911:	What's the problem?
Caller:	Everybody's been shot.
911:	Who's been shot?
Caller:	Me— and—
911:	With a gun?
Caller:	Yes.
911:	Who did it?
Caller:	I don't know.
911:	Is that a house or an apartment?

Caller:	It's a condominium. . .
911:	Okay. Now you say everybody's been shot. I already got you help on the way, but when you say everybody's been shot, how many?
Caller:	Uh, me.
911:	Where are you shot at?
Caller:	In the living room—I've crawled to the phone.
911:	I mean what part of your body, ma'am.
Caller:	I think my stomach—they're coming back in . . . please (inaudible)
911:	Who did it? Give me a description of them!
Caller:	Why are you doing this? Please— (inaudible). Please, please, I don't even know your name. Please . . . please, Larry. I don't even know your—

The Crime

Charles Wayne Smith and his son, Steven Smith, ran a book-making operation out of a condominium in DeKalb County. Lonchar became $10,000 in debt to the operation, and on October 18, 1986, visited the condominium, accompanied by Mitchell Wells and an unidentified third accomplice. At the time they visited, four people were in the condominium. The three murder victims, Wayne Smith, Steven Smith, and Wayne's companion, Margaret Sweat, were in the living room. Richard Smith (another of Wayne Smith's sons), the aggravated assault victim, was in a bedroom. At trial Richard Smith testified that he heard a knock on the door and then saw Lonchar enter the living room. He added that Lonchar displayed a badge and identified himself as special agent Larry Lonchar. Wayne Smith and Steven Smith were then handcuffed.

Richard Smith heard four or five shots from the living room, and then Wells came to his bedroom, shot him several times and left. He pretended he was dead while the condominium was ransacked.

Shortly thereafter, afraid he would bleed to death, he picked up the extension telephone in the bedroom and heard Sweat talking to the police. Then she yelled, "They're back." Richard Smith crawled to the living room and saw a man wearing a trench coat leave the condominium.

Wayne Smith was shot in the chest, the back, and the head. Steven Smith was shot in the chest and in the head. Margaret Sweat was shot in the shoulder, stabbed in the neck 17 times, and stabbed in the chest three times. Richard Smith was shot in the back and was grazed on his head. Of the four occupants of the condominium, he was the only survivor.

Lonchar showed up at his cousin's house that evening wearing a trench coat. His hands were cut. He asked if Wells had been there earlier that day and responded to the cousin's affirmative answer by threatening to kill Wells. Lonchar complained to his cousin that he "couldn't kill the bitch," and told him he had cut her throat. His cousin drove him to Chattanooga, where he caught a plane to Texas. He was arrested at a Western Union Station in Mission, Texas, in June of 1987 when he went there to pick up money that had been wired him.

The Trial and Conviction

Lonchar's attorney informed the court that Lonchar wished to absent himself from the trial as soon as the jury was selected. The attorney stated that he had advised Lonchar against such a move, but that was Lonchar's desire nonetheless. The court adjourned to its chambers and discussed the matter with Lonchar and his attorney, outside the presence of the state's attorneys. Lonchar stated to the court that he did not have a case, that the outcome was a foregone conclusion, and that he had not been assisting his attorney anyway. He stated further,

> I just repeat the way I feel, you know. My presence is irrelevant. And like I say, I haven't been assisting [my attorney] and I am not going to

start assisting him, and I am asking, you know, like I say, I realize at times I will have to be present. I realize that and I will cooperate. But as far as, you—I have read that the law says once the jury is impaneled that I don't have to be present, you know. I don't want to cause a scene where you have to handcuff me and chain me to the seat and gag me and all that. However, I feel, you know, if that is my only alternative, then I will, I mean, that is what I am asking, you know to avoid all of this, you know. I know what is going to happen in this case and, you know, there is nothing I can do about it.

Lonchar stated that he understood his right to assist his attorney and present evidence but that he was "just being realistic . . . I have no case, Your Honor."

The court stated, "I will give him a chance to think about it. Obviously, I do want him during the *voir dire* [the questioning of prospective jurors by a judge and attorneys and selection of an impartial jury], which may take some period of time, and at that point, I will reconsider it, and I will ask him to reconsider."

After the jury was selected, the court addressed the defendant as follows:

THE COURT. Mr. Lonchar.

MR. LEIPOLD. Stand up.

THE COURT. You recall the discussion that we had yesterday morning, sir?

MR. LONCHAR. Yes, sir.

THE COURT. You will recall both the Court's request and your attorney's request that you remain in the court-room, but that I told you that that was the decision that I would probably allow you to make. I wanted you to sit through the *voir dire* process and I wanted you to have an opportunity to reconsider that issue.

I am going to allow you, if you wish, to withdraw yourself during those parts of the trial that you think is — that you want to be excused from, if you wish to do so. I want to advise you, however, that, obviously, you would not be here, first of all, to assist your attorney in responding to questions and certainly you would not be here to evaluate what it is that your attorney does in your behalf. If you want to voluntarily give up those rights then you are, in fact, giving up a very valuable right that you have, and I am sure Mr. Leipold is going to do an excellent job, do the best possible job that he can do on your behalf, there is no question about that. There is, however, no question that it is always better to have your client with you in court, both for strategic purposes and also for information purposes. Mr. Lonchar, do you understand what I am telling you?

MR. LONCHAR. Yes.

THE COURT: Now, are you telling me that you still want to be absent from certain parts of the trial?

MR. LONCHAR. Yes, sir.

THE COURT. Do you understand that there may be certain parts of the trial which I will have to direct that you be here, for identification and for certain other purposes, do you understand that?

MR. LONCHAR. Yes, sir.

THE COURT. All right, sir. I will at any time give you the opportunity to come back into Court whenever you wish to come back into Court and I will do whatever is necessary to facilitate your re-entry back into Court out of the presence of the jury. So, you can come back in whenever you'd like. Do you understand that, Mr. Lonchar?

MR. LONCHAR. Yes, sir.

Periodically throughout the trial, the court asked the defendant if he wanted to return to the courtroom for the remainder of the trial. Lonchar declined, and except for a few brief instances in which he was returned to the courtroom to be identified by a witness, the guilt-phase evidence was presented in his absence.

On June 25, 1987, Lonchar was convicted in the Superior Court of DeKalb County, Georgia, on three counts of malice murder and one count of aggravated assault. He was sentenced to death for the murders and to twenty-one years imprisonment for the aggravated assault.[6]

Postconviction Chronology of Events Leading to His Execution as Reported by the *Battle Creek Enquirer*

October 18, 1986: Murders of Charles Wayne Smith, his son Steven Smith, and Margaret Sweat in DeKalb County, Georgia.

June 25, 1987: Found guilty of the murders by the DeKalb County court in the State of Georgia.

June 29, 1987: Sentenced to die in Georgia's electric chair with the first execution date scheduled between August 10-16, 1987. The execution was stayed because of an automatic death sentence appeal to the U.S. Supreme Court.

July 1, 1987: Mitchell Ward Wells, who pleaded guilty to his part in the murders, was sentenced to two life sentences plus 20 years.

August 29, 1988: Execution is stayed by the U.S. Supreme Court because more time is needed for review.

March 21, 1990: Scheduled to die at Georgia Diagnostic and Classification Center in Jackson, Georgia. But against his wishes, his Decatur, Georgia, lawyer, Mike Mears, filed an appeal. Mears said his client's desire to die indicated insanity. Under Georgia law, an insane person cannot be executed.

May 10, 1990: Scheduled to die May 18 but his execution was stayed again as his sister of Battle Creek pleads for his life. Again Lonchar shows no objection to being electrocuted. His sister also claims he is insane.

July 3, 1990: Newest execution date is stayed by the Georgia Supreme Court because Mears filed a petition with the U.S. Supreme Court claiming Lonchar is not mentally competent to be executed.

February 9, 1993: Scheduled to be executed on February 24, 1993, at the Georgia Diagnostic and Classification Center in Jackson, Georgia, after the U.S. Eleventh Circuit Court of Appeals ruled in November that he is competent enough to decide his fate.[7]

Although I had seen the many articles about his past execution dates that were scheduled and then appealed, I knew my time for action had come. Join me to get a peek inside Larry's psyche through the letters that we exchanged between February 1993 and October 1996.

Think About It: All Have a Death Sentence

Imagine hearing the judge's verdict pronouncing the death penalty for you, and then *bam!*—his gavel slams finalizing your sentence and destiny. What thoughts would be running through your mind?

For someone who had committed a heinous crime, you may feel that such a verdict is certainly justified. You may also be thinking that the person who took a life should lose his/her life in return as punishment for the crime. In 2017, there were 2,817 death-row inmates awaiting their date with death for their crimes.[8]

Would you be surprised, however, to learn that you have been living with the death sentence hanging over your head since the moment you were born? Who is your judge? God. But you may say, "I have done nothing to deserve such a sentence, and certainly, I have never killed anyone." When Adam and Eve sinned against

23

God in the Garden of Eden, the death sentence was passed to every human. Death became a part of life for your physical body. No one is immune—no matter what one's religious beliefs may be. That death penalty may be cancer, a debilitating disease, a tragic accident, or perhaps just old age. You may not know the exact date like a death-row inmate does, but there is an unknown date just the same. Physical death is a certainty.

What happens after your physical death, however, you *are* given a chance to determine. Will your death result in peace and happiness? Or will you condemn yourself to a future that is even worse than living a life on death row? God has provided a way for you to live in peace and happiness that could very well be eluding you in this life as it eluded Larry. As you follow Larry on his death-row journey, you will learn how this peace and happiness can be possible.

Chapter 3

February 11, 1993

Larry,

I do not know if you remember me. I am your cousin. Your mother and my father Buddy are cousins. Growing up, we did not have a chance to really get to know one another except by sight at family reunions.

After reading a recent article in the *Battle Creek Enquirer* and learning that the date for your execution has been set for February 24, I called your aunt to get your address. Since we never had an opportunity to talk about spiritual matters, I do not know if you are really prepared to die. I could not let you die without sharing Christ with you and the difference a relationship with Him can make in your life. You may already know what I am going to share since your Grandma Emma is a Christian. However, I do not want to take a chance that you have never heard about a peace that only Christ can give you. Why? Because I care about you.

In our society today, people tend to be classified based on the good or bad things done in their lives. The consensus seems to be that our actions determine our final destination after life. A murderer, many believe, definitely deserves to die and go to hell. That, however, is human thinking.

Almost 2,000 years ago, Jesus Christ came to earth as a baby to challenge many human beliefs. He looked at people much differently. He could see inside people and know their pasts without judging them by human standards. What He saw was their deepest needs, and His mission was to meet those needs. Some needed healing. Some needed hope. Others needed to be loved. All people, however, shared one need—forgiveness. That is what Jesus came to earth to provide for all who will believe in Him.

In case you have never read the Bible or may have read it but forgotten what you read, I want to share with you the love that Jesus has for you. Would you do me a favor? Please read all the enclosed booklet *Would You Like to Know God Personally.*[9] Near the end is a sample prayer that you can say to invite Him to be part of your life. If you have never said this prayer, then I am hoping you will.

Larry, as I am mailing this letter, I am praying that when you die on February 24, you will know Jesus as your personal Savior. I want to get to see you again when I get to heaven since we will not have that opportunity on earth. I may never get a reply from you to know your spiritual condition by February 24, but I will be constantly in prayer for you.

Erin

*****

February 21, 1993
Dear Erin,

Thank you for your surprise letter. It was very thoughtful of you!

I'm sorry but I cannot remember you. If I saw your face, I'm sure I would. I asked my mother today about you. She told me more about you. Could you send me a picture of you when you were younger? I am just trying to remember you.

No, I am not a Christian. I wish I was. I envy your faith. I've read the Bible a few times recently (the past few years). And when they strap me in the chair, I'll be praying.

Well, my cousin, I'll let you go. I'm sorry this is so short but I'm not in a "writing mood." I thank you so much for thinking of me and praying for me!

I hope you and the Bible are right that there will be another life after death! Sure hope we meet again!

Love,
Larry

*****

March 20, 1993
Larry,

I am glad to be able to write to you again. It was extremely nice to get another letter since I did not expect to hear from you again.

When I read that you are not a Christian, I began earnestly praying that you would think about all of the things I shared with you and would make the decision to accept Christ's offer of forgiveness before 7 p.m. on February 24. As I was praying that evening for you, my mom called a little before seven and said that your execution had been delayed for at least twenty-four hours so that an appeal could be filed. Your Aunt June called to let her know. I was so relieved and prayed the appeal would be granted because I want to have more time to get to know you and to answer questions that may be keeping you from becoming a Christian. If you had died without a personal relationship with Christ, you would now be so much worse off than being on death row.

The next day, I read in the paper some details of that evening and learned a little of what you went through to be prepared—having your leg and head shaved. I can only wonder what must have been going through your mind. Then, you also were denied to talk with your attorneys face to face. That must have been extremely frustrating.

I cannot even begin to imagine what you, your father, and brothers experienced during their visit with you earlier in the day. How does one say a final goodbye to family? The article said that you had a phone call with your sister. Did you get to talk to your mother? I also read that your attorney said that you really wanted to go through with it but that one of your brothers could not deal

27

with it and was threatening to kill himself. What an emotional roller coaster you must have been on before requesting to appeal your case!

You asked that I send along a younger picture so that you could try to place me. I looked through my pictures and decided to send one of me in the tenth grade (just a few years ago!). Of course, I've "matured" some, now wear glasses, and have a slightly different hairstyle.

I did not share with you in my last letter about my family. I have been married to my husband Dave for twenty-one years. Dave works in the office at the Union Pump Company, and I am an instructor in the Business Department at Kellogg Community College. We have two children, Gregg and Michelle. Gregg is nineteen, graduated from high school in June 1992, and is currently a student at KCC. Michelle is fourteen and in the eighth grade at Pennfield Middle School. My parents, who I am sure you probably remember, still live in Battle Creek and are retired. Dad has been retired for several years since he has had some heart attacks and strokes.

My hope is that you will write to me again. I want to know how you are doing and want to be an encouragement to you in any way that I can. Michelle asked me to tell you that she is also praying for you.

Love,
Erin

*****

April 11, 1993
Dear Erin,

I'm in bad shape mentally. I was looking so forward to finally being free and at peace. But I've informed them all I'll have to do it myself now. I'll try to live as long as I can for them, but there is no doubt I'll end my pain and suffering myself sooner or later.

The psychiatrists are trying to get me to take an anti-depression medication, but I still refuse. I don't like taking drugs (medication).

I'd wrote sooner but cause of my 'deep depression' I don't feel like writing letters or doing anything.

Enclosed is a copy of a letter I wrote soon after the 24th and the articles I thought you would be interested in reading. Also, the treatment by the chaplains. Their actions and others by so-called Christians can make me say one thing. I'm a lot of things but at least I'm not a hypocrite. There are a couple of inmates around me who consider themselves Christians, but I don't. There's more to being a Christian than just reading the Bible and praying. It also consists of acting (being) like a Christian—and they don't. They are hypocrites too.

I envy your faith. I wish we wasn't so far away so you could visit me. I'd like to discuss why I can't ever be a Christian. But the bottom line is religion is based on faith (believing) not on facts. I'm sorry if I offended you, but I'm just being honest.

Enclosed is your picture back. I definitely remember you! It has been many, many years but there is no doubt I remember your face. Thanks for sending it.

I enjoyed learning about your husband and children. I know you have to be proud of them. What is your son studying in college? Thank your daughter for praying for me. Sounds like you have a good life.

Do you have any pets? If so and you have cable, watch a show on the Family Channel called "That's My Dog." It's a game show with family pets (dogs) that are the contestants. I sure do enjoy it. I love dogs.

My mother lost the man she was living with for about ten years on 2-12-93. He was a good man. He took good care of her. Now she is alone, which sure worries me.

I'm tired so I'll close. Again, thank you for your prayers and letters! Take care!

Larry

*****

The following is the letter Larry enclosed. Copies were made using carbon paper so that it could be sent to several people.

Dear

Yes, I'm sorry to say, it's me. I just can't believe I'm still alive. I'm so tired of being incarcerated (27 years of my life). I was looking forward to being free and at peace finally.

I'm very depressed that I'm still alive. They have me on "suicide watch" now. I'd wrote sooner but I just couldn't. Very depressed aren't even the right words to describe how low I've been.

Let me explain why I changed my decision. On my last day, my visiting was over at 3 p.m. I was with my dad and oldest brother. It was the first time I had ever heard my dad say that he loved me. He was on the floor crying. He couldn't even stand up, he was so upset. I've never seen my dad cry in my life. They had to carry him out of the visiting room. My oldest brother wouldn't let go of me. He was crying and holding on to me. Even the guard that was in the visiting room left crying.

I was then taken to the medical center and given another physical, which was stupid as I was given a physical the day before when I was put on "deathwatch." (Deathwatch consists of being put in an isolation cell. Two guards never take their eyes off me. My every little movement is recorded by the guards in a log book.)

I was then handcuffed and chained (legs). Put in a van and driven to the "Death House." I walked right by the "chair." I was placed in the holding cell next to the "chair." I called my sister and brother (couldn't get ahold of the brother who I was informed later by the lawyer was going to kill himself if I died). They were very painful calls, saying good-bye. A lot of crying on both ends.

I then had my head and right leg shaved. They had to do my head three or four times before they were satisfied. Speaking of that, there was two chaplains back there in the "Death House" too, with many guards. Anyways, one chaplain told the guard who was shaving my head for the 3rd or 4th time, "Well, what is this the 3rd or 4th time? Did you get it right this time?" And he laughed. Isn't that amazing? A minister who was suppose to be back there to comfort me, laughing while they are preparing me to die. He never did say one word to me the whole over two hours I was in the "Death House." The other chaplain was making the phone calls for me.

Anyways, during the shaving, Mr. Marable, the man who was in charge of the execution, asked me if I had a final statement. I said I did. When he refused to let me to give it in my cell, I refused to give one.

I then called my reporter friend to give it to her. I was starting to reconsider my decision for the first time on dying. As I couldn't get the picture of my dad and brother crying out of my mind. Then I was upset cause I had just said good-bye to my sister and brother.

After the call to my reporter friend, I was informed that I had a lawyer call (6:15 p.m.). They wouldn't let the lawyer in to see me. Which the lawyer has already filed a federal lawsuit over it as the Dept. of Correction Director had given him permission to be with me in case I changed my mind about dying. But when the lawyer arrived at the prison, the warden refused him permission to be with me but set up the phone call at 6:15 p.m. The warden informed the lawyer when the lawyer told him the Director (warden's boss) had given him permission, "This is my prison. I run it."

The lawyer informed me on the phone at 6:15 p.m. that my youngest brother said if I die he was going to kill himself, as he felt responsible for me being where I am. So, I told the lawyer to give me a few minutes to think of what I'm going to do.

I then asked the chaplain (who was making the phone calls) if I could talk to him for a few minutes. He said, "Sure." I asked if he could come in my cell so we could have some privacy as there were many guards outside of my cell, a small area. Mr. Marable heard my request and said the chaplain couldn't come in my cell. I told him, "All I want is a couple minutes in privacy with the chaplain." He said, "Talk to him through the bars."

The phone then rang and Mr. Marable picked it up. When he hung up, he came to my cell and said, "Your lawyer said you are thinking about changing your decision. I got to know now if you are or not." I said, "That's why I want a few minutes with the chaplain." He said again pounding his fingers on my cell door, "I got to know now, yes or no." His tone of voice and attitude (we still had a half-hour before the execution) pissed me off. It was the "straw that broke the camel's back" that made me stop the execution. So, I informed him I was stopping the execution.

Did I ask for much? That's why the chaplains are back there for.

I was so upset that I didn't die when they transferred me back to the "deathwatch" isolation cell. They sent a psychiatrist to talk to me. He's the one who has placed me on "suicide watch." I'm now back on "Death Row" but every 15 minutes a guard looks into my cell and records what I am doing. I wrote the psychiatrist to take me off the "suicide watch" cause it's senseless. I informed him if and when I decide to kill myself being on "suicide watch" isn't going to prevent it as I'll just cut my wrist and get under my blanket. The guard when he looks in on me will just think I went to bed.

I told the psychiatrist that night, "I walked right by the 'chair' and even when they shaved my head and leg I wasn't scared. It just wasn't normal for me not being scared to die." The psychiatrist said it was normal. He said how some terminal ill people are the same. They have accepted the fact that they were dying. That I also had accepted it and was looking forward to it. So that's why I wasn't scared the doctor told me.

I got to start all over. I gave away everything: my watch, stamps, junk food, writing material, and other stuff. Pitiful. Don't have the money to replace the stuff either.

Plus the hot weather will soon be here. You just wouldn't believe how bad it is in here—90s and 100s in here day and night. The steel and cement bakes in the sun all day so at night they are still radiating heat. So hot I don't sleep or feel like doing anything.

My dad and brother visited me Sat (27th). My mother visited me Sunday (28th). They were all very happy to see me alive. My dad flew back to Michigan after our visit. My brother is staying another week with my mother so she can visit me this coming Saturday.

Why does my family and friends want me to continue to suffer, suffer, and suffer? I hurt every morning when I open my eyes. I hurt so much I just don't know how much more I can endure.

Oh, yeah. On my last day (24th), the warden came to the visiting room and asked me if I'd visit with my judge (the judge who presided over my trial and who signed the "Execution Order"). I agreed. The judge and his wife (she's a minister) are very religious people. He came and visited me for about ½ hour. I told him I hold no animosity toward him. He thanked me for that. He hugged me at the end of our visit and kept his arm around me all the way to the door.

Think About It: Depression

Larry spoke about being in "bad shape mentally" several times in his letters. This was his way of expressing that he was depressed. Would you have similar feelings had you been in his shoes?

Depression has been defined as a "mood disorder that can be accompanied by feelings of severe despondency and dejection, sadness, hopelessness, helplessness, and worthlessness (to name a few). Contributing to it can be a combination of genetic, biochemical, environmental, and psychological factors."[10]

Many stressful life events can act as triggers for depression. Have you experienced the death of a loved one—a parent, spouse, or child? The loss of a job? A debilitating illness? A divorce or other meaningful relationship that ended? Have you ever been physically, sexually, or emotionally abused? Have you lost your freedom? While not everyone who faces these stresses develops a mood disorder—in fact, most do not—stress plays an important role in depression.

I personally went through a time of depression after my father died in 1994. It took me a while to realize why I could cry so easily, could not sleep well at night, and had little patience with others. A friend and colleague noticed the changes in me and suggested that I think about getting some professional help. When I was on a trip and had thoughts that I would not care in the least if the plane crashed since I would no longer have to experience the emotional pain I was having, I knew the time to seek counseling had come. Never would I have considered suicide, but the joy of living was gone.

Through counseling, I learned that the death of my dad was just a trigger to underlying issues that had been simmering under the surface for many years. Anger was one of my major issues. If anyone had told me I was an angry person, I would have laughed in his/her face. Me? An angry person? I get along with everyone—Miss Compliant and Miss People Pleaser. So when my counselor told me I had anger issues, I was shocked. After many sessions, I discovered that most of my anger involved control issues and the loss of personal freedom in several areas of my life. My personality lent itself to allowing myself to be controlled and not setting boundaries with the important people in my life. Treatment also included taking an antidepressant to replenish the serotonin in my brain so that I was in a better position mentally to deal with the issues facing me.

According to the National Institute of Mental Health, depression affects more than 16.1 million American adults, or about 6.7 percent of the U.S. population age eighteen and older in a given year. Youth depression is also on the rise.[11] What I find sad is that two-thirds of these people are not diagnosed and receive no treatment.[12] Do you (or someone you love) currently fall into this two-thirds who are depressed and currently untreated? Not sure? Ask yourself some of the questions below.

Do I get extremely irritable over minor things? Do I cry easily without knowing why? Do I have anger management issues? Have I lost interest in my favorite activities? Do I have a lot of anxiety and restlessness? Have I ever contemplated suicide? All of these are the emotional symptoms of depression.

Depressed people also exhibit some of the following physical symptoms (which are by no means a complete list): insomnia or sleeping too much, debilitating fatigue, increased or decreased appetite, weight gain or weight loss, and difficulty concentrating or making decisions.

Could you relate to four or more of these symptoms? If so, you could be depressed and may need to seek treatment by a professional.

Left untreated, depression can lead to thoughts of suicide, which Larry contemplated, or suicide. Suicide is the second leading cause of death for fifteen- to forty-four-year-olds in the United States. Each 12.6 minutes, there is one death by suicide. Add to that figure the 250,000 who become suicide survivors each year.[13] Depression is serious! If you or someone you know is depressed, be smart and seek help. Not sure where to start? The National Suicide Prevention Hotline is available twenty-four hours a day by calling 1-800-273-8255.

Chapter 4

April 7, 1993

Dear Larry

Thanks for writing back to me and sending the enclosures with your letter. After reading everything, I can better understand how you are feeling, such as your disgust at the chaplain who laughed. It certainly was not the appropriate thing for him to do. You were absolutely right in your thinking about what his duty was supposed to be. I agree that he was acting like a hypocrite. I guess any profession is open to having hypocrites among its number. It's sad to have to say, but there are many so-called pastors and Christians who fall into that category. They really paint a bad picture for anyone who is watching to see how "Christians" act.

The Bible refers to these people as false prophets and deceivers. Not everyone who professes to be a Christian—or even a pastor or chaplain—has had a true, life-changing encounter with Christ. They themselves have been deceived by Satan whose goal is to use them to turn non-Christians off to Christianity so that he can have them instead. Larry, please don't let Satan deceive you through the chaplain. Please don't judge all Christians based on what you saw in him. There are many Christians who act totally different and are sincere. Perhaps, you've just not had an opportunity to meet them. The real test of authenticity of a Christian is whether or not he/she has truly taken that step of faith and accepted Christ's love and forgiveness. Such a person will act much differently than the chaplain you had the unfortunate experience to encounter.

I'm glad that you could remember me—even though it has been many years. It always helps to be able to visualize who you are writing to.

I too wish I lived closer so I could visit with you. I would very much like to know why you feel you can't ever be a Christian. Would it be something that you feel you could write about in more depth to me? If it's because of the crimes you have committed, Christ is willing to forgive any crime.

You may feel that murder is the worst crime and that a murderer does not deserve to be forgiven. Christ does not think so. Some of the men who turned out to be God's greatest leaders were murderers—Saul (later renamed Paul) and King David are two that come to mind. 1 Timothy 2:4–6 says, "For he longs for all to be saved and to understand this truth: That God is on one side and all the people on the other side, and Christ Jesus, himself man, is between them to bring them together, by giving his life for all mankind. This is the message that at the proper time God gave to the world" (The Living Bible) . These verses put no conditions on whether only people who *deserve* to be saved can be saved—they said *all*. That *all* includes you, Larry.

Two or three weeks ago, I called the International Prison Ministry and asked them to send you a couple of books that were written by former prisoners that tell how their lives were changed after they became Christians while in prison. I hope you will read them. The head of the ministry is Chaplain Ray. I know that you have a bad feeling about chaplains right now, but all that I have learned about Chaplain Ray leads me to believe he is a genuine Christian who has a love and concern for prisoners. After you read the books, would you share with me your reaction? The lady I talked with said that he may also be able to talk with you personally—but you would have to request it and have arrangements made through the prison. If you are interested, I can give you his name, address, and phone number.

I can understand concern over your mother being alone since her friend died. I would feel exactly the same way if one of my parents was alone. Not being able to check in on her must make it even more of a concern. Seeing our parents hurting is hard. Over the last three years, my dad has had four strokes. Fortunately, they were all relatively light ones. He has, however, suffered short-term memory loss and has some difficulty using his hands and walking. Seeing him in his present physical condition breaks my heart.

My dad mentioned the other day that he remembered last talking with you at your Aunt June's house during a family reunion. It may have been in honor of her fiftieth wedding anniversary. Do you remember it? He said that he had enjoyed talking with you. From what I recall, it was a two-day celebration. I was there for one of the days but am not sure if it was the same day you were there.

You asked what my son is studying in college. He is planning to get a bachelor's degree in business administration. The classes that he is taking at KCC should all transfer to Western Michigan University. His goal is to someday own his own business. Right now, he's counting the days until May 7 when he'll be out for summer break.

When I read your question about having pets and saw that you liked dogs, it made me smile. Michelle truly loves dogs! She said that she wants to write you about this topic. She is in the band and track. She tells me, though, that her clarinet is an antique since she's using the same clarinet that I played in the band! She had her first track meet last Thursday. Her best events are the sprints.

Take care. Please think about what I've written and write me again. I'll be continuing to pray for you.

Erin

*****

April 16, 1993

Dear Erin,

I am in bad shape mentally. My lawyers are afraid I'm going to commit suicide. So they've been writing letters to the warden expressing their fears. Because of those letters, each week when the psychologist and psychiatrist come in, I have to talk with them. I finally agreed to take some anti-depressant medication. Last week the psychiatrist doubled the dosage. It's not helping as it doesn't change the main reason why I'm so depressed—my wasted life. I didn't realize how much I missed of life things and how precious life is until it was too late. It sure hurts! I can also never forgive myself.

My oldest brother flew down Monday. He's suppose to visit me tomorrow and bring Mom. The lawyers paid for his airline ticket. Sure am looking forward to their visit. My sister is suppose to come down and visit my mother and me in late May. I've decided she will be taking me home. After her visit on Saturday, I plan to commit suicide on Sunday night. I'm so tired of suffering. I wasted this life. Who knows, maybe in death I can get another chance (reincarnation).

Thanks for trying to encourage me in your last letter. Y'alls actions proves to me that you all are what I call *real* Christians cause it doesn't matter what I am y'all have Christian love for me. Tell me why the majority of so-called Christians don't?

I have to stop writing now since I am very tired. Take care.

Love,
Larry

*****

April 21, 1993
Dear Larry,

Your last letter definitely opened my eyes to how depressed you are! Please, however, do not take your life as you are planning to do. It will not solve your issues of suffering and a wasted life like you think it will. You may feel there is absolutely no hope, but that feeling is common with depression.

Spending a majority of your life in prison could easily lead to feelings of depression and the belief that you wasted your life. My guess is that there are many people who *have* their physical freedom who feel just like you. These people may seem to have everything going for them—wealth, good looks, good jobs, and family—but they feel similar to you. Their life has no real purpose and has been wasted. They are in an emotional prison—one that does not have steel bars but is a prison just the same. Many of these people also feel as you do that the only way out is to take their lives. I truly think that it is Satan who is actively at work making them feel as they do. He does his best work through depression.

Larry, your life up to this point may have been wasted. But that does not mean that the rest of your life has to be. Death through reincarnation is not the answer. (There's no proof that reincarnation is a possibility.) Only Christ can give meaning and a new purpose to your life right now if you will let Him. What I am going to say next may sound ridiculous to you at this point. However, if you do come to the point that you will surrender your life to Christ, you will see that what I say is true. When people give their lives to Christ and accept the forgiveness for sin He offers, they become a new person on the inside. 2 Corinthians 5:17 says, "When someone becomes a Christian, he becomes a brand new person inside. He is not the same anymore. A new life has begun!" (The Living Bible). You will think differently and see things in a different light with Christ's help.

Even though Christ may not change your circumstances of being in prison, He can help you tolerate it and use you to work for Him in Jackson, Georgia. How? Only Christ knows the answer to that question and would help you see how after you surrender your life to Him. He can work in ways that you may think are impossible. Perhaps, He could give you a ministry of some kind with other prisoners. Does that sound impossible? Jesus is into doing the impossible. Mark 10:27 states this, "Jesus looked at them and said, 'For people this is impossible, but for God all things are possible'" (NCV).

Your brother told a reporter in February that you were a very smart person and could have done anything you would have wanted to do. However, your intelligence was directed in the wrong direction. The impression I get is that you are regretful and are searching for something to fill the void in your life. You seem to be open to the possibility of Christianity since you have said several times that you wish you could be a Christian. I think that all that is standing in your way are a few questions on issues that need to be addressed. I'm praying that Christ will work in your heart and mind to help you believe. He can make a real difference, Larry. My relationship with Him is what gives my life meaning and focus. If I did not have Christ to lean on, I know that I would probably be feeling as hopeless as you feel.

I want you to know that I am not someone who will give up on you. I can be very persistent! Hopefully, you will see my persistence as love for you. Again, please think about what I have written. I will write again soon.

Love,
Erin

*****

April 26, 1993
Dear Larry,

It's me again. I told you that I am persistent! I cannot get your last letter and the despondency you expressed out of my mind. The Lord has laid on my heart some other thoughts to share with you.

One of the statements that you have made a couple of times in your letters was that if you had gone through with the execution, you would now be at rest and peace. While such a statement would make death look attractive, it is a false statement for anyone who is not a Christian. As the *Would You Like to Know God Personally* booklet I sent mentioned, the Bible talks about both heaven and hell being real places. Below are some Scripture verses that tell what each is like.

The Existence of Heaven

> But Stephen was full of the Holy Spirit. He looked up to heaven and saw the glory of God and Jesus standing at God's right side. He said, "Look! I see heaven open and the Son of Man standing at God's right side." (Acts 7:55–56 NCV)

(In this verse, Stephen spoke these words when he was near death from being stoned by people who resented him talking about Christ.)

And the angel carried me away by the Spirit to a very large and high mountain. He showed me the holy city, Jerusalem, coming down out of heaven from God. It was shining with the glory of God and was bright like a very expensive jewel, like a jasper, clear as crystal. The city had a great high wall with twelve gates with twelve angels at the gates, and on each gate was written the name of one of the twelve tribes of Israel. The twelve gates were twelve pearls, each gate having been made from a single pearl. And the street of the city was made of pure gold as clear as glass. I did not see a temple in the city, because the Lord God Almighty and the Lamb are the city's temple. The city does not need the sun or the moon to shine on it, because the glory of God is its light, and the Lamb is the city's lamp. By its light the people of the world will walk, and the kings of the earth will bring their glory into it. The city's gates will never be shut on any day, because there is no night there. (Revelation 21:10–11 and 21–25 NCV)

(In these verses, John is telling about a glimpse God permitted him to have of heaven so that he could write about it.)

He will wipe away every tear from their eyes, and there will be no more death, sadness, crying, or pain, because all the old ways are gone. (Revelation 21:4 NCV)

(In this verse, John is talking about heaven.)

Jesus said to him, "I tell you the truth, today you will be with me in paradise." (Luke 23:43 NCV)

(Christ referred to heaven as paradise when he was talking to one of the men who was crucified next to him. His words indicate that the man would immediately be with him in heaven when he died.)

Heaven will seem like paradise to us compared to the hard life we experience here on earth. Hell, however, will be much worse than anything we have experienced during our life.

The Existence of Hell

> In the place of the dead, he was in much pain. The rich man saw Abraham far away with Lazarus at his side. He called, "Father Abraham, have mercy on me! Send Lazarus to dip his finger in water and cool my tongue, because I am suffering in this fire!" (Luke 16:23–24 NCV)

(These are Jesus's words.)

> That one also will drink the wine of God's anger, which is prepared with all its strength in the cup of his anger. And that person will be put in pain with burning sulfur before the holy angels and the Lamb. And the smoke from their burning pain will rise forever and ever. There will be no rest, day or night, for those who worship the beast and his idol or who get the mark of his name. (Revelation 14:10–11 NCV)

(John is describing what life after death in hell will be like for those who choose the beast [Satan] instead of Jesus.)

Based on what the Bible says, there will be no rest or peace for those who have not asked for Christ's forgiveness for their sins. The only ones who experience rest and peace after death will be Christians.

Larry, you also commented that religion is based on faith (believing) not on facts. You are right—to a certain extent—in that regard also. We do have to believe or have faith. But we have to base our faith in a belief of the facts stated in the Bible—facts about Christ's unconditional love for us, His death, His resurrection, the existence of a heaven and hell, the ability of Christ to forgive our sins, and many other promises Christ gave us in the Bible. Hebrews 11:1 says this about faith, "What is faith? It is the confident assurance that something we want is going to happen. It is the certainty that what we hope for is waiting for us, even though we cannot see it up ahead" (The Living Bible). Unfortunately, we did not have the opportunity to see Christ when He lived on earth as did His counterparts mentioned by name in the Bible; and we also can't see heaven with our eyes. However, we have to believe that what Christ said is true—about loving us and about heaven and hell. That is where our faith comes in.

Some ask these two questions, "How does one know there is an everlasting life after death?" "How do we know for sure that we don't just die and that's it?" We don't know absolutely for sure. However, our faith in the Word of God helps us believe there is. I would respond to those who are skeptical of a life after death that I would certainly not want to take a chance that there isn't anything after death only to find out when it is too late that there is a hell.

I am not trying to preach, but I have such a heavy burden to share these things with you knowing that you are contemplating suicide. It will not be the easy way out that you are thinking it is. If you feel you have hit rock bottom and nothing could possibly be worse than the life you now have, please think again! Hell would be much, much worse—and would be forever!

Well, I should close so I don't wear out my welcome! There isn't a day that goes by that you're not thought about or prayed for. Please think about what I've written and let God have a chance to work in your life. He loves you and counts you worthy to be His son.

I'd like to send you a "goodie" box if you would like one. Just let me know what types of "goodies" you like or are allowed to have.

If there are any special mailing instructions, let me know that also. I will be looking forward to hearing from you again.

Erin

*****

May 1, 1993
Dear Larry,

I haven't heard from you since my last two letters and hope I get another letter soon. I am concerned about you since you said you are contemplating suicide.

I know that I have shared a lot of information with you in my last few letters. Please always feel free to ask me any questions that you might have about what I have written. I welcome your questions since that is the only way I have of knowing what is on your mind and am not easily offended. Your questions will be good for me. I want you to feel that you can be open and honest.

Take care. I'll be continuing to pray for you as I wait for your next letter.

Erin

*****

May 9, 1993
Dear Erin,

I am sorry that I have not written in such a long time. I have been depressed and not felt like writing.

You asked why I feel I can never be a Christian. I'd really like to be, but like I told you before, religion is based on faith rather than on facts. For example, let's take Adam and Eve and the great flood. The Bible states mankind was created by God. But where is the proof?

I do know I can go to a museum and see proof of evolution. Scientists can prove, for example, how glaciers went across Michigan millions of years ago but there is no proof earth was ever destroyed by a flood.

I've asked many pastors the same thing. I've had some inform me that these are just parables. But then I've had others state the Bible is true, we just have to believe these things happened.

Like I stated before I wish I could become a Christian but I just can't believe there is a God cause I don't see any proof of one. If I could see just one actual miracle, I might be convinced there is a God. Please don't be upset with me. I'm just being honest with you. I'm not going to be a hypocrite.

I'm sure you remembered years ago how some people went to Turkey as they think Noah's Ark is in the mountains. If they would've found it, to me that would've been proof. So, all I can say to you is keep praying for me.

My oldest brother did visit me yesterday but Mom didn't since she did not feel good. She said she will be down this coming weekend. I called her this morning, as today was Mother's Day. I hope you had a good Mother's Day!

Thank you for your offer to send me a "goodie" box but we aren't allowed to receive one except during the month of December.

Enclosed is a book marker for your Bible. Hope you like it. These guys here crochet some beautiful things. Out of the string the cross is made out of, they make doilies, table cloths, table center pieces, just to name a few. Oh, yeah, I saw a guy make "The Last Supper" picture out of it too. Boy was it beautiful! Out of yarn they crochet blouses, baby blankets, house slippers, dolls, hats, scarfs, and afghans to name some. Wish I could do it as it passes time for them plus it helps support (money) themselves.

Thank you for sharing your children with me. I know you have to be proud of them.

Yes, I remember going to the reunion your dad mentioned. I think it was for my aunt and uncle's 50th wedding anniversary. Wish I could remember talking to your dad. I did talk to a lot of people there. We were such a close family (relatives) when I was young. Sure hope your dad is better. It was sad to read he's had four strokes.

Well, I'll close for now. Thank you again for caring, prayers, and writing! It means a lot to me!

Love,
Larry

*****

May 14, 1993
Dear Larry,

First of all, thank you for your wishes for a nice Mother's Day. I had a very enjoyable day with my family. We went to church and then ate dinner out. I also got to spend some time with my mom.

Thank you also for the beautiful cross bookmark! You could not have chosen a better color as red is my favorite color. Each time I use it, I will think of you!

Much thought has been given to how to respond to the questions you raised in your recent letter. I know that until you get satisfactory answers to them, you will not be able to accept Christianity. Many other people get hung up in exactly the same way.

First, I would like to respond to your question as to why some "men of God" would say that the accounts of Adam and Eve and the flood are merely parables and are not true. To answer that question, I would have to go back to a comment I made in another letter about there being men who call themselves pastors (such as the chaplain who so upset you) who are pastors in name only. They have not really had a true salvation experience. Their faith or religion is merely in their head but has never reached down to the depths of their heart (soul). Matthew 7:15 cautions us, "Watch out for false prophets. They come to you in sheep's clothing, but inwardly they are ferocious wolves" (NIV). They are hypocrites and will fool many people and keep people from believing in Christ. They will have to answer to Christ at the Great White Throne Judgment. The sad thing is that some of them do not realize their doctrine is false. Why? Because Satan has blinded them to the truth—just as he's trying to do to you. I'm praying that he'll not have the victory in your life though. I need another brother in Christ. I would be proud to have you fill that role.

You said that you needed just one miracle to convince you. It would be great to see a miracle such as a blind person being made to see, someone being raised from the dead, or Christ walking on the water. God doesn't provide those spectacular miracles for people today, but He does provide miracles for us. We just don't realize what they are when we see them.

The miracle of birth and life itself are the most wonderful miracles of all. I don't know if you've ever witnessed a birth, but it is an experience that lets you know there is a God. When you consider how a sperm and an egg can unite and then divide into the millions of cells that form a baby, much more than chance is at work—it's only by the hand of God that a perfectly formed human baby can be the end product nine months later. And that baby has organs and a body that work together in perfect harmony to allow life itself to be sustained normally for more than sixty or seventy years.

The very fact that we're alive is a miracle too. God provided the exact atmosphere we need to live and a home (the earth) that provides for our needs. The fact that we start breathing on our own after birth is also a miracle. When both of my children were born, it was a confirmation to me that there is a God who still performs miracles! However, man does not view it as a miracle because it seems so commonplace. However, that does not make it any less of a miracle. You, Larry, are also a miracle.

There's nothing that I can do to convince you of these things that prove an existence of a loving God—except pray that God will make Himself real to you and will lift the blinders from your spiritual eyes that Satan is so strongly fighting to keep in place.

I am enclosing a few pamphlets that were written by scientists that discuss both evolution and creation. Please try to read them with an open mind and weigh the merits of each position.

I will close for now. However, please think about the thoughts I have shared with you. Feel free to ask any further questions you have. Michelle asked me to tell you that she is continuing to pray for you.

Love,
Erin

*****

May 16, 1993
Dear Erin,

By the time you receive this, as you know, I'm dead. I'm just tired of suffering. It's worn me out the past 28 years of it. My future (the rest of my life incarcerated) would consist of just more suffering. I wasted my life. I didn't appreciate how precious and short life is until too late. Plus I just never could forgive myself for the pain I caused my family and other people.

I'm not much of a religious person but before I die I'll be praying God forgives me. Also, when you receive this, please say a prayer for me.

I used carbon paper for the above cause of all the letters I have to write.

Mom visited me yesterday. I can't put into words how painful it was saying goodbye. We both cried a lot. My oldest brother visited me today. He just doesn't believe I'm going to do it. What I think is that he just don't want to believe it.

I wish we could've met more recently in my life. But thank you for caring (prayers and letters). It meant a lot to me. Take care of yourself. Goodbye, my friend.

Love,
Larry Lonchar

Think About It: Wasted Life

Have you ever felt like that your life has been wasted—that you are or were capable of doing so much more with it than you have done?

Larry felt that his life had been wasted. He had the brain power and potential, as his brother stated, to do almost anything he wanted. However, his life decisions led him down a path that led to imprisonment for a majority of his life. Many times, hindsight and consequences of past actions show us what we wish we had done differently. If Larry had his life to live over again and knew what he knew at the time of his death about the preciousness of life, do you think he may have made different choices?

What about you? Have you done things you wish you would have done differently and could undo? Is there something you currently need to change in your life? Is there something you have always wanted to do to make a difference in this world? What is holding you back? In most instances, until you breathe your last breath, it is not too late to correct the future course of your life. The choice, however, is totally yours.

Chapter 5

May 27, 1993
Dear Erin,

I'm sorry I haven't wrote in a while. Since my failed suicide attempt, I haven't felt like writing letters or doing anything. I cut my wrist. I did a lot of damage. I crippled my left hand. The doctor who sewed me up said it's 50-50 that I will ever get the feeling back in the palm of my thumb and a couple finger tips. That doesn't bother me too much. What does is the pain I'm in (not much at the moment cause he put me back on pain pills). He said I'll probably have that pain the rest of my life. If that's true, my life sure is going to be short. It's so hard on me. I'm feeling somewhat better though. Now all the mental pain I'm in having to live with every day plus the physical pain too will make me have them kill me.

After my failed attempt, they took everything from my cell, even the basics like: washrag, towel, tooth brush, toothpaste, sheets, blankets, to name a few. All I was allowed was the boxer undershorts I had on, not even socks or t-shirts. After a few days of that, they gave me everything back but my razor when my lawyers raised a fuss with them.

But they still wouldn't let me out of my cell for a few more days. Then for the next week they only let me out for one hour a day. Also, all this time I was on "suicide watch" which consisted of the guard looking in my cell every 15 minutes to record what I was doing. They moved me right by the guard's booth too. Finally I convinced the psychiatrist to take me off. That I wouldn't try to commit suicide again. That I'd let the state kill me.

Well, it's in the 90s down here and going to get worse. It's just like an oven in here day and night. I just don't think I can last too much longer. I'm tired of suffering.

My oldest brother, Tom, has been down here the past month visiting mom and me. He's going to stay a couple more weeks too. Sure alright with me!

Thank Michelle for praying for me. In her letters to me, she says that she really wants a dog. I think y'all should let her have a dog since she is old enough to take care of one.

Well, I'll close. Thanks for your prayers and caring!

Love,
Larry

*****

June 1, 1993
Larry,

It was good to hear from you again—but not that you tried to commit suicide. I am sorry to hear about your hand and the pain you've been experiencing. I'll be praying that you get the feeling back in your thumb and fingers and that the pain will lessen so it is tolerable (or that it may eventually leave).

After you said that your sister would be taking you home, I was quite sure you would be attempting suicide. Then getting your suicide letter left no doubt. My heart ached since I did not know if you had died or not. I believe only the Lord knows why your suicide attempt was not successful. There have been and *are* many people praying for you. The Lord hears those prayers and answers in His way. He's still waiting for you to come to grips with the knowledge that He *loves* you and wants you to love Him in return. I strongly believe that is why you are still alive.

Would you do something for me? Would you for the next thirty days say a prayer to God? It might go something like this, "God, I need to know if you are real. Satan has me confused right now. Show me in some way that you are real so I can believe in you. Please give me an open mind where spiritual things are concerned." My prayer will be that you will agree to do this and that God will work in some way to let you know that He *is* real and He *loves* you. To give you fair warning, however, it may not be a real easy thirty days if you faithfully do this, though, since Satan will also be working very hard to try to discourage you in every way he can. I merely ask that you don't give up during the thirty days if you truly meant what you said about wishing you could also believe.

Another thought just occurred to me to share with you. Jesus is willing to accept you just as you are—with all your thoughts (right or wrong) and ideas. He just asks that you believe in Him. When you do and give your life over to Him, He will replace any incorrect ideas (beliefs) with those that are correct—one at a time. You do not have to act or believe perfectly to be saved; you just have to be willing. There are no Christians I know who have not had to change some ideas or beliefs as they have grown in the Christian life. Only God has the power to change us. When we become Christians, we actually welcome His intrusion into our lives. Just start small by acknowledging that there is a God. He'll take it from there.

At this point, I know of nothing else that I can do that would be more effective than to continue praying for you. Only God can save you. However, you need to have a mind that will be open to look at Christianity objectively and give God a chance to work.

Enough preaching! Now on to something a little lighter!

My son Gregg plays on the church softball team on Tuesday evenings. So far, they've had a losing season. I'm not sure they've won any games. My husband Dave is on a different church softball team than Gregg. His team has won two games (one by forfeit), so they're not doing much better.

You mentioned Michelle's hope for a dog. I do agree that she's old enough to take care of one. The main problem is that Gregg is allergic to a majority of dogs. We had a poodle for thirteen years. It was difficult at vacation time to find someone to take care of her since she was very temperamental. Maybe someday Dave will change his mind. She always keeps hoping and is very persistent.

You would probably really enjoy being around Michelle. She has a very positive attitude, likes to talk a lot, loves to tease, and is very easy to please. She's not like a typical fourteen-year-old who can be moody and hard to get along with. We are very close and enjoy each other.

Well, guess I had better close for now. Dave's team is starting its game at church in a few minutes.

Please write soon.

Love,
Erin

*****

June 20, 1993
Dear Erin,

I received those books from Chaplain Ray. Thank you! I wondered who ordered them. I haven't read them yet but I will. Haven't felt much like reading.

I did read the pamphlets you sent me though: "Testimony of a Former Skeptic" by Hendrik Hanegraaff[14] and "Were You There?" by Ken Ham.[15] Let's discuss them. Their proof is: "Where do we put our faith and trust? In the words of scientists who don't know everything, who were not there when the earth came into existence? Or in the Word of God—the God who does know everything—and who was there?"[16] What kind of evidence is that?

Right they are that nobody was there at the beginning to say that's how earth came into existence. But using their same argument, how do we know God was there at the beginning? Their proof is just by saying God was there. Then the scientists' evidence is the same, they say the Big Bang.

The same pamphlet says, "Reading of the Bible indicates that the creation was only thousands of years ago."[17] You can go to any museum and prove that wrong. Fossils are millions of years old. (Dinosaurs lived hundreds of millions of years ago.)

Then it states, "We can't prove, from a strictly scientific perspective, the Flood of Noah. We would do well to trust the testimony of the One who was there to see the fossils laid down."[18] Their proof is we have to trust this is the way it happened cause the Bible states it. They even admit they have no scientific evidence of the Flood of Noah.

One pamphlet states, "In fact, if you undermined the first few chapters of Genesis, the rest of the Bible becomes irrelevant."[19] I've had different pastors tell me the Flood and Adam and Eve are parables. Others say the Bible is all true. Why is it men of God, who have degrees in religion, even can't agree?

Many Christians believe in evolution, another statement from the pamphlets which would contradict the book of Genesis. And it then states, "If evolution is true, the entire Christian faith is a sham."[20]

You quoted in a recent letter the story of Lazarus and the beggar from Luke 16:23-24. Tell me why was Lazarus already in hell and the beggar in heaven? I've been told by many pastors and the Bible too that first there will be Judgment Day. So, like I just asked, why was Lazarus and the beggar already in heaven and hell?

Tell me why did Jesus's 12 disciples still have doubts about him even after all the miracles Jesus performed? It would take seeing only one miracle for me or the majority of people to believe. How can any person see a man walk across the water with the wind instantly calmed and not believe? His disciples saw this man do all these miracles and still had doubt. But I or others who didn't see him do these miracles are suppose to believe he did them and then believe he's a God? I know I ask a lot of questions. I just need some answers that make sense to me. I will be interested in what you have to say.

And, yes, I'll pray for 30 days like you asked me to in your last letter.

The 4th of July will be coming up soon. Do you and your family have special plans?

Well, I'll close for now. Thank you again for caring, prayers, and writing! It means a lot to me!

Love,
Larry

*****

June 28, 1993
Dear Larry,

I am sorry to have taken so long to respond to your last letter, but we have been on vacation to a state resort park in Kentucky, so I just got to read it a couple of days ago.

Your letter raised some legitimate questions that have made me stop and think about my reasons for believing as I do. It's been good for me! I will attempt to answer your questions in the best way that I know how. Every letter that I write to you is written only after much thought and prayer. Therefore, I'm counting on the Lord to help me answer your questions in a way that will be meaningful to you.

Proof of Evolution vs. Creation

You raised the issue about there being proof for evolution and not any proof for creation. I read the article that you sent along. I agree that the museums do offer visible "proof" that man evolved from an ape. However, from what I have read, scientists have never found a complete skeleton of any of the "ape/men" that are depicted in the museum. They have had to guess what the creature looked like in order to reconstruct it out of the very few bones they have found. Since none of the scientists were actually there to see for themselves what the inhabitants looked like (and there were no cameras back then), they really have no scientific basis for their guesses. I personally believe that it takes more faith to believe in evolution than it does to believe in creation because there is absolutely no evidence that evolution is true. It appears to me that much of evolution is based on guesses rather than observable, substantiated fact.

Evolutionists also try to explain the existence of the world by the big bang theory . Why? I think it is because they want to deny the existence of God. When I look at our universe—the fact that the earth is tilted at just the right degree, the sun is just the right distance to avoid our burning up or freezing, and our atmosphere contains just the right balance of oxygen, etc., to sustain life—I find it hard to believe that it all happened by mere chance. There are many proofs of creation around. The intricacy of each part of the human body is also proof.

Noah's Ark and a Worldwide Flood

The issue of Noah's ark and a worldwide flood is also something that is hard to prove. I don't have the exact quote or a copy of the article I read, but there is evidence that there was a worldwide flood that apparently came very suddenly and with great force. That, scientists feel, could explain why some fossils that have been found appear to be much older than what they actually are. I guess one could argue or debate over the question of how old the earth is, but I'm not sure that it really matters. Again, it's just another way Satan is trying to prevent man from seeing the more important issues in life. One of the brochures touches on the flood a little.

The movie *In Search of Noah's Ark* came out several years ago. Just recently, there was a one- or two-hour special on TV about the ark in which people said that they had climbed to where the ark was and had actually been inside it. Because of the height of Mt. Ararat, most of the year, it is not very visible since it is submerged in snow and ice. It is only after a warm trend that a small portion of the ark can be seen.

Is it Noah's Ark? According to those who have seen it, it appears to fit the description. The Bible said that the ark came to rest after the flood on Mt. Ararat—and that is the location of the sighting. Without an unusual flood of great proportions, how would such a large structure be on the side of a mountain? The real problem with further exploration of the ark is that the different governments involved will not give permission for other than air explorations at this time.

Lazarus, the Beggar, and the Rich Man Question

Another question you raised was about the story of Lazarus, who was a beggar, and the rich man found in Luke 16. You said that people are not sent to hell until after the judgment. I had to really think about that one. I finally went to my pastor to see if he could give me more of an explanation. You really keep me on my toes! Hopefully, his explanation will help you understand the situation better. (I learned something new in the process also!)

Verse 22 says, "Later, Lazarus died, and the angels carried him to the arms of Abraham" (NCV). The verse does not specifically say heaven. From the pastor's extensive study of the Bible, he believes that until Jesus came to earth to give His life on the cross, those who believed in God went to a special place called paradise when they died that closely represented heaven but was not actually the real heaven. After Jesus's death, Christians who die go directly to heaven. This belief is based on 2 Corinthians 5:8 that says, "We are confident, I say, and would prefer to be away from the body and at home with the Lord" (NIV).

Now, to address the judgment issue you raised—I can understand why you could get a bit confused about it. Judgment *is* a reality according to Hebrews 9:27: "It is appointed unto man once to die, but after that the judgment" (KJV). There are actually two judgments mentioned in the Bible—the Judgment Seat of Christ (for Christians) (2 Corinthians 5:10) and the Great White Throne Judgment (for nonbelievers) (Revelation 20:10–15). Christians will be judged by Christ for what they did for Christ *after* they became a Christian (1 Corinthians 3:10–15). They are not judged for wrongs (sins) committed while living on earth since Christ has forgiven their sins and forgets them. Psalm 103:12 verifies this, "He has taken our sins away from us as far as the east is from the west" (NCV).

God also made a place called hell that is reserved for those who refuse to believe in Him. When a man dies, his soul goes to hell, a temporary residence until the Great White Throne Judgment when Satan and all who denied Christ will be judged for their sins. Revelation 20:10–15 (NCV) explains what happens at this time,

> And Satan, who tricked them, was thrown into the lake of burning sulfur with the beast and the false prophet. There they will be punished day and night forever and ever. Then I saw a great white throne and the One who was sitting on it. Earth and sky ran away from him and disappeared. And I saw the dead, great and small, standing before the throne. Then books were opened, and the

book of life was opened. The dead were judged by what they had done, which was written in the books. The sea gave up the dead who were in it, and Death and Hades [place of the dead] gave up the dead who were in them. Each person was judged by what he had done. And Death and Hades were thrown into the lake of fire. The lake of fire is the second death. And anyone whose name was not found written in the book of life was thrown into the lake of fire.

The book of Revelation can be a little hard to understand and interpret, but these verses do make it clear that there is a hell and a lake of fire that will be worse than hell. Exactly when a person enters hell is not the most important issue. What *is* important is that hell and the lake of fire will be a reality—a very real, *everlasting* reality. It's not where I would want to be. I doubt you would want to be there either.

Another question you posed was why did some people in Jesus's time, who actually saw the miracles, choose not to believe in Him—including His disciples? Jesus's disciples' "unbelief" was just temporary. They believed in Him but sometimes temporarily forgot the miracles they had seen—such as when they questioned Him about how he would feed all of the people who had gathered to hear him preach or forgot that, with His power, He could calm the storm as He walked on the water out to them. Their belief in Jesus, however, was real. If they had doubted and not believed, do you think they would have risked their lives serving and preaching about Him?

For others who saw the miracles and chose to not believe He was the Son of God, it all comes back to Satan's influence in their lives. Satan is a real and very powerful force in the world today. His mission is to stop people from believing in Christ! How does he accomplish his mission? By making people doubt, through evolution and unbelieving—yet convincing—pastors. There are so many devious ways he has to blind people to Christ and to make them doubt and turn up their noses at the salvation He gave His life to provide for them. Why does Satan do it? Because he *hates* God. God is his archrival since Satan (originally named Lucifer) was ousted from heaven after his attempt to overtake the throne of God. He will be allowed to roam the earth until the judgment day when he will be cast in the lake of fire as his final punishment.

Thank you for taking on the thirty-day prayer challenge that I gave you. I will also be praying that the Lord will answer your prayer. He loves when someone seeks Him with a sincere desire for an answer.

On a lighter note, you asked what my family is planning to do on July 4. Since it falls on Sunday, a good share of the day will be spent in church. We will go to Sunday school and the morning service. In the evening service, Michelle, one of my friends, and I will play an accordion/clarinet trio of "America the Beautiful." This will be Michelle's third time playing her clarinet in church. She did one solo but did not like playing by herself. She feels, just like me, that there is safety in numbers! After church, we will probably go to the airport and see the fireworks sponsored by the Kellogg Company, which are always breathtaking. The International Hot Air Balloon Championship is all next week at the airport, so we are looking forward to seeing the balloons take off. I love seeing the bright colors and the variety of shapes as they inflate. On the last night is a balloon illume—the balloons are tethered and all illuminate at different times. That is one of my favorite events. I'll send you some pictures.

Until next time, take care. Please think about what I have written and let me know if you have any other questions.

Love,
Erin

Think About It: Hypocrites

It was extremely important to Larry that he not be a hypocrite. What is a hypocrite? "A person who pretends to have virtues, moral or religious beliefs, principles, etc., that he or she does not actually possess, especially a person whose actions belie stated beliefs."[21]

It is impossible to live in the world and never experience dealing with a hypocrite. What is sad to me is that those who are hypocrites give many people excuses for why they will not make certain decisions—especially the decision to believe in Christ and experience His forgiveness of sins and promise of eternal life in heaven.

If you do not have a relationship with Christ, is there someone from your past or present that you are using as an excuse for not believing in Christ? Do you think your reason is totally valid after reading this chapter? Have you ever asked that person why he/she acts or believes in that manner? Do you think you will have a valid excuse when you stand before the Lord and are asked why you did not believe in Him? In addition to the verses in Revelation 20, Romans 14:11 clearly states that you *will* one day stand before Christ, "'As surely as I live,' says the Lord, 'Everyone will bow before me; everyone will say that I am God'" (NCV).

If you are a Christian, are you acting in any ways that would cause someone to label you as a hypocrite and give them an excuse to reject Christ? If so, what do you need to change in your life to not be a stumbling block to those who are watching you who do not yet know Christ as their personal Savior?

Chapter 6

July 7, 1993

Dear Erin,

Thank you for answering my questions. I will be asking those same questions to some ministers and see how their answers compare to yours.

My mother visited me last Saturday. She now has arthritis in her hip and is in constant pain plus it affects her walking. It sure tears me apart to see her like this. I pray she gets better. I said in my prayer that if this is the way you can make me a believer, heal my mother and I'll take it as a sign that there really is a God.

Received a letter (copy) that the Attorney General wrote my trial judge when the lawyers wrote him requesting he don't sign the "execution order" without a hearing in front of him. The Attorney General pointed out that the law states the judge's job is to sign the "execution order" without holding a hearing.

The reason he hasn't signed it yet is the judge who I went in front of on June 23rd is holding up the official rulings until she (judge) hears arguments on if she can dismiss my appeals with prejudice, which means if I do change my mind, too bad. I can't file an appeal. The judge didn't know during the hearing on the 23rd if she could rule like that. The Attorney General admitted in the letter I received today that the judge can't rule like that. If I want to change my mind, I can sign the appeal papers. So the judge will be issuing her (official) rulings any day. My trial judge should then sign the "execution order." I should die near the end of the month.

My brother visited me Monday (4th). He sure is upset about my decision to die and just don't understand it. I cried trying to explain it. You just won't believe the last days, how hard it is. I remember when they were shaving me (prepping me for the execution), all I was thinking was I wanted my mother. So, when you read how I was crying when they put me in the "chair," it will not be from fear but knowing I'll never see my mom and family again.

They don't know it, but I'm not going to let them visit me this time on my last day. When the time was over last time, my brother wouldn't let go of me, my dad was on the floor crying and, of course, I was crying. No, I can't go through that again.

I'm expecting a visit tomorrow from Mary from my attorney's office (she was visiting some other guys today). I talked to her for a minute as I was up there in the visiting room talking to a psychologist. Mary said she'll visit me tomorrow. I'm going to have her mail this letter and a couple more I have to write. That way her office will pay for the postage since I'm out of stamps at the moment. Last year they changed the policy. We use to be able to receive stamps through the mail. Now, however, we can't since there is the possibility that LSD could be put on the back of them. It sure hurt me (us) when they changed the policy. The little money I receive (from Mom) I'm spending more on store "goodies." Since I don't have long left to live, I'm eating (enjoying) the "goodies."

Well, I'll let you go. Take care! Thanks for caring!

Love,
Larry

*****

July 11, 1993
Dear Larry,

As always, I enjoy going to the mailbox and finding a letter from you.

I am not at all surprised that you will be asking the same questions that you asked me to some ministers and compare their answers with mine. I really encourage you to do that. Just be sure that they are genuine Christians. Since you seem to be able to detect hypocrites very well, I will be praying that the Lord helps you to see and believe only the truth.

What an emotional visit you and your brother had! I can understand why your brother would be upset with your decision to die and not understand it. He loves you and wants to have you in his life as long as possible. I can understand your side too. You are worn out from your years on death row.

Your experience in February was an extremely difficult time for you and your family. It is understandable that you wanted your mom with you when you were being prepped for your execution. I think for anyone who is close to his/her mother, your reaction would be normal. Our mothers are the ones who offer us unconditional love and comfort. Shedding tears is okay . It does not mean that they will be tears of fear. I am sure it will be hard for your family to not be allowed to visit you on the day of your execution since you do not want all the emotional turmoil you experienced last time for yourself or for them. As a mother, I cannot even begin to imagine how I would emotionally handle my son being executed. My heart goes out to your mom. You have to do, however, what you feel is best for all of you.

It appears you are hoping that your execution date is sooner rather than later. If it does end up being set for the end of this month, I have a lot of praying to do for you between now and then since I know you are not spiritually ready to die. Please keep up your thirty-day prayer for God to make Himself real to you even beyond the thirty days if necessary. Please let me know when you get the judge's ruling.

I had to smile when I read that you are splurging on "goodies" from the store and enjoying them. That is one pleasure you can have!

How is your hand feeling? I am hoping some of the pain is gone and that the doctor was incorrect when he said you might have it the rest of your life. Are the antidepressants helping any?

There is someone from church who would like to write to you. Do you mind if I give her your address? I noticed on your return address a different cell number. Is 104 your new cell?

Michelle and I are curious as to what a typical day is like for you. Sometimes, we wonder what you are doing at various times of the day. When is your birthday?

Michelle, my mom, and I are getting ready to take off for the day to make our annual visit to Shipshewana, Indiana, to a flea market. It is one of the highlights of our summer. We spend the day shopping and then eat at one of the Amish restaurants. Fun day!

Keep me updated. I will be waiting to hear again from you soon.

Love,
Erin

*****

July 24, 1993
Dear Erin,

Sorry it's taken so long to reply to your last letter. It's been over 90 degrees for the past 26 days, including a lot over 100. It's like an oven in here. Plus there isn't any relief in sight the weatherman says. Being so hot in here, I sure haven't felt like doing anything.

My hand doesn't hurt any more. I still don't have feelings in parts of it. The doctor said I might not regain it, but what the heck, it's not hurting so it doesn't bother me.

To my surprise, the anti-depressant medication is working. I get depressed maybe one day out of the week. Before I use to be lucky if I *wasn't* depressed one day out of the week.

However, it still doesn't change my plans. I wrote a letter to ask them to set my execution date. So, I've decided to die. I'm not going to change my decision this time. I'm so tired of suffering. By living, all my life would consist of is more suffering. Plus there are so many other reasons why it's best that I die.

I didn't tell Michelle yet. But I know I'm going to have to. How do you think I should handle my upcoming death with her?

They killed one of us the end of June. The man they killed before him was a real Christian. When they asked him if he had any final words, he thanked them for he was going to be with his God. He was very calm the witnesses said, no sign of fear in him. I sure envy that faith!

In answer to a question in an earlier letter, yes, I've seen an actual birth of a child. Not in person but in biology class. It was a film that showed it from the starting to the actual birth. You stated there was a God cause, "it's only by the hand of God that a perfectly formed human baby can be the end product 9 months later." Then why are there so many deformed babies?

I hope Michelle likes her angel that I sent. I was planning on getting her a Shar pei doll made. But I can't afford it now. My dad was supposed to send me $50 but didn't. He plays one lotto ticket for me each Saturday. I won $500 with my numbers, and we were supposed to have split it.

So Dave and Gregg are on the church softball teams, hey? It doesn't matter if they aren't big winners if they are having fun. That's what is important. Do they play other church teams?

Did you all go see the fireworks on the 4th? They are at the airport now, hey? I remember them at Bailey Park. When we were kids, we never missed them. I do hope you send some pictures of the hot air balloons like you said you would. I'd return them. As you can guess by now, I enjoy looking at pictures.

Michelle didn't mention that Gregg is allergic to dogs, the majority of them. I understand now why she can't have a dog.

I always loved to bowl when I was younger. Do y'all like to bowl?

No, I don't mind you giving my address to anybody. I like getting letters. I feel bad that it's taking me so long to reply to them. Yes, my new cell is now 104. They moved me there when I tried to commit suicide as they can look into the cell from their booth. They said I can move back downstairs soon, which I'm looking forward to, as it's a little cooler down there.

My birthday is September 3. I'll write what a typical day on death row consists of in my next letter. Please remind me if I forget.

Well, I'll close. You take care. Again, thanks for caring! And your prayers are sure needed cause I know I'm a lost sinner.

Love,
Larry

*****

August 10, 1993
Larry,

It was good to hear from you again. It was such encouraging news to hear that the antidepressant is working! What antidepressant are you taking? I was just wondering since my dad had been on one, and it seemed to help him feel better emotionally. He seemed to want to sleep a lot though. Does it have that effect on you?

I am sorry to hear that your mother is experiencing so much pain from her arthritis and can understand how it must be tearing you up inside. I've shed many tears over my dad's condition. It does hurt. I have been praying that she will feel better. Larry, the Lord is certainly able to heal her or help relieve the pain she is in. However, the Lord's ways are not always our ways. He may not choose to reveal Himself to you in exactly the way you requested. Perhaps, He has another way in mind.

Many times, I have prayed for something and spelled out the way I thought He should answer. He always has answered my prayers, but not always according to my stipulations. Most of the time, the answers have far exceeded my expectations. I have slowly learned to leave the methods in His hands as He will do what's best for me.

One recent example of how He answered prayer in a very unexpected way happened about three weeks ago. I had been praying that Gregg's girlfriend, Jenny, would become a Christian. She had been coming to church since January and seemed to be leaning toward making that decision. She, however, had some questions to be answered. Every time she had an appointment with our youth pastor, she either couldn't keep the appointment or had an excuse. The last time she had an appointment, she was ill all day long. That was so discouraging for me because I felt that she was very close to becoming a Christian. I even commented to Dave and another friend that Satan had the victory again this time! I was really wrong! Gregg went to her house after he got off work. While he was there, one of Jenny's friends called and told her that she was having a lot of personal problems. Through that call from her friend and the conversation she had with Gregg afterward, she became a Christian. The Lord works in His own way and in His own time frame. But He *does* work!

I want you to know that I am praying just as earnestly for you, Larry. I know Satan is powerful and is working to keep your spiritual eyes blinded to the Lord's love and forgiveness. However, I know my God is much more powerful. I am praying Satan's hold on you will be broken and that you will be able to experience the forgiveness and the joy and peace that only He can give. The Lord has placed within me a real love for you—the love of a sister for a brother. I'll never stop praying for you as long as you live.

I've been thinking about your waiving your appeal. I really can't say that I blame you as I'm sure prison life on death row is very hard to handle—especially with no chance of parole. As I was lying in bed thinking during the night about you, the thought struck me that Jesus was sentenced to death row and was executed in a terrible way. Crucifixion on a cross was one of the most horrible death sentences a person could receive. Nails were pounded (actually spikes) through His wrists and feet. From the weight of the body and His positioning on the cross, all of the bones and joints in His body were probably dislocated, and breathing would have been extremely difficult. On top of all the physical pain, He was also spit at, called names, and laughed at. We know, however, that He had not committed a crime deserving of such a death. Why did He endure it? Because of His love for us.

There is not one feeling we can experience that He did not also experience during His human existence on earth. He knows what you are going through and what you will experience later. He's there to comfort you and go with you down the road when the execution takes place. No one else can know like Jesus knows or can love you like He does. The man who was executed in June that you said was a Christian did not go through it by himself. Jesus gave him the calmness you said he experienced. He had a better—much, much better—future ahead of him in heaven. The moment his life ended in the chair, He was at "home" in heaven with Jesus—forever.

You mentioned that you know you are a lost sinner. To come to the realization, you must believe to some degree that there is a God. You can experience the same calmness and peace that the Christian man you talked of experienced if you would just let go of the idea that you can't be helped or saved. I don't want to offend, but I think there is a stubborn streak in you right now that is preventing you from acknowledging Christ's power to save you. If it is because of your belief in evolution, that does not have to stop you. As I mentioned in a previous letter, Jesus takes us from where we are at and begins there to work on us. If you have thoughts, ideas, and habits that are contrary to those a Christian should have, He will help you to realize that and to change.

You commented on how miserable you have been this summer with the ninety to a hundred-degree heat. We have had a few ninety-degree days here that were very humid. It can be unbearable when you have no way to escape it. However, leaving this life without becoming a Christian will not be a way to escape from the heat. You'll just be trading one misery for an even worse existence. Once death occurs, there will be no appeals that can change the decision you made. I care too much for you to see you die without the Lord's forgiveness. I wish you could see inside my heart to see how much I yearn for you to become a Christian. No amount of yearning on my part, however, can make you take that step. It is a personal decision only you can make. Please give the Lord a chance.

You asked my advice on how to approach Michelle about your upcoming death. She has known from the start that one day it will happen. We've talked about you a lot. Since she is very much like me emotionally, I think the only way she will take it well is if she knows that you are a Christian. We'll both be brokenhearted if you die without giving yourself to the Lord. We both want to be able to see you in heaven since it will not be possible on earth.

You asked why God would allow deformed babies. I think the babies became deformed many times because of environmental factors—the mothers' use of drugs, alcohol, etc. What may have started as a perfect baby was altered because of choices that the mother may have made during pregnancy. I'm not saying I have the total answer, but that is my theory. I read somewhere about parents that had one normal child and then had two that were deformed. They finally figured out that the deformities were caused by an insecticide or pesticide that the home was using to avoid tick bites that could cause Lyme disease. We just never know, I guess.

I can't believe the summer is passing so fast! Dave and Gregg's teams played their last games a week ago. Michelle went to band camp last week where they learned their marching routine for the football games. She was so glad to be home as it was a rather grueling week physically. She starts back to school on August 30 and will be in the ninth grade. I start back to work in a week, and then classes start on August 23. Gregg is not real excited about going back to school.

You asked if we like to bowl. We do but only get a chance to bowl a couple of times a year—even though we don't live far from a bowling alley.

We did go to the airport on July 4 and saw the fireworks. They lasted about twenty-five minutes, were synchronized to music, and made the sky explode with brilliant colors. An estimated 250–300,000 people were there! In addition to the hot air balloons and fireworks, there was a performance by the U.S. Air Force Thunderbirds in the afternoon and a carnival to draw the crowd. Enclosed are some pictures from vacation as well as of the balloons.

You wanted me to remind you to tell us what a typical day is like for you. I hope by now you've gotten to move downstairs where it is cooler.

Did you get a chance to read either of the books from Chaplain Ray? I hope so since I think they will provide some encouragement for you.

Well, I am about "talked" out for now. We'll be looking forward to hearing from you again real soon. Take care and keep praying.

Love,
Erin

*****

August 31, 1993
Dear Erin,

Sure got a smile out of looking at the pictures. Thank you for sharing them with me. Those balloon designs are amazing!

The anti-depressant I'm taking is a Zoloft, which the doctor said is relatively new. No, it doesn't make me sleep.

My sister Tina and oldest brother Tom are now down here. Good timing too as they will be here for my birthday (last one), which means a lot to me! Plus it sure means a lot to Mom to see them again.

It was good to hear that Jenny became a Christian! Hopefully, your prayers will be answered regarding me.

Doing time here isn't hard except during the summers. Most of my pain and suffering is mental. Hopefully, by dying I'll finally be at peace. I will write about a typical day for me in my next letter since I am tired.

Well, school is back in for you. Back to work for you. Ha! But I believe you enjoy teaching, cause that's what kind of person you are. I bet Michelle was excited about going back to school.

If you have cable and *Showtime*, watch a movie called "The Last Light" that is about a death row inmate and a guard friendship that develops.

You all take care. Thanks for caring!

Love,
Larry

*****

September 15, 1993
Dear Larry,

Fall is quickly coming to Michigan. It is a beautiful time of the year, but I face it with mixed emotions. I *love* seeing all the trees turn brilliant colors since they are gorgeous. However, I also know that winter is creeping close behind in its footsteps and with it the cold and snow.

My semester is getting underway. It normally takes about a month to get back into the swing of things after having the summer off. You were so right in your last letter about my love of teaching. Interaction with students is also a plus of the job—at least most of the time! ☺ When you are doing something you enjoy, it does not seem like work.

I did not have a great start to the semester since I missed the first week of it because I had pneumonia. The following week, I was only allowed to work part-time. Dave and I went to a concert the Friday night before classes started. By the time it was over, I was chilled and running a fever and had a hurting back. I laid in the backseat for the 90-minute drive home feeling terrible. The next day, I felt worse so went to the emergency room and discovered I had pneumonia. So glad that I did not wait! The ER doctor gave me an antibiotic and a decongestant. The antibiotic started working in twenty-four hours. The decongestant, however, was full of caffeine and had me wired so tight I could not even sleep. When I called my regular doctor on Monday, he put me on something else and told me I could do nothing but rest. My family watched me like a hawk to make sure I rested. I am slowly getting back on my feet.

We do not have *Showtime*, so I cannot watch *The Last Light*. Even if we did, I am not sure that I could watch it. Right now, it is hard for me to watch anything about prisons—and especially death row.

You will be happy to know Dave relented, and Michelle is finally going to get a dog—a poodle. It will be the family dog. However, she and Gregg do not know about it. So please do not mention anything to her in any of your letters. It will be born in October and be picked up mid-December after my semester is over. We thought that would be a better time so the puppy will not have to be alone for long periods of time during the day when we first get her. Both children will be very happy. It has been ten years since our other poodle died.

Since I have a lot of catching up to do for work and am trying to conserve my energy, I will make this letter shorter and say goodbye for now. I am still waiting to hear what life on death row is like.

Love,
Erin

*****

October 11, 1993

Dear Erin,

You asked me what a day consists of here on GA's death row. It's about time I answered it.

Georgia's death row is in G-House of the prison. (Regular inmates are housed in units A-F.) I am in G-4. There are four separate 2-floor cell blocks each consisting of up to 30 men. We are separated so we can't mingle with men in the other blocks. Each cell block has 3 groups which consist of up to 10 men.

Your bathroom is probably bigger than my 6 by 8 feet cell. We have a steel bed with a mattress that is about 2 inches thick, a toilet, a sink, and a shelf. When I wash up in my sink, my bed gets wet. There are four holes in our cell walls. One hole is where we plug in to get the volume of the TV. The other three holes are for a rock, country, and soul radio station.

Each cell block has five TVs across from our cells by the windows. About four years ago, cable got installed. Each TV can be viewed by up to six cells. We are allowed to watch whatever channels we want. We have to tell the guard who then turns the channel. We generally take turns deciding what will be watched. However, in some cell blocks, the inmates who have the most "power" generally determine what channel the TV is set to. The TVs are shut off at 3 a.m. and back on at 6 a.m. So we spend a lot of time watching TV. I love watching movies plus I am a big game show nut.

Starting at 6 a.m., they open one group of cells for three hours. You can come out of your cell. Not much to do as you only hang-out in your block. Besides talking with the other guys, you can play cards, chess or checkers. I talk to everybody but I only have a couple I consider friends. Most of these guys are back-stabbing, no-good snitches. A different breed of inmates then what I was used to in Michigan's prisons. The men on death row are all ages (elderly people to a 19-year-old kid). They are children rapists, women rapists (all killed them too), murderers, etc. The 19 year old killed both his parents and sister by stabbing them to death when he was only 17. These are not the people to become friends with. It hurts when you do and then they are executed. The few guys I hang out with are like me, they like sports.

If you want a shower, you have to take it while your group is out for the three hours. Oh yeah, the shower has bars on it too. When you take a shower, they lock you in it. After the three hours, you are locked back up. Then they let another group out for three hours. This goes on until 9 p.m. So two groups will be out twice a day and the other group only once. But it rotates each day. We talk to the same guys, follow the same routines, day after day, month after month, and year after year. So, as you can see, besides 3 or 6 hours a day, we are locked in our cells. Think about what it would be like to live in your bathroom 18-21 hours a day.

Each cell block is allowed to go outside twice a week for a three hour yard period. Our yard is behind the prison and consists of two separate areas since they only allow up to fifteen men in one yard area. Each area has a volleyball court and one basketball rim to play half-court basketball. It seems we always lose a volleyball in the barb wire. The yard area has a fence around it with a lot of barb wire and a big cable wire crisscrossing it to prevent a helicopter from landing. There is also a big field and woods by the yard. I sure do enjoy it when I see deer in the field. I've seen a skunk too.

Our food is the same each month. They have four weeks on their menu. Then it starts over again. I very seldom eat their food. I survive mainly on junk food. On the weekdays, it's brought to us around 7 a.m., 11 a.m., and 4 p.m. On the week-ends and holidays, we are only fed two meals a day.

As far as our mail goes, it is opened but not read. It has to be opened so that the guards can check to be sure there are no "illegal" items that have been sent. We do not get mail on weekends. Before I decided to commit suicide, I tore up all my letters so that the police would not read them when they found my body.

Like I stated earlier, it's the same routine and food day after day and so on. I don't call it living but existing. So, when they kill me next month, they really aren't ending much of my so-called life.

What the majority of the public and prison employees forget, we are still human beings—not just a number. My number is EF209811.

Even though we are murderers, we have family and friends who care about us and who suffer too when they kill us. In Michigan prisons, the staff considered you more like a human being but not down here. They are wrong, too, cause it's repeated in the New Testament "God does not show favoritism." [Acts 10:34 NIV] So, when I feel they disrespect me, I disrespect them. I don't care if it's a guard, sergeant, or even the warden. They show me respect, I give them respect.

Mom and Tom visited me Saturday. Their visits mean so much to me! Mom was finally feeling better. She's been sick for the past six weeks.

I received a letter from the Senior Assistant Attorney General. The lawyers won't let them move up the hearing so it will be on the 29th. (Did I tell you that I have now fired all of my lawyers?) I'll then die a few weeks later. The hardest part is knowing I'll never see my family again. It sure upsets me when I think of it. At least I know I'll always be with them. I'm going to be cremated. When any of my family dies, some of my ashes will be buried with them.

Sad to read about your sickness. Sure glad you went to the hospital. A lot of people die from pneumonia. They now have a pneumonia vaccine. You only have to get it once. So, consider having it.

I can't read books any more. But I pass a couple hours a day reading the newspapers and magazines.

Well, I'll close as I want to write a few lines to Michelle before I go to bed. So, you take care!

Love,
Larry

*****

October 30, 1993
Dear Larry,

Thank you for your description of life on death row. I can only imagine how extremely bored and confined you must feel to be in such a small enclosed space eighteen to twenty-one hours each day. I did not realize that your cell was so small. No wonder when you wash up, your bed gets wet. It is good to know that you do get out of your cell at least three hours a day and can mingle with the other guys and play cards, chess, or checkers.

Is listening through the port in your cell wall the only way you hear the sound of the TVs? If not, what would get to me the most is the constant noise from the TVs that are on twenty-one hours a day, especially if they are on different channels. I do understand, however, that they provide some of the only enjoyment and distraction from prison life that you get. Sometimes all that I can tolerate is having our TV on for three or four hours in the evening if the volume is loud. Does the talking and probably shouting from other inmates get to you? I would honestly be ready to scream if I had to live with continual noise and in such a confined space! One must get used to it after a while, but it is hard to imagine living in an environment with continual noise and no way to escape from it.

For you to hardly ever eat your meals, they must taste pretty bad. When you can't afford the goodies from the prison store, do you go hungry a lot of the time? I read that one man who had been in prison for many years and was then exonerated was actually allergic to food on the outside at first. All that he could eat for quite a while was bread without getting sick. It surprised me that on the weekends and holidays, you only get two meals. You must be hungry a lot, or your body has become so used to being hungry that, after a while, it does not bother you as much.

Getting to go outside twice a week must be a welcome relief for you so that you can breathe some fresh air. There are not many options of things to do outside, and some days are probably nasty, but those outdoor days must be considered special. The prison air must also get pretty stale smelling with so many men in such small quarters, especially if they do not take advantage of the showers when they can. It would be easy to not care about hygiene after a while since there is no one to impress unless a visitor is scheduled to come. The cable running over the top of the recreation area to keep helicopters out was a surprise, but it makes sense.

With so much time in your cell, reading and writing letters must also play a big part in your day. You mentioned that you can no longer read books. Why is that? Reading books would be a great way to pass time and allow your mind to go to different places away from the prison. I personally love to read. I am glad you can at least still read magazines and newspapers. Do inmates share the magazines and newspapers?

Getting the news that the lawyers will not let the court move up your execution date must have been very upsetting to you since you are looking for a release from your pain. Knowing that you will soon be saying goodbye to your family must really hurt deeply. It is their love that must be sustaining you through this nightmare called death row. You sound comforted to know that you will get to be with them after your death since your ashes will be buried with each of them. Do they know this yet? Please do not be upset, but I am glad that your date did not get moved up since you do not yet know Jesus. You would have no peace in death without Him.

Next semester will be a different one for me. I applied for and received a sabbatical leave in order to develop a new desktop publishing class, which will be done from my home office. When I went to a conference a couple of years ago, I was introduced to PageMaker, a graphic design software that can be used to create publications such as newsletters, brochures, flyers, greeting cards, and posters that previously were designed only by graphic artists. While I will only receive half pay while off, it is something I am very excited about doing. Normally, we have to develop classes during the summer with no pay. I believe it was approved because it will allow us to add a new class to our associate degree programs once developed. I will be the only one teaching it. One week of my time will be spent in Wisconsin to learn the software.

Tomorrow night will be a fun night for the children since it is Halloween. We normally have around a hundred trick-or-treaters. My mom, Michelle, and I give out candy and enjoy seeing the different children who come to our door.

Goodbye for now. I will look forward to your next letter.

Love,
Erin

Think About It: Emotional Prison

You may or may not be locked in a physical jail or prison with steel bars like Larry was as you are reading this book. Perhaps, you are thinking to yourself, "Thank goodness I am not in prison. I am so grateful to have my freedom!" However, you may still be in a "prison" and feel helpless. How you may ask?

Have you ever felt like you were in an *emotional* prison and did not have the "key" to get out? When I was depressed and going through counseling, I remember one session when I took my picture and overlaid prison bars in front of me. I gave it to my counselor and said, "This is how I feel emotionally." The doors then opened for discussions as to why I was feeling like an emotional prisoner. Finding the reasons why gave me the "keys" to open my "prison" door.

If you are currently in an emotional prison, is it time that you find the keys to your freedom? Seek out a professional counselor or someone qualified to help you work through your issues. Have you failed to set boundaries? Do you let others control you? Are you a people pleaser and want to avoid conflict at all costs? Do you have anger management issues? Have you resorted to addictions such as alcoholism or drug abuse to help bring temporary relief from your inner pain? Any of these reasons (or perhaps others) could be reasons for your dilemma.

Will you take the steps to regain your personal freedom? If you know someone who may need to get out of their emotional prison, perhaps you could be the one to help push them in the direction of seeking help. I know from personal experience just how beneficial counseling from a completely objective professional can be. Since I was in my midforties when I sought that help, I know that it is never too late!

Chapter 7

The letter below was written by my close friend to Larry who knew he needed some encouragement.

November 10, 1993

Dear Larry,

Erin asked me to write to you today since I am her closest friend. This is probably the most unusual letter you will ever receive. Be assured that it comes directly from the heart of someone who cares deeply for you—who truly loves you.

My love is not like any love you've ever experienced during your life. How is it different? It is *totally* unconditional love. I give it to you just because you're *you*—not because you've done anything to deserve it. My love is sometimes hard to comprehend because it is not like the love of a biological mother or father or family member. I will never disappoint you, misuse you emotionally, or withhold my love because I care too much for you. You see, I created you and have loved you since even before the day you were born. I've waited many years (over forty to be exact) for you to return my love. But I'll never give up waiting.

I do wish you would let me show you just how much I love you. If you would accept my love, I can give you the mental peace you are so desperately seeking. I know how you are suffering so, and I know *exactly* why. You see, *nothing* is hidden from me. I know what you were thinking as you tried to take your life and knew how you were hurting inside as well as physically afterward. Even though I knew what the final outcome would be and hated to think of you hurting so, *you* had to make the choice. I also knew why your attempt was unsuccessful. You see, as the creator of life, I am in control of life and death. I knew that your death at that time would have caused you much more misery than you felt you were already experiencing. I wanted you to have another chance to get to know Me.

My "phone" lines have been kept very busy these last few months. You would not believe the incredible number of people who care about you and have "called" me on your behalf. There isn't a day that goes by that I don't get several "calls." You are really very fortunate to have so many Christians that are concerned about you and are so persistent. I needed to let you know that you are loved by more than just Me.

Larry, I also want you to know that there isn't anything you've done that I would ever hold against you. I do not hold grudges and can forgive *any* offense. You've already paid a great price through the sacrifice of your freedom and the mental anguish you've experienced. I am unlike anyone you have ever known who may have had a hard time forgiving and forgetting. Sometimes, people can't understand why I would even bother and be interested in them. I guess I'm sometimes just beyond understanding. But that's because I am God.

I never *force* anyone to return my love. But I'm patiently waiting, hoping that one day very soon, we can truly become father and son. I will love you as you have never been loved before. You'll not be disappointed. It will be the most life-changing decision you will ever make—one that will bring you the peace of mind you are craving. I would be there for you on your execution day also—holding you close. I'll be there that day anyway. However, I'd rather not be there as just an observer but as your personal friend to help you through the time.

I've said that I love you—but words are cheap. You may be wondering how serious my love is. I *willingly* died for you. That's the greatest sacrifice that one can give. I know all of your reasons for rejecting me. None of them is good enough. As I've said before, *nothing* you've said, thought, or done can cause me to withhold my love or my salvation from you. Only your continued decision to reject me will I hold against you—for eternity—not because I want to but because you will have chosen to have me do so.

Larry, I'm offering you an unconditional pardon and parole. Why? Because I care for you. I am the only one who can truly understand you and deliver you from your mental pain and suffering. In my thirty-three years on earth, I suffered rejection, abuse, and cruelty. I endured hunger, thirst, and pain. Then, I endured a most painful and humiliating execution on the cross of Calvary to fulfill My Father's (God's) plan of salvation. My death was necessary to provide the only way for you and others to reside in heaven with Me and My Father. I died, but because I have power over death, I rose from the grave. Because I am the risen Son of God, I have power to forgive your sins and give you new, eternal life. All you have to do is to confess that I am Christ and believe in your heart that I died for you and that God raised me from the dead. Will I hear from you soon? I am only a short, sincere prayer away. I'm available twenty-four hours a day with no appointment necessary.

What is the price for this unconditional pardon? I just ask that you love me in return. It's so easy but yet sometimes so hard because Satan is so intent on keeping you from believing in me. However, I am stronger than Satan. I can help you if you'll only surrender and give me a chance.

Larry, I died for you. Who are you going to die for? Me or Satan? Please give Me a chance. By choosing Me, you have everything to gain and nothing to lose. As I have said, only I can offer you peace. If you choose Satan, you will find that he has lied to you about death being the easy way out of your mental torment. With Satan, you have *everything* to lose and will never find the inner peace you are seeking.

I'll be waiting with outstretched arms for you. Remember, I love you.

Eternally yours,
Jesus

*****

November 15, 1993

Dear Erin,

That sure was a beautiful letter you wrote from Jesus. That letter will be saved! Thanks!

My hearing got postponed because the lawyer got mugged over $17 that he had on him and got his jaw broke. So, it's wired shut for three weeks. I was very upset when I was informed. I'd have had an execution by now if it wasn't postponed. Who knows when the hearing will be rescheduled.

They had "Media Day" last Tuesday for the third year in a row when they let the media come back here on death row. The media also requests to interview certain inmates. However, it is up to the inmate if he wants to talk to them. All the press requested interviews with me cause of how close I came to dying in February. There were five TV cameras (five different news stations) and two newspaper reporters. I agreed to talk cause I wanted to inform the victim's families and public why I stopped my execution in February. I also wanted to inform them I've now resolved the reason. I'm in the process of rescinding the appeal papers I signed on the night of my scheduled execution.

Mom visited Saturday and is feeling pretty good. She sure is looking forward to her trip to Michigan. It has been years since her last visit there. She can't wait to see her mother and grandchildren. I won't have any visits while she is gone. That is why she did not want to go at first. But I told her that I wanted her to go. I am glad she decided to go.

It was in the 80s today. Plus I got to enjoy it as today was our yard day. It is always nice to get to be outdoors for a while.

I can't read novels anymore cause of my lack of concentration, which is cause of my depression. I start a book. The next day when I pick it up to continue reading I've forgot what I had already read. I was hoping that it would improve, but it hasn't.

Sounds like your sabbatical leave is going to be a nice change for you. Hope you get the summer off cause of it too.

Boy, Michelle sure will be happy when she gets her dog! I sure won't give away the surprise. I'm sure happy y'all are doing this for her. I sure would like to see the look on her face.

It's very thoughtful of you and Michelle wanting to send me a Christmas package! Every year they eliminate something off the list. So, we are not allowed to receive much now. Hopefully, they will not eliminate goodie boxes completely in the future since it is the only time of the year we can have them. These are the things we can have this year: peanuts, bags of candy (no candy bars), cookies, and cakes. That's not much, is it? My favorite cake is angel food cakes. Plus I like pound cakes and any kind with fruit (for example: strawberry or cherry). I don't like chocolate or coconut. The package can't weigh over 12 lbs. I'm allowed to receive it on December 1st and can't receive it postmarked after Christmas Day.

Well, it's late. I'm sure sleepy but I have to write Michelle. You all take care! Thanks for caring!

Love,
Larry

*****

December 4, 1993

Dear Larry,

Michelle and I always look forward to going to the mailbox and finding a letter from you!

I had to type this letter since I have tendonitis in my right-hand thumb—probably because I write so much each day both at work and to you. I'm supposed to give it a rest for three weeks and see if it will feel better. I sure hope it does since the alternative doesn't sound very appealing—a splint for two or three months that would be very limiting.

It is good to hear that your mom is feeling so much better. Your prayers for her from last summer have been answered.

My dad is doing much better physically. Emotionally, he's still down at times. I heard on the radio just the other day that people who have lost some of their physical capabilities through strokes go through a grief period similar to losing a loved one. I am sure he wonders from day to day if he will have another stroke and how much more of his capabilities he might lose. He doesn't share his feelings much, though, so it is hard to tell what he's thinking. I just keep praying for him. The Lord can help him through these rough days that he has—just like He can help you through your tough emotional days.

I'm glad you liked the letter from Jesus. Even though I wrote it, He laid it on my heart during the middle of the night and gave me the words. Would you believe I got up right then and wrote it? Every thought that was expressed about Jesus and His care for you come directly from the Bible. Many of them were paraphrased, but the facts are true. He truly loves you and cares about you.

Boy, nothing like rubbing it in about your nice weather! It's hard to remember when it was even in the sixties around here! Glad you got to get out and enjoyed the nice day. It was hovering in the thirties here. Brrrr!

I wish you could be with us when we take Michelle to pick up the puppy two weeks from today. I can hardly wait to see her reaction. She kiddingly asked her dad this morning when he was going to get her a dog. However, she can no longer say dog since Dave told her he did not want to hear the word *dog* again. So now she refers to it as a "furry, barking thing." ☺

It's going to be easy to surprise her when we go to pick it up since we are buying it from a lady in Delton. We have had a standing family joke since last summer about Delton. She commented that she likes everything we do together. Dave told her that he bets she would even be excited if we told her we were going to Delton, which you probably remember is a very small town about thirty minutes from us. She told us she sure would be excited since she had never been there before. So now, we joke about Delton. On the day we go to pick up the dog, we are going to tell her that she's going to have an exciting day since we are going to Delton to see their Christmas decorations. She'll fall for it and not be suspicious. I am sure she will have an exciting day though! When we originally scheduled the pickup date, the calendar was clear that day. Now, she has a puppet performance at a nursing home at 2 p.m. We will probably have to drag her there after she has that puppy in her arms!

Michelle and I had fun last Saturday shopping for the items for your goodie box. We're going to be packing it today and sending it out on Monday. You should, hopefully, get it this week. We were glad that you told us you don't like chocolate since we love it and would have definitely put some chocolate in the box. We tried to select a variety of items. What happens if some kind of food is sent that wasn't specifically on the list? A couple of things were in bags, but we sent them anyway. Hopefully, those items would just be removed, and you would get the rest of the goodies.

How often are you allowed to have visitors or make phone calls? You said that your mom always visits and that you have called her and your sister. I wish that I lived closer to Georgia since I would come and visit you. If you would ever like to call Michelle or me, we would love to talk to you. Our phone number is enclosed. Just call us collect. If you give us an idea when you might call, we'll make sure we are home. Saturday mornings or Sunday afternoons are generally pretty good times to reach us.

Well, guess I need to close for now. I want to get this letter in the mail today and also need to do some baking for your goodie box! If I don't hear from you before Christmas, I'll be remembering you. I thought a lot about you on Thanksgiving Day. Do you get anything special at the prison on the holidays?

Take care and write soon.

Love,
Erin

*****

December 8, 1993

Dear Erin,

To my great surprise, your Christmas box arrived today! Since you said that you were going to mail it Monday, I wasn't expecting it until next week. Did you send it special class or something?

What can I say? I really can't. I sure did not expect you to buy that much stuff. Boy, I couldn't believe it. There wasn't one item that

I don't like! I wasn't suppose to have received the home baked goodies. But I got lucky—my normal guard was on "riot detail" practice.
The guard who inspected the stuff is one of the "good guards." He
gave me everything but the gum since gum isn't allowed in any prison
as it can be used to jam the locks. Items we get that we cannot have
can be sent back, destroyed, or donated to under privileged families.
I had it donated since I think it is a real good plan. I tell you I sure
will stretch the goodies far so I can enjoy the stuff as long as I can.

But it also made me feel sad. You spent all that money on me,
and I can't do anything for you. I sure didn't expect you to spend
all that money. But then it shouldn't have surprised me being a real
Christian as you are. Since you sent me so much food, I won't have
to buy any stuff off the inmate store here. Now I can get better
Christmas presents made for you and Michelle. I was already getting
something made, but I now can afford something better. Anyways,
don't tell Michelle but send me her shoe size. (I haven't forgotten
you. I'll ask Michelle (ha!) for the data I need for your gift.) If you
send it right away I might be able to get the gifts up to you two by
Christmas. I hope so. It still won't come close to being equal to the
Christmas present you two sent me!

Sure wish I had money. Some of these guys make some beautiful stuff. Over the years I've saved a little money each month to get
mom something beautiful (blouses, bedspread, house slippers, doilies
and other things). Wish I could do more for her.

Well, they executed one of us last night. He was a 17-year-old
soldier when he and another soldier got drunk. They robbed and
killed a taxi cab driver. They killed the other guy a few months ago.
One of the witnesses to the execution said on the news that he was
so scared his face muscles were twitching. Plus it looked like he was
going to cry.

There was a lot of protestors as Amnesty International and
other groups was fighting his case. They was real upset that we (USA)
is one of a couple of countries in the world that executes our own
people. On the rock station this morning, the DJ really made jokes
about the execution. He said, "They executed one freak last night,
who's next?" Then you could hear electricity popping and sizzling

in the background with his laughing. Some other guys said he made some other jokes about it, but after I heard the first one I didn't listen any more.

On the news last night I found out something I didn't know. After the execution, they even do an *autopsy here* on the body. They cook us (electric chair) then they cut us open. They did a special a couple weeks ago from their visit here on Media Day. This station showed the electric chair plus the switches and how it works. I did see this stainless table and drain, which I thought they laid our body on to cool off. I bet that's where the autopsy is done.

A couple of years ago before they executed a guy, he thanked them during his last statement. He was a Christian. He was so real calm the witnesses said. He thanked them cause he said he knew he was going to be with his Lord. Then he got a last-minute "stay." So they took him back out of the chair. A couple hours later when the "stay" was lifted by the U.S. Supreme Court, they strapped him in again. He again thanked them. The witnesses said it amazed them how calm he was. That's the kind of faith you have and I wish I could have.

You are right. I sure wish I could see Michelle's face on the 18th when she gets her puppy. If you can, take a picture of her and her dog for me.

How is your thumb? Boy, you sure must use it a lot to get tendonitis in it. I hope resting it helps.

Sure glad your dad is doing better! But it's sad he is still down emotionally. Keep me updated.

When my execution is scheduled, the reporter from the Atlanta newspaper is going to write the article on our interview from media day a few weeks ago. I saw another reporter on TV last night who was also here on media day. She was a witness to the execution last night. If I can track down the article, I will send it to you. A reporter from the *Battle Creek Enquirer* wrote me wanting to know if he could call me for an interview. But I don't know if I'll be allowed to talk to him.

I'm allowed two phone calls (10-15 minutes) a month. Since I help clean up the cellblock, I get three. I always call mom with one, my dad with another, and the third to a brother or my sister. But since my oldest brother and sister are down here and I can't reach my other two brothers, I will try to call you if I'm not allowed to call the reporter. If I'm allowed to call him, I'll call you guys next month. Don't get me wrong, your call is more important. But if the reporter gets permission and sets this call up, you see why I have to call. I'll try to let you know what day and time I'll be calling. We are only allowed to make collect calls. You said it would be best to reach you on Saturday and Sunday afternoons. At least the phone rates will be cheaper then.

It was our yard day today. It was nice, in the 60s. I played a lot of basketball.

Well, it's late so I better close. Want to write Michelle. I sure get some smiles from all the jokes that she sends me in her letters. Again, thanks for caring!

Love,
Larry

*****

December 17, 1993
Dear Larry,

I am happy you got your goodie box so quickly and that you got to keep everything except the gum. If you could have seen us packing it, you would probably have laughed. We had a lot of fun doing it. Even my mother got into the act.

I couldn't find any pound cake other than chocolate at the store. Knowing that you really didn't care for chocolate, I decided to bake one for you (not knowing that you weren't allowed home-baked goodies, I did wonder, though, if they were acceptable). One of the men in the bakery gave me a couple of tins and some plastic storage containers to send them in, which I thought was really nice since it would protect them in the mail. The angel food cake was in a foil container, and I wasn't sure if the boxes were sent through any kind of scanner that would detect metal. I called the airport to see if a foil container would set off the airline security system, and the agent told

89

me it probably would. So my mother gave me the plastic cake carrier. (By the way, Michelle said to tell you that she was glad that you preferred angel food cake over "devils" food cake!)

Once we got everything in the box, we weren't sure what it weighed. I stood on the bathroom scales with it, and it weighed fourteen pounds. When Michelle held it on the scales, it only weighed ten pounds. So we figured it was somewhere in between. Then, my mother suggested getting it weighed at a store where there was a postal scale. It weighed twelve and a quarter pounds—unwrapped. So we took out a package of Chex Mix, which we weren't sure if you could have anyway, and it then weighed eleven and three quarter pounds—unwrapped. We thought surely we would be safe. After we got it stuffed with newspaper, wrapped, taped, and took it back to mail it, it weighed twelve and a half pounds. (I couldn't believe that we had added three-quarters of a pound to the weight just in wrapping it!) We took the chance that it would still be okay. Obviously, it was. The gal at the store said that it would go to Georgia by air if we sent it first class. I didn't think you would get it so fast though!

After sending it, we prayed it would get to you before the cakes had a chance to get old and that what we sent was acceptable since we added a few things that were not on the list. I'm glad the normal guard was on riot detail practice and the other guard let you keep everything except the gum. We are happy you liked everything. God sure answers prayer! Did they bring the box to you before or after it was unwrapped? I imagine that it was already inspected before you got it.

It's really thoughtful that you want to send Michelle and me something for Christmas. *Anything* you send would be special to us since we consider you to be one of our special friends. We were not, however, expecting anything. You asked what Michelle's shoe size is. She wears between a 7 ½ and an 8. I would go with size 8 since that is the size of the roller skates I got her for Christmas.

Michelle and I were talking, and we decided that the *very best* gift we could ever receive from you is to hear that you have decided to become a Christian. We sure hope that one day you will write us with this news. It will definitely be one of the happiest days in our lives (and it will be for you too)! When you care about someone, you want the best for them. In the meantime, we're going to keep praying.

How great your mom finally got to come to Battle Creek after waiting for so long. I assume she'll get to spend Christmas here. It should be a special time for her. My mom and dad saw her the other day when they went to your aunt's house. I want to get over to see her too.

We're having Christmas Day at our house as we do every year. My mom and dad and Dave's parents will be coming for dinner. My brother and his family are going to Florida for Christmas. Wish you could be here with us. Christmas Eve is reserved just for our immediate family. One of our Christmas Eve traditions is to have a special birthday cake to celebrate Christ's birthday. We started doing that when Gregg was small and have done so every year. It's one way we make sure to give Christmas the right emphasis. Another tradition is to read the Christmas story from Luke. Christmas and Easter are my two favorite times of the year. I'm so thankful that God sent Jesus to us on that first Christmas and that Jesus so willingly gave His life for us and rose again on Easter. Jesus in my life is what makes life worth living.

The details that you shared with me about the execution special on TV were ones that I did not know. How did you feel after watching the special? Did you wish you hadn't watched it? I sometimes feel that the less I know the better when it pertains to something I may have to experience that I am not looking forward to. I can't understand why they feel the need to do an autopsy afterward. It seems that the cause of death should be obvious enough. I would think that there would have to be a special autopsy area that met the standards of a regular morgue. That local radio DJ's jokes were definitely in bad taste. I can't imagine that the station would let him get away with it. He obviously is a crude person with a warped sense of humor. I wouldn't have listened to any more of his sick jokes either after I had heard the first one!

I can't imagine why anyone would want to be a witness at an execution. I sure wouldn't want to be! You mentioned the witness said that the last man was terrified, while the Christian man was real calm. That is the difference that Christ can make in a life. My guess is that the terrified man did not know Christ or what was in store for him after he died. If I didn't know Christ and knew I was going to die, I would be terrified too. The Christian man, however, knew that what awaited him on the other side of the chair was far better. I can understand why he thanked them. I so hope that when your day comes, you'll be a Christian man and that any witnesses will be able to see the peace in your life that Christ can give you. Remember that He said that He wants to go through the experience with you. You can count on what He says.

You continue to make the comment that you wish you could have the kind of faith that Michelle, I, and the other Christian man had. Are there any more questions you need answered that would help you get beyond your issue of Christianity being based on faith? I will try my best to answer them if any come to mind.

Tomorrow is the big day for Michelle. We're going to tell her tonight that we're going to Delton first thing in the morning to see some unique Christmas decorations that a lady makes and sells and that we want her to go along to give us her opinion since we are going to get a big wreath for the front of our house. Of course, she'll want to go. Dave thinks that the reality she is getting a dog will not sink in until it is handed to her and told it is hers. You'll probably be able to hear her in Georgia afterward! I am planning on taking a camera and will definitely get a picture of her with the dog to send to you.

My thumb is doing much better. I've been making a real conscious effort to not use it too much. It was three weeks yesterday. The reduced activity and medications are working. And I'm glad.

Since it is suppertime, I need to sign off. Take care. We'll be looking forward to hearing from you again real soon—whether by letter or phone call. You'll be in our thoughts and always in our prayers.

Love,
Erin

*****

December 22, 1993

Dear Larry,

I do not have a lot of time to write but knew you want to hear about Michelle's puppy experience. We pulled off a good surprise on her!

As I already wrote you, she was told we were going to Delton to pick out a Christmas wreath for the front of the house. When we pulled in the driveway, there were about twenty poodles of all different sizes running around in the fenced-in yard. Michelle thought it was great. We told her that she got an added bonus of getting to see all the dogs. As we went in, Kris, the breeder, called the twenty dogs in and let out twenty different poodles! She must have had a special room for them because only one or two were in the same room that we were.

We asked Kris if she could show us her wreaths. She said, "Sure, I'll be right back." She was in on the surprise and came out holding our little puppy in her arms. She had her dressed in a red and white Christmas sweater that said, "Merry Christmas" and had the cutest bow on top of her head and a gift tag attached to her. She asked Michelle if she would like to hold one of her newest puppies and play with it while we looked at Christmas wreaths. Well, of course, she was enthralled with holding the puppy so much so that she did not notice that the tag had her name on it! We finally had to tell her to read the tag. She read it, looked up a little confused, and asked, "Is this *my* dog?" What a smile broke out on her face when she realized she had finally gotten her wish for her own "furry barking thing." She held her the entire way home. And I was right. It was *extremely* hard for her to go to the puppet performance right after we got home.

Gregg was working that day. After dropping Michelle off, we went to the store where he was working and asked him if he was at the point that he could take a short break and was allowed to. I am sure he was wondering why we would want to take him out to the car. He was equally surprised to find out that we now had a puppy. It was not something that either of them thought would ever be a possibility with Dave's insistence that there would be no dog.

We named her Ginger since she is a red apricot color. I have never seen a dog that is such a deep reddish color. She is absolutely adorable! All of us are having fun with her. However, she is considered the family dog since we all love her. I will be sending the pictures after we have our Christmas pictures developed.

Need to go so I can get this in the mail to you. We will be thinking of you on Christmas.

Love,
Erin

*****

January 4, 1994
Dear Erin,

Well, I sure hope you had a good Christmas! My Christmas was a lonely one since my mom was in Michigan visiting her family. Normally she comes and visits me on the holidays. I am glad she got to go see her family but I missed seeing her. She should be back home by now.

I am not doing so well right now. Last Tuesday while playing basketball I was knocked on my back (to the cement). Then later a 200+ pound guy fell on me. Instead of going down with the weight, I let my back muscles accept the weight. I'm on two different kinds of medication for it now. This past weekend I was finally beginning to feel better. Then yesterday while I was bending over to wash my face a sharp pain hit me in the back. I fell to the ground. Now I am back to square one. It hurts to walk, sit, and lay down. Sure didn't sleep too well last night. I'm scheduled to see the doctor in the morning.

I wish I could've seen Michelle's face when you surprised her with the dog. I'll be looking forward to seeing some pictures.

Your gifts and Michelle's will be mailed this week and you will receive them next week. Enclosed is a note that is not to be read until they come. Wish I could do more for y'all! Would you please do me a favor too? Would you call my sister-in-law and ask her if she would drive over and pick up my nephew and niece's presents? I'll write her too. By sending all of this at once, it won't cost me as much postage. I had to save for a couple weeks to send this one box. She is a Christian too. Sad to say her and my brother have separated recently. The children, I'm sure, don't understand it.

I'm still eating the goodies from y'all! Did Dave make that peanut brittle since it said "Dave's Specialty—Homemade Peanut Brittle." Boy, it sure was good! It sounds like you guys had a work detail getting the box together! What cakes did you bake? I thought they were all store bought. They did not last long as I sure didn't want them to go stale. Ha! Trying to make my goodie box last as long as I can. It makes my enjoyment last longer too plus saves me money since I don't have to buy that much stuff from the store to eat.

You are correct that a lack of faith is my greatest issue in believing there is a God. I still need proof (like a miracle) to help me believe the things in the Bible happened. I will be thinking of any other questions I have and you know I will definitely ask them. In my heart, I hope there is a God. I still pray. But I can't completely believe there is a God. I'm sorry!

It is late and I need to turn in and hope to be able to sleep some tonight. I will write again tomorrow.

Love,
Larry

Think About It: Pigeonholing and Judging Others

You have now had seven chapters to get acquainted with Larry through his letters. Think back to the time when you first picked up this book and read about his criminal history. What were you thinking about him at that time? Do you still feel the same way or have your thoughts toward him changed in any way? Do you "see" him any differently than being just a murderer?

How easy it is to pigeonhole and judge individuals based solely on looking at or reading about them and then placing them in one of the "boxes" we have created in our minds. He or she is a criminal, an alcoholic, a druggie, a food addict, abusive, a homeless bum, or whatever other labels you easily attach to others. You may offhandedly make the comment, "Oh, that Joe Blow is a druggie." If you spoke the rest of your thoughts, you might also add, "Why can't he control himself?" Does this ring true for you?

Dictionary.com gives one definition of *judging* as "to form an opinion of; decide upon critically."[22] Critically *should* mean that the decision is based on evidence and careful thought. Too often, however, just the opposite happens when one judges—the outcome is actually critical or demeaning in nature. Opinions are often formed based on first impressions only. How often have your first opinions been negative and eventually proved incorrect? What assumptions have you made that proved false once you got to know the person? Would you have been slower to judge if you could have first "walked a mile in that person's shoes"?

The Bible has this to say about judging others in Matthew 7:1–5 (NCV),

> Don't judge others, or you will be judged. You will be judged in the same way that you judge others, and the amount you give to others will be given to you. "Why do you notice the little piece of dust in your friend's eye, but you don't notice the big piece of wood in your own eye? How can you say to your friend, 'Let me take that little piece of dust out of your eye'? Look at yourself! You still have that big piece of wood in your own eye. You hypocrite! First, take the wood out of your own eye. Then you will see clearly to take the dust out of your friend's eye."

Reinforcing the message of this verse is Romans 2:1–3 (NCV):

> If you think you can judge others, you are wrong. When you judge them, you are really judging yourself guilty, because you do the same things they do. God judges those who do wrong things, and we know that his judging is right. You judge

those who do wrong, but you do wrong your-
selves. Do you think you will be able to escape
the judgment of God?

Why would God want those specific verses to be in the Bible?
Could it be that when we judge another, it is sometimes because we
might see a little bit of that person's actions that we don't like in ourselves? Judging can also be a way to make one feel superior. Think back
to the unspoken thought about the "druggie" being a person with no
control or willpower. The person making that judgment might not
be a "druggie" but might have another addiction—food, gambling,
gossiping, alcohol, smoking, pornography, etc. Should a person who
has one addiction be judging someone with a different addiction or
vice? That is what is meant by considering the "wood" in your own
eye before judging another for the "speck of dust" in his eye.

God is the only One who can judge correctly. Why? Because as
the Creator, He sees our heart and mind and knows the *true* person.
He knows what life experiences have contributed to who we are—
our hurts, our abilities, our passions, and our true character. What is
amazing, however, is that He loves each of us just as we are. His great
love gives Him the patience to accept us and work with us to help
us change into the person He knows we *can* be and He created us *to*
be. Have you ever thought that when you judge another, you are also
judging God, the Creator of that person?

A New Testament story comes to mind from John 8:1–11 about
a woman who was caught in the act of adultery, brought before Jesus,
and harshly judged by the Jewish leaders and Pharisees. By the law
and their judgment of her, they told Jesus that she should be stoned
to death for her sin and wanted to know if He agreed with them.
Jesus saw through their self-righteousness and attempt to trap Him
in order to find some fault in Him. His eventual response is recorded
in verse 7, "All right, but let the one who has never sinned throw the
first stone!" (NLT). Gulp! Talk about these judgmental hypocrites
getting put in their place. No one was qualified to cast a stone at her
and shamefully left the scene. Jesus then forgave her and told her she
was free to go but admonished her to stop her lifestyle of adultery.

Has learning more about Larry's past, how he viewed himself, and how it affected his future made you think any differently about him than what your initial impression might have been? Does he seem more *human* to you now? Have *you* ever gotten angry and done something you wish you had not done in the heat of the moment? Have *you* deeply regretted choices you have made? Chances are that the end result of your choices was not actual murder—or perhaps you are reading this book and you did take another's life. You may be saying to yourself, "Well, I would never murder anyone!" But have you "murdered" by hating or seeking to hurt another's reputation or self-esteem? The Bible says in 1 John 3:15, "Anyone who hates another brother or sister is really a murderer at heart" (NLT). Have *you* ever been unfairly judged? How did it make you feel when you found out? Is this what you want to do to others?

Everyone has a past. It would be impossible to find a person with the "perfect" past that carries no baggage from childhood into adulthood. Sometimes, one is aware of how the past affects his/her present circumstances. Knowing is the first step to dealing with issues and breaking the cycle. Often, however, the person may be unaware of the effect the past has on current behavior. Rather than judging the person, seek to know, understand, and help the person when possible or if asked.

Perhaps you are the person who has carried with you "baggage" from your past that is still affecting you and are tired of carrying the load. How can you identify and/or seek to deal with these past issues? First, be open to input from others who know you well and that you can trust to be truthful with you. We all have blind spots that we do not readily recognize that are operating in the background of our lives and influencing our behavior. Others can more readily recognize our blind spots since they see our overt behavior in certain circumstances that brings out the worst in us. If the person offering feedback knows you personally, he/she may be aware of what is motivating the behavior. Be willing to seek and listen to feedback. Hopefully, the person giving feedback will "speak the truth in love" as instructed in Ephesians 4:15.

Once you identify your issue(s), seek to get help. If you are dealing with a deep-seated issue, it may take getting professional counseling. You may be thinking, "I cannot afford counseling." Think again. There are counseling centers that operate on a sliding-scale fee for treatment. Depending on your income, it could even be free. Check out the resources in your community.

What about you? Are you quick to judge others? Has the Lord convicted your heart about doing so? Do you have any baggage you are still carrying around? If so, maybe it is time to deal with it so that your past does not continue to control your future—like Larry's past controlled him. How freeing would that be to you?

Chapter 8

January 5, 1994

Dear Erin,

Well, I'm writing this letter from the "hole" (segregation). I was sentenced to 30 days today. So Mom can't visit me while in the "hole." She sure is going to be upset! Our visits mean so much to us as we know we don't have that many left.

I was found guilty today for hitting an inmate who told on me. It used to be only a 14-day sentence. But since there are so many fights, they are hoping 30 days will be a deterrent. But stupid me continues to punish myself. I hate myself, so my last 28+ years I'll do things to hurt myself. I'd got found "not guilty" today if I didn't confess to it as no guards saw it. But, like I stated, I just have to punish myself.

We are not allowed any family visits but can have lawyer visits. I am not expecting any lawyer visits because they are mad at me. I'm not allowed any books but the Bible. I got lucky today though. The lieutenant that checked me in is "cool." He let me have a book called, *Hungry for More of Jesus* by David Wilkerson. Have you read it? I prefer reading about the New Testament, especially about the life of Jesus. I think Jesus was a great preacher similar to Billy Graham. I'll start reading it and make notes and questions to ask you about what I read. OK? I'll sure have time to write letters too.

Is there any way you can send me some Bible lessons? They must come first class. I'm not allowed in the "hole" to receive anything but first class mail. (No newspapers, magazines, etc. that come second or third class.)

I am also not allowed any food from the store. Since I seldom eat this so-called state food, I sure will lose a lot of weight. Mom knows how I eat so she knows I'll be going hungry most of the time. Well, they have water. I'll be drinking a lot of that. Sure wish you could send me some food!

I sure hope my Christmas goodies don't get ripped off from my cell while I'm in here. If so, I'm sure I'll be back in the "hole" when I find out who did it. Nice future, hey? (Pitiful, suffer, suffer, and suffer is all I do.).

I didn't get to see the doctor today cause of my move to the "hole." I'll see him tomorrow. Besides my back problem, I'm coming down with the flu. Sure am coughing bad. I very seldom get sick. When I do, though, (every few years) I sure get sick. A few years ago I had to use a breathing machine daily that sprayed medication into my lungs. Wish I could use it this time. It would get me out of the "hole" a few times a day. But I know the doctor isn't going to order it cause he knows it will make these guards mad. A lot of work, taking me up to the hospital and returning me. Well, I'm in the right spot to get rest.

Maybe I can get Michelle to write me once a week and cut out some interesting articles from newspapers and magazines. Sure helps out as it gives me something else to read. There is no doubt within these 30 days I'll re-read the New Testament and the book I mentioned earlier. Even reading letters and replying to them will help pass time.

I already made a chess set out of paper (ha!) and played a game with another guy that is 5 cells away. We holler out moves. I'll make a deck of cards out of paper tomorrow. It will help pass time too.

Too bad you live so far away. You could get in for a visit as a "para-legal." The lawyers arrange that. All they do is type out a letter stating you work for them and are assisting on my case. Then they call down and inform these people when you will be there. They could do that every day. Ha! I do have a couple Christian friends who have been doing this once a month for years with me. So, I'll write them tonight and inform them of my situation. They will be down to visit. But it's only once a month. Oh well, better than nothing, right?

Well, I'll go. Want to write Michelle. You and your family take care! Thanks for caring!

Love,
Larry

*****

January 11, 1994
Dear Larry,

Received your letter yesterday. I am very sorry to hear that you are in the "hole." Is it as bad as it sounds? From what you said in your letter, it sounds like solitary confinement. Are the living conditions worse than normal? I'm sure it's going to be hard to not get out and be able to talk to and be around others for the three weeks you have left. Is this the first time you've been in the "hole"? Michelle and I are planning to write you as much as we can. She had quite a bit of homework last night, but I think she is planning to write tonight. She's thought of something to send to help you occupy your time, but I'll let her tell you in her letter.

I hope that by now you've had a chance to see the doctor and are starting to feel better. I can't imagine an over 200-pound person falling on me. It must have been really painful! Were any ribs broken, or do you just have strained muscles? It can take quite a while to mend when muscles are involved. I'm praying that you will get relief from the pain soon as I know how constant pain can wear on you.

I would be glad to see that your niece and nephew get their Christmas presents. The box has not come yet, but we're sure looking forward to its arrival. It's hard not to open the envelope until the box arrives, but we'll wait! As soon as it comes, I'll give your sister-in-law a call. It's too bad that she and your brother are separated. It must be very difficult for the children to understand and accept. How old are they? It is great that she is a Christian.

You asked in your letter if I would send you some Bible lessons from the New Testament. I would *love* to! I went to our Christian bookstore today and found a short Bible study. Since you are not allowed to have any books except the Bible, I photocopied the pages. At the end of the study, all of the Bible verses for each of the three chapters are given for you.

You said you were allowed to take a New Testament with you when you were moved. The first four books of the New Testament—the gospels (meaning "good news")—focus on Jesus and His ministry while He was on earth. They are a great place to start. I'll try my best to answer any questions that you have about things in the New Testament or the book the guard gave you by David Wilkerson. Our local bookstore is ordering a copy of the book for me since I have not read it. It should be here next week. David Wilkerson is a Christian. I read one of his books, *The Cross and the Switchblade*, and enjoyed it. The story is about how a teenage gang leader came to know Jesus Christ and how his life was changed through David Wilkerson's ministry. I'm looking forward to reading *Hungry for More of Jesus*.

I found some other things at the bookstore today, but I'll send them after I have read them.

Did you get the flu like you thought you were? Sure hope not as that flu that is going around seems to be bad this year. When you get sick, you really get sick! I'll be praying for you. Dave fought a cold all last week, and Michelle is fighting one now. Her throat is really full, and now her nose is quite stuffy. She told us yesterday that her throat only hurts when she has talked too much. So when she mentions that it is hurting, we ask her if that tells her anything. She loves to talk! She's also fun to tease.

You asked what I baked that was in your goodie box. I made the pound cake, strawberry cake, and peanut butter fudge. We must have disguised them well enough in the containers the store bakery provided to allow you to have them! Dave is our expert peanut brittle maker! He got the recipe from an Army buddy when he was in basic training. Our family and coworkers always look forward to crunching on his peanut brittle. It never lasts more than a day or two.

Did you get your deck of cards made? What card games do you like to play? You must be a chess fan. That's one game I've never played. Michelle and I like to play card games though. She's quite a game player and is *very* competitive.

Ginger seems to have adjusted quite well. She's almost potty-trained and generally goes to the sliding door downstairs when she needs to go out. Michelle is so happy to have her. Gregg is the one who really surprised us though. He had never mentioned much about having a dog, but he sure loves her. When we only had her for a couple of days, he was feeling bad that she kept going to Michelle all the time and wouldn't follow him around. It still bothers him that she seems to prefer females. He makes sure, however, that he gets his fair share of nights with Ginger sleeping in his room with him. Michelle tries to get out of sight and sound range every now and then so Gregg can have Ginger time. Since Gregg is a night person, he plays with the dog a lot after Michelle goes to bed. She has stolen all of our hearts! There have been a lot of laughs, cuddling, and "Kodak moments" since she's been around. Michelle has taken at least two rolls of film already. We'll send more pictures as we have them developed.

Michelle and I both always look forward to each letter that we get from you. It's hard to believe that we've been writing now for eleven months. We're glad that we've had a chance to get to know you better.

I'll be praying that you will be able to endure the next three weeks.

Love,
Erin

Excerpts from Letters from January 16 to 20, 1994

Dear Larry,

How are you making out? By the time you get this letter, your time should be half over! I've been thinking of you and praying for you several times each day.

As Michelle told you in her last letter, your box arrived. We both really *love* the slippers. Tell whoever made them what a good job he did. And they're so warm! The temperature has been below zero the last couple of days. (Last night, the temp was supposed to get from -15 to -30 below!) So they have felt really good! The sizes for both of us were perfect as well as the colors. You'll never know how much your gift means to both of us!

Dave and I dropped the gifts off to your niece and nephew. I had some Christmas paper handy, so I wrapped them since I know how much kids like to open gifts! The Barney was adorable, and the white slippers were so feminine. I'm sure they'll both like the gifts. I also enjoyed talking to your sister-in-law.

I've been thinking a lot about your last letter and the section where you commented that you hate and continue to punish yourself. I really haven't known how to respond since I'm not a psychologist or psychiatrist. I do know, however, that you are not the only one who feels this way. Most of the time, we have negative feelings about ourselves because of the way we've been treated by others, how they have talked to us, and the messages they've given us. Before long, we begin believing these things about ourselves—that we're no good, that we'll never amount to anything, that we deserve everything we get, etc. Usually, we regret the things that we have done but can't undo them. It's sometimes hard to live with the thoughts, and we start hating ourselves.

Not having had a chance to know you during the first forty-one years of your life, I really do not totally know what you've been through—nor do I necessarily need to know. Christ, however, knows—and that's what's important. Being in and out of prison as you have been for most of the last twenty-eight years would, I'm sure, be extremely hard on your self-esteem. My guess is that you are constantly treated as a nonperson with no rights and told degrading things. After a while, the principle of self-fulfilling prophecy takes over—we become what people tell us about ourselves and expect out of us.

No human being has been able to live a life that's been perfect (except Christ when He was on earth). We've all done and said things that we regret but can't take back or undo (that's sin). Everyone has sinned—it doesn't matter what the "crime" was; we're all just as guilty in God's eyes. We *all* deserve to be punished for our sins. Without Christ, it is easy to hate ourselves for we have no reason not to. We are unloving and many times unlovable.

I'm glad, however, that God is merciful and loving. Even though we deserve to be punished, He chooses to forgive us. Jesus died on the cross to take the punishment for any sins we've committed in the past or will commit in the future. Because of Christ's sacrifice, God not only forgives us but also forgets our sins. When He looks at someone who has asked for His forgiveness, He doesn't see a sinner anymore—He sees a "new" person. This new person may not always be perfect, but He never stops loving him/her.

A negative self-esteem can only be changed by God's love and forgiveness into a more positive one. I know my self-esteem comes only from God and how highly He views me. He considers me a precious gift and promises to always love me unconditionally—something we as humans aren't capable of doing since we tend to either not ever forgive or forgive and leave the handle of the hatchet sticking out so we can quickly grab it up again. Jesus wants to show you how much He also loves you. I'm praying that you'll come to the point where you can give in and let Him show you that unconditional love. His love can give you an inward joy and sense of peace that you've never before known and can help you learn to love yourself more.

Well, so much for my sermon! I hope you realize that I share these things with you because I care about you. I pray every day that you will discover for yourself what I'm talking about.

How are you coming with your reading of the New Testament and the book by David Wilkerson? I just got my copy of his book yesterday and have read about the first fifty pages. Let me know of any questions you may have. I'll do my best to answer them.

I did some more searching for another Bible study for you and finally found one that I think you will like. It is called the *Uniqueness of Jesus*. You may find some overlap between the one I sent last week and this one, but there are also some differences. Since you can't have books, I'm going to send it in parts. There is a twenty-page introduction at the beginning and then five Bible lessons that go along with the introduction. I'm sending half of the intro pages now and the first two lessons. Each day, I will send more of the study to you.

I've been reading a new book entitled *He Still Moves Stones* by Max Lucado, one of my favorite authors. It is a series of short stories that focuses on the miracles of Jesus and relates these miracles to the present to show how God uses these miracles to also speak to us today. The ones that I'm enclosing relate to two of the incidents from Bible Lesson 4 and may help you interpret the lesson even better.

I also found a small book by Josh McDowell that I'll be sending you in three or four installments over the next several days. I figured it will take about six days to get everything to you. That way, you'll get some mail each day for a while.

Eventually, you will also get a couple of lessons from another study called *Meeting Jesus*, which our youth pastor gave me yesterday. It is a little more in-depth than the previous studies I have sent. Therefore, please write me if you run across questions that you don't understand and want more explanation on. I'm praying that Christ will work in your heart as you study about Him and that you will see Him in a way that you have never seen Him before.

Have you been playing chess much with the guy five cells down from you? What kind of card games have you been playing with the cards you said you were making?

Michelle had a birthday bowling party today, and her birthday is just two days from now. I can't believe my "baby" will be fifteen! She'd get upset if I told you all about her party, so I won't—but I would call it crazy bowling! I'm sure she'll be writing you about it soon. She's one that always shows a lot of excitement over special events, so she could hardly wait for her party!

Since she had perfect attendance this semester, she doesn't have to take the semester final exams. She said that she was going to school even if she was sick, so she didn't have to take exams. Fortunately, she made it! Therefore, she gets Tuesday through Friday off this week. It will be nice having her home.

I need to go for now. Take care and write soon. I'm praying that God will use your study of the Bible to let you see that He is real and that He cares for and loves you.

Love,
Erin

*****

January 19, 1994
Dear Erin,

Hope this letter finds you all well! Myself, my back is better except when I'm in one position too long (like when I'm sitting here writing this letter). Then when I move, it really bothers me. Yeah, the doctor said I did sprain some muscles.

No, I didn't come down with the flu like I thought I was. I had those bad coughs for a few days and that was it. Looks like my white corpuscles defended the flu germs early! Sure was alright with me.

I thought my food problem was resolved too, but I was wrong. Like I told you before, I very seldom eat this so-called food they serve us. These years I've been on death row I've survived on the store goodies I could afford to buy. After a week in the "hole," they noticed I'd only eaten one meal and had a physician come talk to me. He asked why I wasn't eating. I told him why. He asked if there was any food I'd eat. I informed him I can eat the "brown bag" meals they give the regular inmates who work outside for lunch that consisted of sandwiches and a fruit. Since these people didn't have to cook anything, I knew they couldn't mess up sandwiches. The doctor said he'd see what he could do.

Well, the next morning and lunch (no supper), I received at each meal two "brown bags." Each one consisted of three sandwiches, two oranges, and a little can of juice. (The doctor must have told the kitchen to add one extra sandwich, fruit and juice as the workers don't get double.) Boy, I thought my eating problems were over! That day I received a total of 4 cans of juice, 8 oranges, and 12 sandwiches. But since I'd shut my eating (engine) off, I just wasn't hungry. I ate one sandwich and an orange all that day.

Anyways, the doctor came to my cell the next day. He informed me the deputy warden had canceled the order. I sure don't understand that. The doctor prescribed them as treatment for a problem. I told him I sure don't know how they could cancel the doctor's order. I'm lucky the sandwiches were wrapped in cellophane. I just finished today the last sandwich, six days later. I still have a few oranges left. Got to stretch them too.

Thanks for copies of the Bible lessons. I found out I could receive the book you made the copies from as it is religious material. I didn't think I could have anything but the Bible. I asked this local ministry if they had a Bible course and they sent me one plus many other religious books, and the guard gave them to me. Plus I asked the chaplain if he had any Bible courses. He said that he sure did and would send them down to me. So I now have plenty to read and lessons to do. It sure will make these last two weeks go by faster.

You shouldn't have ordered that book *Hungry for More of Jesus* since I'd have sent you my copy. I didn't realize that he was the author of *The Cross and the Switchblade*. (I read that many years ago). I've read half of it. Could've finished it in one day, but I have to stretch things. I read from that, the Bible, do Bible lessons, write letters, and read my trial transcript each day.

I am glad your Christmas presents arrived. Michelle said she loves the slippers and that they fit too. I am glad that you like yours too. I think they came at the right time with the cold weather y'all are having! Who got the funny looking kind (the ones that I had to send instructions with)? Mom likes those the best. Wish I could've sent you two something more.

It's been cold down here the last week. That's ok with me. I can get under the blankets. The heat is what really gets to me. Hopefully, I won't be alive when summer arrives this year.

Sure got a smile out of reading Michelle's and your letters regarding Ginger! I bet she'll be chewing on those slippers too. (Ha!)

It's in the Bible that He'll answer prayers and take care of His believers. Explain to me why other Christians, like you, have bad things happen to them (accidents, death, injury, sickness, finance problems, etc.) when they are real Christians.

Yes, I made the deck of playing cards but haven't used them in days. I've gotten other things to do—plenty of reading and Bible courses. My favorite card games are pinochle, spades, hearts, poker (ha!) gin rummy, 500 Rummy (just to name a few.) I'm real good at all of them. Since math was my favorite subject in school, it gives me an advantage.

You sure are a good cook! I didn't realize you baked both the pound cake and strawberry cake and made the peanut butter fudge. And Dave made the peanut brittle, hey? And y'all aren't overweight. Ha! Boy, it has my stomach talking now thinking of them. Well, two weeks and two days from now I'll be out of this "hole."

The guard just told me when I asked that it is now 2:15 a.m. Since the last pick up for mail is at 3 a.m., I will not be able to write Michelle tonight. Hope she is not hurt when she does not get a letter when you get this one. Tell her that I will write her tomorrow.

Thanks for caring!

Love,
Larry

*****

January 27, 1994
Dear Larry,

Michelle and I both received your letters on Monday. They must have caught up with each other over the weekend! At first, we were surprised that they were in separate envelopes and then realized they had been written on separate days. She was happy that she had one too, although she would have understood!

We were glad to hear that you didn't get the flu and that your back is feeling better. It usually takes quite a while for strained muscles to completely heal so you'll probably be reminded occasionally that they are still not feeling 100 %. Dave strained his back muscles lifting a photocopier, and it took his back a whole year along with some physical therapy to get back to normal. Occasionally, it still tightens up on him.

You asked in your letter why bad things happen to Christians. I guess from a non-Christian perspective, it would seem like Christians should always have good "luck" or good things happening to them. However, that is not what the Bible indicates. In James 1:2, Christians are told, "Consider it pure joy, my brothers, whenever you face trials of many kinds" (NIV). In Isaiah 43:2, we are told, "When you pass through the waters, I will be with you; and when you pass through the rivers, they will not sweep over you. When you walk through the fire, you will not be burned; the flames will not set you ablaze" (NIV). Both of these verses speak of difficult times and use the words "when" and "whenever." This means that hard times will come into the lives of Christians.

Sometimes, Christians (because we're human) and non-Christians wonder why the difficult times are necessary. It isn't the way God originally planned it when He made the earth. It is the result that sin has had on all of creation. *Everyone* has to die since our bodies eventually wear out. How one will die, most do not know. Diseases are a result of Adam and Eve's original sin in the Garden of Eden. Hard times also were passed upon all men as a consequence of their sin. Man, however, has a free will and does destructive things to his body that may ultimately cause death—wrong eating habits, drugs, alcohol, not taking care of his body, etc. Sometimes we, as Christians, also do not make wise choices and have to suffer the consequences of our choices. So even Christians can expect to encounter some hard times during their lifetimes.

God doesn't leave Christians without hope, however. Even though we can expect to have difficult times, we have a source of strength to see us through those hard times that a non-Christian does not have. Isaiah 43:2 (stated above) reminds us that God goes *with us* through trials—He is our protector. Isaiah 40:27–31 gives Christians further hope in rough times,

> People of Jacob, why do you complain? People of Israel, why do you say, "The *Lord* does not see what happens to me; he does not care if I am treated fairly"? Surely you know. Surely you have heard. The LORD is the God who lives forever, who created all the world. He does not become tired or need to rest. No one can understand how great his wisdom is. He gives strength to those who are tired and more power to those who are weak. Even children become tired and need to

rest, and young people trip and fall. But the people who trust the *Lord* will become strong again. They will rise up as an eagle in the sky; they will run and not need rest; they will walk and not become tired. (NCV)

Christians will have difficult times, but we can have peace during those times because of another promise God has made in Isaiah 26:3, "You, *Lord*, give true peace to those who depend on you, because they trust you" (NCV). Philippians 4:13 shares where a Christian's strength and stamina in hard times come from, "I can do all things through Christ because he gives me strength" (NCV).

What purpose do trials or hard times such as sickness have in a Christian's life? The answer is given in James 1:3, "Because you know that these trials will test your faith, and this will give you patience" (NCV). The Lord knew that our patience and perseverance through the trials would help mature and grow us as Christians and force us to rely more on Him for strength.

Many times, the trials that we experience can serve another purpose. They can help us be more sympathetic to others who are experiencing similar trials. When we have successfully made it through a hard time with God's strength, we can encourage others to not give up but to rely on God to see them through.

I have had my rough times, but I know they have strengthened my faith and drawn me closer to God. He's seen me through every one and will continue to do so as long as I live on this earth. Only in heaven will we live a trouble-free existence.

When Christ lived on earth, He did not have a trouble-free existence. He had problems too. He was misunderstood and mistreated. His strength to endure, however, came from God. He was our example. Since Christ experienced hard times, we also can expect to have hard times—even as a Christian. He told His disciples that they would have hard times while in this world, and they did. Yet their faith and their love for Christ saw them through those times.

Does this make any sense to you in terms of an explanation? It probably sounds a little crazy from a non-Christian perspective, but everything I've written I've found to be true in my life. If you come to the point where you can believe in God, you'll know what I've said is absolutely true.

You have certainly gotten a lot of Bible lessons to do! I am glad you found out that you could have religious books and took advantage of the opportunity. I will be waiting to hear more from you regarding the lessons.

I'll be glad when you can leave the "hole." Hope you get some more food that you can eat. I couldn't believe the warden would cancel the doctor's orders either! It seems like the main job of your warden is to see how miserable he can make life for prisoners (at least, that's the impression I get from TV and from you).

My dad has a new neurologist now. He's going to have a nerve biopsy done soon, and it will be sent to Mayo Clinic to see what type of neuropathy is causing his numbness in hopes that they can get to the bottom of his problem. He was so encouraged yesterday. We are too since he's quite unstable when he walks.

Ginger is always good for a few laughs. Yesterday, I was talking with my mother on the phone and had the phone cord stretched from the kitchen counter to the table where I was sitting. It was right in the path she takes to get to the family room. She came bounding out of the living room with a sock in her mouth and ran right into the phone cord. She didn't realize it until she tried to jump over the step that goes down into the family room and the phone cord bounced her back into the kitchen. You should have seen the *very* confused look on her face! I couldn't help but laugh! Yes, she does like the slippers you sent me! Anytime she can reach them, she drags them around. I have to remember to put them up high enough so she can't get to them. As I said before, I really like them. I got the yellow and peach pairs (two of my favorite colors), and Michelle got the rose and red ones. They sure felt good last week when it was so cold!

On February 7, Dave and I are going to the Bahamas for six days. I can hardly wait to get to the warm weather! We've never been there before and may not get a chance to go in the middle of winter again since I normally do not have the time off. Michelle will be staying with my mom and dad, and Gregg will be holding down the fort at home.

Well, guess I had better be signing off for now so I can work some more on my sabbatical project. Take care.

Love,
Erin

*****

January 27, 1994

Dear Erin,

By the time you receive this, I'll only have a couple days left to serve here in the "hole." So, when you write again, put G-2-59, the new cell I'll be in when I get out.

The doctor put me back on pain pills and muscle relaxers yesterday. My back was starting to get real bad again.

Last Friday another doctor stopped and asked me why I was not eating. By then I had been in the "hole" for 16 days and had ate two or maybe three meals in that period of time. So, I told him why not and what the other doctor tried to do for me, but the Deputy Warden canceled his order. He said he'd talk to the other doctor and do something. Whatever the Deputy Warden told the first doctor, who I am sure told the second doctor, must have made him "back off" cause I never heard from him again.

This past week was a good week for me. There were some meals I could eat. But this last week will be another long one, plenty of water drinking for me.

Let me re-read your letters from the 16-20th so I comment on everything you wrote about or asked me. Glad to hear you liked your slippers!

Thank you for wrapping and dropping off the gifts to my niece and nephew. I received a letter from my sister-in-law today. Sure is sad to read how much their separation is hurting her and the children! I'll be writing my brother on that subject. He knows how much it hurt our family when my parents separated. Ok, I have to accept that he doesn't want to be with her any more, but he's ignoring the children too. That I can't understand and will tell him a few words (ha!) about it. (Few words is the nice way of saying what I'm really going to say.)

Michelle told me all about her birthday and bowling party. I sure got a smile reading all about it. Her happiness just overflowed from her letter. I hope y'all will share some of the pictures with me. I'll return them.

Wow, it sure did get cold in Battle Creek! It was even unusually cold down here for two weeks.

Thought I just saw a flash. My little mouse might be back to visit. I can't believe how fast he is!

I'm playing chess with another guy as the previous guy got released. This guy can't play too good so it's not interesting to me but we are passing time. That's why I'm playing.

Well, now to the part I saved for last. I saved it for last cause I might offend you, which I'm really sorry for.

The good news first. (Ha!) I had already completed the two Bible courses that I received from the chaplain before I received yours. Total of 24 lessons. And I'll be surprised if I made a mistake on any of the questions.

By this weekend, I'll have read the Josh McDowell book, *Christianity: Hoax or History* plus the 20-page introduction to the Bible study of *The Uniqueness of Jesus*. I read every verse in the Bible studies you sent me. But the bad news, and again I'm sorry, I probably won't answer the questions. You see, with the first two Bible studies I just completed, I had to read plus look up verses and read them to answer the questions. But the answers didn't have to be in your own words. However, in the studies you sent me, they ask in your own words (explain) what this verse means. In the other two studies, the question called for a certain answer, not what I think this verse means to me.

You see, Erin, I don't ever want to be a hypocrite. I can't say what something means to me if I don't believe. I hope you can understand what I'm saying. You spent your money for me to do these study courses and now I'm telling you I won't answer the questions. I know you aren't happy with me. Try to understand that I'm trying to believe. Like I said, I'll read everything plus look up and read every verse that the questions refer to. So, your money isn't wasted. I just can't put into words yet what the verses mean to me if I don't fully believe in them. Sorry again! I really do think before I die that I'll answer them. I sure hope and pray so.

Well, I'll close for now. I want to write Michelle. Again, I'm sorry! You all take care!

Love,
Larry

Think About It: Self-Esteem

Larry stated at the beginning of this chapter that he hated himself so much that he confessed to fighting with the other inmate because he always felt the need to punish himself. When did his self-hatred begin? Was it when he was involved in the murders that landed him on death row? Or did it begin much earlier in his life?

His hate of himself is the extremely negative side of self-esteem. Self-esteem is simply how you think about yourself and view your worth. Generally, low self-esteem, such as Larry's, begins in childhood. It is affected not only by family dynamics or dysfunction but also by significant adults and peers as one enters school.

Children have a real need to feel loved, approved, and accepted. When they are not, the false assumptions about themselves that they pick up from those who are closest to them become their mental reality. Children who feel unloved may assume that they *are* unlovable. Those who are constantly criticized—told they are stupid, will never amount to anything, are ugly, or continually get negative comments—will soon begin to *believe* these things about themselves. Some children have even been told by a parent that it would have been better if they had never been born. As I wrote to Larry, what one is told and believes about oneself may eventually become self-fulfilling prophecy.

Do you recall the statement Larry made about his childhood? He said, "When my family fell apart, I fell apart." He was eleven when his parents divorced. That was also the time that he began getting into trouble by committing minor crimes that eventually led to his death-row conviction. In an earlier letter, he commented that his dad had never told him that he loved him until he was close to being executed. How many children go through life feeling unloved by one or both parents? How many children are the victims of divorce and think they must have been the cause of it? How many children are abused either physically or emotionally? How many are being bullied by peers? Too many!

What negative behaviors can result from low self-esteem? According to an article dealing with self-esteem in young people,[23] the following are several common behaviors exhibited by children/teens with low self-esteem that when not dealt with will most likely be carried over into adulthood:

- Poor academic performance
- Dropping out of school
- Criminal behavior
- Cutting
- Teen pregnancy
- Early sexual activity
- Alcohol and drug abuse
- Eating disorders

My father, who grew up in a poor family in Mississippi, was physically and emotionally abused as a child by his father. (Fortunately, he had a mother who loved him but, unfortunately, could do little to prevent the abuse.) Of the seven children, he was treated the worst. After finishing fourth grade, he was not allowed to continue going to school so that he could pick cotton for $1 a day that would be given to his father. At one time, his father actually gave him away to a relative for a time. When he was sixteen, he left home hoping to find a better life in Michigan with an aunt and uncle, Larry's maternal grandparents.

The abuse definitely left its scars, and his emotional comfort as a teenager was found in my mother and alcohol. Fortunately, my mother had enough "fight" in her that she protected my brother and me from his alcoholism by teaching us to leave him alone until he was sober. A person who comes from a home where abuse was frequent can carry the pattern into marriage and family. I am so glad, however, that my dad broke that abuse cycle, which I think was probably because he knew what it felt like and how much he hated it. His childhood, however, did have an impact on his self-esteem. It took the threat of divorce and coming to Christ for him to be able to finally control his alcoholism.

I was also fortunate to grow up in a home where I knew my parents genuinely loved me. Despite that, I learned to become a "pleaser" and "stuffer" since my father believed "children should be seen and not heard," expected complete obedience, and a majority of the time was convinced that his opinions were totally correct. Although the abuse cycle was definitely broken, not everything from his (or anyone's) childhood could be put behind him when he became a parent.

I saw the consequences of disobedience since my brother was more free-spirited than I was and was not afraid to talk back. Even though there was no abuse, I did not like to be punished or to be the one to create conflict in my home. To me, being a "pleaser" and "stuffer" was a normal part of life and became part of how I thought of myself. Both had their "benefits." Only later on in life did I realize they were actually negative benefits. Another outcome was that I subconsciously developed an aversion to being controlled.

My actual journey with real esteem issues began as a junior higher when a boy that had liked me in the seventh grade decided that he no longer "liked" me as a girlfriend in the eighth grade. As a junior high gal is prone to do, I sent out a "scout" to find out why. The answer I got back was devastating. He said that it was because I was "ugly." From that day on, I viewed myself differently. However, I never told *anyone* about his comment.

Years later, I realized that it was at that moment I made an unconscious decision to do things that I could control to compensate for being "ugly." It came in the form of overachievement, perfectionism, and weight control. It was good for my career but really wore me out as a wife, mother, daughter, employee, friend, etc. Although I was never anorexic or bulimic, I wanted to keep my weight under control and would get on the scales quite often and cut back on what

I ate accordingly if I had gained a pound. I also wanted to make myself look as nice as I could, which meant my hair and makeup always needed to be as perfect as I could get them before leaving the house. If I did not feel I looked good or had a "bad hair" day, I would be down on myself and feel ugly the entire day.

When I hit my fifties, I could no longer handle the pressure I was putting on myself, became very depressed, and had to seek professional counseling. Getting over thinking of myself as being ugly and instead seeing myself as the beautiful woman God created me to be has been a journey as has been my struggle with perfectionism. There are still times when these tendencies surface. What is important, however, is that I have made progress!

One must also consider what your Creator thinks of you. He knew as humans we would have days when we needed to know His thoughts about us. There are several self-esteem-building verses from the Bible that provide encouragement when we are down on ourselves. Let's look at a few.

> I knew you before I formed you in your mother's womb. (Jeremiah 1:5a NLT)
>
> I will praise you for I am fearfully and wonderfully made. (Psalm 139: 14a NIV)
>
> See, I have written your name on the palms of my hands. (Isaiah 49:16a NLT)
>
> The *Lord* your God is with you; the mighty One will save you. He will rejoice over you. You will rest in His love; He will sing and be joyful about you. (Zephaniah 3:17 NCV)
>
> God even knows how many hairs are on your head. (Matthew 10:30 NCV)
>
> Also, the Spirit helps us with our weakness. We do not know how to pray as we should. But the Spirit himself speaks to God for us, even begs God for us with deep feelings that words cannot explain. (Romans 8:26b NCV)

> But God showed his great love for us by sending Christ to die for us while we were still sinners. (Romans 5:8 NLT)
>
> For we are God's masterpiece. He has created us anew in Christ Jesus, so we can do the good things He planned for us long ago. (Ephesians 2:10 NLT)
>
> But you are a chosen people, a royal priesthood, a holy nation, God's special possession. (1 Peter 2:9b NIV)

What about you? Do you feel good about yourself and have a positive self-esteem? If so, you are indeed blessed! It may possibly be hard for you to understand why others could have a low self-esteem. My challenge to you is to try to understand that others' lives have been different than your life. There may be some deeply suppressed memories that have not even surfaced that they are unknowingly carrying around that still haunt them and perhaps paralyze their mental growth. The most important thing you can do is to encourage them to seek help and to not judge them. A quote from Dr. Chuck Swindoll in his book *Growing Strong in the Seasons of Life* is worth remembering, "Discouraged people don't need critics. They hurt enough already. They don't need more guilt or piled-on distress. They need encouragement. They need a refuge."[24]

If you fall into the negative self-esteem category, you are not alone. My questions to you are as follows: "Are you tired of living your life like you are? Are you tired of having your past define your future? If so, what are you going to do to take even some baby steps in the opposite direction?" It is not mandatory that you live the rest of your life feeling about yourself like you presently do. There are resources available to help you learn the root cause(s) of your low self-esteem.

A good starting place for getting help is a relationship with Jesus. You need Him on your side to help you fight the battle and give you hope. With His direction, He can give wisdom as to who might be your best source of help. If you are not sure where to start the search for help, one option is a church pastor. Another option may be your family physician who may be able to recommend a counselor. The advantage of having a counselor is that you have a completely *objective* individual who you can talk with that will keep your discussions confidential. Whoever you seek out for counseling, however, be sure to find someone you feel comfortable with who is properly qualified. As I mentioned in a previous chapter, do not automatically think that you could never afford counseling.

From experience, I know how freeing it is to finally get things "off your chest" that may have been there for years. Be ready, however, to put into practice what you learn. If you do not take this step, you will have wasted your time and money.

If you are a reader and would prefer to explore some issues bothering you, there is also a multitude of books available by certified psychologists that examine how your past is impacting your present and future. But again, be selective in which authors you read. Not everyone who writes a book is necessarily an expert in the field. Look at his/her credentials, beliefs, and counseling experience. Three excellent books that helped me immensely along with counseling are *Father Memories* by Dr. Randy L. Carson, *The Mom Factor* by Dr. Henry Cloud and Dr. John Townsend, and *Self Matters* by Dr. Phil McGraw (read it *and* actually complete the exercises). Together, this trio of books explores how your childhood can still be affecting you as an adult.

Three other books that helped me improve my self-image and deal with my "pleaser" personality were *Do You Think I'm Beautiful* by Angela Thomas, *People Pleasers: Helping Others Without Hurting Yourself* by Dr. Les Carter, and *Boundaries: When to Say Yes and When to Say No to Take Control of Your Life* by Dr. Henry Cloud and Dr. John Townsend. Reading alone, however, may not be enough to get you where you need to be. It may, though, be the start you need to put you on the path to healing.

My challenge to you is to "Just Do It©" as the Nike slogan says!

Chapter 9

February 1, 1994

Dear Erin,

By the time you receive this letter, I'll be out of the "hole." Eating plenty of junk food (chips, cookies, etc.) Ha! Plus mom will be visiting Saturday morning! She will smuggle me in a sandwich. Everybody does it. The guards don't care as long as it's not drugs, which some do. I told her to double up this time on the sandwich! But besides the food, it sure will be good to see her again! Just sitting next to her without talking even means so much to me! Probably cause I know there isn't going to be many more. Wish she could visit every weekend. However, that is not possible since she can't afford to pay anybody to bring her down. Now a paralegal brings her every two weeks.

These guys sure are going to miss me when I get out on Friday. Besides telling them how to make chess and checker sets out of paper, which helps us pass a lot of time playing, I make puzzles for them to solve, which also helps to pass time. I even gave them some addresses of people they could write in England and the USA that would be pen pals for them, which sure is important to inmates.

As you can see, I did the enclosed Bible lessons. They were too easy. Plus you took all the fun (time) out of it by looking up and printing the passages. I also read and looked up all the passages in the other two Bible courses you sent me. But I told you in my last letter why I didn't answer the questions.

I was very interested in Josh McDowell's *Christianity: Hoax or History*. He has an address where he invited us to write him with comments and questions. I plan on doing that too! When I get his reply, I'll send it to you.

Since I've been in the "hole," I've written close to 50 letters. I had that many stamps cause we use to be able to receive stamps in the mail. They sure hurt us when they changed the rules on getting stamps. We now have to buy them from the inmate store.

After getting out of the "hole," they are moving me to another cell block so that I will not be with the guy who I got into the fight with. That means that I have lost my shower job. It helped some during the summer since I could take at least five showers a day. Now I'll be down to one or two. Boy, am I going to be really suffering. It's like an oven. I always have to get up a couple times in the middle of the night and pour water over me. It helps a little. Sure rough sleeping being that uncomfortable.

When I was young, I used to go to church regularly. But at that age, I didn't understand (like I do now) the meanings of the sermons. I also love those classic movies about the Bible—*The Ten Commandments* with Charlton Heston as Moses, *The Greatest Story Ever Told,* and so on. Plus I still know most of the words to my favorite Christian songs: "The Old Rugged Cross," "Amazing Grace," "Silent Night," "Are You Washed in the Blood" to name some off the top of my head. And like I said, it's been over 20 years since I sung most of these and still know most of the words. Surprised, I bet, hey? Back then I had some faith. Sad I lost it!

Well, I missed the Super Bowl. Did you all watch it? I love all sports. Hope my back gets better.

By the way, don't blame me if Michelle now wants a ferret! Ha! You all take care. Thanks for caring!

Love,
Larry

*****

February 6, 1994
Dear Erin,

I have been busting my store goodies budget since I got out! Everybody has been commenting on how thin I am. When you lose 20+ pounds, what I figure I lost, it shows.

Sure was good to see mom yesterday! But it upset me to see how much pain she's in. She has to go back to the doctor tomorrow. They think she has arthritis in her hip, unreal!

I did not get your last letter until I got back to my new cell. Plus they gave me some other things they had kept from me. The last week of my stay over there they didn't allow me anything. I had so many packages of Christian books, Bible lessons, and articles they gave me on Friday. Glad they kept my *USA Today* newspapers. I'm starting to catch up with the news I missed. That earthquake in LA was unreal. It's sure sad too. Going to take years to repair the damage.

There is a small Christian ministry run by two retired men and a lady that sends Bibles and free Bible courses to anybody who wants them. The lady, Sister Millie, who I correspond with, always sends some beautiful greeting cards for me to send to my mom for special holidays (Mother's Day, Valentine's Day, Christmas, her birthday, etc.) She knows how much mom means to me. I never even have to ask her to send them either.

Well, I'll let you go. Take care! Thanks for caring!

Love,
Larry

*****

February 18, 1994
Dear Larry,

Hello from sunny Battle Creek! Yesterday and today make me think spring is on the way. The temperature has been around fifty-five degrees both days—a real heat wave. It felt good to be outside yesterday and not have to wear a heavy coat! I washed the car in the afternoon, and then, Michelle and I took Ginger for her first official walk on her leash. She appeared to enjoy it. I imagine things are starting to warm up in Georgia too.

Last Saturday, Dave and I returned home from our trip to the Bahamas. Boy, it sure was hard to leave. Every day, the temperature was in the eighties and sunny. We spent a lot of time just relaxing on the beach, soaking up the sun, and reading. (I read four books that week between flying and lying on the beach. I *loved* it!) We were both ready to do nothing for a while. I have enclosed a few pictures we took so you can see what it was like there.

We did a lot of walking since we did not rent a car. I would not have driven even if we did have a car since they drive on the opposite side of the road and *fast!* The first day there, a bus picked us up at the airport, and Dave and I were in the front seat. I about had a heart attack two or three times when I'd see a car coming toward us that looked like it was on the wrong side of the road! By Friday, we were getting a little more used to the traffic flow.

A part of our tour package was a day cruise to another island where we had an opportunity to go snorkeling, had a picnic lunch, and listened to some native entertainment aboard the boat. We found out that the native music has only one volume—*loud*. After a while, the songs sound pretty much the same. That is one thing I won't really miss. I had snorkeled one other time, but it was Dave's first time. He really loved it and couldn't believe how many different kinds of fish there were. The last night there, we got to take a sunset dinner cruise, which was a nice way to end our stay.

While we were gone, the East Coast was hit with an ice storm that delayed many flights. We made it to Charlotte, North Carolina, okay but had to wait an extra two hours for our next flight to Pittsburg—which meant we missed our connecting flight to Kalamazoo. Fortunately, we got on the last flight into Kalamazoo but were three hours late returning.

I found out that you never want to fly with a cold. On Saturday when I woke up, I felt that I might be getting the beginnings of a cold. By the time our first flight was ready to land, my ear was plugged so bad it was hurting to the point that I felt like crying; a few tears actually escaped. By the time we reached Kalamazoo, the pressure had built up inside my ear enough that it felt like it could burst. It was Sunday before it finally unplugged. What a relief! It was worth it, however, since the trip was so enjoyable.

I'm glad you're out of the hole now. I couldn't believe that you lost twenty pounds! I'm sure you have hit the goodies hard! Were your goodie boxes still there when you returned? I hope so. You'll have to eat extra to put on those lost pounds. The sandwiches your mom brought must have really tasted good!

Gregg is probably going to be on needles and pins for most of the day today. It looks like the store he works for is going to be closing—maybe even today. I told him that it will be sad if they close; however, the Lord will provide another job for him. What has been nice about this job is that he doesn't have to work on Sundays. I'll let you know what happens.

I did not see the Super Bowl, but Gregg and Dave watched it. Gregg had several friends from church over that night and made a party of it. Michelle and I went to my parents' house and watched something else.

You did a great job on the Bible lessons you sent back. The teacher in me would have given you an A! I understand why you do not feel you could answer the questions that asked for a response in your own words. I'm not upset with you for feeling that way. You said that eventually you will probably answer them. That is all I ask. I think that at this point you know what needs to be done to become a Christian. Now, it's up to the Lord to continue working in your heart so that your head knowledge becomes "heart" knowledge and you can believe what the Bible says is true. You're actually only about eighteen inches from becoming a Christian—the distance from your head to your heart! We'll be continuing to pray that you can take that trip soon.

The reason I wrote out the OT verses in the lessons is that I wasn't sure if you had just a New Testament or the whole Bible. Sorry I took away the fun of looking them up. I am impressed with the amount of Bible knowledge you have. You also know quite a few of the old hymns. I love Christian songs. Songs tend to stick with me much longer than just hearing words spoken by someone. It's amazing that twenty years later, I can still remember words to songs

I heard as a teenager. Many of my friends say they still remember the songs from their teen years too.

I am glad that you have a lot of Christian people who care for you and visit you. How thoughtful of Sister Millie to give you greeting cards to send to your mom on special occasions. That is a ministry of love to you and the other inmates.

Did you write to Josh McDowell yet? I'll be interested in hearing what he has to say. Since he had difficulty believing there was a God, I am sure he'll be able to relate well to how you feel.

I am glad your back is feeling better. The exercises should really help. They sure helped Dave. The exercises I have been doing for my back the last few months have made it feel much better. Is your mom feeling any better? There must be some medication that can help ease the pain.

I did not realize that your mom could visit every weekend. What hours of the day can visitors come? Is it just on Saturday or also on Sunday? I'm full of questions, aren't I? I am just curious.

Do you like your new cell block? I wondered why they had to move you to another cell block. Sorry to hear that you lost your shower job though. I can imagine that it is quite disappointing as well as hard on you during the hottest months.

Michelle and I have been enjoying watching the Olympics. The ice skating events are our favorite to watch. Dave likes to watch the skiing events too. That was something else about the attack on Nancy Kerrigan! Have you been watching them? If so, what are your favorite events?

Well, I'll be going for now. I think that I've answered all the questions from your letters. If I missed something, ask me again.

Michelle didn't get a chance to write yet, but you should be hearing from her in the next few days. I'll be looking forward to hearing from you hopefully very soon.

Love,
Erin

*****

February 21, 1994

Dear Erin,

Thank you for sharing the pictures from your trip with me! Boy, it sure is beautiful there! And it sounds like you two really had a good time. Got a smile when you wrote about your trip on the bus and the cars coming right at you. So, Dave really enjoyed snorkeling, hey? Boy, I bet he did. And I know there sure was a lot of pretty color fish to look at. Sure sounds like the cruises were real nice too. A nice honeymoon vacation sounds like to me! I know it took some adjusting when you got home going from the nice weather back to cold weather.

Also thank you for the beautiful Valentine's card!

It was nice all week down here, high 60s and low 70s. I sure dread the hot weather which will soon be upon us though. But I shouldn't be around to suffer through much of it. On February 10, my para-legal visited me and informed me that they have re-scheduled my hearing for April 19. So I should die in May.

Yes, my goodie boxes were still there in my cell when I got out of the 'hole." I ate a lot the first two weeks out. But now I am back on my budget.

Did Gregg's store that he works at close? If he doesn't find another job, he can work yards and stuff again as winter is almost over.

You asked about our family visits. Visiting hours are from 9 a.m. to 3 p.m. on weekends and holidays. Mom normally comes on Saturday mornings since Charlie died and usually stays for 3 hours. Now she can only visit me twice a month.

My new cell block is ok, but it really hurt to lose my shower job as I mentioned in my last letter. Plus I don't have control of the TVs like I did in the other block. If I did, I'd be watching the Olympics, which I love. I have not gotten to see any of the Olympics since the majority of the guys do not want to watch it. So, all I see is the highlights of it on the news. However, I like watching *all* the events. The luge looks like fun. I also like watching the ski jumping, but I wouldn't want to do it myself. Ha! I believe Tonya Harding was involved in planning the attack on Nancy. You can bet your house that she won't win any medals even if she's perfect. The judges will be biased against her.

I did write Josh McDowell and got a very short response back, which was disappointing. I am enclosing the response with this letter.

Tell Michelle I said hi and that I will write her this week when I get her letter. Well, I will let you go. You all take care!

Love,
Larry

*****

March 5, 1994

Dear Larry,

Even though it is only forty-five degrees, it's another beautiful, sunny Saturday. The sun makes all the difference in attitude! Thursday and Friday were about the same. It's *so* nice to take a walk around the neighborhood without freezing!

Ginger *loves* her walks. Yesterday, she was really into it—just prancing along and acting like she was having the best time of her life. The more I'm around Ginger, the more I feel what a perfect match she is for Michelle and our family as far as personality goes. She really fits in.

Michelle starts track practice on Monday, so we are going out today to get her some track shoes. She wants spikes this year since she feels it will help her run better. She's really our competitor. When practice starts, however, she's going to be kept quite busy since she'll have practice every day from three to four thirty and track meets on Mondays and Wednesdays beginning in mid-April until the end of May.

Gregg worked his last official day with the store open yesterday. He has this coming week off and will then get to help pack up and tear down the shelving in the store. He hasn't said too much about it, but I imagine he's feeling a little sad. Yesterday, the store owner let the employees buy whatever they wanted for 50% off. He bought quite a few things for us.

He's going out today to put his application in at some grocery and department stores. I think he'd like to work stock. At any rate, he found out he can get unemployment until he finds work. It will pay about 70 % of his average weekly salary. I was surprised since I thought part-time workers weren't eligible for unemployment. His plans are to mow lawns again this summer too. His official acceptance to Western Michigan University for the fall semester came today. Since his ultimate goal is to have his own business, he plans to pursue a business administration degree with a major in accounting and a minor in business management.

Thanks for sharing the brief generic note you received from the Josh McDowell Ministry saying that he would not be able to call you. I was quite disappointed in the response you got. My guess is that your letter did not make it to Josh. I am going to follow up on it. Did Penny send you anything else in the envelope or just the note? She did sound sincere in wanting to answer any questions you have. However, I know that's not what you wanted.

My dad is having a nerve biopsy on Monday morning at seven and a hemorrhoidectomy at 9 a.m. on Tuesday. They decided to do both while he was off his blood thinner so he wouldn't have to be taken off it twice. When he's off it, the risk of having another stoke is much greater. He'll have to stay overnight on Tuesday for observation. I'm certain he will be quite uncomfortable for a few days afterward! Hopefully, however, it will help him get back to normal.

Sorry to hear your mom is in such pain with her arthritis. Hopefully, the doctor can find the medication that will work for her to relieve the pain. It's so hard to watch our parents get older and their health to start failing. I think you feel about the same way I do when you see your mom hurting. There are days that it really tears me up inside. I'm just thankful, though, that my dad can still walk and talk. I know it could be so much worse. His brother who had a stroke cannot talk.

The Olympics sure went by fast. I'm sorry you didn't get to watch them. We watched them every night; however, I was beginning to get a little tired of them by the time they were over. It seemed like the people I wanted to see were always the last ones they had on near 11 p.m. I'm not much of a night person, so occasionally, Dave and Michelle would have to wake me up when it was time to watch. I was most interested in seeing Nancy Kerrigan and Tonya Harding after all the publicity. I felt Nancy got gypped out of the gold. The Russian gal's program wasn't as "clean" as Nancy's, but she still got the gold medal. That's the bad thing about ice skating—the judging is so subjective. Maybe I should have been one of the judges, huh? Oh well, they didn't ask me! Nancy will be sitting pretty financially with all the endorsements she'll get. I couldn't believe Disney is paying her $2 million! It will be interesting to see if Tonya Harding is actually indicted for the attack on Nancy since I think she was a part of it.

It's nice the paralegal brings your mom to visit twice a month. Somehow, I had the idea that visits were only one weekend a month. It's good that people can come any weekend and stay for as long as they want to (between nine and three). I imagine the three hours she stays goes by too fast. I sure would like to be able to visit you at least once. Guess if I'm going to be able to, the Lord will have to work it out. Maybe someday we will at least get to talk on the phone.

You mentioned that if you had been in your other cell block that you would probably have gotten to watch the Olympics. Are there different "politics" in your new cell block? Who decides what programs are watched? I thought you took turns choosing programs. It doesn't seem right that you never get to watch what you want.

So your hearing is set for April 19. I thought it would be coming up pretty soon. I can't say I'm looking forward to it; but since you seem to be wanting it, I'm glad for your sake. Be sure to let me know the results.

I'm coming along quite well on the computer course I've been working on. Starting the middle of this month, I am going to take four weeks of a microcomputer class to learn a couple other programs that I want to know more about. I also have some work-related books I want to read.

Well, I am signing off for now since it's almost time for supper. Dave fixes supper for me on Saturday night. It's always the same menu, but I sure won't complain! I feel really fortunate to have a husband like him. He's one of a kind.

Michelle is looking forward to receiving her letter. Write soon and take care. As always, I'm praying for you. You're special to us.

Love,
Erin

*****

March 10, 1994
Dear Larry,

Are you surprised to be hearing from me again so soon? As you read my letter, you'll find out there's a special reason why.

When I saw the response you got from John McDowell's ministry, I seriously doubted that Josh had even seen your letter. Well, I called Penny, his administrative assistant at his Dallas office, and talked quite a while with her. I was correct that he had not seen your letter. After we talked, she faxed your letter to him at his Julian, California, office where he spends most of his time when he's not traveling. (He just happened to be in for three days this week.) He's on the road a majority of the time.

After I got a surprise call from Penny today asking me to find out if you could receive phone calls, I called the prison and talked with your counselor. He told me that you could receive a call but that Josh's name needed to be on your Receipt of Funds list. He said that when a call came in, the security would check the list, and if you had less than 800, you could receive the call. I really did not understand exactly what the receipt of funds list is or what the 800 represents. Maybe you could explain it to me. Anyway, it sounds like a call from Josh to you might be a possibility. However, his name needs to be added to your list. Are there any certain hours of the day that calls have to be received? I really need to have this information as soon as possible as Penny will be seeing him in Dallas on March 21 to 23.

Would you find out and get a letter out to me just as soon as you can since your letters normally take about a week to get to me?

I'll be looking forward to hearing from you soon.

Love,
Erin

*****

March 16, 1994
Dear Erin,

I received your letter today regarding the phone call from Josh. The counselor is wrong; or if he's not, nobody has heard of what he told you. We are only allowed to receive calls from our lawyers. Then we still have to call them. The lawyers call down here and inform these people they want to talk to us. The message is then relayed to the guard in G-2, and he informs us. Then the guard calls collect to the lawyer. Nobody here, and some of these guys have been here over 10 years, have heard of these people letting somebody call directly in to us.

The Receipt of Funds list the counselor was referring to is my list of people that I am allowed to call. We get around that by putting on our phone call request form the name of somebody on our Receipt of Fund List but put down the phone number of who we want to talk to.

What you could do is call and explain the situation to our chaplain. He could approve a phone call from me to Josh. But the best way is to have Josh call my lawyers. They would then call down here and go through the process I mentioned earlier. The lawyer could set up a three-way phone hookup then switch my line over to him. A lot of trouble either way. You shouldn't do it. I'm a lost cause. I'll be dying soon, *I'm really sad to say*, a non-believer. Plus you know that I still want to see evidence of a miracle to prove there is a God.

Since I've been out of the hole, I've moved back away from God that I had moved toward while I was in the hole. In the hole, I was contemplating God a lot—reading the Bible, doing Bible courses, and reading other religion material. Since I've been out, I haven't done any

133

of those things. *I'm sorry* cause I know this will hurt you. You just have to accept the fact I'm lost. And I'll be dying a lost sinner too.

It really means a lot to me that you tried to save me. If only it was 20 to 30 years earlier. I have given up on this life. I'm just waiting to die, which hopefully will be very soon. *Again, I am deeply sorry.*

Mom was scheduled to visit me this past weekend but couldn't since her doctors put some kind of gadget on her last week that monitors her heart. A couple times a day she has to call a number then put part of the gadget to the phone, which then relays the data to the doctor. We are waiting on the results now as they took it off her this week. Hopefully, she'll be able to come down this weekend. We sure are worried. Why would the doctor want this test unless he thought something was wrong?

How did the nerve biopsy and hemorrhoidectomy they did on your father come out? Yes, we are alike in that it really tears us up to see our loved ones suffering!

Has Gregg found another job yet? Sure good to hear he's been accepted at Western Michigan. What kind of business does he want to own? That sure made sense to take advantage of the 50% off items from Gregg's former store.

It was just in the news that Tonya Harding pled guilty today. It was a plea-bargain. A very good deal for her cause they could've convicted her of being involved with the planning of the attack. But being a home-town hero and having money got her this plea-bargain. She was guilty.

In the other cell blocks, they do take turns on deciding what's going to be on our TVs. In this block, they don't. A few guys with the most seniority run (choose the programs) the TVs, which is unfair. But since I'm not going to be here long, I won't "rock the boat."

I'm sleepy, so I'll close. You take care! *Again, I'm sorry.* Thanks for trying!

Love,
Larry

*****

March 20, 1994
Dear Erin,

My mom visited me yesterday. She told me about your dad's death. I'm really sorry. So don't worry about writing me for a while. I hope Michelle is handling it alright. At least you all have your faith to help you all through this. Knowing he's now in Heaven has to comfort you all some. But I know there will always be some hurt. Whenever you write again and, if you want to, will you tell me what he died of? I was told he was going to the operating room to have those tests you told me about but he died on the way to the operating room. Mom and I was also wondering how old he was. Another reason why I'm glad I'm dying soon. I know how much it would hurt me to lose any of my family.

Well, I'll let you go. Again, I'm really sorry! Take care!

Love,
Larry

*****

March 29, 1994
Dear Larry,

Thanks for your letter expressing sympathy on the loss of my dad. It meant a lot to me. I feel like my world has been turned upside down for the last two weeks. Without the Lord's support and comfort and the support of friends, I know we would not have been able to bear up as well as we have.

You asked what happened. First of all, instead of just one day in between his two surgeries, his cardiologist insisted on at least a week between them. So he had his nerve biopsy the week before. His hemorrhoid surgery was at 8 a.m. the following Tuesday, March 15. Because the second doctor considered him to be at high risk because of previous strokes and heart problems, he wanted him to be kept overnight for observation. He also gave him only a local anesthetic for the surgery since that would be easier on his heart. Dad seemed to be doing okay after his surgery. Later that day, he started running a temp. However, by the next morning, it was pretty much gone. Since he had not had a very good night—the Demerol had made him have nightmares—the doctor decided that he should probably stay at least one more day. My mom spent the night with him at the hospital on Tuesday to make sure he got his medications on time and got everything he needed and because Dad wanted her to stay. I spent most of Tuesday with him also. It touched my heart when Mom told me later that she had crawled in bed beside him and snuggled up close to him to warm him up that night because he was cold. I am so happy that she got that special time with him.

On Wednesday, I went up to see him at 1:30 p.m. He was sleeping when I got there and seemed to be resting well. A few minutes later, he woke up and complained that his heart was bothering him. This wasn't totally unusual since it happened quite regularly. My mom asked the nurse if she could give him some nitro that she always carried in her purse and was finally told to go ahead. He took a couple and decided he felt better sitting up in a chair. He hadn't been sitting up for long before his eyes rolled back in his head, and he blacked out for a few seconds—we guessed it was a seizure. My mom ran to him to keep him from falling out of the chair, and I ran for the nurse. The patient in the bed next to him probably thought I was a track athlete when I jumped over the bed and sped past him. My heart was pumping and my imagination running wild since I had never experienced the sight before. All I could think was, *That's my dad. I have to get him help! I hope he is not dying!* When I got back to the room, his eyes were open. I breathed a sigh of relief!

The nurse made him get back in bed and immediately called his cardiologist who ordered him to be put into the progressive care unit so that he could be monitored more closely. While they were getting him ready to move, he started crying—I think because he was so scared he was going to have another stroke. My heart was breaking to see my dad crying, but I was trying to be strong for him even though sobs from deep within me were threatening to erupt. I was so glad that I was there to be able to hug him and comfort him while my mom was getting his personal items ready to be moved. In those brief moments, I got to hear him tell me one last time, "I love you." All I could do was squeeze him even harder and relish the hug I got from him. I will always wish I had said "I love you" back to him, but I was too choked up to even talk. My hug had to speak for me. I'll *always* treasure those words and his hug.

The staff decided to leave him in his bed and move the entire bed to the other floor. His cardiologist arrived at the exact time they were going to move him. Just outside his room, Dad had another seizure that was worse than the first one but again came out of it. The doctor went in the elevator with him to the sixth floor. Mom and I took the stairs and got to the floor as they were bringing Dad out of the elevator. He had just been wheeled out when his doctor hit dad's chest and began calling his name. He began having another seizure that he never came out of. A Code 100 call came over the intercom, and hospital personnel seemed to appear out of the wall. They got him to his room, and I saw the doctor start to do CPR to revive him. I remember so vividly standing just outside the door with my emotions in high gear and thinking (and must actually have been speaking my thoughts), *No, this cannot be happening! That's my dad! I still need him!* At that point, my mom and I were escorted to a waiting room.

The next thirty minutes seemed like an eternity, and life came to a standstill. During our wait, we called the immediate family and our pastor. I was so glad that Dave and our pastor and his wife were there with us when the doctor finally came out and said, "He didn't make it." Gregg and Michelle made it to the hospital about ten minutes after we found out. They both took it extremely hard since they had a very close relationship with their papa. It took us about three hours to locate my brother. When he found out, he really fell apart. I appreciated that the hospital allowed my dad's body to remain in the room until my brother came so we could go in as a family and say our initial goodbyes as the reality of his death hit us. It all felt like a nightmare when I recall it. I still can't believe it's actually true. I think we're still in the stage of being numb.

That night was the most unusual night I ever experienced. After my mom's sister and husband and my cousin left us, we were all physically and emotionally exhausted. All of us wanted to be together that night to comfort one another. We pulled out our hide-a-bed in the family room and lined up our recliners; and Michelle, Gregg, my mom, my brother, and I held hands all night. In the background, an instrumental tape by Dino called "Peace in the Midst of the Storm" played continuously. The music offered us some quieting peace in the midst of our "storm" that night.

I so dreaded making the funeral arrangements—especially selecting his casket. The thought kept going through my mind as we got closer to having to make that decision, *I do not want to pick out a casket that my dad is going to be put in. I just want to wake up from this nightmare.* Unfortunately, it wasn't a nightmare—it was reality. Mom, my brother, and I agreed on everything. Having so many friends—over a hundred during the two hours of visitation— pay their respects on Friday at the funeral home helped us through.

Your brother Rob came on Saturday morning when my mom, brother, Gregg, Michelle, and I went to the funeral home to spend some time alone with my dad. I was glad we got to have that hour by ourselves to say some of our last goodbyes since it helped make the funeral easier. His service was beautiful. Two of our pastors sang songs that were Dad's favorites, and the message was so good. My dad would have been very happy with it. After the service, it was touching to watch as Gregg slipped one of his senior pictures into my dad's suit pocket. I thought I would have a really hard time during the service, but the Lord gave me a special peace I didn't think could be possible.

I can remember wondering when my grandma died how my mom could keep it all together. I just knew I would fall apart if I lost a parent. When I was younger and would go to a cemetery with my parents, I always left with tears in my eyes thinking about the time I might lose one of them. I had heard older Christians say, "The Lord gives us the grace and strength that we need when we need it." I was somewhat of a skeptic about that and would think to myself, *Well, He better have a big dose of both for me! I know I will be one to really test His resources.* His Word, however, has proved itself true to me in the last two weeks.

My mom is living with us right now. She'll be welcome until she decides she wants to go back home. Her being here has greatly helped me. I can hardly stand the thought of her having to go back to an empty house and live. When I go to her house to get something she needs, it chokes me up to see my dad's empty chair. I cannot bring myself to sit in it right now. Gregg said that he would be glad to go live with her for a while if she would like him to. There's no rush. Dave doesn't mind her being here. The last week, we've been kept busy with taking care of insurances and getting bank accounts changed to my mom's name. I never realized there were so many details to take care of.

We just finished writing seventy thank you notes for all the food, flowers, and cards that were given to us. I was happy that most friends sent plants rather than cut flower bouquets since plants last longer. We put the cut flower arrangements out at church the next day and gave them to some of Dad's special friends after the evening service. I couldn't bear to part with hardly any of the plants, so now, my house looks like a greenhouse—I did share some with my brother and mom. Gregg and Michelle also each got a plant. Mom gave me some of my dad's money to buy a plant stand to display some of the plants. That will always be special to me! She said that dad would have smiled to see me keeping all those plants! He always loved plants and had a green thumb!

Well, I'll write again later. A friend is here to take my mom and me walking at the mall and out to lunch. She sure has been good to us. She's expecting her dad to die real soon from cancer. We'll have to help hold each other up in the days ahead.

I know you told me to just give up on you in your last letter. I *can't* do that. I've just given you completely to the Lord. I can't save you anyway—only *He* can. I will comment more about your needing proof of a miracle in my next letter. Just know that I'm still praying for you and care about you.

Love,
Erin

*****

April 3, 1994

Dear Erin,

Hope these few lines find you all well!

I wanted to call you and Michelle last Saturday. I'd called sooner after your father died, but I had already used my allotted phone calls for the month of March. So today while filling out the phone call request, I couldn't find your phone number. I know you've sent it to me. I'm sorry, as usual I've misplaced it (and so many other items). If you would still like me to call, please send your number again. Sure wish I could've called you so I'd found out how y'all are doing. I just don't know what to say, but I'm deeply sorry.

Thank you for sharing your sad experience with your father with me. My mother sent me the obituary on your father out of the newspaper. I thought it was a good picture of your dad. You have your faith to comfort you. I envy it. If I lost one of my family members, it would devastate me. I'm just not mature mentally. I believe it (my maturity) was harmed cause of my incarceration when I was 14 years old on to the present.

I received my official notice last Friday informing me my case is scheduled for April 19 at 10 a.m. I'm sure I won't be alive next month at this time. What are your feelings regarding cremation?

Well, I am sleepy and think I need to go to bed. I will write to Michelle tomorrow. Thanks for caring and not giving up on me.

Love,
Larry

Think About It: Grief

Grief has many faces. Look around you and notice the uniqueness of each person you see. Each one *will* experience grief in some way during his/her lifetime, and the way it is handled will be as unique as the individual. No two will process grief in *exactly* the same way.

What is grief? It is the natural response to a loss. Normally, grief is associated with the death of a loved one. However, according to the *Grief and Loss Fact Sheet* published by www.beyondblue.org.au/the-facts/grief-and-loss, "One can grieve the loss of a relationship, miscarriage, pet, job or way of life. Other experiences of loss may be due to children leaving home, infertility, loss of freedom (such as incarceration or a debilitating illness), and separation from friends and family. The more significant the loss, the more intense the grief is likely to be."[25] If you have experienced grief, you will be able to relate to what I am about to describe in some way.

"Have you ever cried over something so much that you run out of tears? Your swollen eyes just give out and dry up while a current of unrest still gushes through your soul."[26] This quote by Lysa TerKeurst, founder of Proverbs 31 Ministries, so succinctly described my feelings after my father died. I felt like the bottom had literally dropped out of my world. At first, shock and numbness were my companions. Not having my father any longer seemed surreal—more like a nightmare that I was hoping to wake up from and breathe a sigh of relief that it was just a dream. He was there to hold and communicate with one minute and then was suddenly gone. It is good that God insulates us and helps us get through the initial days following a death when so many decisions are required in a very short amount of time when we are emotionally spent. The support of family and friends is also very helpful and comforting.

While I did not realize it, grief has five stages according to David Kessler on www.grief.com.

- *Denial and shock.* "Denial is nature's way of letting in only as much as we can handle." Common feelings during this period are numbness, feeling overwhelmed, and having thoughts of how or why we should go on. Emotionally, it is a little like feeling you are in a boat that is lost at sea in a storm and your compass is not functioning. Eventually, however, a shoreline becomes visible and the feelings you are denying begin to float to the surface, while other feelings, such as anger, also develop.
- *Anger.* Included in one's anger may be the loved one who is the cause of your grief, doctors, friends, your family, your-

self, and perhaps even God. "Underneath anger is pain, your pain. It is natural to feel deserted or abandoned . . . Anger is strength and it can be an anchor, giving temporary structure to the nothingness of loss." Anger allows one to temporarily place blame, whether justly or unjustly, to help "explain" the loss. Our human tendency is to *fear* anger and stuff it since it makes *guilt* surface. Instead, *embrace* it. It is perfectly normal to feel angry, and it is important to healthy grieving that it be felt and worked through.

- *Bargaining.* This is the "if only" or "what if" stage. How easy it is after a loss to go back in time and think about how things might have turned out differently *if only*? *If only* I would have handled things more tactfully. *What if* the diagnosis had been made sooner? *If only* I had noticed sooner the signs that my child, spouse, or friend was acting abnormally. "*What if* I had left my gun at home so that I wasn't tempted to use it when my anger flared (in Larry's case)?" "The 'if onlys' cause us to find fault in ourselves and what we 'think' we could have done differently . . . We remain in the past, trying to negotiate our way out of the hurt."[27]

- *Depression.* It is the rare person who will not experience depression after a significant loss. At this point, "our attention moves squarely into the present. Empty feelings present themselves, and grief enters our lives on a deeper level, deeper than we ever imagined." When it happens, keep in mind that it is *not* mental illness or not unusual. It would be unusual to not experience depression. How long will the depressed feelings last? It will vary with each individual and depend on how severe the loss. Many well-meaning friends or family members who have never gone through a similar loss may tell you to just "snap out of it" or "it's time to get on with your life" after what they consider to be a reasonable time to grieve. Grief, however, does not have a timetable. Eventually, it will gradually subside as acceptance, the next stage of grieving, is reached.

- *Acceptance.* Does acceptance mean that one is "all right" or "okay" with what has happened? No. Someone or something that was very important and valued was taken away and will never be a part of life again. At this stage, one begins to accept the "new normal" as reality and makes the necessary adjustments. Slowly, but surely, we begin to live again and develop new connections, relationships, and perhaps interdependencies. However, if one does not let grief run its course, acceptance will take much longer.

David Kessler gave some excellent insight that is worth remembering.

> People often think of the stages as lasting weeks or months. They forget that the stages are responses to feelings that can last for minutes or hours as we flip in and out of one and then another. We do not enter and leave each individual stage in a linear fashion. We may feel one, then another and [move] back again to the first one.[28]

When going through a grief recovery program after my dad's death, I learned three words that have stuck with me and that I always share with others who are grieving in any way—time, talk, and tears! All three are essential to healthy grieving.

For me, the grief feelings came in waves, which is typical, and often when I least expected them to hit. A trigger would be seeing a father and daughter together either in real life or on TV, going into the greeting card aisle and seeing birthday or Father's Day cards knowing that I no longer had someone to buy one for, glancing from a distance the profile of someone who reminded me of my dad, or seeing his empty recliner when I would go to visit my mother. Easter was two weeks after my dad died. After church, we ate dinner at a restaurant with friends. All was okay until I noticed one empty chair at our table. Bam! The tears welled up inside like a dam wanting to burst. My dad *should* have been sitting there with us. After that holiday, no extra chairs were present at our table. Memories of the past could also make the tears begin to flow. Although it has been twenty-three years, tears flowed while writing this chapter. My husband referred to my sad times as my "dad moments." While these were my triggers, you may have experienced others.

At times, grief caused my anger to be directed at God. In addition to losing my father, years later, my daughter had two miscarriages. A couple of years into their marriage, my son-in-law went through a bout with cancer and then radiation therapy that the doctors said would mean no biological children for them. When Michelle became pregnant, our family was thrilled and felt that God was giving us a miracle child despite the prognosis. When she miscarried about ten weeks into the pregnancy, this ecstatic grandma-to-be was devastated! I was angry at God for over a year feeling He had played a cruel trick on us to get our hopes up and then dash them and for denying Michelle and her husband a family. Every time a friend or relative would so happily announce a new child was on the way, my heart ached. Yes, I tried very hard to put on a good front and congratulate them; but on the inside, I was secretly thinking to myself, *Lord, it is just not fair*. Finally, after a very painful year that involved moving through the stages of grief, acceptance came that God may have had reasons beyond my understanding for having the baby naturally abort. Because I so wanted to be a grandmother, it was hard to accept that not having a grandchild to love may be my reality.

When Michelle miscarried her second child, the hurt was not as severe, but was still there. When they eventually decided to adopt an infant, hope was renewed. Two weeks after the final papers were submitted to allow them to be considered as adoptive parents, Michelle discovered she was once again pregnant, and the adoption process was placed on hold. Her third pregnancy resulted in a beautiful baby boy who is his grandma's pride and joy!

This experience taught me the lesson of Isaiah 55:8, "'My thoughts are nothing like your thoughts,' says the Lord, 'And my ways are far beyond anything you could imagine'" (NLT). If I can be absolutely honest, I felt ashamed that I had gotten angry with Him and doubted His ability to give us their precious son and our grandson. Even if He had not worked in that way, however, I had made up my mind to accept whatever He chose for our family. Perhaps that surrender was what the Lord was waiting for all the time.

I also think of Larry's family and the grief they experienced after his arrest, incarceration, death penalty sentence, and finally his death. Do you recall the raw emotions displayed by his brother and father on the night of February 24, 1993, when they thought the execution would happen that night? Can you imagine what it would have felt like emotionally if Larry was your child or brother whom you loved so very much? I clearly recall what an emotional roller coaster I was on as his cousin as I wrote to him, waited out the appealed execution dates, and then learned that his execution was a reality. We had become close friends over the years of writing, and my grief afterward was real. For his immediate family, it was an extremely hard ten years.

Are you going through a time of grief right now that seems to be sucking your energy and life away? Have you experienced grief in your past and can recall how it felt? If so, your grief experience can be used in the future to help others who are grieving. The grieving need friends who will come alongside them to let them know they are not alone and that what they are experiencing is normal.

If you have never experienced grief or even the same type of grief, be careful that you do not say that you understand exactly how the person feels. Until you have walked the road of grief and suffered the same type of loss, it is impossible for you to understand another's loss. It is okay to admit that you cannot imagine how they feel. However, you can listen, help where and when help is needed, and be patient. It will also be extremely important to not rush them through the grief process.

Do you need some grief support or know someone who does? Check out Internet resources on grief such as www.grief.com, www.griefshare.org, www.beyondblue.org.au, and www.stephensministries.org and their four-booklet *Journeying through Grief* series by Kenneth C. Haugk. There are also local agencies that provide free grief recovery programs. You do not have to walk the grief journey alone. Take advantage of the resources that will help you better understand how to process your grief.

Chapter 10

April 5, 1994

Dear Larry,

Thank you for your thoughtfulness in having Sister Millie and Karen send me sympathy cards on your behalf. My heart was deeply touched. Both wrote a personal note along with it, which was nice. You mentioned Sister Millie is the one who sends the lovely cards to your mom. What a ministry she has!

After I sent my letter off last week, I reread your letter of March 20 and realized that I had not answered all of your questions. Sorry about that, but I wasn't thinking real well that day, and the letter was hard to write. Each day is getting a little better. Tomorrow, it will be three weeks—it seems like we've been in a vacuum during that time. I guess the Lord does that to keep you safe and help you through the grieving process. When I'm tempted to feel sad, I just keep focusing on the fact that Dad's in heaven and having a wonderful time!

You had asked how old Dad was. He had been sixty-seven exactly one month since his birthday was on February 16, and he died on March 16. I can't recall if I told you that we had an autopsy done. The preliminary results that appeared on the death certificate indicated a massive heart attack. The final autopsy report takes about four to six weeks to get back. The doctor will explain it to us then. We have not yet gotten the results back from the nerve biopsy. Hopefully, we'll at least learn what was causing the numbness in his legs.

Michelle, my mom, and I are going to get away for a couple of days to the Holidome in Ft. Wayne, Indiana, since it is spring break. I really need a change of pace. Michelle and my mom will probably play a lot of pool—that was a prerequisite for selecting a motel! They sure enjoy it. I think I'll be content to just curl up and read, sit in the hot tub, and play a little shuffle board or Ping-Pong. My mom needs to get away so she can relax a little. It seems that most of her waking hours are spent taking care of insurance and financial details. She's really organized though! She seems to be doing well. We're keeping close tabs on her. She's really a strong person.

Michelle appears to be handling my dad's death quite well. When she says anything, it is usually something funny she remembers—which makes us laugh too. My dad used to always love having her to rub the top of his bald head and would always exaggerate how good it felt. He loved her Steve Urkel impressions too—she'd call him Carl and my mom Laura, which always made them laugh. If you have ever watched *Family Matters*, you will understand the humor. Remembering the good, fun times helps to make things easier.

She is sure loving track this year. Practice is every day after school from three fifteen to four thirty. I thought she might get tired of it, but she is eating it up. Her coach this year actually teaches them a lot about running technique. She had the second best time in both the 200- and 400-meter runs last week, which made her happy. She's going to go out for the longer runs this year so there won't be as much competition. When things calm down, she'll be writing again. Right now, she hardly has a spare minute.

Gregg found another job working at a grocery store in the meat department. It is not his favorite job since it is rather boring, but he is going to wait until his probation is up and see if he can transfer to a job as a stocker.

I know I still owe you an answer about your desire to have "proof" there is a God through a miracle. You will definitely get one in my next letter.

Well, I need to be going for now. I want to work on the computer a little since I have not touched it in three weeks. I'll be waiting to hear from you again soon.

Love,
Erin

*****

April 10, 1994
Dear Erin,

I am glad that I waited a day to write since I received a letter from you as well as one from Michelle!

I am happy that you, your mom, and Michelle got away for a few days. I hope you all had fun! Tell me all about it. No, better yet, I'll have Michelle tell me all about it.

I want to call you but have to wait until after the 21st of this month to know when exactly I can call you. You were very helpful telling me in one of your letters when it's the best time to call. Just don't interrupt any plans. If I don't catch you all at home, I'm allowed to try again.

Being it will be after my court hearing on the 19th when I call, I'll be able to tell you all about the hearing. If you're home for the Channel 41 evening news on the 19th or 20th, I might be on it as most of the time they will report any news on me. When I was scheduled to die last time, they sent a reporter to be a witness to my execution. He was interviewed on the Atlanta station right after I stopped my scheduled 7 p.m. execution at 6:30.

Mom visited me yesterday. She said she was going to call her doctor Monday morning since her heart has been acting up. She told me that she has to take four nitro pills each day. I now know she has a heart problem as everybody I know who takes nitro pills has had a heart attack. It sure has me worried!

Sounds like Michelle really loves track—maybe a scholarship in that field? As expensive as college is, I'm sure a full or partial scholarship would sure be helpful. Hope Gregg will get to transfer to a job that is less boring after his probation period. Sounds like he needs to be kept busy.

We have a new warden that begins May 1. We are all optimistic that he'll make some good changes.

Did you send me the two books by Chuck Colson—*Born Again* and *Life Sentence*? I have given them to two of the other guys to read.

I will be looking forward to your answers about cremation and miracles.

It was 85 degrees today which makes me feel tired. Sorry about the short letter. You take care!

Love,
Larry

*****

April 17, 1994
Dear Larry,

Michelle and I will be looking forward to your call after the twenty-first. In the meantime, just know that I have been praying for you ever since you told me that your hearing was scheduled.

You asked me what I think about cremation. Personally, I wouldn't choose cremation for myself or anyone else since I can't stand the thought of a body being burned up. I feel like we are not showing much respect for the deceased. Since the Bible does not say anything about it either, it's a personal decision each person has the freedom to make. I'm glad my dad did not chose cremation as it would have made his death that much harder to handle.

Larry, I always appreciate your honesty about why you cannot become a Christian. One of the reasons you said makes it difficult for you to believe in God is that you have no "proof" that He is real, and seeing a miracle would be the proof you need. True—He doesn't work the outstanding miracles that He did in Bible days, but I've seen Him work miracles in my life and the lives of others. I'd like to share some of them with you so you can perhaps see that He is still just as active today as He was in Jesus's days, but in a more subtle manner. Please, please, keep an open mind as you read the "proofs" of miracles I am sharing with you.

I have seen the hand of God protect me and provide for me so often in my life. Sometimes, I'm sure He's done so, and I haven't even realized it. There have been times, however, when there has been no doubt that He has intervened and worked a "miracle" on my behalf. One of the earliest instances I recall is when I was a teenager. I had just gotten back in town from Western Michigan University and decided I needed to get some gas. I stopped to wait for some oncoming traffic and then made my left turn into the gas station. As I was turning, I heard brakes start squealing very close to me. When I looked up, a semi that I had not seen coming was just feet from crashing broadside into me. Normally, I would have panicked. Just before impact, however, my foot hit the accelerator, and I escaped being hit by the semi. I avoided the crash but not the adrenaline rush after an *extremely* close call. My racing heart and trembling hands took a few minutes to calm. Others who had witnessed what happened were very surprised I hadn't been hit—especially the two passengers that were in my car! I thanked God many times for intervening on our behalf.

A few years ago, our family went to Cadillac, Michigan, for an overnight getaway. Since Dave grew up in Cadillac, we often went there. The kids and I decided to go shopping at Kmart. On our way back to the motel, we had to stop for a red light. Right ahead of us was a semi carrying a big roll of steel. I had the choice of either pulling up alongside the semi or staying behind him at the light. My normal instinct is to pull alongside so I can get ahead of a semi as I dislike following one. This particular night, I had the feeling that I should just stay behind. I'm so glad I did! A few seconds after we stopped at the light, the steel roll that was on the flatbed of the truck rolled off and would have smashed onto the top of my car. Fortunately, no other cars were beside the truck either. As I sat and watched in disbelief the steel roll fall off, I thanked the Lord for His intervention in keeping us safe. Some may call it luck; but I call it a miracle from God.

Another instance is a little more personal. A couple of years after Gregg was born, we decided we would like another child. My prayer was that the Lord would give us a girl. It really looked like we may not be able to have any more children as two years later, we still had only one child. Finally, it appeared our prayers were answered as I was pregnant. However, about two weeks after I learned the great news, I came very close to losing the baby when I went to work in the kitchen at our Christian camp. I was heartbroken at the thought. The Lord was good, however, and took care of the baby. Eight months later, Michelle was born. She has indeed been God's gift to us in so many wonderful ways! (As I write this, I am close to tears thinking of how good He was to allow us to have two children to love.) I believe all children are miracles.

Dave lost his job at Clark Equipment Company when it moved to Kentucky because he chose not to move and was unemployed for ten months. Needless to say, he was getting quite down about it since he had put his resume in at many places but with no luck. I had suggested that he might want to go back to school and get his bachelor's degree in business since most businesses were so degree conscious—many would not even let him leave a resume if he did not have a degree. His two-year degree in business management helped but was not enough. Until about nine months into his unemployment, he was not receptive to the idea. Finally, he decided that maybe that's what he should do. On his very first night of class, a man who had worked with him at Clark told him about the job opening at Union Pump. He had the job within two weeks. Coincidence? We don't think so. God engineered the circumstances and provided Dave's job at just the right time. He gave him a job that he's really come to like. God cares about *every* detail of our life.

A year ago last October, Gregg and a friend were pulling out onto I-94. At that time, he had a sporty car that was quite low to the ground and not easy to see. He had just gotten off the entry ramp when a semi sideswiped him. (It seems like semis are dangerous to us!) I shudder to think how seriously he could have been hurt—or even killed. However, he was protected from any injury. The driver's side of the front of the car was quite dinged up, but Gregg and his friend were unharmed. Later that night as I realized how close he had come to death, I just sobbed with gratefulness. I *know* God intervened and protected him.

This may seem insignificant but still demonstrates God's protection. Just last week, after we had had our seven inches of snow, I was driving near the library. When I came to the stop sign at an intersection, I hit a patch of ice and could not stop. I *knew* I was going to hit the car in front of me and was bracing myself for the impact. At the moment that we would have collided, the car pulled away from the stop sign to turn. I don't know if the driver knew how close he came to being hit, but I sure did! My heart felt like it was pounding out of my chest, but I was thanking the Lord for His perfect timing! I could rattle on with more instances, but I think you can see what I'm saying about God working in lives today.

I've enclosed part of the first chapter of a book written by Billy Graham entitled *Angels: God's Secret Messengers*. It describes a few occasions in the lives of other people when they have seen God at work firsthand. The smaller article, "His Mysterious Ways," was written by the son of one of my church friends. I don't feel anything happens by mere chance or luck.

I have also seen God at work in your life in the last year—although you may not even have realized it—in the following ways:

1. The fact that your brother called your attorney when he did on the night of your scheduled execution was no accident. Your decision to appeal was, I believe, because of all the prayer going up for you from Christians and was engineered by God to give you more time to learn of Him and His love for you.

2. When you attempted suicide and were experiencing a lot of pain from your injury, God gave you relief from the pain. Hadn't the doctors told you that you might have to learn to live with it?

3. Last February, we barely knew each other. I knew you were in prison; but when I heard that you were scheduled for execution on the twenty-third, God touched my heart and prodded me to write to you. I have learned to listen to His

prodding since He always has a special purpose. I am so thankful I did! He gave Michelle and me a special friendship with you. This is proof that God still "talks" to people today. He gives one the urge to do things that one normally wouldn't have the courage to do and then directs the person along the way as he/she obeys Him. He knew we needed each other and then gave us time to develop a friendship. He truly is in control of every aspect of our lives.

4. When your hearing was postponed in October, I feel God was at work then also. If your date had been set and the execution carried out shortly afterward, God knew you would not have been spiritually ready at that time. I know you were disappointed, but God knew how much more disappointed you would have been to not have accepted His forgiveness and to have died without knowing Him. He has prolonged your life for a reason, has His hand on you, and is at work in your life.

5. You mentioned that when your goodie box arrived, the normal guard was on riot practice detail and that the "good" guard was on duty and let you keep some of the things that you might otherwise not have been allowed to keep. God's timing is perfect. He knew who would be on duty and when the box should arrive. I had prayed that you would be able to keep some of the things I was unsure about sending but wanted you to have. To me, it was not an *accident*.

6. When you were taken to the "hole," I know it was no coincidence that the particular guard you had was on duty and gave you the book by David Wilkerson. My guess is that he is a Christian. God knew you needed that guard, on that day, and He wanted you to have that book. To me, that's evidence that God is real and that He cares for *you*.

7. Would you have been open to searching the Bible and asking for Bible lessons last year at this time? My guess is that you probably would not have been. Where did the desire come from? I believe God placed that desire within you.

He is a personal, caring God, and He loves Larry Lonchar. He's patiently waiting for you to come to the point where you can believe He is real and can return that love.

Are you at all convinced about His existence? I'll be continuing to pray that God will make Himself real to you. I don't exactly know how that will come about, but He does and will work it out in His way and in His time. You'll *definitely* know it's Him.

Michelle is having a great track season! She went to an all-day sixteen-school track meet on Saturday. All of the events were four-person relays. Her freshman 440-meter relay team took a first—the only first that Pennfield received. She got a medal for it and was thrilled. Last Thursday, she came in second in the 100-meter dash. Yesterday, she got a first in the 100-meter dash, a third in the 200-meter dash, and a first in the 440-meter relay. Was she ever wound up after the meet! She said that she has almost enough points to qualify for a varsity letter in track for this school year. They get points each time they place and for extra things they do—such as helping out at junior high track meets. She'd probably be upset if she knew I told you about her track meets since she always like to tell things first. So don't mention it. I'm sure she'll write you about it too. I just feel so happy for her and thought you'd like to know.

I hope the new warden proves to be a refreshing change for everyone at the prison and that he has a little more compassion and understanding than the current warden. That can go a long ways.

I have given you enough to think about for one letter so will close for now. My prayer is that you will consider what I have written about miracles and that it will help you see some proof of God's existence.

We will be waiting—but not eagerly—to hear the results of your hearing. Remember that you are loved and continually being prayed for.

Love,
Erin

*****

April 24, 1994

Dear Erin,

Mom visited me Sunday. She told me you had called her. I'm very sorry I haven't wrote sooner. My hearing was postponed. I've been so upset! These people have moved me to another cell cause they think I might try to commit suicide again. I sure have contemplated it.

The lawyer called me Friday, the 15th, and informed me that the judge postponed. I slammed the phone down in his ear. Then Monday, the 18th, I had a pastor visit. I had him call the lawyer and tell him to call me, which he did. I told him his firm had seven days to get my case transferred to Judge Craig and to have the court hearing rescheduled, at the latest, during the month of May or I was going to write the Attorney General, judge, Bar Association, and the media. In my letters I will mention reasons #2 and #3 on why I stopped my execution when I did—there was more than just family pressure. I know I have not told you this before. My two lawyers would be in big trouble if I told what they did.

Reason #2—One lawyer told me that he'd smuggle me in some sleeping pills so I could commit suicide. "Just don't let these people kill you."

Reason #3—Another lawyer said he'd give me a thousand dollars if I wouldn't let them kill me.

When I was informed at 6:15 p.m. by one of my attorneys that my youngest brother said he was going to kill himself if I let them kill me, I decided to stop my execution. I did not want my brother to kill himself (which now I believe he won't), and I would just commit suicide. I asked the attorney for the sleeping pills a year ago. I haven't heard from him since. I decided the thousand dollars would pay for my cremation. When the one lawyer would not give me the pills, I asked the other lawyer for the thousand dollars he said he'd give me. I would just commit suicide without the pills. He paid my mom $50 a year ago. As you know, I went ahead and tried to commit suicide anyways.

I've told the lawyers over and over to not lie to me. It really bothers me when people lie to me! Not only did they lie about the pills and money, they told me a couple other lies—that they was going to file a suit against these people on the conditions we live in and was going to send a lot of law students from their office down to visit me during the summer so I could get away from the heat and be in the air conditioned visiting room.

I am in the process now of writing the letters. That is why I haven't called you this month.

I wrote my friend at the Atlanta newspaper and told her I had a story for her and to send me her phone number again. I should be hearing from her any day. However, since it is a state holiday today—Confederate Day—and tomorrow is a federal day off for the Nixon funeral, I may not hear from her until the end of the month. I will then call her when I hear from her.

I'm not saying her phone call means more than yours. I just want to put the pressure on the lawyers as soon as possible. Hopefully, they will withdraw from my case like I told them to do and I can get to court sooner. I sure do not want to be here for the heat another summer!

Thank you for your view on cremation. I wondered exactly what the Bible says about it. The chaplains I talked to are against it too. I'm not in favor of it either but this is the less cost I'll be burdening my family with.

Thanks also for sharing with me your "miracles." If there really is a God, then he sure is looking out for you (taking care of you). To you and other Christians, you all consider them "miracles," but to us non-Christians, we would say you're lucky. Don't be offended. I'm just being honest and pointing out how others (non-Christians) would view them.

I read recently where this man had won $20 million in the Florida lotto. A couple years earlier when he lived in Ohio he won a couple million in their lotto. A mathematician said he really beat the odds by winning two. He said the odds to win once was many millions to one but the odds to win two was so many billions or trillions to one. A lot of us would call him a real lucky person. I've known other people where good things happen to them all the time, but yet they weren't Christians. We call them "real lucky." I am sure you have heard the adage, "Some people have all the luck."

Like I said, don't be mad at me and don't give up on me cause your "miracles" and other things you write does make me give religion more thought.

A pastor has visited me twice. He brought me *Evidence That Demands a Verdict* by Josh McDowell. I started reading it today. Have you read it? He also hinted that he'd like to witness my execution. By our conversations, I know he believes in capital punishment.

There is another question that I need to have answered. Please tell me why a loving God would condemn a person to everlasting punishment in hell. If Gregg or Michelle did something wrong, you might be upset with them but would forgive them because you love them. You wouldn't keep punishing them for what they did. So why would God do that?

Maybe I will be calling you before you receive this letter. Matter of fact, I know I will as May 1 is Sunday. I'll be allowed my new allotment of phone calls. I hope I catch you and Michelle home.

When do you start back working again at KCC? I know you can't wait!

Well, I'll let you go. You all take care! Thanks for caring!

Love,
Larry

*****

April 26, 1994
Dear Larry,

I talked with your mom on Thursday evening to see how your appeal hearing went. She told me it had again been cancelled and that you were very upset about it. Did you ever find out why it was postponed? Would you be upset with me if I told you that I was relieved that it was postponed? I'm not looking forward to your death since I consider you a close friend and will miss you. I know that's selfish on my part, but I can't stand the thought of you dying without the Lord.

I know that you're dreading the hot summer months ahead. However, the Georgia heat will not even begin to compare with the heat you would experience in hell—with no relief ever in sight and no opportunity to change your mind about there being a God. As long as you're alive, there's still hope, and I'll never give up hope! I know the Lord can still work miracles, and that's what I feel it's going to take.

I did not request the two books by Chuck Colson be sent to you. Josh McDowell must have asked Prison Fellowship to send them. You mentioned that two other guys were reading them. Did you get to read them too? I hope you will read them if you haven't. You may find them interesting.

Speaking of Josh McDowell, he called me on Thursday evening inquiring about you. I was so surprised when I answered the phone and found out it was Josh! We didn't get to talk long as he was in between flights at the airport. He travels all over the United States and the world and said that he has spent a lot of time in Russia lately. Did you know he grew up in Union City, Michigan? Anyway, he would like to come visit you if you'll let him. I sure hope you will consent to let him come. Since he at one time, as I mentioned before, did not believe there was a God, I'm sure he could answer your questions better than any other Christian could. He knows where you're at since he was there before too. Josh sounded like a very sincere and caring person that you would feel comfortable talking with. As a favor to me, I hope you will consent to let him come. He asked me to fax him your reply and the execution date so he could work out a time in his schedule. (I know you don't know the date since the hearing was postponed, but I didn't know that when I talked with him.) He is aware that his visit has to be worked out through the chaplain and has to be during the weekdays at certain hours. If you agree to his visit, will you let the chaplain know you'd like him on your visitor's list?

You mentioned that you were concerned about your mom because she has to take four nitro tablets each day. Usually, taking nitro does indicate that there is some problem with the heart. It does not always mean, however, that the person had a heart attack. Dave's mother takes Nitrostat, and she has not officially had a heart attack. The doctor described her problem as being similar to a migraine headache—the muscle around her heart tightens up similar to the muscle in a person's head when a migraine headache occurs. Taking a nitro helps her heart relax and allows her to breathe a little easier. Maybe your mom's problem is somewhat similar without being an actual heart attack.

The weather here has been beautiful the last week. Yesterday was in the low eighties, and today is in the seventies. We've had very little rain and lots of nice sun! When it was in the eighties yesterday, it was beginning to get a little warm. The evening was beautiful though. It was about the first night we could sleep with the windows open and felt so good to have the fresh air coming in!

We had some bad news last night. Dave's brother who lives in Grand Rapids has only been given one to three weeks to live. He was diagnosed with pancreatic cancer five and a half years ago. It has been in the last two months, however, that he really went downhill. His stomach has stopped working, so the only nutrition he is getting is intravenously. We're going to go see him tonight. However, I'm not really looking forward to it since he's lost so much weight and only weighs 104 pounds. Walt is a Christian, though, and has had the Lord's help through his illness. He's not been in any pain either. As a result of his cancer, he has had an opportunity to talk to many people about the Lord, and several have been saved because of his positive attitude and testimony. A lot of sadness is hitting our family all at once. I'm so thankful, however, that I have a Lord who cares about me and helps me through these hard times. I think about the *Footprints* poem when hard times come.

I have to sign off for now. I'm enclosing our church's weekly prayer sheet. As you will see, your name is on it and has been for many weeks. A lot of people ask about you and are praying for you.

I'll look forward to hearing from you. Take care.

Love,
Erin

*****

May 6, 1994

Dear Larry,

I so enjoyed your phone call of a week ago! It was just too short! I wish we could have talked longer. Michelle thought it was neat to get to talk to you too. She wondered if you got the joke about the oldest quarterback being George Washington. That was one she dreamed up—most of the time, it is easy to tell the ones she makes up. Your call was a bright spot in an otherwise very dreary, rainy day. It sounded like you were in a room with an echo. Are you on a speaker-type phone? Are all of your calls monitored? After writing for over a year, it was good to get to hear your voice. Did we sound like you expected?

Our last letters to each other crossed in the mail since they were written only a day apart. First of all, I want you to know that I do *not* easily give up on anyone! You are entitled to your opinion on luck versus miracles. We both have differing opinions on various topics we've discussed since February of last year. So you are stuck with me! ☺

I need some time to think about how to answer your question about why a loving God would condemn a person to everlasting punishment in hell. That letter will come soon.

I was surprised at the offers your two attorneys made to you. They sound like they are not very honest. Why do they want you to commit suicide instead of letting the state execute you? (By the way, I hope you're not seriously contemplating suicide again. Please don't!) Were you planning on sending a copy of your letter to them before you send it to Ms. Westmoreland to see if they will get off dead center and try to get your hearing sped up? I'm sure they wouldn't be too happy to have many people know what is in the letter. Have you heard from the Atlanta reporter yet?

I can understand how upset you must be with people lying to you. It upsets me too when I get lied to. As I was reading your letter and your comments about being lied to, I thought of someone else who has been lying to you—for probably most of your life. That is Satan. He is described in the Bible as being the Father of Lies (John 8:4) and a Deceiver (Revelation 20:7–10). He's really done a good job on you and many, many others. He's deceived you into thinking there is no God and no hell. Since you are really upset now about the attorneys lying to you, you're going to be indescribably upset when you discover how Satan has lied to you. I sure hope you make that discovery while there is time to change your mind!

You mentioned that the pastor who visited you hinted that he would like to be a witness to your execution. Did he come right out and ask? What did he say that makes you think he wants to be a witness? I was somewhat surprised. As I thought about why he may want to be a witness, it may very well be so that he can be around so he can pray for you. You should ask him why he wants to be there. I would like to know too.

I've not read *Evidence That Demands a Verdict*, but I did thumb through it. Our pastor read it, though, and felt it is a good book since it is broken into segments that do not take too long to read. The book *A Ready Defense*, I believe, presents a summary of some of the information in the two volumes of *Evidence that Demands a Verdict*. I read most of the *A Ready Defense* and think it was good since it presents evidence from non-Christian and Christian historians to support the historical evidence of Christ and the authenticity of the Bible. The last chapter, "Still Changing Lives," is also very interesting. I especially liked the testimony of a death-row prisoner, Ernest Gaither, that was on page 457. I am trying to figure out a way to get the book to you! Have you put Josh on your visitor list with the chaplain?

Dave's brother died a week ago. His funeral was on Monday. Since he was so thin, it was a closed-casket funeral. The service was very nice, but it still doesn't seem like he should be gone. Dave has been struggling quite a bit emotionally this week. On top of my dad's death, it makes it a little harder to handle. But we're making it through—day by day.

It doesn't seem like Mother's Day is Sunday. I think I still feel a little numb emotionally to really enjoy the day this year. Dave and the kids are taking me and both of our moms out for dinner on Sunday after church. My brother is also coming. Will your mom get to come visit you this weekend? It would be nice if she could come on Mother's Day.

I don't start back to KCC until the middle of August. I've been working when I can on the computer but haven't made a lot of progress lately since I've been helping my mother clean and rearrange her house. We've worked pretty steadily the last week and a half. Since my dad had required so much care, she really hadn't had a chance to do much in the way of housework. Many things had piled up that needed to be sorted through, discarded, or put away. We painted the spare bedroom and moved her room into it so she could be more centrally located in the house. She felt too isolated in the other bedroom.

We have another very beautiful day today with temperatures in the sixties. I walked a couple of miles in the neighborhood this morning, which felt good. Michelle is raking the lawns of widows in our church, a project the youth group takes on twice each year, and then is going miniature golfing in the afternoon. Gregg has several lawns to mow. Dave is videotaping a sixty-fifth wedding anniversary open house at church. I'm trying to do as little as possible—maybe sit outside and read—since my days have been very busy the last couple of months.

I'll be looking forward to hearing from you soon. Take care.

Love,
Erin

*****

May 7, 1994
Dear Larry,

This will be a very short letter since I have been keeping very busy with track and school. When you told my mom in your last letter that you do not believe in miracles, I knew that I had to share with you about a TV special I recently saw. A gal was walking on the grounds of her college campus and saw a guy who was hiding in the bushes. She was immediately concerned. When she went into her dorm, she called the police to report him. The police arrived soon enough to catch the guy. When asked why he didn't do anything to her and why he didn't leave the bushes, he replied, "Why would I want to move an inch when there were two huge guys walking with her, one on each side, the whole way to her dorm? I was afraid if I moved or made any noise whatsoever, they would find me and pound me into the ground!" The girl was immediately stunned and replied, "There were no huge men walking on either side of me. I was alone!" That right there is proof of guardian angels and a miracle that saved the gal from being attacked.

Please think about this further evidence of miracles. I believe that everyone has a guardian angel . . . believer or unbeliever. If God knew that a miracle would make an unbeliever start believing in Him, why would He want to withhold a miracle from that person?

I will write more to you about my track season in my next letter. Of course, you can expect that letter to be longer!

Love,
Michelle

*****

May 8, 1994
Dear Larry,

In your April 25 letter, you asked why a loving God would condemn a person to everlasting punishment in hell. The point you raised about a parent punishing a child but then forgiving him is a legitimate one. I guess to answer that question, one has to go back to the book of Genesis to the beginning of creation. Here is my best shot at answering that question.

When Adam and Eve were created by God, their Father, He created them as human beings with a free will (not as robots). It was their *choice* to obey or disobey God—just as children have a choice whether they will obey their parents or not. While having nearly full control of the Garden of Eden, their exquisite home, they had only one restriction—to not eat from the tree of the knowledge of good and evil; if they did, they would die, both physically and spiritually because of their disobedience (Genesis 2:17).

Until Satan entered the picture, they had no desire to eat from that forbidden tree. Satan, as I mentioned before, is a deceiver. He convinced them that God was lying to them about dying if they disobeyed. They listened to and believed him and ate the forbidden fruit. True, they didn't instantly die; however, their bodies did begin to die physically—a little each day—and their close spiritual connection with God was severed. Their sin, in essence, put a chasm (or uncrossable barrier) between them and God. Without realizing the full consequences of their disobedience (sin), they chose to no longer be true children of God but became children of Satan by their own free choice. Their action was comparable to the case of the child divorcing his parents that was in the news a while back.

The Bible clearly states that Satan has his children and God has His in John 8:44, "For you are the children of your father the devil, and you love to do the evil things he does. He was a murderer from the beginning. He has always hated the truth, because there is no truth in him. When he lies, it is consistent with his character; for he is a liar and the father of lies" (NLT). Also look up 1 John 3:10–12. These verses start out saying, "So now we can tell who are children of God and who are children of the devil" (NLT). Clearly, God has made a distinction between those who are His children and those who are Satan's. The only ones condemned to everlasting punishment are the children of Satan. God does not condemn His own children.

You probably know the story of Satan's fall. He was one of the greatest and most honored angels in heaven. But he was also conceited and thought he was better than God—his creator—and decided to overthrow God.[29] Of course, God is mightier than Satan and quickly squashed his rebellion and condemned Satan and his league of angel followers to eventual eternal damnation in the lake of fire. He's been upset with God ever since and has worked hard to diminish God's authority over man.

His first human victims were Adam and Eve. He's very convincing and works in many ways—whatever way he knows will work on a particular individual. In your case, he's worked very hard to convince you that there is no God. Adam and Eve soon found out that Satan was wrong and had lied to them. They did indeed die, although not instantly. Cain was the next victim. He killed his brother Abel out of jealousy. Why did God banish him rather than forgive him? He would have been willing to forgive him, but Cain was not willing to have God do so. God looked at Cain's heart and knew he wasn't sorry for what he had done.[30] Had he confessed when God asked him about Abel, I truly believe he would have been forgiven and not banished. Cain made his own choice.

Because God is a holy God, He cannot tolerate unconfessed sin. Since no sin can enter heaven, He created hell as the place for people who choose to live for Satan and reject God and His offer of forgiveness. God is, however, a God of love. He loved Adam and Eve and every human being born after them and didn't want the fellowship between them to be broken. However, He didn't *force* Adam and Eve to obey Him—just as he doesn't *force* people today to believe in Him and obey Him. Because Satan is so active in our world today, many continue to believe Satan's lies and never come to see the love that God has for them.

Because God is a God of love, He made a special way for man to be able to escape hell and the consequences of their willful sin. For Adam and Eve and those who lived *before* Christ came, God made a way for them to be forgiven by sacrificing animals and confessing their sins. He then forgave them, and they became His children. He made it even easier to become one of his children when Jesus willingly came to earth, shed his blood, and sacrificed His life to pay the penalty for our sins (but you know the story). John 1:12 says, "But to all who believed him and accepted him, he gave the right to become children of God" (NCV).

When we become a child of God's, He forgives us for all past, present, and future sins. True, we may have to deal with the consequences of our sins and actions while we are alive (as children have to deal with the consequences of their misbehavior), but we are not condemned to hell because of them. So God doesn't willfully send men to hell—He gives them a choice. They choose to accept or reject His free gift of eternal life in heaven and make their own choice to become His sons or children. 2 Peter 3:9b says, "But God is being patient with you. He does not want anyone to be lost, but he wants all people to change their hearts and lives" (NCV). That is one of the reasons He has delayed His promised second coming so long—to give as many as possible the opportunity to make a choice to choose God. It breaks His heart when He is rejected.

Not only does He provide a way to escape the eternal punishment, but also He will provide as many possible opportunities for a person as He can. The hard part, though, is getting a person to recognize God's work and to realize the circumstances in his/her life as being arranged by God. I can't (and God won't) force you or anyone to believe and act on what He has offered through Jesus Christ's death on the cross.

I'm reminded of a story that I heard not long ago that illustrates my point. A flood hit a man's town. At first, the flooding was minimal. When a person stopped by in a van to offer help in evacuating his home, he refused it saying that it wouldn't get much worse. The flood did get worse, however. As the waters rose and the man was forced to the second floor of his home, a rescue worker came by in a boat and offered to help him get to safety. He again refused, not believing things would get worse. Finally, as he was on the roof of his house, a helicopter flew by and offered to get him out of the area. Again, he refused the help that was offered. Eventually, the flood waters swept him off his roof, and he died. As he stood before the Lord, he couldn't believe that he had died and the Lord had not helped him. He asked the Lord why, since He was a loving God, He would let him die like that without helping him. The Lord responded, "Oh, but I did help! I sent a van, a boat, and a helicopter. But you refused all three. There was nothing more I could do."

You remind me of the man in this story, Larry. The Lord has sent many concerned and caring Christian people to you to help show you His love and truth about Satan. He has given you extra time. Why? Because He cares for you and loves you (even though you're not even His child at the moment), and He's not willing that Larry Lonchar perish. However, you haven't yet accepted His offer of help—His offer to give you peace after death and a really good life in heaven with Him. Please don't wait until it's too late and then be shocked and really sorry.

God is like a parent. He will allow us to suffer the consequences of our actions when we do wrong, but He will also forgive us if we ask Him to. *He* doesn't condemn people to an eternity in hell—*people condemn themselves* because they refuse to believe in God and return His love. So much for another of my sermons. Please know that it's because I care about you that I have to express my feelings, even if what I sometimes say is somewhat blunt. I'm glad we can both be open with each other.

Feel free to let me know if you have any questions about what I have written. You made me think really hard on this letter! Remember that you are loved.

Love,
Erin

Think About It: Luck or Miracle?

Do you believe in miracles? Or is just luck and chance at play when something very unexpected and unexplainable happens in one's life? Do miracles happen only in fairy tales and movies? Or only to selected characters of the Bible whom God loved? Can miracles happen in the twenty-first century?

Luck is defined as "a combination of circumstances, events, etc., operating by chance to bring good or ill to a person."[31] Miracle, on the other hand, is defined as "an effect or extraordinary event in the physical world that surpasses all known human or natural powers and is ascribed to a supernatural cause."[32] Larry felt very strongly that miracles happened only for the benefit of believers, while luck was for unbelievers. Do you agree or disagree with his logic?

The Bible records many supernatural events—the parting of the Red Sea so the Israelites could cross to the other side on dry land to escape the Egyptians,[33] the shutting of the mouths of lions when Daniel was thrown into the lion's den for not bowing to the statue of the king,[34] three men being thrown into a fiery furnace yet coming out unscathed by the fire or even smelling of smoke,[35] a friend of Jesus brought back to life after being dead for four days,[36] and a raging storm that threatened to sink the disciples' boat being instantly calmed by three words, "Peace, be still."[37] There are many other situations you may have heard of whether you are a believer or not. If you are an unbeliever, you may be thinking, "Larry was right. All of these supernatural events happened to people who loved and believed in God."

Upon further examination, however, you will find instances in the Bible when unbelievers also experienced miracles—a demon-possessed man was freed of the demons that were destroying him mentally and physically[38] (a believer cannot be possessed by demons since they will not reside where Jesus resides), a commander of the Syrian army (Naaman) was healed of leprosy by dipping seven times in the Jordan River,[39] the centurion army officer whose servant was healed from a distance by Jesus merely speaking the words,[40] the blind were given their eyesight,[41] and a Roman soldier's severed ear was reattached with a touch by Jesus.[42] Does this provide proof if you believe luck is only an option for unbelievers?

There are instances in the Bible when angels are used by God as part of miracles. One of them is found in 2 Kings 6. In this passage, the king of Syria is enraged that Elisha, one of God's prophets, has been telling the king of Israel about all of his tactical moves against the Israeli army. When he found out where Elisha was living, he was determined to get rid of the "snitch." One morning, Elisha's servant walked outside and saw that their city was surrounded by the Syrian army and was petrified. When he told Elisha about the huge army, Elisha asked God to open the eyes of the servant to see who else was there. When he did, he saw that God had provided an even larger army of angels with horses and chariots of fire to fight and defeat the Syrian army and protect Elisha.

Does God work miracles today? If you believed the true story Michelle shared with Larry about the college gal who was protected from the guy who would have harmed her, you have proof that God still performs miracles of protection today.

My mother shared with me that in her younger years, she was diagnosed with a cyst or tumor in one of her female organs and was referred to a surgeon to have it removed. While praying and watching a religious program on TV, she felt an unexplained sensation start at the top of her head and move to the bottom of her feet. When she went to the surgeon, he told her that whatever was there was gone. She is convinced the sensation she felt was God's healing hand moving over her. She also shared with me a story she saw on TV about a pastor's wife who had a definite diagnosis of cancer and was referred for surgery before starting chemo. When the surgeon did some further testing before surgery, he told her that the tests revealed that she was cancer free. God is still in the healing business today.

Think back over the various miracles presented in Erin's letter to Larry. Can you see God's hand was at work in Larry's life, an unbeliever?

How about you? Have you or someone you know experienced any unbelievable or supernatural events? What were they? Were they miracles or just luck?

Chapter 11

May 17, 1994
Dear Erin,

It sure was good talking to you and Michelle! I was uptight and realized afterwards I shouldn't have been, sorry. I assure you I'll call again. And I hope Michelle wasn't too disappointed as I didn't talk to her much, but I will in my next call. I deeply apologize for not asking on the phone how your mother was doing. Even though I was uptight, I shouldn't have forgotten that. Have you all received the final autopsy report?

Sure is sad to read about Dave's brother dying! He couldn't have been too old either since Dave isn't old. Was he in his 40s or 50s? I'm sure it's some comfort knowing he was a Christian. That's why he wasn't afraid of death. He knew he was going to be with his Lord.

Yes, I agree, a lot of sadness is hitting you all at once. The "Footprints"[43] poem is the answer! I've had a copy of it for many years. It's the best poem I've ever read. I never could understand a lot of poems in English class but the meaning of "Footprints" is very clear to me.

I will be sharing what you wrote about why a loving God would condemn someone to eternity in hell with some ministers and see what they have to say.

No, my mom didn't visit me on Mother's Day. She had visitors for the weekend—Charlie's relatives from Virginia. All of his relatives still stay in touch with her. I called her though. Sure hurts me knowing I'm not out there to have been with her! I didn't appreciate these things until too late. The pain just tears me apart. I can never forgive myself, so death I hope will end my pain. How was your Mother's Day?

I requested to see the doctor tomorrow as my left eye has been bothering me for days. All I do is rub and rub it.

I'm still reading *Evidence That Demands a Verdict*. I read some of it each day. If you have some books to send me, send them to Chaplain Harrell here. Add a few lines saying they are for me. He'll get them to me. That's how I received *Evidence*. The pastor brought it to Chaplain Harrell who then gave it to me.

By your letter of May 6, I assume you believe in capital punishment. You stated that we have to accept "the consequences of our actions while we are alive." Moses killed. So why didn't he die? (God forgave him.)

But God wants us to repent and become a Christian, right? How can we do it if we are dead (executed)? There is this one death row inmate who spent over 15 years here on death row. I know him. He came close to being executed a few times. But finally a court ruled in his favor and he ended up with a "life" sentence. He's now free and living in Michigan. He's also a minister, which he couldn't have been if he was executed. Plus Jesus's life teaching was all about love and forgiveness. Executing us shows no love or forgiveness.

These other so-called Christians use the statement from the Old Testament, "An eye for an eye, and a tooth for a tooth" as one argument that the Bible supports capital punishment. But Jesus replied to that in Matthew 5:38-39 "Ye have heard that it hath been said, an eye for an eye, and a tooth for a tooth: but I say unto you that ye resist not evil; but whosoever shall smite thee on the right cheek, turn to him the other also." (KJV) Otherwise, I interpret that he's saying not to seek revenge (punishment) when somebody does us wrong (killings).

Then Jesus replied to the saying: "Thou shall not kill" in Matthew 5:21(KJV). And then he said "Love thy enemies . . . if ye love them which love you, what reward have you?" (Matthew 5:44, 46a KJV).

I'm sure you've heard of Charles Manson. The following night after killing all those people at Sharon Tate's house, they killed a couple with the last name of Labianca. Their crimes are referred to as the Tate-Labianca killings. Well, Charles "Tex" Watson, the person with the girls who did all the killings (Manson didn't kill anybody) is now a Christian. A couple of years ago, he was up for parole and the Labiancas' only daughter came and testified at the parole board hearing requesting that he be given parole as she stated that she was a Christian and her God has taught her to love and forgive Tex Watson who killed her parents. To me (I watched it on TV), she is a real Christian. (He didn't get the parole and probably never will.) Could you do that?

On my last day, Chaplain Harrell and LaVelle will be with me right to the end. You can call them to find out how my last hours were as they will be the only ones with me besides the guards.

I will go for now to make sure this letter gets in the mail as it will be picked up soon. Take care. Thanks for caring!

Love,
Larry

*****

May 24, 1994
Dear Larry,

It was good to hear from you again last week.

I had to smile when I read that you were uptight before calling us. I felt the same way the night before when Dave told me you had called and would be calling back. After I thought about it for a while, though, I came to the same conclusion that you did—I shouldn't have been! After writing each other for so long, the phone call seemed very natural. We were glad to hear that you may be able to call again! We'll look forward to it. Michelle was not disappointed that you didn't talk to her longer, but she is also looking forward to another call.

Glad you have an appointment to see the doctor about your eyes. Were they itching? Maybe he will have some drops you can use to make them feel better. My mother has trouble with her eyes itching in the spring because of the pollen and other things in the air. She puts a hot washcloth over her eyes, and it makes them feel better. I also have trouble with allergies in the spring. However, I just get headaches instead of my eyes bothering me. I don't know which is worse.

You asked how my mom is doing. I think she's going to be okay. She moved back to her house a week ago Saturday, the day before Mother's Day. That was *real* hard for both of us! My brother stayed with her all last week. Last night was her first night alone, and she sounded this morning like she did okay. I know it's going to be lonely for her though. That's the hardest part of it all. I try to do something with her each day, and she's been going to Michelle's track meets. I think eventually she'll find some things to do to fill her time, such as volunteering more at the Red Cross and Volunteer Bureau. She's also going to be the official secretary for the Children's Church Ministry at church, which will involve doing a lot of photocopying. My hope is that she'll develop a good friendship with another widow.

Probably of all the Mother's Days I've had, this one wasn't my favorite. Dave got me some gorgeous flowers, and both Gregg and Michelle were very thoughtful. We ate dinner out with my brother and his family, my mother, and Dave's parents. The meal was great! What made the day a bummer was seeing my mom so down after having moved back home. It made me cry several times during the day and was so frustrating since there was not anything I could do. We knew her moving back was necessary and healthy for her, but it still hurt seeing her sad. Based on what you have written about your feelings toward your mom, I think you can understand how I felt. By Monday, she was doing better, and we got to talk a lot last week, which helped a lot.

I am going on the annual ladies bike trip with about twenty ladies from our church the end of June. We start at the church and ride about a hundred miles in two days and end up at Lake Michigan where we stay in a cottage right on the lake. I've gone four or five times but did not go last summer because my back was bothering me. Last Friday was the first time I rode my bike in a year, and my back seemed to do okay. I'm looking forward to the bike trip.

We received the final autopsy report on my dad. It not only showed that the main cause of death was a massive heart attack but also indicated that he had had one or two small heart attacks a couple of days before he died. I was surprised by that. He had not had any other strokes—just the four we already knew about. In addition, there was hardening of the arteries in both his heart and kidneys. The nerve biopsy that he had done a week before he died showed nothing to indicate what had caused his neuropathy that was making his walking so difficult. He would have been devastated by that information, so I'm glad he didn't have to hear it. The Lord was merciful in taking him when He did so that he wouldn't have to suffer any more. But I sure do miss him! I still never know when one of my "dad moments" is going to hit. The strangest things can bring them on. I'm sure not looking forward to Father's Day this year. It's going to be a hard one. We have decided to plant a tree in his memory on Father's Day.

I'm sorry you inferred from my statement that we suffer the consequences of our sins while on earth that I believe in capital punishment. That couldn't be further from the truth. As you pointed out, the Bible says that we are not to kill. I feel man has overstepped his bounds when he deliberately kills another through capital punishment. I can hardly stand to even listen to or read about accounts of those who have been executed. It tears me up inside. As I've mentioned to you before, your impending execution is really weighing heavily on my mind. I'm really dreading that day and praying that you will accept God's offer of forgiveness.

All the points you made through the Scripture you quoted are good. I agree with them. It seemed like I sensed a lot of anger being expressed. The point I was trying to make with my statement is that God does not hold any of our sins against us *if* (for the reasons I stated in my letter) we will confess them to Him and ask His forgiveness. God forgives us, but man generally does not. It is man that instituted capital punishment, and the laws of the land and man determine how one pays for the consequences of his sins. God forgets and forgives our sins when we take the steps to become a Christian. As you pointed out, man is not so forgiving. Our nature is not the same as God's. However, He can give us the grace to forgive someone who takes the life of one of our family, such as the LaBianca daughter did.

It's really hard to predict how I would react if one of my family members was murdered. I'm sure at first I would be very angry. After all, Christians are human. I would hope that I could eventually show Christian love to that person and be able to forgive. I couldn't do it on my own, however. It would take God's help. I learned from my dad's death that God does give you the strength and ability to hold up and handle things you never thought you could handle. Would you be able to forgive the person who would take the life of one of your family members? I don't think you could without God's help.

Gregg gave his notice at the grocery store last Friday. On Saturday, the assistant manager asked him why he was leaving. He told him that the only job he really wanted to do was to stock shelves. As they talked and he learned that Gregg had been head stocker at Kennedy's, he called the head stocker at Felpausch to ask him to talk to Gregg. They're supposed to talk tonight while he is at work in the meat department. He seems pretty excited about it. His desire is to work the night shift from 10 p.m. to 6 a.m. so that he can still do his lawn jobs and get to play softball. I'll let you know what happens!

Guess I had better be going for now. I'm supposed to pick Dave up for lunch in a few minutes. I will look forward to hearing from you again soon.

Love,
Erin

*****

June 1, 1994
Dear Larry,

We have had a beautiful spring in Battle Creek. It's so much nicer and warmer than last year. Yesterday, Memorial Day, was around eighty-five. We spent the afternoon with my brother and his family and my mom. First, we attended a special memorial service at the cemetery for all those who had died in the last year. It was okay, but they started it earlier than they said it was going to start, and we missed half of it. Afterward, we all went bike riding on the bike path that they built a few years ago that goes around most of the city of Battle Creek that covers about fifteen miles and had a cookout at my house. It was a very enjoyable day.

Michelle had her final track meet, the all-city meet, of the season tonight. Her 400-meter relay team took fourth, and she got another medal. Due to a bad handoff that made her go out of the handoff zone, her 800-meter relay team got disqualified. She was quite disappointed because they would have gotten another medal. Immediately after her last event in the track meet, we had to rush to get her to her band concert that started at eight—the time we left the track meet. Fortunately, her band was playing last. We got there ten minutes before she had to play, and she still had to change from her track clothes into her band uniform. I felt like I ran a track meet tonight too! She has just one week of school left and will be writing you shortly afterward since she has a lot to tell you and feels bad that it's been so long. She asked me to thank you for her last letter and the articles you sent.

Gregg got the full-time stocker job at the store and started last night. He is working from 10 p.m. to 8 a.m. three to four days a week. It was the shift he wanted since he's a night owl. He seems happy with it and liked his first night. Because he works nights, he gets fifty cents an hour more. He'll have a pretty good summer income when he combines that with his lawn mowing but will also be very busy! His church friends are now home from college so he's enjoying seeing them again. We have several here tonight that are playing video games. It's nice to have them around again. They call me their second mom, and I call them my second, third, and fourth sons. They ask me every so often which number they are. I tell them that depends on how much they come to see me. We have a good time joking around.

Dave's brother Walt was fifty-five, nine years older than him; his sister is six years older than he is.

Dave just got home from his softball game so I need to be signing off. He happily told me his team won both of their doubleheader games. His first game started at eight fifteen. Gregg's team lost their game tonight.

I'll be looking forward to hearing from you again real soon.

Love,
Erin

*****

June 7, 1994
Dear Erin,

Hope this letter finds you and your family well. Sorry I haven't wrote in a while. I'm so far behind in my letters. All I want to do is sleep. I'm sleeping more hours a day than I am awake. My eyes are ok now. I figure it was cause of the high pollen count.

The chaplain brought me the book today you sent. Plus he informed me that Josh McDowell will be visiting me on the 16th of this month. It's all set up. Looking forward to that visit! Sure hope he can convince me there is a God! I sure would like to be a Christian before I die.

Thank you for telling me how you feel about capital punishment. I have done some more thinking and want to share some other thoughts with you.

I watched *Witness to an Execution*. Did you watch it? Overall it was a pretty good story. But it didn't really address the issue of capital punishment like they hyped it up to do. Plus the execution itself was a second or two. So it didn't give the public a good view of what an execution is really about. Eyes burning out, parts of the body smoking, and so on, which really would turn the public against it if they could see what actually happens during an execution. I feel the public should view a real execution. They did a poll regarding the show. High 70% wanted execution but high 70% didn't want to watch one. Why not? This is what they want (execution). Don't make sense, does it? Everything else is public—our arrest, trial, sentencing—so why not the end results the public wants?

Oh, yeah, I forgot to mention something. I read an article in the *New York Times* newspaper last week about the execution on March 31 here in Georgia. He was scheduled to die at 7 p.m., but the courts held it up until they could hear the lawyers' last-minute appeals that pointed out that under a new Georgia law he couldn't be sentenced to death if his case was tried now since he is mentally retarded. One of his jury members (the only black member) also testified at the hearing that she was bullied by the other 11 jury members to vote for the death penalty. (If one jury member holds out—votes no—the person gets a life sentence.) If she'd known that, she said that she would've voted against the death sentence. Another juror testified that it was real racial in the juror room. One statement she remembered was said a few times, "It's just one less nigger." Also, the victim's family didn't want him to be executed.

The Georgia Supreme Court denied his last day appeal on the grounds of the unfair (racial) jury. The U.S. Supreme Court voted 6-3, the dissenting opinion stated how racial it was and couldn't understand how the majority couldn't agree on that. He was executed at 10 p.m. Sad that all the testimony did not save him. The article stated, to show how much consideration he got at the clemency hearing, that when they issued their decision they didn't use his name but Inmate Larry Grant Lonchar. The reporter asked, "How could they make a mistake like that?"

I think that anyone who believes in Jesus Christ can't believe in capital punishment but the majority do and use the verses in Matthew 5:38-39 that I quoted in a previous letter to justify their belief. Jesus' teaching was all about love and forgiveness. He wants us to repent and become a Christian. We can't if we're dead. Look at Moses. He killed but God forgave him and look what he became. He couldn't have become that if they would've put him to death when he killed. At least, I can say one thing I'm not and that is I'm not a hypocrite, which I see the majority is.

Another example, a couple years ago in Atlanta a church was robbed. The guy robbed the church's secretary. The TV news had an interview with the pastor of the church. The pastor pulled a gun out of his pocket and said, "I wish I'd been here. The guy wouldn't be robbing people anymore." Here was a man of God with a gun talking like if he would've been there he would have killed the thief! That is definitely not a Christian attitude!

I have some other opinions on capital punishment but will share them in my next letter since this one is getting long and I am tired.

I do, however, have another question to ask you. Adam and Eve had two sons, Cain and Abel. Cain killed Abel. "And Cain went out from the presence of the Lord and dwelt in the land of Nod, on the east of Eden. And Cain knew his wife" (Genesis 4:16-17 KJV). The Bible says that God created Adam and Eve, who had two sons. Where did Cain's wife come from?

I am looking forward to Michelle's letter. It sounds like she had a good track season. I'm sure she'll tell me all her summer plans too.

Good to hear Gregg got the stocker job he wanted. Boy, working all night plus doing yard work and his recreation sure seems like a lot on his body. But when you are young, a person can do these things, lucky him. (Ha!)

Got a kitchen worker smuggling me in some sandwiches. They cost me two stamps each one, so I can afford to buy a couple a week. They sure taste good!

Well, I'm sloppy as usual so I'll close. Tell Michelle and everybody Hi. You all take care!

Love,
Larry

*****

June 16, 1994
Dear Larry,

I was happy to get your last letter. When I read that Josh was coming to see you on the sixteenth, you wouldn't believe how *ecstatic* I was. That made my day! I had been praying that it would work out that he could come visit with you. The next day, I called his office in California and talked to Terri, his assistant, to see what time he would be coming so I could be praying for both of you. What a bummer it was when she told me that he wasn't going to get to come after all. The rest of my day was ruined, my tears flowed, and I was *extremely* disappointed!

179

Did you get word from the chaplain that he wasn't going to be able to make it? I sure hope so. I don't know if you got any explanation as to why he didn't come. Terri told me that he had to cancel everything for the entire week because of something of a personal nature that came up. It must have been really necessary because he already had his airline ticket purchased to come! He even had to cancel going to a friend's wedding on the seventeenth. It must have been something serious, or I don't think he would have cancelled all his plans. My concern is that you will understand and not hold it against him.

Terri mentioned that Bylle Payton might visit you on the sixteenth instead. She said that he had been on death row for ten years and had talked with you once before—about three years ago. He was providing the transportation from the airport to the prison for Josh. Did he come? Terri and I are both praying that Josh will be able to reschedule his visit. In the meantime, I hope that you will continue reading his two books that you have. They may be able to answer some of your questions and help to convince you that there is a God.

You asked in your last letter where Cain's wife came from whom he married after he fled to the land of Nod. The only explanation that I can give is that he married his sister. Genesis 5:4 tells us that Adam and Eve begat sons and daughters. We do not know how many years transpired between Cain and Abel's birth and the time Cain fled. Women were not really considered very important in Bible days and were rarely mentioned in Scriptures. Therefore, it seems perfectly logical that daughters were born to Adam and Eve after Cain and Abel were born. Those daughters could certainly have been of marriageable age and could have moved away from home or went with Cain. I firmly believe that Adam and Eve were the first two people on earth and all other people descended from them.

Since reading your views on capital punishment, I have a question for you. Do you think there are some innocent men on death row? I also watched the movie *Innocent Victims* that was a true story about a man accused of killing a mother and her two children. The district attorney was so sure of Tim Hennis' guilt that he railroaded the suspect into a guilty verdict. After fighting a huge legal battle,

Hennis' guilty verdict was overturned. Do you think this happens very often? Do you personally know of any cases where an innocent person was wrongly convicted due to manipulations of the police or attorneys?

You've probably received Michelle's "book" by now. She had writer's cramp when she finished. Her hand was still a little sore today. I told her that she had better not wait so long to write next time!

We finished the first day of our garage sale today. She was quite happy that she made about $31 out of the $150 in sales and is hopeful that more young mothers with children will come tomorrow so she can sell more of her toys and items that she has outgrown.

The weather today was in the mid-nineties and very humid. The heat index was about 109 degrees. I can begin to realize a little of what you must be experiencing in Georgia—only I imagine it's even hotter and more humid. I really feel for you! Fortunately, we did have air conditioning at my mother's house to escape to when there were no customers. Speaking of air conditioning, they built a new county court house and jail in Battle Creek that is scheduled to open in the next couple of weeks. I heard that the entire facility is air-conditioned. It must be so because there are no windows in the cell block wings. Sure wish you had air conditioning to help beat the heat.

Gregg bought a new (used) car yesterday. Ever since he sold his Mazda RX7 last spring, he's regretted it because his truck is not very comfortable to drive. He bought an '87 Mazda RX7 with 56,000 miles, which I guess is low mileage. His friend is going to buy his truck in August. He hopes to get quite a bit of his loan paid off while he's working full-time this summer. (Yes, Gregg is finding out that working nights is a little taxing on his body. It's harder than he thought, especially when he doesn't always get adequate sleep during the day since he has lawns to mow and a girlfriend to see.) In the fall, he's planning on working thirty hours a week (three nights), which is still considered full-time. Sure hope he can handle that and school too! He says he can, but we'll have to wait and see.

Gregg wants to have the downstairs of our tri-level as his "bachelor pad." It has two rooms—one will be his bedroom and the other his "relaxing space." Dave finally relented after being assured that he did not have to do any of the work. The very next day, the big move began. First, Gregg and one of his friends had to clear everything from his bedroom and move it downstairs. Next, Michelle was switched to Gregg's former bedroom, which is larger, to make way for our office that had to be moved from downstairs to upstairs to make room for Gregg's bedroom furniture. Needless to say, things were quite a mess for three days. There were times I just sat on our deck and breathed deeply to relieve some of my stress since I hate messes. It all came together, though, and everyone is resettled and happy. I was exhausted.

I am looking forward this Thursday–Saturday to our ladies bike ride and am hoping the weather cooperates!

Glad your eyes are feeling better. Itchy eyes are terrible. What do you think is causing you to sleep so much?

I'm happy you have an opportunity to get sandwiches a couple of times a week since you don't like the regular food. What kind of sandwiches do you get? How do you like the new warden that took over last month?

Well, it's getting late, and I have to get up early tomorrow for the garage sale. I'll be thinking of you and praying for you next Friday when you have your hearing. Please let me know the results of the hearing as soon as you can. Remember that we care for you.

Love,
Erin

*****

June 21, 1994
Dear Erin

I received your letter yesterday. Then Michelle's novel came today. Ha!

Thank you for informing me on why Josh didn't visit on the 16th. Even the chaplains here asked me why he didn't come. Yes, it sure sounds like something serious came up. No, I'm not mad. I sure was looking forward to it though. I was prepared too! (Ha!) I had finished both of his books. He'll reschedule it I'm sure.

Oh yeah, Bylle Payton didn't visit me. And I sure don't remember him ever visiting me. He might've visited here but not with me.

So you have a question for me to answer this time? The table has turned on me! (Ha!) I watched the movie *Innocent Victims* which was a true story about Timothy Hennis' wrongful prosecution on three charges of murder and the sentence to death. It was sad that the local police department set their sights on one person and used only the evidence that could back up what they wanted but that is what goes on more than the public might think.

I *know* that innocent men have died on death row. I was here with a guy who did ten years on our death row for a murder he didn't do. He was poor and black. The prosecutor took his case to the grand jury a couple of times trying to get an indictment but couldn't as there just wasn't enough evidence. So after a year, what the prosecutor and police did was take some hair found on the victim and sent it to the FBI crime lab. Well, the report came back saying the hair could match any Negro male's arm hair. But the police testified the report said it matched his, so the grand jury indicted him. He was tried and sentenced to death.

After a few years, a big Atlanta law firm took over his appeal. Some lawyers and law firms across the nation will do this. Anyways, they discovered the FBI report on the hair and that the police officer who testified had lied. Like I stated earlier, he did ten years here before he was freed. I was in the same cell block with him. I heard he had filed a lawsuit, but I don't know how that came out.

Then another guy here got his trial conviction and death sentence "overturned" and was given a life sentence instead cause he was black, had killed a white woman, had an all-white jury, and a lawyer who was a member of the KKK and who referred to him during the trial as a nigger. This is the reason why the majority of these southern "hick town" cases get overturned. The police and DA (prosecutor) will do anything to get somebody for a murder. It helps the DA get re-elected and makes the public think the police force is doing a good job. A poor person ends up with a court-appointed lawyer who the majority of the time hasn't tried a murder case before. I'm sure you read how the anti-capital punishment people always use that reason why the poor and minorities are the people on our nation's death rows—inexperienced lawyers.

So the new jail is finally opening, hey? An ex-guard from the county jail corresponds with me. He told me all about it. The lawyers even went to Battle Creek to talk to him last year about my case. I haven't heard from him in a few months so I hope he's alright! He's in poor health and in his 80s.

My hearing is two days from now. I'm sure hoping it goes my way so I'll die in a couple weeks. Sure don't want to suffer through another summer down here. It's been in the 90s the past couple of weeks. But it's going to get hotter every day for the next month. The humidity gets so bad that if I don't wrap my stamps in cellophane the glue on them will be sticking to something. I have to put them in hot water to unstick them. Then use toothpaste (ha!) for my glue.

So far the new warden has made some changes. However, those changes have been for the guards. We are not sure what other changes he will make.

The guy who was smuggling the sandwiches transferred. So no more sandwiches. Sure was good while it lasted. The sandwiches were peanut butter, baloney with cheese, and once in a while a tuna fish. My hearing is at 10 a.m. so I know that I'll have sandwiches for lunch that day. The guards will bring them. That's ok with me!

So Gregg has a new car and bedroom, hey? Michelle called it his "bachelor pad." She also was happy for it too as she liked getting a larger bedroom.

How was the ladies bike ride? I am looking forward to hearing about it.

Well, I'm going to close for now. I'm really sleepy. Why I'm having more than usual problems expressing myself.

Love,
Larry

*****

June 23, 1994
Dear Erin,

Well, my hearing is completed. The judge ruled in my favor. She granted my request to dismiss the lawyers and the appeal papers that were filed last year. With that ruling, she vacated the "stay of execution." So now, a new execution date can and will be scheduled.

I'm writing my trial judge tonight requesting that he sign the "death warrant." When he does that, I will know what week that I will be executed. These people decide which day out of the week that the execution will be held. They always pick the first day of the week the judge schedules it for.

My trial judge is a Christian and his wife is a preacher. I read in the paper about that a couple years ago as he was attending a theology seminary himself. He visited me last year on my scheduled "last day." It really bothered him that I was going to die. I told him I sure didn't hold no animosity toward him. The jury convicted and sentenced me to death. He had to do his job as the judge. He sure thanked me for telling him I didn't hold anything against him.

Well, I'll close as I have some letters to write. Tell Michelle I will write to her over the weekend. You all take care! Thanks for caring!

Love,
Larry

*****

June 29, 1994
Dear Larry,

Thanks for writing me so soon after your hearing. I was anxious to hear how it went. I had a feeling that it would happen this time. Please let me know as soon as you can when you hear from the judge. I assume your mom will find out shortly after the date is set. If she doesn't mind, would you ask her to call me collect and let me know? Otherwise, I'll just wait to hear from you.

I'm sure it's very hard to wait the next two or three weeks— especially since you know what you have facing you.

I'm glad you took Josh's cancelling his visit so well. You must have been doing a lot of reading to finish both books! Did they answer some of your questions? I'm still praying he will be able to reschedule his visit.

The bike trip last week was fun despite not having the best weather. Thursday was overcast when we started out to ride forty-eight miles, but we didn't get any rain until about 1 p.m. when we stopped for lunch. By the time we got back on the road, it was raining pretty hard, so we rode the last two hours to get to our motel in a downpour. Needless to say, we were all pretty wet even though we wore our rain gear. With our shoes squishing as we walked into the motel, we sounded like ducks and looked like drenched cats. Since it was still raining on Friday and I did not have anything to prove, I rode in the van that carried supplies and luggage and was an encourager. The fellowship with the other nineteen women was the very best part of the trip. I really needed to get away and just have fun. It helped give me a different perspective on things.

There was a very bad storm last night that blew the top out of one of my mother's trees. Electricity was out a couple of hours at our house and about five hours at my mom's. We had a cleanup party tonight. You wouldn't believe all the twigs and leaves that covered the yards.

It's getting late, so I guess I had better be going. Write again soon. Remember that you're special to us and we're praying often for you.

Love,
Erin

*****

July 7, 1994

Dear Erin,

Thanks for answering my question about where Cain's wife came from. I will be asking some other ministers for their view too.

I received a letter that the Attorney General wrote my trial judge. The lawyers wrote him requesting he don't sign the "execution order" without a hearing in front of him. The Attorney General pointed out that the law states his job is to sign the "execution order" without holding a hearing.

The reason the judge hasn't signed it yet is that the judge who I went in front of on June 23 is holding up the official rulings until she hears arguments on if she can dismiss my appeals without prejudice, which means if I do change my mind, too bad. I can't file an appeal. The Attorney General admitted in the letter I received today that the judge can't rule like that. If I want to change my mind, I can sign the appeal papers. So the judge will be issuing her official rulings any day. My trial judge should then sign the "execution order." I should die near the end of the month.

Michelle told me about your family vacation that you'll be taking soon to Mackinac Island and the Mall of America in Minnesota. Sure sounds like it's going to be fun. Drive carefully too!

The ladies bike ride sounded like fun. Too bad the weather wasn't better.

I am expecting a visit from Mary, the paralegal, tomorrow and am going to have her mail this letter and a couple more. That way her office will pay for the postage. I'm all out of stamps. The little money I receive from Mom I'm spending more on store "goodies." Since I don't have long left to live, I'm eating (enjoying) the goodies.

Well, I'll let you go. Take care! Thanks for caring!

Love,
Larry

Think About It: Capital Punishment

Capital punishment—are you for or against it? For most, there is no neutral ground on this controversial topic.

Capital punishment is currently legal in thirty-one states. "The annual number of U.S. executions peaked at 98 in 1999 and has fallen sharply in the years since. In 2016, only 20 inmates were executed and only 5 states–Alabama, Florida, Georgia, Missouri and Texas––

accounted for those executions."[44] Research indicates that support for the death penalty seems to be falling in the last two decades. However, slightly more Americans favor it (49%) rather than oppose it (42%). In addition, men typically support it more than women.[45]

The cost to maintain a death-row inmate varies by states.

> In Texas, for example, one death penalty case costs the state about 2.3 million dollars . . . One reason the execution of death row inmates costs so much is that some of the inmates spend decades waiting for the death penalty to be administered. This is because of the extended trial process involved and the length of the appeal process. They spend their entire stay on death row in special buildings separated from other prison populations. These special buildings require additional upkeep and more guards. In the long term, this costs states millions more a year than they would have paid had these inmates been sentenced to life imprisonment instead.[46]

Other reasons are the requirement to appoint death-qualified defense lawyers, more pre- and posttrial filings by both prosecutors and the defense, lengthier and more complicated jury selection practices, the two-phase death penalty trial, and more extensive appeals once a death sentence had been imposed.[47]

Do you feel the much higher costs of maintaining a death-row inmate are justified? Would life in prison without parole be a better choice?

In a 1993 interview with a reporter from the *Atlanta Constitution*, Larry was quoted as saying, "Capital punishment, it's the easy way out. I don't deserve that. I'm tired of suffering day in and day out. Doing time doesn't bother me. I know what I've done and I know what I've done with my life. Maybe it's best I continue suffering."[48] Have you ever thought about capital punishment as being the "easy way out"? For most, being executed is the ultimate price to pay for a crime. If you were in the shoes of a murderer and had the choice, would you rather spend an average of fifteen years on death row or spend the rest of your life in prison with no chance of parole?

Research also states that a majority of death-row inmates are minorities. The deathpenaltyinfo.org website presented the following statistics that give pause for much thought:

- The jurors in Washington State are three times more likely to recommend a death sentence for a black defendant than for a white defendant in a similar case. (Prof. K. Beckett, Univ. of Washington, 2014)
- In Louisiana, the odds of a death sentence were 97% higher for those whose victim was white than for those whose victim was black. (Pierce & Radelet, Louisiana Law Review, 2011)
- A study in California found that those convicted of killing whites were more than 3 times as likely to be sentenced to death as those convicted of killing blacks and more than 4 times more likely as those convicted of killing Latinos. (Pierce & Radelet, Santa Clara Law Review, 2005)[49]

In Larry's opinion, many minorities and poor are sentenced to death because of lack of money to acquire adequate legal representation and are assigned pro bono lawyers who may be inexperienced. The statistics presented above also prove that the race of the victim can determine whether a death sentence judgment is issued. Racial prejudice definitely plays a strong role in who may be sentenced to death. If you are not in the minority population, try putting yourself in the shoes of one who is. Would your feelings about these statistics be upsetting and seem unfair?

When asked if there were innocent men on death row, Larry's response was, "Yes, I know there are." "How many are sentenced to death in the United States for crimes they did not commit? A new study believes the figure is 1 in every 25—or 4.1 %. Since 1973, 144 people on death row have been exonerated."[50] In a 2015 survey done by the Pew Research Center, "about seven-in-ten adults (71%) said there is a risk that an innocent person will be put to death, including 84% of those who oppose the death penalty. Even a majority of death penalty supporters (63%) said there's a risk of taking an innocent life."[51] With the advent of DNA testing, hopefully, less people will receive wrongful convictions. Imagine that you had been arrested and wrongfully accused of murder and knew that you were innocent. Or suppose after spending years on death row, DNA testing or other evidence proved you were indeed innocent? How would you react?

A big argument that arises (and Larry had strong feelings about) is whether capital punishment is biblical. Can a Christian support it? Even among Christians, there is not a clear answer and are split opinions. For further information on differing views among Christians and the Scripture used to either support or reject capital punishment as being biblical, check out the following website that provides a view of each stance: https://religionnews.com/2017/04/28/is-the-death-penalty-un-christian.[52] You are encouraged to do further research if you still need to settle in your mind where you stand on the issue. If you are a Christian, can you biblically support your position for either stance?

So where do you stand on the issue of capital punishment? If you were a strong advocate of capital punishment before reading the chapter, has having a more close-up encounter with Larry through his letters and insights changed your mind at all? If you are anti-capital punishment, were your views solidified more, or do you now feel differently?

Chapter 12

Larry waited almost one year from the time he filed to have his appeal lifted before an execution order was granted. The excerpts from our letter exchanges from July to December 1994 will highlight his thoughts, feelings, and concerns during that time. A letter from my husband Dave begins the chapter.

July 15, 1994
Dear Larry,

Over the past year and a half that you and Erin have been corresponding, it's been good to get to know of you a little better. Many letters have come and gone. As Erin has told me things from your letters, you impress me as an individual who wants all the facts before making any decision. This reminds me of myself. The more information I have, the better. It just makes sense. This goes for my work and my personal life.

None of us have seen Jesus, so why should we believe in Him? Good question. God gave His word, the Bible, to tell us of Himself and of Jesus. It's a guide, a yardstick to measure our lives by. It tells of Christ's love for us and His death for *our* sins and how *all* of us can be forgiven and have everlasting life. Jesus tells of the people of his day who had seen Him and believed and how even more blessed would be those who believe and who had never seen (Him) (Matthew 20:29). That's me, Erin, Michelle, Gregg, and *you, Larry,* if you accept Christ's gift of salvation. What a promise!

Larry, I sometimes get too tied up in my underwear looking for facts and figures about a subject or decision and miss the simple stuff.

Often, the answer is right there in front of me, but I just can't see it. I'm blind to it. Many times, I really don't have all the answers I think I should have. I have to rely on faith that the way I'm proceeding and the facts I do have are right. It's amazing how things work out, and I'm happy I proceeded rather than just doing nothing.

Here's a final thought. I like to cover my bases as much as I can and have as many options available as possible. When it comes to being a Christian, I sincerely believe that Jesus died for me, forgave my sins, and gave me eternal life in heaven when I die—all because I asked Him to do so. I also realize some folks struggle with asking Jesus into their life for various reasons. Because I like to cover all my options, if I was struggling about making a decision concerning becoming a Christian, I would give the following some real serious thought. What would I have to lose? Becoming a Christian doesn't cost anything. There are and will be questions about a lot of things pertaining to the Bible and the things of God. That's where the faith part comes in.

When looking at the decision real close, a person might think about the chances of being a Christian and whether it is really the way he/she should go. Let's say that being a Christian has only a 10% chance of being right. Most betting people would steer clear of those chances. The stakes in this choice are as high as they come. To say the chances are too slim and the right decision is to go with the higher percentage in this example is a choice that God has given each of us to make. The question I pose is, what if you are wrong? The Bible clearly states that an eternity in hell awaits those who do not accept Him as their savior.

Larry, I know you and Erin have discussed at length how to become a Christian. I also know you have had and still do have many questions concerning the Christian faith. I can only tell you God's ways are not men's ways. We only think on human terms, and God thinks and acts on a higher plain. Yet He still loves and cares so much about us that He let His son die for us. Wow! We continue to pray for you that the Holy Spirit will work in your thoughts and heart to the point you will realize that Jesus is the way, the truth, and the life; and no one can have eternal life without Him.

I also have enclosed a couple of short devotionals from a booklet I read. Hope they are of some use.

Yours in prayer for you,
Dave

*****

August 8, 1994
Dear Dave,

Thank you for your thoughtful letter and devotionals from a booklet, which I did read.

I read everything now on religion. I would sure like to die knowing I'll be spending eternity in heaven. But I'm not going to say I'm a Christian until I can honestly say I believe there is a God. I can't say that yet. Foolish me!

You are right, though, why it's still so foolish not to believe even if it was only a 10% chance there is a God. Sure, a bettor would always bet on the 90%, but it's only common sense if it was only a .000-1% chance to believe when there is so much at stake. I mean, if there isn't any God, what did we lose? Nothing!

But if there is a God and we didn't believe, look what we lost, heaven. And that's why you are out there, a happy Christian man. And I'm a sad, dumb, stupid, and many other adjectives man. So, I envy your faith!

Well, I'm sleepy and worn out from playing basketball today, so I'll close. Take care of yourself! Again, thank you for caring!

Larry

*****

August 8, 1994
Dear Erin,

Mom visited me yesterday. She informed me that you had called her since you hadn't heard from me, so you were seeing if anything was wrong. I'm real sorry. I was planning on having the lawyers mail a letter to you (and pay the postage), but they informed me that they would not be mailing any more letters for me. So I had to wait until mom got her check to send me my monthly money so I could buy stamps.

You asked me if my mom visited me on my scheduled last day in February of last year. No, she didn't visit me then or will she come this time. She agrees with me. It would be just too hard on her. Our last visit a couple days before my last day was hard enough on both of us. Her doctor had her sedated on the actual scheduled execution day so she could handle it. On my last day, she'll really be in bad shape. With her health issues (bad nerves and high blood pressure), she just wouldn't be able to handle saying goodbye hours before my death. I can't put into words how hard it was on my dad and brothers saying good-bye. No way could my mom handle it. And I'm not going to put my dad and brothers through it again either.

You also asked if it was Chaplain Harrell who was laughing back there in the "death house" when they were preparing me to die. When I discussed this with Chaplain LaVelle, his explanation about the incident changed my opinion. So I don't hold any hard feelings on Chaplain Harrell or LaVelle now. I've never met Chaplain Hood.

Well, has Michelle put any dents in your car yet now that she has her driver's permit? Just teasing! I'm sure she takes driving serious like it should be and is a good driver.

My birthday, September 3, is fast approaching. Another year of my life wasted. It hurts so much. Just didn't realize how short and precious life is until too late.

I appreciated the letter from Dave. Since I want to drop him a few lines, I'll let you go. Again, I'm sorry for taking so long to write. Thanks for caring!

Love,
Larry

*****

August 12, 1994

Dear Larry,

I was very happy to receive your letter today. It made really good time in getting here. Earlier in the day, I was wondering why it had been so long since I had heard from you but had a feeling it was because you did not have any stamps. As I am writing my letter, Michelle is sitting on the floor of the office beginning her letter to you.

Thanks for explaining about your mom not visiting on the last day. I was just concerned that she would be upset to not get to see you. If she's visiting a couple of days before, that's good. I'll really be praying for both of you because I know it's going to be an extremely difficult time. It sure would be for this mom! Sure wish I'd been able to visit you.

Dave and I celebrated our twenty-third wedding anniversary on the seventh. How quickly the years have flown!

Believe it or not, our car is still in one piece—with no scratches or dents! Michelle is doing an excellent job of driving although she's a little nervous yet driving in heavy traffic. I'm sure she'll be ready in January to get her license.

I'm glad that you were able to discuss the laughing incident with the chaplain and to get an explanation of what went on. There is nothing worse than harboring ill feelings toward someone.

Gregg is continuing to fix up his "bachelor's pad." Dave finally got cable hooked up so they can watch the TV that Jenny bought for him to use. He also bought a love seat that just fits the space he had, a compromise between Dave and him since he wanted a full-size couch to stretch out on. Since it was also a hide-a-bed, it was a great compromise and only cost $20 at Goodwill! He also bought a new desk, since he did not like the bright turquoise desk he inherited from Michelle. Can you imagine that? He's really happy with his new living quarters downstairs.

Well, guess I had better be going for now. I'll be looking forward to hearing from you again real soon. Take care and keep studying and reading the Bible. Don't forget that you can ask God to show you that He is really real. He'd love to do so. We love you.

Love,
Erin

*****

September 3, 1994
Dear Erin,

I received your *beautiful* birthday card yesterday. Thanks! Mom sent me the $15. That was very thoughtful of you too! It sure will come in handy. I can buy some extra stamps now. Sure can't use that excuse anymore on why I haven't wrote in a while. ☺ So I'll write more often now. Mom visited me today so that made my birthday more meaningful.

Just recently I saw a man spraying something on the guard's booth window. I thought he was washing the window. Boy was I wrong. To my amazement when the stuff he sprayed dried after a couple of minutes, the window was now a one-way mirror. We can't see inside the booth, but he can see us. I sure don't like that. ☺

Michelle told me about Ginger's new diet—her and Gregg's orthodontic retainers. She should be out of the chewing stage by now. That was one expensive meal!

Oh, yes. Thank you for the "I Said a Prayer for You Today" card. I have it in my Bible. It means a lot to me cause I know you mean everything on that card. I'm going to give it to Mom when I die. It's sure beautiful!

I am glad this 3-day weekend is about over since we only get fed two meals a day, no mail, and no outside yard.

Well, I'll let you go. Y'all take care!

Love,
Larry

*****

September 15, 1994

Dear Erin,

Long time no letter from you. Are my bad habits rubbing off on you? ☺ I'm sure you are quite occupied now that you went back to work, so I understand. You sure do keep yourself occupied. You are getting your necessary rest, aren't you?

Well, my middle brother, Rob, moved to Georgia last week to live with my mom. She (me too) is so happy that he is living with her. She told me he's sure helping her out a lot. I just hope he stays down here and can find a job quickly! Mom needs him so much! He and Mom visited me Saturday.

I am going to tell you something, but don't tell anybody else, ok? I sure don't want it to reach mom since she already has enough worries now. Rob told me Saturday when mom left the visiting room to use the bathroom that he is dying. Isn't that something? It sure has me so upset!

He was shot in the back of his head over 20 years ago. The buckshot is still in his head. He was working at the hospital painting earlier this year when he passed out and was unconscious for three hours. They took some x-rays and found the buckshot in his head. The doctor said he probably at the most has a couple years left. If they operate to remove it, the doctor said that there is about an 80% chance that he won't survive the operation. He's having headaches already. Unreal, hey? I worry about my mom and other brothers, and now I have this. So I'm sure not sleeping well.

My youngest brother, Steve, is hooked on drugs. The only end result to that is death or jail. He won't be able to handle jail and would commit suicide. My oldest brother, Tom, is smoking at least two packs of cigarettes a day and working seven days a week and not eating well. All that is bad for his heart, which isn't normal. He has a bad heart. The doctors told Mom when he was young that he wouldn't live long. He's proved them wrong so far, but working, smoking, and not eating well sure isn't good for his heart. Sure glad I'm dying soon. I just hope I go first before any of them. Selfish me, hey? But I'm not as strong as they are mentally. Well, enough of that stuff.

Billy Graham is coming to Atlanta next month. Rob said he's going to that. Mom said she would like to go so badly too but can't. The arthritis has her where she can barely walk. She said she'll watch him on TV. Rob is a Christian. Mom believes in God too. But her actions don't support a Christian lifestyle. It makes me feel a little better that she believes in God, the Bible, and Jesus Christ. But by not living a Christian lifestyle has me not considering her a Christian. A real Christian just doesn't say they believe in God, the Bible, and Jesus, but they act and speak like God expects them to.

Keep an eye on Michelle. She's at the age where "peer pressure" becomes part of her life. But I think she'll be alright. As long as she keeps her faith, she isn't going to let "peer pressure" make her do anything stupid.

Well, I'll let you go. Thanks for caring!

Love,
Larry

*****

September 24, 1994
Dear Larry,

So you wonder if your bad habit of writing rubbed off on me, huh? I'll bet you received my letter about the same day that yours went out. But you're right, it has been a long time since I have written. The first few weeks of the semester have been very hectic for me, but I think I'm finally caught up.

I appreciate your concern about me getting my necessary rest. You're quite perceptive. Actually, sometimes I think I've been overdoing the last few months. There are just so many things to attend to between work, church, and family—and I like to spend some time with my mom too since she gets lonely. I am being pulled in many different directions. Keeping busy is also a way I may be dealing with my grief. Hopefully, the pace will slow down just a bit. I'm beginning to look for things I can cut out of my schedule, which should help.

Glad Rob finally made it to Georgia to live with your mom. I know that she needs someone to live with her to help her out and be company for her. I imagine he'll get to visit you more often now that he's so close. That will be nice for you. Hopefully, he can find a job very soon.

What a shock you must have had when Rob told you he is dying! I really feel for you and know how upset you must be. It's always hard to understand why so many things seem to hit at once—Rob, your mom, and other two brothers. What's so frustrating is when a solution to a problem is out of our control. We just have to sit back and watch things happen. I know I felt like that with my dad when I would see him doing things that I knew were not good for his health or went against what the doctors had told him he could do. It is all part of life, and it seems the older we get, the more things there are that can affect our family. I was happy to hear that you feel Rob is a Christian. I will be praying for your mom.

The only way I've been able to handle hard things is to give them over to the Lord and ask Him to give me the strength and mental fortitude to handle them. Even then, I don't always do real well. I still have my blue days. Guess those are the times I try to take things back over and handle them myself. It's probably hard for you to relate to what I'm saying since, as far as I know, you have not yet accepted that God is real and given control of your life over to Him. I hope that someday soon, however, that will happen. In the meantime, just know that I pray every day for you. You're still on our church's prayer sheet every week too. So many ask about you and really care about you.

Michelle bought another hamster about seven weeks ago. We discovered it was a female when she started putting on weight and four babies were born a few days later. We've been having quite a time with our "babies." They are now almost as big as their mother. We've had to separate them into five different cages because they've been fighting. Two of them were getting "beat up" by the more aggressive ones and had bleeding bellies. I thought that the two injured ones might be able to stay together, but the minute I put the second one in the cage, they started fighting! Now, they both have a home to themselves. We also took Snuggles, the mother, out because she was beating up on the first baby. I think she had had enough of the babies too when we heard a rustling sound behind our bed one night and found that she had gotten out of the cage and "run away" from her brood. I had to chuckle at that! On Tuesday, when they're six weeks old, the local pet store is hopefully going to buy them from us—for fifty cents each. They really get a good deal because they can sell them for $10 each. Since none of Michelle's friends were allowed to have one, I hope the pet store will take them so they will have a home and not a home with us!

Thanks for being concerned for Michelle. I know the teen years can be difficult with peer pressure and all. I'd be quite surprised if she ever succumbed to peer pressure as she's very strong in what she believes is right and wrong. She's also *very* conservative and picky about who her friends will be. She has only a small circle of friends, and they are all Christians and think the same way on issues. I'm really grateful for that.

Being a Christian has definitely influenced her values. In the fourth grade when she did not like the rock music being played on the bus, she actually wrote to the school superintendent (who was also our next-door neighbor) to complain about having to listen to it. Shortly afterward, the music on the bus was stopped. When the other kids on the bus found out why they could no longer have the music, she took a lot of heat for the letter she wrote but handled it just fine. It took a lot of courage for her to stand up for what she believed.

I've shared the new news that I have, and it's almost suppertime. I am being pampered tonight since Dave is fixing supper. I am fortunate to have him.

Take care. Write again soon.

Love,
Erin

*****

October 2, 1994

Dear Erin,

You are right. In my last letter I wrote how my bad habits are rubbing off on you, as I hadn't heard from you in a while. I received a letter from you the next day. Now I have two letters to reply to. I better get my lazy self going.

Sure got a smile reading about the hamster "babies." Did the pet store buy them? (What a rip off to buy them for 50 cents and sell them for $10!)

When I talked to my mom on Tuesday, she told me Rob worked 12 hours on Monday. He saw some guys working on the roofs of Mom's apartment complex, so he asked them if they needed any help. They did, so he had a job about a week after arriving down here. He told me Saturday he only worked two days last week cause of rain. He really likes the guys and they like him. His boss is trying hard to find him a car. He said he'd pay for it and take so much out of his paycheck each week. Sure hope he has found one this week since he's paying a neighbor of mom's $10 a day to use her car to drive to and from work. He said when he gets a car he'll visit me every weekend. Plus it will mean a lot to Mom. He can take her to visit me and other people, to the store, and to get her out of the apartment.

Mom also told me that my grandma, her mother, is in bad shape. My aunt told mom that they don't expect her to live much longer. Sure is sad! It hurts me I'm not out there to say goodbye. We always were close. She has had a good life and is a real Christian.

Enclosed is an article that I consider *real* evidence on evolution. Showed it to a pastor last week when he visited me. He also believes Adam and Eve and the flood are parables. I've had other religion leaders tell me the same thing. Then I've also had some tell me that they aren't parables but everything in the Bible is true. Why I stay confused, who am I to believe? Let me know what you think about the article and please return it.

They discontinued our cable TV cause of politics—the tight governor's race. The challenger (Republican) has stated all Georgia's prisons will be more of a punishment. (We are treated like animals now). He said all cable TV will be removed. I do not think he or the public know that we (inmates) pay for our cable by the profits from the inmate store. So, it's not like the taxpayers are paying for it. Anyways, the governor doesn't want the media or his challenger to find out not only do we (death row inmates) have cable TV but we also have the premium channels (HBO, Showtime, etc.) Maybe if the governor gets re-elected, we will get our good channels back next month. The TV helps pass the time for us.

Well, I'll close as I want to write Michelle a few lines. Should've wrote these earlier. I slept all morning and watched football all afternoon and night, sorry. Tell everybody "Hi."

Love,
Larry

*****

October 13, 1994
Dear Larry,

Did you think I had fallen off the face of the earth since I have not written in almost three weeks? It has been a very busy three weeks. Dave and I took a weekend color tour to Cadillac, my mom and I went to Grand Rapids to spend a night and Christmas shop, Michelle has had marching band competition and football games that we go to so we can see her march, plus midterm is here, and I spent many hours grading papers and figuring midterm grades. Finally, I can see the light at the end of the tunnel before the holidays hit.

I have mixed feelings about the holidays this year since it will be our first ones without my dad. I hope the workshop on "Getting through the Holidays" that my mom and I are going to soon gives us some good ideas.

If the inmate store is paying for the cable TV for the prison, then I do not understand why it should be taken away, other than because of politics. Many seemingly unfair things happen under the guise of politics. Hopefully, your current governor will get reelected, and you will get it back. Do you still have regular TV?

When I talked with my mom tonight, she told me that your grandmother died today. My heart goes out to you and to your entire family. I've lost two grandmothers and know how it feels. I'll be thinking of you and praying for strength for all of you in the coming days, weeks, and months as you grieve her death. I was quite sure your grandmother was a Christian. She is now in a far better place and really enjoying herself. I know it will be hard for you not to be able to be with your family at this time.

I read the article you sent about evolution and am returning it as you requested. After reading it, my only comment is, where did the oldest ape-man have its beginnings? If man evolved from a single cell, who created that cell to begin with? Everything has to have a beginning and a creator. If the formation of the earth and the universe is accredited to the big bang theory, where did the matter that exploded come from? The only response I can have is that God created it. I feel you're willing to keep an open mind and am praying every day that God will speak to your heart and provide the evidence you need to believe in Him.

You mentioned that you have talked to several religious leaders about the Bible and get conflicting opinions and are confused about who to believe. I feel a *true* Christian and pastor would have to believe the Bible is 100% true and that the stories of Adam and Eve, the flood, etc., are not just parables but *true* events. If a "pastor" chooses not to believe even one small portion of the Bible, how can he believe that any of it is true—how would he ever be able to know what is and what isn't true? I think his congregation would also be very confused. You aptly labeled those who tell you the Bible is full of parables as "religious leaders." Do *you* truly feel that they are true Christians?

There are many who are masquerading as "pastors" who may be truly good people but have not met Jesus. They have the "head" knowledge but not the "heart" knowledge. The Bible says that God has reserved His harshest punishment for those false religious leaders who have led others astray by their false doctrine. They will be held accountable to God himself for what they are preaching (2 Peter 2:1). Actually, I strongly believe they are acting under Satan's influence rather than God's. Since you really do not get to observe their lifestyle after you talk with them, it is probably very hard for you to assess the extent of their "Christianity." I know a person's walk and talk are strong indicators to you of his/her claim to be a Christian. I would be very leery about believing those who say that *any* portion of the Bible is untrue.

Guess I had better close for now as it is after 10 p.m., and tomorrow is another workday. I will be looking forward to your next letter. As always, you are in our prayers.

Love,
Erin

*****

October 31, 1994
Dear Erin,

Hope this letter finds you and your family well. It is Halloween night. Did you have a lot of visitors? Boy, when I was young, it was one of my favorite nights.

I didn't know Grandma had died until I read your letter. Mom had written me that day but our great postal system delivered it to me ten days later. It sure hurt me to read about Grandma, even though Mom told me she was in bad shape and to be prepared for her death. If there is a heaven, I know she is in heaven. Did you or your mother go to the funeral?

It is a real good idea you and your mother are going to a workshop for people who have lost a loved one. I sure agree with you it's going to be hard on you all without your dad. Let me know what you learn.

Boy, is my sleeping messed up. I have so much on my mind. I haven't gone to sleep before 3 a.m. in close to a month. Two nights ago it was 5:30 a.m. when I turned my cell light off.

Thank you for your opinion on the article I sent on the oldest ape-man bones they recently found. I'm not trying to be funny or trying to offend you, but I could ask the same questions regarding

God. Where did he come from? Who created him? I mean all of a sudden there was a God? Like you said, everything has a beginning. Also, Jesus is God's son. How was Jesus created before he came to earth? I am still hoping I can find evidence to convince me there is a God. I also pray every night asking for that proof. If you find any other books on creation vs. evolution, I would appreciate you sending them to me. I read that kind of material very thoroughly. Sure wish I could hear a debate on that subject.

Since I have waited a long time for the judge to issue an execution order, I wrote him a letter asking him to do so soon. Would you type it for me and make some copies?

The lack of sleep is catching up with me, so I will say goodbye for now. Thanks for caring!

Love,
Larry

*****

November 8, 1994
Dear Larry,

I'm sorry you had to hear about your grandmother from me. I just assumed that you would already have heard before my letter reached you. My heart goes out to you since I know the heartache of losing a grandmother. You asked if my mom or I went to the funeral. We didn't get to go to the funeral because the same day your grandmother died, one of my cousins (on my mother's side of the family—her sister's grandson) was killed in a car accident. Both funerals fell at the same time. My mother and I felt that my aunt really needed the support because she wasn't doing well emotionally, so we had to be with her. What a hard decision to have to make—seems there have been a lot of those hard decisions lately!

We did, however, go to your grandma's visitation. She was dressed in a very pretty light purple dress, and her hair was done very nice. She looked so natural and peaceful lying there. It looked to me like she had lost some weight since I had last seen her. There were lots of beautiful flowers. You would have been satisfied with the decisions the family made. I heard that a Baptist minister was doing her funeral service. I'm sure it was nice. I believe she was a real Christian too. Remember that you *can* see her again if you decide to commit your life to Christ. I know she would be waiting with outstretched arms for you—just as Christ would.

The workshop on "Getting through the Holidays" was very good. We had already done some of the things that they suggested, such as changing your normal way of doing things. For Thanksgiving, we are going to eat out—not a very popular decision with Gregg and Michelle. Dave's parents will join us since they are also grieving the death of his brother. For Christmas, Mom and I decided that we would decorate the small shrub that we planted in Dad's honor last summer with some miniature lights. He always said how much he liked a green Christmas tree. They usually had a silver artificial one. Last Saturday when we went to Frankenmuth to the huge Christmas store they have there, I bought a special ornament for my tree in memory of my dad. Today, we're going to the cemetery and put out a Christmas wreath. I know it's a little early, but we have to get the stand in the ground before it freezes.

Your question about who created God was a fair enough one to ask. You will probably have a hard time accepting my answer because it requires faith. Faith is defined in Hebrews 11:1b as "knowing that something is real even if we do not see it" (NCV). The Bible says that God *was* even before the beginning of time—He does not have a beginning or an end. He is referred to in the Bible as being eternal or everlasting, which means having no beginning or no end. Such a concept is hard for us as humans to understand since we measure everything in time. Believing that something had no beginning but has always been and will continue to be forever is difficult to believe. Genesis 1:1 says, "In the beginning, God created the heavens and the earth" (KJV). Psalm 90:2 states more about His eternal nature, "Before the mountains were born and before you created the earth and the world, you are God. You have always been, and you will always be" (NCV).

You also questioned how Jesus came into existence before He came to earth. John 1:1 says, "In the beginning was the Word, and the Word was with God and the Word was God" (KJV). The Word is another name for Jesus. John 14:8–9 provides further evidence, "Philip said to him, 'Lord, show us the Father. That is all we need.' Jesus answered, 'I have been with you a long time now. Do you still not know me, Philip? Whoever has seen me has seen the Father'" (NCV). One of Jesus's purposes in coming to earth as a man was to put God in a human body to help make it easier for man to see what God is like through Jesus. Since these verses are from the Bible, which is the Christian's authority, we believe God is eternal and has always existed. As I said, it requires faith to believe this explanation.

I'll continue to be on the lookout for other books about evolution versus the Christian faith. If I find one I think you'd like, I'll send it in care of the chaplain again. I was glad to hear that you're still open to God and are asking Him to reveal Himself to you. I know He honors all serious, heartfelt requests such as yours.

Michelle and I are planning on going shopping soon for your goodie box for Christmas. I assume we can still send the same types of things that we did last year. Let us know if there is anything you would especially like or cannot have. We love putting your goodie box together!

Now for the hard part of my letter. I'm sure you are disappointed to get your original letter to the judge back untyped. I'm asking you to not be upset but to try to understand the reasons why I did not type it.

First, I have done a lot of thinking and praying about your request. I know, to you, it probably seems like a very small request. To me, however, it is not. By typing your letter to the judge asking him to sign the execution order, I feel I am helping to speed up your execution. As a Christian and because of my convictions, I do not feel that the Lord would have me type your letter. As far as I know, you are still not a Christian. I, and all those who are praying for your salvation, have left you in the Lord's hands and have asked Him to bring you to Him in His own time. I do not feel that I have the right to perhaps shorten that time and, therefore, be the cause of your dying without having had enough time to come to realize that there is a God and to accept the salvation God wants to give to you.

I don't think you would want that to happen either if you only realized what a much worse fate awaits you after death if you do not accept His love and forgiveness. If you already were a Christian, I might feel differently about typing the letter because I know I would be helping you out of a bad situation into a much, much better situation—living in heaven. Can you understand what I'm trying to convey? As a Christian, I feel that after I have prayed about something and asked the Lord for his guidance that I will feel a peace about a decision. I have no peace whatsoever about typing the letter—just a very definite feeling that what I would be doing is wrong. I do have a peaceful feeling about not typing it, however.

Another reason that I am very hesitant to type the letter is that I know it would not be what your family would like. I do not want hard feelings against me where they are concerned—because we are family.

I will be waiting for your reaction to my letter. I truly hope you can understand that my decision was made out of love for you.

Love,
Erin

*****

November 21, 1994
Dear Erin,

Hope this letter finds you all well! First of all, let me tell you that I am not mad or disappointed that you didn't type that letter to the judge for me. After I mailed it, I thought of that same reason. I just used carbon paper to make the copies.

Sorry to hear about the death of your cousin! I sure can understand why you were with his family.

It brought tears to my eyes to read about your description of Grandma at the funeral home. I'm so immature. I couldn't have handled being there at her funeral. Another reason why I'm hoping I die before any of my immediate family.

I sure hope you all have a good Thanksgiving, but I know it will be difficult to have a happy holiday since it will be the first one without your father. The "Getting through the Holidays" workshop was just what you needed. I am glad you and your mom went to it. Rob said that he will visit me on Thanksgiving. His visit gives me something to look forward to that day.

Thanks for your explanation about who created God and Jesus. You are right that a lot of faith is required to believe they always existed. I will definitely be keeping what you said in the back of my mind. Right now it is hard to grasp.

You mentioned shopping for my Christmas goodies. We better follow the rules on what I'm allowed to have this year as I doubt if we can get that good guard again. The following is from the memo on what we are allowed:

Cakes—my favorite is angel food and cakes with fruit (like strawberries) ☺.

Cookies—I like any kind but chocolate unless they are Oreos

Candy—hard candy individually wrapped, no foil. M&Ms are allowed (I like the plain). I like most any kind of candy.

Nuts—clear factory-sealed packages (I'm not fussy about the kind either). ☺

I sure loved that homemade peanut brittle Dave made last year. I might be allowed that. Oh yeah, the other rule is that all packages must be received between 12-1 and 12-31.

It is sad to tell you this. I'm not even getting a package from my family this year because Mom said that money is short this year. But don't worry. I'll get my three packages I'm allowed. My Christian friend Robbie always sends me one. Then a paralegal is going to send the third one. The lawyers pay for these for inmates who do not have anybody.

Well, they are coming to pick up the mail, which will be the last time until Sunday night. Tell Michelle I'll mail her a letter and one for you then. You all take care.

Love,
Larry

*****

November 28, 1994
Dear Erin,

I'm depressed so I thought I'd write you and Michelle, hoping it will cheer me up some. The following is just between you and me, ok? I'm really ashamed to tell anyone, but I consider you family and can share it with you. Last weekend, Thanksgiving weekend, was a four-day weekend for state employees here in Georgia. On holidays and weekends, we can have family visits. I have two brothers and a mother that are only a 30-minute drive away from me and nobody visited me.

Then Friday, I received a manila envelope from my mom. It had some Christmas cards in it which I asked her to send me so I could send them to family and friends. I'm "up" cause it's Friday and I know I would have a visit the following day or Sunday. Well, my mood sunk when I received the envelope. On the outside of it mom had written, "Rob has to work this weekend so we can't come down." No letter at all!

I've told them over the years how much their letters and visits mean to me! Mom used to write me twice a week and found somebody to bring her down to visit me every other weekend. Since Rob has moved down here 12 weeks ago, I've received three visits and four letters from her. She also used to send me $25-$30 each month since she knows I don't eat the food here. This is the third month she hasn't sent any. It sure hurts me! It guess all this hurts so much cause I know if the shoe was on the other foot, say it was one of my brothers, I would be visiting him as often as the rules allowed and doing anything else for him. Not only because he's my brother in prison but he's also dying, which I am. I'm not cheering myself up writing this stuff so I'll stop and talk about other things.

Oh yeah, I'm sure you are close to sending my goodie box, which sure will come in extra handy (food) for me in December. Friday they made some guard movements. That guard who last year replaced the regular guard for a day when your Christmas box arrived is now the guard in charge of our mail. So that means he will be passing out all our Christmas boxes this year, which sure is great! He'll let us have stuff that we aren't supposed to receive, like he did for us last year.

I received a letter from my friend who's a reporter at the Atlanta newspaper. She's going to do an article on my fight to die. A week ago Sunday on "60 Minutes" she saw a story on a Texas death row inmate fighting to die too. She said she'll be interviewing me in about two weeks if these people let her.

If it is not too late, would you see if you can find the issue of *Life* magazine that I've enclosed a picture of? Then cut out the article on Jesus for me. I'm still searching. Hopefully, I'll find Him before I die.

Well, I'll close as I want to write Michelle. I will tell her I'm sorry for not writing last Sunday like I told you I would. Thanks for caring!

Love,
Larry

*****

December 3, 1994
Dear Larry,

I am happy this letter still finds you still speaking to me! Having to send your letter back was by far one of the hardest things I have had to do! But, as I tried to explain, it's because I truly care about you that I did. I am so glad that you understood.

Sorry it's been so long since I've written. So much has been happening that my energy has been zapped. By the time I get done with the things I have to get done each day, it's sometimes ten thirty or eleven at night. I was very happy to have the four-day break at

Thanksgiving. The last month has been especially stressful for me at work since our computer lab has acquired a virus, and we are our own technicians. My officemate and I have spent hours in the lab. Our lab had been virus-free all semester until about three weeks ago. Now, about 90 % of the computers are infected, and we haven't found any software to clean them with. Students are getting very frustrated—and so are the teachers! I leave the lab every day with a tension headache. Things that are out of my control really bother me. I've been after our computer support people to do something, but they are dragging their feet. I guess when it doesn't affect you directly and you don't have to deal with the situation daily, the urgency isn't there. It's gotten to the point I dread going into the lab every day. Sure hope they do something soon with the end of the semester fast approaching!

I'm glad you consider us family and feel you can share your feelings and disappointments with us. We all need someone we feel will listen to us and that we can get things off our chests too . I know how disappointed and hurt you must have been to not get your visit on Thanksgiving from Rob as I know you were really looking forward to it. Disappointments on holidays always seem greater. It must seem to you right now that your family does not care like you want them to care. When we are alone, family is especially important to us. Has Rob visited you since Thanksgiving? Did he say why he didn't come to visit?

It must also be very discouraging to not receive the regular letters and monthly checks from your mom. Do you feel you can express your feelings to her and ask her why she doesn't at least write? Probably having an extra person living with her does require more effort on her part and cost. Do you think that perhaps another reason she has slacked off is that she may be trying to distance herself a little bit so that when the time comes that a date is actually set, she'll be able to handle it better? I know that the last couple of times that I talked with her she said that she felt every time the phone rang after your June hearing, a bomb was going to be dropped on her—that she was going to find out that a date had been set. I'm just guessing, and I may be way off base. However, that may be part of the reason—hard as it is for you when you long for the closeness right now. We all react to hard situations in different ways. What do you think?

While I've got my "psychologist" hat on, I also wanted to respond to your comment about your being immature because you cried when you read about your grandma. There is nothing immature about crying over the loss of someone you love. It's all part of grieving for the person. It's the person who doesn't cry that's not "normal." Men are taught not to show their real emotions from the time they are small children and are told "boys don't cry." That's crazy. It's unhealthy not to cry and to stuff our feelings inside. It's through tears, talk, and the passing of time that we get through the grief process. That's why I'm glad you shared your feelings with me. If I had not cried and talked about how I've felt during the last several months, I don't know how I would have handled my emotions. Fortunately, my mom is a good listener. We talk together often. So don't stop talking.

Did you get your box? You didn't mention what the weight limit was so we assumed it was the same as last year and limited the box to twelve pounds—well, actually twelve and a half pounds. It was fun shopping for you. Since I didn't know which guard would be checking the box, the only homemade item was the peanut brittle. My mom and I made it this year since Dave was sick that day. It should still taste good, though! Have you gotten any other boxes yet? Hopefully, you'll get the other two that you're expecting.

I'll look at the library for the article about Christ from *Life* magazine. From the write-up in the newspaper about it, it doesn't sound like it would be very helpful—but I may be wrong. Once classes are over, I'm going to go to our Christian bookstore and see if I can find another book to send you via the chaplain.

If you can, would you send me a copy of the article that the Atlanta newspaper is planning to do about you? I'd be sure to send it back.

I need to be going for now since I have some papers to grade and need to get prepped for tomorrow. Maybe I'll even get some of my Christmas cards done. Remember that we love you and that you're special to us. I think of you each day and pray for you. I'm confident that the Lord is going to answer my prayers. As always, I'll look forward to hearing from you again real soon.

Love,
Erin

*****

December 7, 1994
Dear Erin,

I received the "Big Goodie Box" today! Boy, am I going to have big fun eating it! ☺ I sure can't thank you enough. Michelle told me in her letter that as you were packing it she was saying, "I know he'll like this, that, this, that—" ☺

There is some bad news too. That ex-mail guard gave it to me, so there were some things I didn't get. The good and new mail guard was eating lunch. When he came back, I asked him why he didn't pass out the Christmas boxes since he's the mail guard now. He said since December is more work with the Christmas boxes that the former mail guard is helping him out. Bad luck, hey? I did get to keep a few things I shouldn't have received. However, the item that I didn't get that hurt the most was the baggy of peanut brittle! When my mom comes this weekend, I'll have her pick up the stuff I couldn't have. Then every time she or Rob come to visit me, I'll have them wrap up a few pieces of peanut brittle and bring it in their pockets. So, I will eat it! ☺

I hope my Christmas present to you all arrives before Christmas. It's coming from a company. I know you all will enjoy it. I bet you have no clue what it is, hey? ☺ Let me know when it arrives and exactly what it is so I'll know they sent the right one. Boy, I bet you are curious! ☺

Last year when they let the media into the prison, one free-lance writer also interviewed me. She had just left the surviving victim from the family I killed. He was shot but lived, his dad and brother died. He asked her to ask me why I killed his dad and brother. I was honest and told her what to tell him. I got a copy of the article she wrote yesterday. I sure wish I didn't read it. I cried. It sure upset me! I couldn't even lay down until after 5 a.m. this morning. A big reason why I can never forgive myself and why my pain because of the crime will never go away. Hopefully, dying will end my pain.

I'll send the article if you want to read it. You decide, but don't let Michelle read it! I just hope the article won't stop your love for me as it brings reality to the crime. Not that it goes into detail about the crime, but it goes into detail of the pain I caused the victims' families. She was also supposed to have written a story on our interview but her paper she worked for went out of business before it was published.

What plans do y'all have for Christmas Day?

This letter turned out longer than I figured. I'll let you go as I want to write Michelle a thank you letter too. Again, thank you so much for caring!

Love,
Larry

*****

December 13, 1994
Dear Larry,

How nice to get your Christmas card and letter yesterday! Your card is on our front door along with the others cards we've received from friends. Yours is the most special one though! I haven't gotten around to getting my cards out yet but hope to this week.

Thanksgiving really wasn't as hard as I thought it was going to be. We just decided to remember that Dad was having the best Thanksgiving he'd ever had with Jesus and was the happiest he had ever been. That sure helped. I did go to a florist and get a beautiful peach rose and set it on the kitchen table in his honor for the day. My mom said she looked at it a lot that day and was happy to have it there. It was a comfort for me too.

I can't believe that Christmas is creeping upon us so fast and is less than two weeks away. Our tree is finally up. When the lights from the tree reflect off the special laser disc ornament I bought in honor of my dad, it is beautiful! My mom did let me put a small string of lights on the shrub that we planted last spring in my dad's memory, but she did not want any other Christmas decorations up at all.

You asked what we will be doing for Christmas. On Christmas Eve, we celebrate with just our immediate family. I always get stocking stuffers for Gregg and Michelle, and they open them that night. The main focus of the evening, however, is celebrating Christ's birth by reading the Christmas story and then having a piece of a special birthday cake for Jesus after we sing "Happy Birthday" to Him. The birthday cake tradition began the year Gregg was old enough to understand the true meaning of Christmas.

We'll be going to church Christmas morning since it falls on a Sunday. My brother and his family will be joining us for dinner and the rest of the day. Maybe he'll decide to come to church with us since he and his family came to the special Thanksgiving service. It was so nice to all be there together. That would sure be a nice gift.

The computer virus in our lab is gone! Finally, we got someone to listen to us and take what we were saying seriously. I had called my supervisor and told him that I was at the height of my frustration about the problem. He had also gotten a few calls from students. The solution ended up being quite simple. We had to delete all the virus scan software and reload it. Then, it didn't detect the virus any more. Sounds strange, doesn't it? The computer technician said that it was reflecting itself on all the computers. It wasn't actually there, but the computer scan software thought it was. All went well after the issue was fixed, and the semester ended on a good note.

Now that the semester is over and grades have been posted, I am so glad to finally have some time to finish getting ready for the holidays. Since classes for the winter semester do not begin until the middle of January, I will enjoy having a couple of weeks to myself to relax.

I am not sure if I will have a chance to write or will hear from you again before Christmas. If not, you will definitely be in my thoughts. Hopefully, you will get some family visits too.

Love,
Erin

Think About It: Loneliness

Have you ever been in a room full of people and yet felt all alone and experienced a deep ache inside? Have you wished that someone in the room would take the time to "see" you on more than just as superficial level—as more than just someone in the crowd? If so, you have experienced loneliness.

Wikipedia defines loneliness as "a complex and usually unpleasant emotional response to isolation. It typically includes anxious feelings about a lack of connection or communication with other beings."

God created us with a deep heartfelt need for social interaction with others. In Genesis 2:18, after He created Adam, He said "It is not good for the man to be alone. I will make a helper who is right for him" (NCV). It was then that Eve was created. We were created to live in relationship with others and need at least a few people we can connect with on a heart level who understand us and who we can talk to and vice versa. Many times, that may be family, a trusted close friend, or both.

In today's social-media-oriented society, feelings of isolation and loneliness are becoming more prevalent. We choose to communicate more informally via text, e-mail, tweets, and Facebook with our "friends." Picking up the phone or seeing a person face to face and having a personal, deep conversation is becoming a less common way of connecting. Perhaps, it is because we have a busy lifestyle or feel others do not have the time to talk. Some may brag about how many friends they have on social media; but, if asked, a majority would probably have to admit to having feelings of loneliness.

It is often easy to spot those who may have the potential to be lonely—a widow or widower, a single person, one who is homebound or in a nursing home, a homeless person, a prisoner, or others that you can think of to add to the list. Often, it is assumed that if one does not fit in any of these categories, loneliness should not be an issue. I have found that is an incorrect assumption.

There are spouses in marriages who are lonely and children who are mistreated or abused and do not feel loved. Outside the family are others who also do not feel loved or who do not fit in at school or elsewhere, have handicaps, are different in some way, or are bullied. Even those who seem to have many friends and are considered to be popular and have it all together may fall prey to the predator of loneliness. A key factor that determines one's level of loneliness is how connected and loved one feels with at least one or two significant others in one's life, be it friend or family.

Through Larry's letters, it is easy to read between the lines and see his loneliness. Imagine being confined to a small space for eighteen to twenty-one hours per day with most social contact being with those you may not trust or those who treat you merely as a number. Although he connected outside the prison with others via letters, it was not the same as connecting with someone he knew loved him and had his best interests at heart. His visits from his mother and brothers were his only break from loneliness. When they did not come, a piece of his heart was broken from the disappointment. After writing for a year and half, Larry and I also developed a trust and friendship at a heart level that he did not want to lose, as evidenced by his comment to not stop loving him if I read the article written about the surviving victim and the pain Larry had caused his family. What he did not realize at that point in our friendship is that I would never have given up on him. The family/friendship connection was one that I also needed, so it was mutually beneficial.

I have lived with loneliness at various times in my life—when good friends have moved away, a loved one has passed away, life circumstances took "good" friendships in different directions and left me feeling wounded, or busyness has interfered. It is easy for me to be in church or at a social function and feel lonely and isolated since most friendships seem to be only the "Hi, how are you today?" type, where there is no connection at the heart level. I was recently at an overnight girlfriend "retreat" and found that others felt the same as I did when I made the comment about feeling isolated. It takes time to cultivate a real heart-level relationship; and many are so busy, including myself at times, that we do not take the time to listen and connect. Hurt from past relationships can also make it hard to trust enough to once again pursue a close friendship.

So what is the solution to loneliness? If you are not a Christian, God first wants to fill that place in your heart that only He can fill. Become connected to Him at a heart level. Next, look for someone whom you can trust and can feel safe opening yourself up to being a friend to—especially if you are recovering from being wounded by a friend—and allow yourself to get to know that person on a deeper level. Even having one close friend can make a difference in your level of loneliness. Who knows? Perhaps, you will be an answer to someone else's loneliness.

Chapter 13

January 3, 1995
Dear Erin,

Sorry I haven't written in a while. Been really upset about Mom's mental and physical condition. The doctors got her hooked on the prescription drugs. I've asked my brothers and sister to get her some help before it's too late. If I was out, I sure would do it. Since I'm not, it just makes me hate myself more for not being able to help my mom.

I like the way you spend Christmas Eve. Sure nothing wrong with singing Happy Birthday to Jesus! When Michelle and Gregg have children, they'll continue doing it. You all know the real meaning of Christmas, the birth of Jesus, not what the majority of our society celebrate, Santa Claus. That's why our society is in such bad shape.

Well, I sure hope you all had a nice Christmas and New Year. I'm expecting a letter any day now from you or Erin telling me all about it. Maybe some pictures, too? (Hint) I received the beautiful Christmas card from y'all, thanks! I'm still enjoying the goodies y'all sent me! ☺ Has the Christmas present from me arrived yet?

To my surprise, my brothers Tom and Rob visited me on the 24th—my Christmas present I guess! If so, it meant a lot to me! But, when I asked Tom if he wanted to talk to the staff writer of the Atlanta paper, he got upset. It sure hurts me to see the pain on his face when my execution is mentioned. The writer asked me if he would talk to her. Both brothers said that they would come back next week during our three-day "holiday" and would try to bring mom. None of them came though. My hopes were crushed again.

Thanks for making the copy of that article out of *Life* magazine for me. I haven't read it yet but will before my next letter to you. How come you didn't comment on it? I sure respect your opinion!

I also received the book you sent, *Handbook of Christian Apologetics.* Thank you. I'm looking forward to reading it and will give you my opinion on it. I also hope it will convince me there is a God! But I'll probably go to my death without that. Pitiful!

To close on a positive note, I will tell you about what happened when I was watching the Bowl Game between Ohio State and Alabama over the weekend. The game got stopped for a few minutes cause a dog ran onto the field. ☺ Every time somebody would try to catch him, he'd run off. It sure was something. He was scared as there were so many people. They never did catch him. He finally found some empty space at the end of the field and ran off. He got plenty of TV coverage too. ☺ Bet that does not happen very often!

I've got a gift on its way to Michelle for her birthday. I won't tell her so she will be surprised when she gets it.

Well, I am sleepy as usual so will close for now. Tell Michelle I'll write her soon. Tell her "hi" and everybody else too.

Love,
Larry

*****

January 15, 1995
Dear Larry,

Now that the holidays are over, I have some free time to write. Everyone except me is back to school and work. I am enjoying a few free days before starting back for another semester.

I am glad that your brothers got to come and visit you on Christmas Eve and can understand why it was really special to you. Likewise, I can imagine your disappointment that no one came to visit over the New Year's weekend.

Are your brothers and sister trying to get your mom some help? It can be easy to get addicted to prescription drugs. That happened to one of my cousins, and it took her a long time to get herself straightened out again.

We had an enjoyable Christmas and New Year's. I took some pictures that I will send to you. However, I am waiting until after Michelle's birthday to use up the rest of the film in the camera so I can get them developed. Speaking of Christmas, we got the video (*Where Jesus Walked*) you had sent to us. We have not had a chance to watch it but are looking forward to it. Have I told you that Dave and I went to Israel with a group from our church about twenty-two years ago? What a trip! It made the Bible cities and events come alive. We visited many places on the video, so it will be even more special to us! Thanks so much for your thoughtfulness. Your gift means a lot to us!

You asked for my comments about the article in *Life* magazine. I felt that a majority of it was quite fundamental. However, other parts were way off base—I'm sure you know which parts I am referring to. I'll be interested in your reaction to the *Handbook of Christian Apologetics* and am praying that it will help to convince you that there is a God. I agree with your comment that it would be pitiful if you go to your death without believing there is a God. And it will also be unnecessary. Please read it with an open mind and let God speak to you through the book. My greatest hope is that 1995 can be a year of a new beginning for you. You have come to mean so much to me, and I cannot stand the thought of your dying without knowing the Lord.

Do you remember watching *Bonanza* years ago? We are watching the new version of it tonight. Sure seems strange to see Michael Landon's and Dan Blocker's sons on the show!

Since it is getting late, I am going to sign off. Michelle has some time off next week, so she will be writing then. Take care.

Love,
Erin

*****

January 29, 1995

Dear Erin,

Sorry it's been a while since I have written. A few things have happened that has my mind off in "space." Received a notice informing me the judge signed the "Dismissal Order." Then I received a "registered letter" informing me that the "Stay of Execution" has been lifted. The lawyer had already called Mom, Tom, and my dad with the news that my execution will soon be scheduled and he doubts if they can stop it. Tom called my mom crying after he got his call. The rest of the family is upset too. Mom and Rob visited me this weekend and were trying to talk me into stopping my execution. They didn't. I just have too many reasons why I have to die.

I signed up to attend a weekly Bible study that is taught by a Jehovah's Witness. To my amazement, he told us what I've told you and others—if God is such a loving God, He wouldn't punish his children for eternity. They do not believe in hell but believe the non-believers just won't be resurrected when Jesus returns. He also stressed how we all are sinners, nobody is better than another. He's used the same example I've used. Like I told you, "If Michelle did something wrong, you'd punish her. But you still would love her." I'm not expressing this like I want, but I know you can understand what I'm getting at.

I am also reading other religious material (Bible, and so on). Don't have much longer to live. Sure hoping I can die believing in God!

I'll sure call you on my "last day." I'm not going to mention the latest news to Michelle. You can tell her.

We watched that Bonanza show too. That's the second one with the real Bonanza's sons playing in them. They both were ok. Sure not as good as the original show though.

Wasn't much of a Super Bowl game today like I expected.

Well, I'll close for now. I promise I'll write again soon.

Love,
Larry

*****

February 1, 1995

Dear Larry,

As I sit down to write this letter, I realize it will be one of the last ones I may get a chance to write to you. Rob called me last night and told me the execution order has been officially signed by the judge and that it would be carried out in the next two to three weeks. My heart is really heavy with this news because you are very special to Michelle and me. Just the thought of what is ahead brings a tightness to my throat and tears to my eyes. I know I am losing a good friend, and it is hard to accept.

Rob asked me to write to you on behalf of your family to ask you to change your mind because you were dying for something you didn't do. I know we've never discussed the details of your being on death row, but I had heard from family that you were more than likely innocent and were covering up for someone else. It takes a strong, loving person to do that. I'm not asking for the details of what happened, but just stating what I was told. I know how strongly you feel about wanting to die, but Rob wanted me to express to you how much they wish you would not go through with it. They love you. I told him I would do as he asked.

As Michelle and I were discussing Rob's call and his comment that you were innocent, she made a very good observation. She said, "Mom, Larry is doing just what Jesus did. Jesus died for something He didn't do and so is Larry if what his brother said is true." I've thought a lot about her statement today and feel the comparison is a good one. You must really care enough for the person you are covering for to be willing to suffer and die in his place. It's the perfect picture of what Christ did for each of us. If *you* can love someone that much, just think of how much more Christ loves *you*. He willingly died on the cross to pay the death penalty for each of us. What a sacrifice He made for us—just because He loved us and wanted us to have a way to go to heaven.

Do you still have the letter from Jesus that I sent you about a year ago? I'm enclosing another copy of it in case you do not have it. Please take time to read it and think seriously about what it says. The *only* way Michelle and I will be able to accept your death is if we know you died a Christian. We both want to see you in heaven.

Dave asked me to share with you an illustration. Since Christmas is still a recent memory, his thinking was along those lines. Do you remember as a child how you anticipated Christmas? Most of the anticipation was focused on the gifts under the tree. Even though you didn't know what was wrapped in each package, you hoped that all of them would have something good inside because someone who loved and cared for you had provided the gifts. When Christmas morning came, you didn't have much of a decision to make as to whether or not you would take and open the gifts with your name on them. You were eager to do so, even if you weren't sure what was inside because you had been told it would be something great. If you had decided to not open the gift, you would never have known how good the gift really was, would you? Because you accepted and "tore" into the gift, it became yours.

Becoming a Christian is similar. God is offering us inner peace and a new home in heaven as a gift. Jesus told us that when He said in John 14:2, "In my Father's house are many mansions . . . I go to prepare a place for you" (KJV). It's the only home we'll ever have that is free! Normally, there's a really large price tag attached to a gift of a new home. He has a gift "box" with your name already on it. He's holding it out to you—just waiting for you to reach out and take it. In many previous letters, we have told you about how real and good God's gift of salvation is. We are praying that you'll believe and take it soon.

I wish you could have seen Michelle's face when she opened the birthday present you sent her. She was so happy! It will definitely be one of her cherished possessions! You couldn't have chosen a more perfect gift.

A lady who writes to you and lives near me sent a picture of you last week. I was so glad to get it! She had prints made from the one you sent her. I saw a small photo of you in the newspaper a couple of years ago, but this is much better and helps me to visualize you more accurately. I've also shown it to many people at church who have been praying for you, and they were also happy to be able to see you.

Michelle and I talked quite a while last night. She's writing you a letter with some of her thoughts. These are *totally* her thoughts. I think you will see from her letter how much you mean to her.

I am going to close for now as I have many things to do to get ready for classes tomorrow. I wanted to be sure that I got your letter written though. I'll write again soon and will be looking for a letter from you real soon.

Love,
Erin

*****

February 1, 1995
Dear Larry,

I want to start this letter out by telling you how much I appreciated the birthday present you sent me! I love it and am going to find the perfect spot to hang it in my room so I can look at it every time I walk in my room. Snoopy was so appropriate too since I *love* dogs! I certainly wasn't expecting it. It was a great surprise!

Ever since Rob called with the news about the execution order, it has really got me to start thinking about some things I want to tell you. Since I care about you so much, I knew I had to write you and tell you these things.

In the next couple weeks, not only will you be making one life or death decision, but also you will be making two—one physical and one spiritual. You can choose two deaths, which is a one-way trip to hell with no second chance and no layovers. Not only will that happen, but also the hearts of me, my mom, dad, and everyone else who's praying for you will break in half. On the other hand, you can choose one death and one life. I hope with all my heart that if you choose the physical death, you will choose the spiritual life and eternity with our loving God and Savior, Jesus Christ. There are a lot of things I can be happy about, but nothing will make me happier than to see you accept Christ as your Savior.

You've mentioned to my mom that you just want to end it all and get out of the pain and misery of prison and everything else. Well, if you choose the physical death along with the spiritual death, your misery will only be beginning. Hell will be so much worse than the pain you're facing now. You have it good compared to what you will face in hell. You may have seen comics in the newspaper depicting hell and having people in the comic smiling. The only one who will be smiling is Satan. This won't be a smile of happy greeting, but a smile of satisfaction that he has tricked someone, caught them in his trap, and prevented them from true happiness—heaven. Satan will not welcome you with a big hug but will watch you eventually be thrown into the blazing fire where there will be gnashing of teeth with no way out forever and ever and ever. It's not going to be like it is here on earth where you can walk away from bad situations. In hell, you would be stuck—never again would you be able to be relieved. This is definitely not a place I would want to be.

Imagine that there was someone in the prison who you disliked very much. Would you want to make them happy? I know I wouldn't. I would try to stay away from this enemy as much as possible. I wouldn't want to do anything to make him/her happy. I certainly wouldn't want to spend the rest of my life with this person. If you choose not to accept Christ as your personal Savior, you will be making your greatest enemy, Satan, extremely happy and will be spending the rest of your life with an enemy who will laugh at you because you fell for his trickery. Satan is trying to deceive you so this can happen. My mom said that you hate liars. Would you want to spend the rest of your life with someone who is lying to you, trying to trick you and bring you much pain and misery? I thought you wanted to get away from that.

If it is a fact that you don't believe there's a God and that's keeping you from coming to Christ, think about all the people in the Bible who gave up their lives because of taking a stand for Christ. People were willing to die rather than to deny knowing Christ and stop preaching about him.

You mentioned that it was a shame that we will never get to meet each other. This doesn't have to be so. Even though we may not get to meet on earth, there is a way that we *could* meet in heaven.

It's not too late! Jesus will welcome you, just as enthusiastically now as He would have twenty years ago! ☺ Remember what 1 Peter 5:8 says, "Your enemy the devil prowls around like a roaring lion looking for someone to devour" (NIV). Don't let yourself be his next victim. After the switch is hit, there will be no chance to change your mind.

I hope you carefully read the copies of a couple different devotionals that I am sending and the Bible verses that go along with them.

I certainly couldn't end on a serious note, so I'll tell you a few jokes! ☺ The answers are at the end of my letter.

1. Why do bees hum?
2. What goes Ha, Ha, Ha, plop?
3. What goes A, B, C, D, E, F, G, H, I, J, K, L, M, N, O, P, Q, R, S, T, U, V, W, X, Y, Z, burp?
4. Why did the turtle cross the road?
5. How do you know when an elephant's in your refrigerator?

You would laugh if you could see Ginger frolicking in all this snow we got! We have so much that you can't even see her legs. All you can see is her body and head! She gets so wet; and when she comes in from outside, she runs right up and jumps in someone's lap.

Don't forget that I'm praying for you *every* night!

Love,
Michelle, Ginger, Snuggles

Answers to jokes:

1. They don't know the words.
2. A man laughing his head off.
3. A man eating alphabet soup.
4. To get to the Shell station.
5. You see the elephant's footprints in the butter.

*****

February 3, 1995

Dear Larry,

This letter will be short after my last longer letter, but I wanted to answer your questions since I do not know how much longer we have to write each other.

We all enjoyed watching the *Where Jesus Walked* DVD you sent us for Christmas. It definitely brought back memories for Dave and me from our Israel trip. Michelle enjoyed seeing places in Israel for the first time. Thanks again for sending it to us. It is too bad that you cannot watch it since I am certain you would have liked it.

I can't tell you how disappointed I was to hear that the Bible study you are attending is being taught by a Jehovah's Witness. The Jehovah's Witnesses, I know, are very enthusiastic and sincere. But they themselves are being blinded by Satan to the truth of the Bible. Do you really feel that with their views on there being no hell, they are true Christians? I know that is really important to you. True Christians believe that all parts of the Bible are true. The Jehovah's Witnesses are considered to be a cult—not a true religion. The Bible speaks in Mark 13:22 about there being false prophets who will arise and try to lead others astray with their false religions. They will lull people into believing things that are clearly opposite of what the Bible teaches.

The Bible is God's only guidebook. Are they using the Bible? If so, how can they justify saying there is no hell when the Bible clearly states there is one. I've written you previously pointing out the references that say there is a literal hell. Anyone who adds to or takes away from the Bible is, in effect, lying. They are acting on Satan's behalf rather than God's. Satan is using them to try to persuade you that there is no hell—he's really quite clever. He knows what you already think and is sending along someone who will confirm your thinking so he can continue to confuse you.

You also brought up again that a loving God would not condemn his children to eternal punishment. As I have written before, He doesn't; we condemn ourselves by not choosing to accept the way out He provided through Jesus' death on the cross. It was because of His love for us that Christ came as a sacrifice and scapegoat for our sins. Would you do me a favor? Please don't continue going to the JW Bible study or doing their course. Aren't there any Christian Bible studies you could get involved in? I feel that in the last two years we've gotten to know each other quite well and have developed a trust. I wouldn't try to lead you to believe something that isn't true. I care too much about you to do that. I'm going to be looking for some information about the Jehovah's Witnesses to send to you. Since your time on earth may be short, I do not want you to believe false doctrine. It is your future life that is at stake.

I had a dream about you the other night that will probably make you smile. In the dream, I came to visit you at the prison. Within the prison was a cafeteria and small shopping mall. You were allowed to go eat at the cafeteria with me and really enjoyed all of the good food to choose from. Next, we leisurely walked through the mall and did some window-shopping and talked. The part of our conversation I remember most vividly was when you told me that you had accepted Christ. I was ecstatic! Too bad I had to wake up. Pretty weird dream, huh? I am taking that as a sign from the Lord, however, that I am going to get to see you and that you are going to be a Christian when I do. I believe the Lord can speak to us through dreams.

I told you this letter would be short, and it is already longer than I expected. So I will sign off for now. Praying for you as always.

Love,
Erin

*****

February 9, 1995
Dear Erin,

First of all, thank you for your two letters and the pictures from Christmas. I sure loved them. The pictures brought a smile to my face—the outfits that Michelle had Ginger dressed up in were something! Looks like everybody had fun too. Seeing the pictures also hurt some cause they remind me of what I also lost, a chance to marry and have a family. Life offered so much, but I didn't realize or appreciate it until too late. Pains me so much.

Yes, I still have the letter from Jesus you composed for me. I've sent that letter to everybody I know. You sure have a way with words. When I die, I'll leave it with my dad along with the February 1 letters from you and Michelle.

Rob was wrong. The "Execution Order" hasn't been signed yet. He must have misunderstood the lawyers when they called him. The judge signed the "Dismissal Order." He said that my trial judge can now sign the "Execution Order." They were expecting him to do that a week ago. But it doesn't surprise me he hasn't yet. He's a Christian. Signing the "Execution Order" really bothers him. When I was scheduled to die in February of 1993, he visited me on my last day. When I told him I didn't hold anything against him, he sure thanked me and relief showed on his face too. The jury sentenced me to death; he didn't. A minister who visited me last week who knows him said, "He's really struggling with it." So that is why he hasn't signed it. But the Attorney General will pressure him into doing it since it's his job.

As I said, I will call you on my last day. Visiting ends at 4 p.m. I'll then be taken to the medical section and given a physical. Then I'll be chained feet and hands and put into a van and driven to the "death house." During that time I'll be prepped for execution (head and right leg shaved, showered, and get new clothes with the right leg cut out for the wires). I will also be able to make my phone calls during that time. So expect my call from 4:30 to 6:45 p.m. since the executions are usually at 7 p.m.

Josh McDowell's staff assistant sent me a letter and three books, which had to be donated to the prison. So the Chaplain brought them down to me and asked which one I wanted to read first. I had already read *More Than a Carpenter*. So I chose *Answers to Tough Questions*. I am still searching for the proof (answers). Before I let them kill me, I want to consider myself a Christian! I'll continue reading the Bible, these books, and any other materials.

Glad you got the video. I wish I could see it too. It would be very interesting to go to Israel.

I didn't return to the Jehovah's Witness Bible study. After contemplating it, I realized I couldn't believe in what they teach. As much as I doubt a loving God would condemn his children to eternal punishment, the Bible in many places states that there is a hell.

Been cold and even snowed down here the last few days. That's ok with me. I get under my blanket and sleep good!

Hopefully, your dream of me will come true! Sure tells me how much I'm on your mind for you to be dreaming of me. This also has a sad side. Cause again, I'll be hurting people (y' all) when they kill me. This bothers me! I've hurt so many people now. This is another reason why I hurt cause I can't forgive myself for the pain I've caused others.

Well, I'll close now. Tell everyone at church "hi" and how much it means to me knowing they are praying for me! You all take care! Thanks for caring and for your prayers.

Love,
Larry

*****

February 18, 1995
Dear Larry,

Thank you for explaining to me what the lawyers actually told Rob. Probably the words that stood out most to him was "execution order" and whatever else was said did not register. It appears that you will have longer than just two or three weeks. I'm glad you could give me a time frame for your phone call. I'll make sure I'm here during those hours since I wouldn't want to miss it.

I can understand why the judge is having a hard time signing the execution order. I sure would have a struggle signing it for someone too. He sounds like a very caring, Christian person. His struggle is coming from his convictions, and he more than likely realizes you are not a Christian and knows what further implications that has for you beyond the chair.

How happy I was when I read that you quit going to the Jehovah's Witness bible study! Your time could be better spent reading some of the books that have been sent to you by Christian authors—those sent to you from Josh McDowell's office sound like good ones. Did you get a chance to read the *Answers to Tough Questions* yet? I hope you also get a chance to read the second book.

Would you believe that I've had two more dreams about you? The second was quite a lot like the first one. In the dream, you again told me that you were a Christian. The third dream was just last night. It was different. In this dream, you were released from prison for a few days to come visit us. Then you had to go back. It was hard seeing you leave since I knew what you were going back to face. Dreams are really strange sometimes, aren't they? My family tells me that I'm noted for having strange dreams! I don't think the first two are strange, though. I'm hoping they are a sign from God to let me know that you're going to come to the point where you will believe in Him and surrender your life to Him. I continue to pray for you each day. You mentioned that you felt sad that you would be hurting me. If my dream comes true, I'll be sad but glad at the same time—glad because I know you'll be with Jesus and out of your suffering.

I knew exactly what you meant when you said how nice it is on a cold night to snuggle up under a warm blanket. That is one of my favorite winter activities! The last couple of days have been nice here—in the forties. It's supposed to still be nice tomorrow and then rain on Monday and Tuesday. Most of our snow is gone—and I have a smile on my face! I even washed my car on Thursday afternoon and took Ginger for a walk. She loved getting out. After the extremely cold weather we have had the last two or three weeks, this is a real welcomed relief. I'm ready for spring!

I am going to sign off for now. Gregg and Jenny are here tonight, and I want to spend some time with them. Michelle will be home around seven thirty, and our Saturday night tradition is to watch *Dr. Quinn, Medicine Woman*. Take care and write soon.

Love,
Erin

*****

February 27, 1995

Dear Erin,

Sorry I haven't written in a while. It's unreal how lazy I've become. I even refused my anti-depressant medication tonight cause I didn't want to get up, put my pants on, and walk ten yards to get it.

Mom and Rob visited me Saturday! Mom was feeling pretty good, which I was glad to see. It hurts me to see how unhappy Rob is. Mom said he misses his children in Michigan, and it is tearing him apart. His ex-wife will not even let him talk to them. A co-worker who is going to be traveling offered to drop him off in Michigan if he paid for the gas. I hopefully talked him out of it since there is a warrant for his arrest in Michigan for not paying child support. He left on Saturday saying he wasn't going to go. Not only might he get arrested if he went, but he probably wouldn't come back to Georgia. It means a lot to Mom to have him living with her.

I'm sure the trial judge hasn't signed the execution order yet cause he's waiting on me to write him and request he do it. I did that the two previous times. Like I said in a previous letter, he is very reluctant to do it. I'll write him if he hasn't signed it by summer when the oppressive heat arrives. If my brothers weren't down here, I'm sure I'd have written him by now.

You'll be happy to know that I'm starting to believe. I'm still reading the *Handbook of Christian Apologetics*. The authors use the argument of why would the writers of the Bible be willing to suffer so much like some of them did if this all was something they made up. I agree with that argument plus others in the book. But then I was knocked back when it stated that Genesis has to be true. You know my feelings towards Genesis. I've seen bones of prehistoric humans (evolution) that contradicts humans (Adam and Eve) being created. So this is the main obstacle in my not becoming a complete believer.

Boy, you must really have me on your mind for you to have had two more dreams with me in them. I also hope it's a sign from God and they become true that I'll tell you I'm a Christian.

I have had tendonitis in my knee for a while. It is getting better but still hurts some when I sleep. I never put in for a sick call to have the doctor look at it since I would not be allowed to go unless it was swollen and really hurting. I'm living with it.

Well, I see by all my scratch outs that I'm losing my concentration. That is why I struggle to read the books. I read a page or two then start drifting. I really am forcing myself though cause I want to read these books. I will close now while you can still understand what I am writing. Thanks for caring and your prayers! Tell everybody "hi."

Love,
Larry

*****

March 2, 1995
Dear Larry,

Would you believe that it's only 5 a.m.? I woke up early and was thinking of you, so I thought I would get up and write since it has been a couple of weeks. I am sure I will be dragging by the time my class gets out at eight forty-five tonight!

The reason I woke so early is because I had another dream about you. This was different from the others. This dream took place at the prison—only I know the surroundings were definitely not realistic prison surroundings. At first, in the dream, I was talking to you on the phone—which was nice. Then someone opened a door, and we got a chance to chat face to face to each other. Michelle and my mother were also there. We really had a good visit and had a chance to give each other a friendly hug. When I asked you how this could happen, you just said that the time must be near. Since getting your picture, you must be on my mind even more. At any rate, it was nice to "see" you!

You said in your last letter, "You'll be happy to know that I'm starting to believe." That was an understatement! I'm *extremely* happy that you have come to this point. Even though I know it is just a start, it is the first step that so many of us have been praying about for a long time. My prayer now will be that that tiny seed of faith you've realized will continue to grow and take root in your life. Since Mark 10:27 states, "All things are possible with God" (NIV), I'm confident that it is going to grow into the faith you need to become a Christian. You too can be praying for this from God. Remember that He knows what is hanging you up and can provide the answers you need to get past the Genesis and creation issue. Just continue to keep an open mind and heart and invite Him to show you the truth in a way you can accept. Since I've always believed in creation, I can't fully understand how you feel.

I think you gave Rob some wise advice to stay in Georgia since there is a warrant out for his arrest. I agree that your mom certainly needs him too. Plus, I know that you enjoy his visits.

It is good that your knee is starting to feel better. I know how painful tendonitis can be since I have had it twice—once in my thumb (which took a year to heal) and another time in my upper leg (which took about six weeks to heal with an anti-inflammatory). The key is to "baby" it until it feels back to normal.

Battle Creek got hit with an ice storm last Sunday night. I felt *so bad* that our Monday classes had to be cancelled! It was nice to just be able to be lazy most of the day. There were two reruns of *Columbo* on in the afternoon, so Michelle and I watched those and at the commercials made some peanut butter cookies—Dave's favorite. Our favorite is chocolate chip, but we thought we had our favorite too many times lately, and it was time to "share." What's your favorite kind of cookie?

Michelle took Ginger in for her yearly checkup yesterday, and she passed with flying colors. She had gained a little over a pound from last year. She said that all the treats were probably showing up!

I've been trying to be nicer to myself lately—to balance work more with pleasure. My mom and I have been getting out to the mall two to three times a week to walk. Yesterday, we walked a little over three miles. It does us both a lot of good. I enjoyed the article you sent me on prayer walkers a few letters back. I do that a lot—especially when I'm walking by myself. I just shut everything out and have a talk with God. You don't know how many times I've prayed for you while I've been walking. Actually, whenever you come to mind, I send up a short prayer on your behalf.

Well, it's getting close to six thirty, so guess I had better be signing off since I have a class at eight and still need to have breakfast and get ready. I'll be looking forward to hearing from you again real soon.

Love,
Erin

*****

April 4, 1995
Dear Erin,

Every time I write I have to apologize for taking so long to reply to your letters! The psychiatrist increased my anti-depressant medication last week. It seems to be starting to work. I haven't been sleeping as much as I was. Hopefully, I will come out of this laziness since I still have books that I want to read.

I've been real upset the past month. *If* I get a visit this weekend, it will have been six weeks since my last visit from any of my family. It sure hurts me too! I have three brothers and a mother a 30-minute drive from here, but I can't get a regular visit from any of them. Sure don't understand it either. They tell me how much they love me and don't want me to die, but it does not feel like they do when I do not get visits from them. I had to use all my phone calls last month calling Mom to find out what's wrong since when they don't visit I just know something is wrong and I really worry.

One of my neighbors is scheduled to die Thursday. They'll move him out of our cell block tomorrow and put him in an isolation cell in the hospital wing here where he will be on "death watch" for his last 24 hours. Two guards will not take their eyes off him. Here is a guy who I talk to every day, play cards, basketball and so on with, and in less than 48 hours he'll be in a box six feet in the ground. Unreal!

A few weeks before that, they moved a guy's personal property out of his cell and said he's not coming back. He is dying of AIDS and is in the prison hospital. Sure is sad since he was such a friendly guy. It is also a painful way to die.

Thank you for the beautiful card and the Psalm 103:1-4, 8-13 poster. If only I could fully believe! Cause like the Psalm states, "He forgives all my sins" which I sure need to help me to forgive myself. Because right now I feel if there is a God, heaven, and hell that I deserve to be in hell! I don't deserve to be in heaven with people like you! You and I are like night and day. You are *good* and I'm *bad*! I have the poster hanging by my bed so I can see and read it all the time. I am hoping that it will sink in to my head!

Sure good to hear you are trying to be nicer to yourself! That walking with your mom at the mall sure is good. But also try to give yourself more time just to relax around the house, a couple of extra hours to sleep, or like you stated when your class was cancelled, just be lazy.

I sure would have enjoyed watching *Columbo* with you and Michelle since I really like that show. The cookies would also have been very good! My favorite cookie is oatmeal—but I like almost any kind!

The weather and temperature has been nice the past couple weeks, but the pollen count has been unreal. Last year for the first time it really bothered me. This year it is not. ☺ I am sure you are glad the snow and cold are behind you. What has the temperature been like in Michigan?

Well, I need to close so I can write some other letters. Again, I am sorry for not writing sooner! Thanks for caring and your prayers!

Love,
Larry

*****

April 11, 1995
Dear Larry,

It was so good to go to the mailbox and find another letter from you! I know that you have times when you do not feel like writing. I just appreciate it when you do send a letter.

You mentioned that you bet I was glad that the snow and cold were behind us. The day before your letter came, we had snow! I couldn't believe it! It thundered and rained this morning, turned to sleet, and then was a real wet, messy snow. By afternoon, it had started to melt. What unpredictable Michigan weather!

I've been contemplating what you said in your letter about feeling that you deserve hell. Without Christ's forgiveness, that would be a true statement. However, in God's eyes, all of us deserve hell because all of us have sinned. God doesn't look at one sin as being worse than another sin. Basically, a good person who has sinned just once—even if it was something relatively small—is as unworthy of heaven as you feel you are. For in God's eyes, any sin makes a person unworthy of heaven since God hates sin of any kind. But He *loves* the sinner! Because of His love, He decided to be merciful to us— which means to not give us what we deserve, which is hell. That's why Christ came to die on the cross so our sin could be forgiven. His mercy is extended to *everyone* who asks—and *everyone* who asks is unworthy for all have sinned (Romans 3:23).

Why He would want to be merciful to mankind is sometimes very hard to understand, but He doesn't ask us to understand everything—just accept it as His gift of love to us. When we accept His free gift of salvation, He *completely forgets* whatever we've done prior to that time—even though we can't forget what we've done. (That's what those verses in Psalm 103 that are on the poster tell us.) After we're a Christian, we will still remember what we did because Satan will try to keep making us feel unworthy so we don't experience fully the joy Christ wants us to have.

Satan also works overtime on people like you who haven't yet become a Christian but are seriously considering the possibility—he doesn't want to lose you! He's doing that to you right now by trying to convince you that you can't become a Christian because of what you've done and make you feel unworthy of heaven. Please stop listening to him. Remember that he's a liar!

So in response to your statement that you don't deserve to be in heaven—it's not true. God loves you just as much as He loves me. Once we're Christians, there's no such thing as good and bad people in God's eyes. Remember also the thief who was on the cross beside Christ. He acknowledged Christ and asked to go to heaven, and Christ assured him that because of his faith, he would be in heaven with Him that very day. Christ doesn't have favorites and doesn't look on a person's past. He only looks into a person's heart to see if he/she believes in Him and is serious about committing his/her life to Him. That's the key to getting into heaven—a desire to want to and a belief in Christ.

I'm glad you enjoyed the poster of Psalm 103 and have it hanging up where you can read it often. I'll also be praying that it will sink in—into your head and your heart! There's not a day that goes by that I don't pray for you.

Tomorrow's Easter already. We'll be going to the 8 a.m. sunrise service. Michelle and the rest of the puppet team are doing a special Easter presentation during the sunrise service. I haven't seen it yet, so I'm looking forward to it. After the 8 a.m. service, we'll be having a pancake breakfast. Our main service, which is normally at eleven, will be at 10 a.m. tomorrow, and we'll be done around 11:15 a.m. Then, we're going to dinner with my mom and Dave's mom, dad, and sister. In the evening service at 6 p.m., the choir is presenting a musical/drama that Dave has seen and says is really good. Sure wish you could join us.

The Battle Creek paper carried a short story about the man from England that was executed a week ago Thursday. I also heard about it on the radio. Then, when I read in the paper that it took place in Jackson, Georgia, I wondered if you knew him. No wonder you've had a hard time lately! Has any of your family been to see you yet? Sure hope so because I know how important family support is during hard times.

The trees are just starting to look like they might bud soon here. When they do bud, our pollen count will most likely be quite high too! I am glad it hasn't bothered you this year. Usually, I get headaches in the spring when everything starts budding and blooming but haven't had any yet. Maybe I'll be lucky like you are this year, and my allergies won't bother me too much.

Track season has started for Michelle. She is very happy that she's getting to run the 200-meter sprint and the 400- and 800-meter relays. They were supposed to have a track meet last Thursday. She was all primed for it, but it got cancelled because the other school felt it was too cold outdoors. She was disappointed.

Mom and I made it through the first anniversary of my dad's death on March 16. We both did better than we expected, but work for me and working at a blood drive for my mom helped the day pass. Our hard day actually came a couple of days beforehand. We cried with each other and then pulled ourselves back together. It was terrible when it hit while I was at work though. I had to go to my office for a few minutes to get it back together. I called Dave, and he helped talk me through it.

Well, Dave is waiting patiently for the computer so he can write a few checks for the church, so guess I had better "surrender" it. Besides, I do have a lot of papers to grade yet since I "played" this afternoon. Hopefully, I will hear again from you soon.

Love,
Erin

Think About It: Mercy

Do you ever have a day when you are constantly running just a few minutes behind schedule? To hopefully regain some of the precious time lost, your foot presses a little harder on the accelerator, taking you over the posted 35 mph speed limit, which you think is ridiculous anyway. You justify in your mind, *Everyone else always drives faster on this street anyways.* As your eyes move to the rearview mirror, your stomach does a lurch, your pulse starts racing, and you internally groan to see the red and blue flashing lights coming up behind you. As you pull over and are waiting for the officer to approach and issue you the speeding ticket you deserve, you begin calculating the hit to your wallet and the points on your license. After talking with you about hazards of speeding and the merits of obeying the law, however, he surprises you and lets you off with a warning.

He did not give you what you deserved. The officer demonstrated mercy to you.

Mercy can simply be defined as not being given what one rightfully deserves for a wrong (sin) one has done. Just as the speeder broke a man-made law, so humans break God's law each time they do something that goes against the laws He has given us in His Word.

God said in Romans 3:23, "All have sinned and fallen short of God's glorious standard (NCV). Then, He states in Romans 6:23a, "The payment for sin is death" (NCV). In Chapter 13, Michelle described to Larry in her letter that the death spoken of in the Bible is eternal separation from God in hell after our physical death on earth. From just those two verses, the future for every human is very grim. God, however, in His love provided an escape and *mercy* to us through Jesus in the last part of Romans 6:23 that says, "But God gives us the free gift of life forever in Christ Jesus our Lord" (NCV). So even though we all deserve eternal death, God is willing to give us mercy.

In one of our letters, the repentant thief on the cross was referenced when Larry and I discussed forgiveness and heaven. When the thief mentioned in Luke 23 realized that Jesus was Christ, "Then he said, 'Jesus, remember me when you come into your Kingdom.' And Jesus replied, 'Today you will be with me in Paradise. This is a solemn promise'" (TLB). He was shown instant mercy. Max Lucado offers an interesting insight on this passage that is appropriate to close this discussion on mercy.

> Much has been said about the prayer of the penitent thief on the cross next to Jesus. But dare we forget the one who didn't pray? He offered no request. He, too, could have requested mercy. He, too, could have asked Jesus to remember him in the new kingdom. But he didn't. He offered no prayer of repentance. And Jesus did not require one.
>
> Jesus gave both criminals the same choice. One said "remember me." The other said noth-

ing. There are times when God sends thunder to stir us. There are times when God sends blessings to lure us. But then there are times when God sends nothing but silence as he honors us with the freedom to choose where we spend eternity.[53]

Which "thief" represents you?

Before leaving this chapter, ponder on the following questions:

- Is there any human being who is exempt from God's mercy? Why or why not?
- According to Titus 3:4–5a, why do we as humans need mercy?
- Lacey Sturm wrote the lyrics for *Mercy Tree*[54], which references Calvary's cross as a mercy tree. Based on what you know about mercy, why is the name she gave Christ's cross appropriate?
- Think of a time when someone extended mercy to you— did not give you what you deserved. How did it make you feel toward that person?
- Is there someone who has wronged you that you need to show mercy to?

Chapter 14

April 12, 1995
Dear Erin,

Hey, it has only been a little over one week since I last wrote you. Surprise! Surprise!

Mom visited me Saturday. She sure wasn't looking or feeling good. She wasn't going to come but knew it had been six weeks since her last visit. The Christian van that brings relatives to visit us once a month was also coming that day. She knew if she did not come then it might be another month before she could come.

Rob lied to me again when he told me on the phone that he would be down this weekend too. Just like he lied then too saying that he mailed $200 to an inmate that I owe $200. Mom is upset about this mess he has me in too. This guy is getting tired of my excuses; he wants his money back. She knows if I get into a fight over this I'll be back to the "hole" for 30 days.

Seeing Mom in the shape she was in Saturday, the lies from Rob, lack of visits from family and letters was the "last straw." I wrote the judge Sunday night asking him to set my execution date. Hopefully, by the time you receive this, it will have been scheduled.

Thank you for the beautiful Easter card. I hope you all had a nice Easter. I really wish I could make your Easter better by saying I'm a Christian! But as much as I would love to say this cause I know it would mean so much to you, I can't lie to you. I haven't in the past and won't in the future.

I hope you got rested up during your week off for spring break not long ago. I know your schedule so I know you needed it.

Well, I will let you go. Tell Michelle and everybody "hi." You all take care!

Love,
Larry

*****

May 5, 1995
Dear Larry,

I was very happy to hear that you got a visit from your mom even though she did not feel that good. Moms do that for the children they love.

So you finally wrote the letter to the judge requesting an execution order to be issued and a date set. I can understand why you were upset enough at your family to do that and that you do not want to spend another agonizing summer with the intense heat. I can't say that it makes me very happy though. You and I both know that you are not ready to die.

It does not sound good that you owe another inmate $200 and that he is putting pressure on you to pay him. What will happen if no one sends the money to you? I will be praying that you come up with the money to pay the debt. Was it from playing poker?

Gregg just came up to talk to me or rather to show me a receipt for a purchase he made—an engagement ring for Jenny! I'm a little shook right now! I was sort of expecting that Jenny would be my future daughter-in-law, but it still took me a little by surprise. Gregg had to have the ring resized and won't be giving it to her for two weeks. Guess that will give me a chance to get used to their engagement a bit before it's officially announced. Jenny is a sweet gal, and I'm sure she and Gregg love each other just by watching them. He said that it would be a while before they get married since neither of them can afford to be on their own at this point. I expect it to be a couple of years, but I could be wrong. I jokingly told him that he'd have to wait another three and a half years if he wanted to be like Dave and me. We dated for three years and then were engaged for another three years! We certainly knew each other well though! The reason we waited was that I started dating him when I was a sophomore in high school and then wanted to finish college before we got married. He laughed and said that he doubted Jenny would go along with that. The morning sure took a turn I hadn't expected!

I am enclosing a $20 money order to help you out with postage costs because I like hearing from you. Maybe you can also buy a few snacks with it. I called the chaplain to see if I could send it directly to you, and he said it was okay to do it that way.

Well, it's almost five, and we're having a family picture taken at six at the church for a pictorial directory. I need to sign off for now. Write again soon!

Love,
Erin

*****

May 9, 1995
Dear Erin,

Thanks for your letter and for making copies of my letter to the judge. I don't have anything for you to copy this time.☺ Seriously, though, I appreciate you making copies of things I send you.

Mom came to visit me on Sunday but could only stay 1-1/2 hours since she was weak. When I thought she was in Florida visiting my sister like my brother told me on the phone, she was in the hospital in "critical condition." She had pneumonia and was close to going into a coma from being so low on potassium. She had sure lost weight but said she had already gained two pounds and was starting to eat better. It sure upset me! Not only did my brothers not tell me, they also did not let my sister know. When she talked to Mom and found out Mom had been in the hospital, she sure was mad at my brothers. She would have come to Georgia to be with her.

Mom also said on Sunday that the lawyer called my oldest brother on Friday and told him they expect an execution date to be set on me any time. I will let you know as soon as I hear when it is.

Yes, the $200 was from a poker debt. I asked one of my attorneys to borrow it and my mom would pay him back $40 a month when she gets her check. He sent me a letter informing me that he had sent the money. So that's one less worry off me. Rob said he had sent the money but that he would still help pay the $200. So he is going to send $25 from each paycheck to the attorney. Mom said that she will make sure he does it.

So you are going to be a mother-in-law, hey? I'm sure glad you like her! In-laws not getting along has messed up many marriages. Also glad they are thinking clearly and aren't planning on getting married soon since they realize they can't support themselves yet. Boy, you sure played "hard to get"! ☺ Made Dave wait years before you would marry him. Just teasing, I sure understand why you did it.

Thank you very much for the $20! Now I can write you more often. ☺ Seriously, though, I'll spend it all on stamps so I can write more letters to you and other people.

I just finished a Bible study course that Josh McDowell's assistant sent to me. I'm sad to say even though it was a good course that I'm not closer to God. I can't get past the obstacle of Genesis. If I can't accept and believe that Genesis is true, then I'm lost since sin and everything originates from Genesis. I just don't know how I can solve this major problem! What do you suggest?

I read all the things you send me before I go to sleep. Besides being quiet in here then, it lets me have it on my mind right before I go to sleep. Hopefully, I'll have some kind of dream regarding it as I keep on praying to God that He give me some kind of proof (sign) that He really exists—even though by the Bible I'm wrong for requesting this proof.

How has Michelle been doing in track this year? Then again, she probably doesn't want you to tell me so she can tell me. ☺ What are her plans for a summer job?

Well, I'll close for now. Tell Michelle and everybody "hi." Thanks so much for caring and prayers!

Love,
Larry

*****

May 24, 1995
Dear Larry,

Hello from wet Battle Creek! After three days of sunny skies, we're on our second day of rain this week—with a couple more days of rain in the forecast. We should *really* get the flowers this year if the saying is true that April showers bring May flowers. I think we may have to revise that, however, to read April and May showers bring June flowers.

I am glad your mom got to come to see you again. She was *very* sick! Pneumonia can take a deadly toll on the body. Glad she caught it in time! Since she is feeling better, I am sure you are also.

Gregg gave Jenny her ring a week ago today, so it's now official. They're both happy! When I talked to Gregg a few minutes ago, he said they'd like to get married in October. I told him that seemed a little ambitious. My two-year guesstimate was *very* incorrect! He is twenty-one, however, so will have to make his own decisions. Maybe when they do some more thinking, they will change to a later date.

You asked what Michelle's plans were for the summer. I think she's planning on working for my mother—washing windows, cleaning out cluttered areas in her house, doing odd jobs, etc.—to make money to help pay her portion of the car insurance. I offered her a chance to earn some money by doing the washing and ironing, but she has not decided yet. We figured if she could get her car insurance money saved during the summer, it wouldn't be necessary for her to work during the school year.

I've asked my pastor, Brian Spencer, to write to you regarding Genesis and creation. You may already have received his letter. When I took your address in to him on Tuesday, he had just sat down to write it. Hopefully, he may be able to answer the questions you have. He said that you are welcome to write him directly. He is a great person and very easy to talk to. I shared with him the small portion from your letter about getting past the obstacle of Genesis. You asked if I had any suggestions. This is all I could think of—to have Pastor Spencer write to you. I have shared with you all that I know on the subject.

How generous of your attorney to send the $200 to pay off your debt to the other inmate! Not many would do that. Having a plan to pay him back must have helped. Michelle and I are happy that the debt is settled and you now have one less worry hanging over your head.

I've run out of news for now. It's a little after 8 p.m., so I am going to either watch TV or read a book for the rest of the evening. As always, I look forward to your next letter. Remember that you're special to us and that we care about you!

Love,
Erin

*****

June 1, 1995
Dear Erin,

I received your letter of the 24th yesterday as well as the letter from your pastor. Thanks! I will try to write him soon. You know how I am by now in regard to writing letters or, for that matter, doing anything.

I requested to talk to the chaplain last week to get his opinion on Genesis, and he came down and talked to me. A guard stopped me today. He stated he was a Christian and wanted to know if I was since he said he heard I don't have much time left. We discussed my "hang up" with Genesis. Like I stated before, it's the obstacle that's preventing me to fully believe in God.

Would you please send me in your next letter a short verse or saying that you really like? Don't forget to send it! And no, I'm not going to tell you why. ☺

Got a smile when you wrote that you offered Michelle a chance to earn some money from you by doing the washing and ironing each week and she hadn't decided yet. Your wages must have not been high enough. ☺

Also got a smile reading your opinion on Gregg and Jenny's plans. You sounded like a mother. ☺ It is a normal reaction though. What is Dave's opinion on their plans?

Would you believe they gave us French fries on our supper trays tonight? It is the first time since I've been here. Boy, did I enjoy them!

The hot weather is upon us. Reached the 90s last week but it is suppose to only reach the high 80s this week. Sure glad I won't be around to suffer through another summer. How's the weather up there?

I will let you go. You all take care!

Love,
Larry

*****

June 12, 1995
Dear Larry,

Today is an absolutely gorgeous day in Battle Creek. The sun is shining, and the temperature is expected to be in the low eighties— three beautiful days in a row! Ginger and I just got back from a mile walk in the neighborhood. I can't even put my shoes on anymore without her thinking it's time to go for a walk.

The Daniels family has been keeping busy. I finished working on lecture notes for a new book I will be using in the fall. Michelle finished her sophomore year and track season. Gregg celebrated his twenty-first birthday over a two-day period and is keeping very busy with his lawn business. Dave is on "vacation" this week to roof the front half of our house and get some things done at church that he does not normally have time to do when working. He told Michelle that she can earn some extra money by handing him shingles or help-ing lay them out so he can keep nailing. She is planning on doing that. Must be he's offering better wages than I did for doing the laundry!

You asked me to send to you a favorite verse or saying. I'm really curious as to what you've got up your sleeve! My favorite verse is Jeremiah 29:11, "For I know the plans I have for you, says the Lord. They are plans for good and not for evil, to give you a future and a hope" (TLB).

How do you figure you rated the French fries? Did someone goof up? They must have tasted extremely good if you hadn't had any in several years! Did you eat them slowly to savor the taste?

I got a call from Rob at five thirty last night with the news that your execution date had been set for Friday, June 23, at 3:30 p.m. Is that right? He said that it hadn't hit the papers yet but expected it to soon. I really felt bad after his call—couldn't even go to church—but I knew it would be coming soon. Even though I had been expecting it, to hear an actual date makes it so final! I am slowly coming to grips with it this morning, but my heart is struggling with it since you've not yet been able to accept the Lord's gift of salvation.

How I wish I could give you the shot of faith you need to make that life-changing step but know that only the Lord is capable of doing that. I feel I've tried to help you in every way I know how to, so the only thing left for me to do is to keep praying—which I intend to do until the last possible moment. When you call me on your last day—and I will be home and waiting for your call—I so hope you will be able to tell me you are a Christian. It will be easier to accept your death if I know you're going to heaven!

I am glad you got the letter from Pastor Spencer. Did it help at all to answer your questions about Genesis and creation? If not, remember that he's open to having you write again if you have questions. He sure cares about you and asks me frequently if I've heard from you and what's going on. Enclosed is an article that deals with creation versus evolution that you may find helpful in putting things into perspective.

I have done some additional thinking about your hang up about Genesis and now have another thought for you. Larry, I don't believe that *anyone* has all the answers to *every* question about God and the Bible when they make the decision to become a Christian. As a matter of fact, Deuteronomy 29:29a states, "There are some things the Lord our God has kept secret, but there are some things he has let us know" (NCV). Probably everyone has questions about *some* part of the Bible at the time they ask Christ to be their personal Savior. Salvation isn't based on knowing everything there is to know about God and the Bible and knowing the answers to *every* question we might have. If that were so, none of us would be saved. All that is necessary is a basic belief that there is a God and that He sent Christ (because of His grace) to die for us to provide a way for our sins to be forgiven and to go to heaven. Once we can acknowledge that He is God, He will bring understanding to us about the other issues we question.

Normally, a person has time after becoming a Christian to study the Bible in depth with new "understanding" given to him by the Lord. In your case, you won't have that luxury since you have less than two weeks left. However, that will make no difference to our loving God. He will accept you *just as you are* with outstretched arms if you can acknowledge Him as God. He'll personally answer your questions as you begin to spend eternity in heaven with Him. Satan is the one who is putting this Genesis hang up on you. As I've said before, he is fighting *very* hard right now to retain control of you. *Please* don't give him the victory!

You mentioned in one of your letters that you were starting to believe since if so many Christians have been willing to suffer for their faith that they wouldn't have done so if there wasn't some reason for their strong faith. Please let that small seed of faith that you have take hold and grow. Jesus said in Matthew 17:20, "I tell you the truth, if your faith is as small as a mustard seed, you can say to this mountain, 'Move from here to there,' and it will move. Nothing will be impossible for you" (NIV). If you have never seen a mustard seed, it is very small. I know there's hope for you because you admitted that you've started to believe. Give that belief to God and see what He will do with it.

Hebrews 11 is considered the faith chapter that will introduce you to people who made *extremely* difficult decisions because of their faith in God. I hope Christians in America never have to make similar decisions, but I know I would have to choose death if it meant renouncing my faith. I have no doubt that God would give me the strength it would take.

If I don't watch out, you are going to be calling me Preacher Lady! Before you do, just remember the reason I write these things is because I care about you. As I said in a letter a year or so ago, God has given me a love for you as a sister has for a brother. We want those we care about to be happy. You've had so much unhappiness in your life that I think it's time the rest of your life is filled with happiness—but only Christ can give you that happiness.

Since the mailman will be coming by any moment and I want this to be mailed today, I will say goodbye for now.

Love,
Erin

*****

June 12, 1995
Dear Erin,

It has been a couple weeks since I last wrote you. I have not heard from you either. You must be busy. It would not surprise me if our letters cross in the mail.

I know you are not going to like my news. The judge finally signed the execution order. The date is set for Friday, June 23, at 3 p.m. I have only 11 days left before I will be out of my misery of prison and the heat.

I have already talked to the chaplain. He and I are going to be doing a lot of talking between now and the 23rd. During that time, I will also continue reading the religious books I have and keep praying. As I've said before, I hope I can say I am a Christian when I die but I still have a lot of doubts—especially about creation vs. evolution. I just cannot get over that hang-up.

I heard that my dad is going to come visit me on Father's Day. As much as I want to see him, I know it will be a hard visit. I assume my mom and brothers will also come visit me that weekend since it will be my last one. I hope they do not try to talk me into appealing my decision to die since my mind is made up. I will also be telling them that they cannot come visit me on my last day.

I will plan on calling you on the 23rd. Since it will be an afternoon execution, expect my call between 12:30-2:15.

Thanks to both you and Michelle for so faithfully writing to me, encouraging me, and praying for me. You will never know how much that has meant to me to know I am loved by y'all. It was also fun getting to know your family in the process. Tell Michelle to take good care of Ginger!

I feel bad that I will not be able to have the gift made for you using the verse that you sent to me. There just is not enough time left.

I have a lot of last letters to write to my family members to tell them I love them and also want to write my final statement to give just before they execute me. So if you do not get another letter from me, you will know why.

I will look forward to talking to you on the 23rd to say goodbye. Thanks so much for caring.

Love,
Larry

*****

June 16, 1995
Dear Larry,

You were right. Our letters did cross in the mail. We both wrote the same day!

Summer finally arrived in Battle Creek and with it the sun and warmer temperatures. The mornings have been absolutely beautiful—really inviting for me to be outdoors. I have spent a lot of time sitting on the deck, reading, thinking, and praying this week. Bet you will never guess who I have been praying for the most.

You said that your dad will be coming to visit on Father's Day. I am certain that will be an *extremely* hard visit for both of you. Knowing what a hard time he had a couple of years ago, you are probably hoping he does not do a repeat performance. I can only imagine how your brothers will react to not being allowed to see you on your last day. It is your choice though. At least, you can call them that day.

I was glad to hear that you and the chaplain have made plans to do a lot of talking between now and the twenty-third and that he, I assume, will be with you that day. I hope that through your talks you may able to resolve in your mind the questions that are keeping you from surrendering your life to Christ. Remember that Christ can also be there with you in a way that no human can between now and then—and forever after. Christ's presence can make a real difference to you before and during the whole ordeal. (Think about the difference that you pointed out between the responses of Christians and non-Christians who had been executed! There's a reason why the Christians faced death so much differently—Christ!) He's just waiting for the okay from you as He won't force Himself on you.

Resolving the hang up you have about creation is not a deal breaker. What a shame to let your belief about evolution keep you out of heaven! (That's Satan at work!) God will understand and love you despite that belief. He just asks that you have even a *little* faith that lets you acknowledge that He is God and that Christ is your only way to have your sins forgiven and to experience the peace only He can give. *Please* give up your fight and surrender yourself to God's loving arms. You'll find there's no more peaceful and safer place to be!

Don't feel bad that you didn't have time to get the gift made. It is your thoughtfulness to even consider sending it that means so much to me. There is something that you can give me that no amount of money could buy. I'm sure you know what that gift is. Your acceptance of Christ would be the most precious gift you could ever give to me—and to yourself! Losing you will be more bearable for me and a whole lot of other people if we know that we'll get to see you in heaven some day and have a reunion!

It is time to say goodbye until next Friday when we talk. I cannot believe this will be the last letter I'll be writing to you as anything sent after today may not have time to reach you. If you have a chance, would you write a note to Michelle on the back of the picture I sent you of her and Ginger and send it to her? She would so love it if you could. She felt bad that she didn't get to write more often but is writing to you now. Michelle and I will both be waiting for your call. We're sure going to miss you, Larry! You've become a special part of our lives.

We love you. Know that you will be constantly in our thoughts and prayers. Talk to you on Friday!

Love,
Erin

Think About It: Grace

Think back to the scenario of getting pulled over for speeding from "Think about It: Mercy" in Chapter 13. Instead of being shown mercy by the police officer, however, you are given the ticket you deserved. Because you feel that others were driving just as fast as you were when being pulled over, you decide to fight the ticket and must appear before a judge in court. After presenting your case, the judge determines that regardless if others were also speeding, you still broke the law and *deserve* the ticket. As you accept his ruling, his next words surprise you. "Even though you deserve the ticket, I am going to dismiss the guilty charge and strike the ticket from your record just because I am feeling generous today." Do you feel the sense of relief in that verdict? The judge demonstrated grace to you.

A term that has been used in close conjunction with mercy is grace, which involves being given something that one *doesn't* deserve. Because of our sin, we do not deserve a home in heaven when we die. According to 1 John 1:9, "But if we confess our sins to Him, He is faithful and just to forgive us our sins and to cleanse us from all wickedness." God is willing to forgive our sin, which we don't deserve. Ephesians 2:8–9 provides further evidence of God's grace, "God saved you by his grace when you believed. And you can't take credit for this; it is a gift from God. Salvation is not a reward for the good things we have done, so none of us can boast about it" (NLT). What is salvation? It is defined as "deliverance from the power and penalty of sin."[55] The source of our deliverance is Jesus and His death on the cross. The result of salvation is an eternal home in heaven. Since it is free and a gift, all we are asked to do is accept it.

Max Lucado in his book *Just Like Jesus* beautifully describes God's grace. "Our Savior kneels down and gazes upon the darkest acts of our lives. But rather than recoil in horror, He reaches out in kindness and from the basin of His grace, He scoops a palm full of mercy and washes away our sin."[56]

Before continuing to the next chapter, spend a few minutes thinking about the following questions:

- Can you think of a time when you were given something that you absolutely did not deserve? How did being shown grace make you feel?

- Have you ever accepted God's mercy and gift of grace? Do you know without a doubt that when your earthly life ends, you will have an eternal home in heaven?

- Are you like Larry and cannot wrap your mind around the concept that there is a God and/or One who could ever forgive and love you? If so, has the evidence presented throughout this book of His existence and how God's mercy and grace can be part of your life changed your thinking about God's goodness and love for you?

- If you are a Christian and are given the opportunity of talking with a skeptic like Larry, what would you say to convince them of their need for God's mercy and grace?

Chapter 15

June 25, 1995

Dear Larry,

Never would I have guessed a couple of days ago that a delay would be granted and I would be writing to you at least once more. Things really took a turn I hadn't expected! Your desire to donate your organs, which I read about in the newspaper, is certainly admirable and, as you pointed out, may allow several other people to live and benefit positively because of your sacrifice. If your request is granted, it will also help benefit other death-row inmates by changing the manner of execution used in Georgia. Guess we have to wait until Monday or Tuesday to find out the results.

Last Friday was an extremely long and tense day. Many, many Christians were praying for you. Our prayers were answered through the delay to give you more time to consider the claims and love of God and to seek His forgiveness. I still feel the Lord will work in your life and will continue to be praying earnestly for you.

You really attracted a lot of publicity on Thursday and Friday! I saw you on Channel 41 evening news on Thursday. Then on Friday, there was a special news brief at 3 that your execution had been delayed. On Friday evening, you were carried on all of the local channels. Were you surprised to be on the national news covered by Dan Rather? They announced several times during the day that there would be an interview with you on the six thirty news. We videoed those interview spots. You presented yourself well. The *Battle Creek Enquirer* also carried three articles.

When we saw you on TV, Michelle commented that you sure resembled my dad's side of the family. My mother and I had to agree. You have many physical characteristics you inherited from your mother's side of the family!

My heart was sick when I heard you say on Channel 3 that you would be going to hell because that is what you deserve. I knew then why your execution was delayed—you are still *not* ready to die. Do you remember the story that I told you a while back about the man who was a victim of a flood who rejected many rescue attempts and then asked God when he stood before Him why He did not save him? God pointed out all the methods He had used to rescue him that he rejected. Dave's first reaction after hearing about the post-ponement was that God had just sent another rescue helicopter for you. Will you wake up and see it as that?

I don't buy your statement that you don't believe that there's a God because of your belief that there is a hell. When we first started corresponding, you didn't think anything happened after you died—except that you would be at peace and just dead. You've come a long way from that belief since you now firmly believe that you are bound for hell. If you accept the existence of hell, I think you have, perhaps unconsciously, also accepted the fact that there is a God and that He created hell for Satan and his followers. If you believe in a hell that was created by God, then why is it impossible to believe that God also created the earth and the heavens? I think you believe much more than what you give yourself credit.

Please give it some serious thought and analyze what you *really* believe. Also, what happened to your desire to finally be at peace? Have you given up on experiencing that peace you are so longing for? You know that won't be the case if you go to hell as you say you are. Christ is your only way to have this peace.

The TV interviews and newspapers quoted you as saying that you are a cold-blooded killer and deserve hell. Without the Lord's mercy, even the very *best* person on earth *deserves* hell. As I said before, God does not play favorites and judge us on what types of sin we have committed in this life to determine who *deserves* to be forgiven and go to heaven. It's not a matter, at this point, of God forgiving you. You have to be able to forgive *yourself* and stop punishing yourself for something you are already paying society's price for.

God does not think that your act of murder is unforgiveable. Remember Saul (later named Paul) from the Bible? Before God touched his life, he was a regular scoundrel, a respected Jewish leader whose goal in life was to persecute, imprison, and kill Christians. He had many more than three deaths to his credit. Did God push him away and reject him because of his murderous actions? No way! In Acts 9, when God struck him down on the way to Damascus with a blinding light and spoke to him, he had been on the way to persecute and murder more Christians!

What was God's reaction? Did he condemn Saul to hell because of what he had done? No! He chose to use Saul as one of his missionaries. Why? Because He saw the good in Saul's heart. In Acts 9:15b, this is how God described Saul to Ananias, "I have chosen Saul for an important work. He must tell about me to those who are not Jews" (NCV). Saul *deserved* hell, but God had other plans. After being struck down by the blinding light, he realized it was God speaking to him, and his whole relationship with God changed. God is trying to speak to you also, Larry, just as he spoke to Saul. Why? Because you have value to Him.

Another example is the convicted murderer Ted Bundy who killed many more people than you did. In a videotaped interview a couple of hours before his execution, he admitted that he deserved hell for his deeds, but he died a Christian. Why? Because he realized that God loved him despite what he had done.

A person deserves hell *only* if he/she refuses to accept God's unconditional love and forgiveness. Why don't you stop punishing yourself, Larry, and wake up to the fact that your life (and your destination after you die) can be different. If you die and go to hell, it will be because that's what you *want*—not because that's what you *deserve*. You've said many times that you hope you're a Christian when you die. Why don't you *act* on that hope while you yet have another chance?

I hope you don't think I've overstepped my bounds in our friendship by talking this way to you. It is only because I truly care for you that I wrote what I did. If you have a chance to write again, I'd like to know what your reaction is.

I'll be glued to the TV to see what the decision will be on your request to donate your organs. I assume if it's denied, another date will soon be set.

We love you, Larry. *Please* consider what I've said and reconsider your decision to choose hell. That's not the only choice you have.

Love,
Erin

******

July 2, 1995
Dear Larry,

Wow, what an emotional roller coaster week for me after anticipating and preparing for two executions! However, I can't even *begin* to imagine what it was like for you emotionally—***especially*** last Thursday, when you came within one minute of being executed!

Michelle and I were so glad that you called us. It was hard knowing how to end our conversation, though, since we didn't really know what would eventually happen because of your appeal. Your comment to us that you would take the steps to become a Christian before you were strapped into the chair was an encouragement to us. When your sister called us at six fifty-five to tell us that the execution was scheduled to take place at seven, she was having a very hard time. I mentioned to her what you had told us earlier in the day about making your peace with God. She then told me that you told her you would be going to heaven to be with your grandma after you died. I was *so* happy that you had asked her to call me to thank me and to find out that you had asked Christ for forgiveness.

Even though my heart was heavy to hear the news since I consider you a friend and knew I was going to miss you and your letters, what a joy her call brought to my heart! Michelle was jumping up and down, smiling real big, and clapping as she heard me talking to your sister! After we hung up, I hoped that she didn't mistake my happiness over your salvation for happiness over the intended execution. I was positive you would be executed. It wasn't until I called your mom the next morning that I learned your execution had been stayed at six fifty-nine. I know she sure was relieved, and I was glad too. It's not easy to let go of a good friend. I'm sure as 7 p.m. drew closer, you were also beginning to wonder whether the stay would be issued or not. I was surprised that it went all the way to the U.S. Supreme Court!

Wanting to donate your organs and receiving a lot of mail in that regard during the last week must be an encouragement for you. How are you feeling about the stay of execution? I remember that last time after it was stopped, you were really depressed and wished you hadn't stopped it. Do you feel differently this time?

Do you want to know what I think about the stay? (I bet you know that you're going to hear anyways!) Now that you're a Christian, I think God has special plans for you during the months that it takes for the Supreme Court to reach a decision. He spared your life for a special purpose. I'm looking forward to seeing what that purpose is. Perhaps, it is to grant your desire to donate your organs so that others may have a new lease on life. Maybe some of the people who receive an organ may not be Christians but will have an opportunity by living longer to realize their need to do so. Your organ may be a "helicopter" that God is sending to rescue them just as he sent several to rescue you and give you a chance to become a Christian. It could be that God will use you to work in another prisoner's life to lead him to Christ. Only God knows why and what He has in mind. As a Christian, you need to pray and ask Him to show you what His purpose is and be willing to do what He may lead you to do. Does that make any sense to you?

We've shared with our church that you accepted God's gift of salvation. I wish you could have been able to see the excitement that everyone expressed! Many also literally had tears of joy in their eyes. We told our youth pastor and the youth that you appreciated the notes from the young people. Boy, were they excited! We've had a real celebration at Calvary Baptist!

I am wondering what you've been thinking since you made the decision to become a Christian and am waiting to hear from you. I know that living the Christian life in prison may not be easy, but know that Christ is there to help you now. The moment you asked for God's forgiveness and expressed your desire to become a Christian, God sent a part of Him, the Holy Spirit, to live within you and to be with you for your remaining days on this earth. The Holy Spirit's job is to encourage you, teach you, comfort you, and help you to live the Christian life. Look up the following verses in your Bible that tell you about the Holy Spirit: John 14:16–17,26; Acts 4:8 and 31; Romans 5:5; 1 Corinthians 3:16; Galatians 4:6; and Romans 8:16. I'm enclosing a booklet for new Christians that has a lot of good information in it to help you. I will share more with you in a future letter on how to grow as a new Christian.

I read in the newspaper that prison officials have received a couple of anonymous notes from groups of inmates saying that they have plans to harm you. Is that true? Why would they want to do that? What does the prison do when there are threats from inmates? Be certain I will be praying for your safety.

Can it already be July? The world hot-air balloon championship is in town again this week, so we'll be taking in a few events at the airport—the 6:30 a.m. launch tomorrow and the Air Force Thunderbirds performance at 4 p.m. On the fourth, we are going to the fireworks at 10:30 p.m. if it doesn't rain as predicted. Hopefully, your family can visit you over the holiday.

Michelle already wrote you that we are going on vacation to a state resort park that is nestled in the mountains of Kentucky. My idea of relaxing is sitting by the pool and reading. Michelle has plans to play a lot of games while we're gone so I know that will also be part of the routine. I've never seen anyone who enjoys games as much as she does or is as competitive as she is! Well, to be honest, she gets her competitiveness from me.☺ There is one game that I can never beat her at, though, and that is a matching game that has flags of many countries to match up. Two tiles can be turned over each turn. I can never seem to find the one that matches on my second tile. She *loves* playing that game with me! I told her that she could not bring that game!

If we were not going to be 400 miles from the prison and you could have visits from family during the week, we would have tried to get to Jackson to see you. If it would work out sometime that we could come, what has to happen? Will they let anyone other than immediate family visit? Michelle wanted to know if she would be able to visit also since she's only sixteen.

Write soon so we know how you are doing. We will continue praying daily as prayer is still important. Christ can give you the strength to live the Christian life in prison. Remember that we care for and love you.

Love,
Erin

*****

July 12, 1995
Dear Erin,

Hope this letter finds you all well and that you had a nice vacation in Kentucky. I am sure Michelle will give me all the details when she writes to me.

When it was 6:59 p.m., I was certainly thinking my appeal would not be granted. All executions and death sentences are appealed all the way to the U.S. Supreme Court. Then the lawyers also file the 11th hour appeals to them, and it is RARE for them to grant one of them since they accept very few cases. That is why I was so surprised they granted mine. Mine is even rarer cause it was accepted by them not through the regular way they accept cases but by the 11th hour appeal of the lawyers. Now my case will be argued in front of them the latter part of this year. Their ruling should be issued the first month or two of 1996.

Mom and Rob visited me Sunday. It was the first time they saw me since the execution was stopped and both were happy. I, however, am not so happy. The prison officials are retaliating against me. I am on lock down for 24 hours a day, and they are messing with my food and store orders. The reason being used for my lock down is the supposed threats you read about in the newspaper. It has been in the 90s for the last week, which makes it like an oven in here. Boy, the heat gets to me. I am only being allowed one five-minute shower a day. If I wasn't on lock down, I'd be taking a minimum of five a day. Then to add to all of my suffering, I have a toothache. I bet it will have to be pulled. Why I wanted to die so badly! I'm so tired of suffering!

When Rob was here on Sunday, they retaliated again. He had on a new pair of cool-looking tennis shoes. I asked him to let me try them on and did. For that, I was given a disciplinary report for "Possession of Unauthorized Clothing." When the disciplinary report was reviewed (we are given a set of our rights for the disciplinary hearing) by the lieutenant, I pointed out the disciplinary report even stated I took the shoes right back off. So how am I in possession? An hour later, I was re-served the same disciplinary report but the charge was changed to "Violation of Institutional Visiting Rules." Instead of dismissing the disciplinary report, they changed the charges. They will probably ban Rob from visiting me for so long (3, 6, or 12 months).

Thank you for the copies of the Battle Creek paper articles. At least their two editorials were fair. The one Atlanta's paper printed on me *really was bad*. I don't know why they keep using that 1968 mug shot picture of me either.

The plans y'all had for the 4th of July sounded like fun. I hope you will send me some pictures of the balloons. Seeing the Thunderbirds would also be a highlight for me. We were supposed to have been given a piece of watermelon on the 4th of July for dessert, but that did not happen. We did get strawberry shortcake, which was good. Since I had just eaten a lot of strawberries as part of my last meal, I sure was looking forward to the piece of watermelon, which we get twice a year.

This is the part of the letter *I dread writing*. But even though it is going to hurt you and others, I have to write it. I've always been honest with you and always will. Erin, I'm not a Christian *yet*. When they lifted the "stay" after talking to you and Michelle, I didn't have enough time to call you back. That's why I told my sister to call you so y'all could pray for me at 7 p.m. and to tell you how sorry I was I couldn't say goodbye. She told you a white lie when she said I'd accepted Christ and was going to heaven. I didn't tell her to say this though. I'm sure she didn't mean to hurt you. She knows y'all are Christians and how happy it would make y'all feel thinking I died a Christian. It was wrong on her part, but she was trying to ease your pain as well as hers by thinking I'd be in heaven. So, don't be mad at her. You have to admit my death wouldn't have hurt you all as much knowing I would be in heaven, right?

But, Erin, I didn't lie to you on the phone. My plan was when they strapped me in the "chair" to pray to Jesus asking Him to forgive me and to accept me into heaven. All of my last five minutes were going to be spent in prayer to Jesus, confessing my sins, asking for His forgiveness. I also closed my eyes and prayed earlier too when they were shaving my head and leg. I told Jesus how I had doubts about Him and religion (being honest) and asked Him to forgive me for having doubts. I even suggested that He could show me evidence that He is real by stopping my execution since I now had a reason to live—to try to get the laws changed so I and other death row inmates could donate our organs so other people could live. Oh yeah, I also prayed that if He wanted me at 7 p.m. to give me strength to face death and that I would not be afraid. At no time, even at one minute before when I honestly thought I was going to die, was I scared. He answered my prayer, hey?

Well, I'll let you go for now. It's getting late, and I want to finish my reply to Michelle's bible study group who wrote me. I have already worked on it for an hour and still am not satisfied. I have other letters to write to your pastor and a couple of others from your church. It's unreal how lazy I've become. Most of the time I just don't feel like doing anything.

Tell everybody "hi" for me. Y'all take care. Once again, I'm sorry that you must be extremely disappointed. Thanks so much for caring and for your prayers.

Love,
Larry

*****

July 19, 1995

Dear Larry,

I received your l-o-n-g letter yesterday. It sounds like life for you has been quite different since the execution was stayed. I'm sure being unable to be out of your cell has been rather hard on you especially in the very hot weather. Are you still being confined to your cell?

I read your last letter with very mixed emotions. You told me you said the prayers you said but are *not* a Christian. Needless to say, I am somewhat confused. Did you not mean what you said when you prayed? Did you just say the words hoping that if you were executed, they would get you to heaven? If you did not truly believe what you asked Jesus to do, they were meaningless words. It's very clear that you intend to wait until the last minute of your life to make your final decision.

What's the deal? Are you afraid of what being a Christian will mean to you? Do you think you can't be in prison and live the Christian life? Obviously, you're afraid of something about being a Christian. If it's fear, God will equip you with whatever you need to live the Christian life in prison. He hasn't said that it will be easy, but He gives us strength to do whatever we have to do as a Christian (Philippians 4:13 and 19).

You said that when your head and leg were being shaved, you prayed for two signs from God that He is real—that He would stop the execution and that you would be unafraid. You said that you were never scared and the execution was delayed. Since it is almost unheard of that the Supreme Court would stay the execution, obviously God intervened on your behalf and granted both of your requests in ways that I feel borders on being a miracle. Haven't you said all along that you wanted God to perform a miracle for you and then you would believe? Were you being truthful?

Larry, it appears to me that you are playing games with God—and that's not a very safe thing to be doing. God has clearly been working in your life—striving with you, so to speak—so you may come to believe in Him. He's brought many Christian people into your life to pray for you and be your friends and spared your life on three occasions since you've been on death row—His proof that He cares about your soul. However, He gives a warning in Genesis 6:3a where He says, "My spirit shall not always strive with man" (KJV). This was said at the time He instructed Noah to build the ark and before He later destroyed the earth because of the greatness of man's sin. However, God is very patient—He gave men another 120 years to repent and turn to Him before he actually sent the flood, but eventually His patience ended. It could be a very sad thing if you keep playing games with Him now that you do believe—and I have every reason to believe you do based on what you have said to me and what you told me you prayed when you were being prepared for execution.

Last Sunday night, we went to a service at the Gull Lake Bible Conference. The speaker told a true story about two men who went fishing together. Their discussion turned to God. One of the men was an unbeliever. He needed proof that there was a God. While they were talking, he raised his fist toward heaven and shouted, "If there is a God, let Him strike me dead." He died instantly. I guess he got his answer—but how sad he had to get it that way and without a chance to personally get to know God. He'll forever regret his foolish request. Also, look at the story of the rich fool in Luke 12:16–21. He thought he could get by just fine without God. In neither of these instances are we told how long God had been striving with these men—but I'm sure He had given them both opportunity to believe in Him because of what is said in 2 Peter 3:9b, "But God is being patient with you. He does not want anyone to be lost, but he wants all people to change their hearts and lives" (NCV). God isn't in the game-playing business. According to 1 Samuel 16:7b, He knows what's in our hearts and what our real intentions are. "God does not see the same way people see. People look at the outside of a person, but the LORD looks at the heart" (NCV).

You mentioned that many inmates seem to be upset with you—for whatever reason—because the execution was stayed. Obviously, since you are being kept away from the other men, there must be reason to assume that you would not be safe around them. Do you feel your life could be in danger? No man, not even a man on death row, can be sure of when he will die. A death-row inmate can *assume* that he'll know the exact date. *Only God knows for sure.* You'll recall that Jeffrey Dahmer was killed by inmates—I'm sure he wasn't expecting that. Even natural causes, such as a heart attack and heat stroke (look at all the people who died last week during the terrible heat wave), could take a person's life. So even though you are counting on having that last minute to make a confession to God and ask for His forgiveness, you're not assured you'll have that opportunity. You're really treading on dangerous territory and making the biggest gamble of your life—at stake is your soul. Is it really worth it?

Just as you had struggled writing to me about your decision to wait to ask God's forgiveness, I've struggled writing this letter. Right now, I'm feeling somewhat betrayed. You told me on the phone that you were ready to ask for Christ's forgiveness. You told Michelle and me, "I will do it." Since you have always told me the truth, I believed you. I guess that's why I felt it was okay to tell others at church—especially after talking with your sister. It will be hard to face these people (my friends) and tell them that you aren't a Christian after all. However, I know that the Lord will give me the strength to do what I have to do, and He'll provide the right time to do so. I just feel sad that I have to tell them. We will, however, keep praying for you and caring for you.

We had an enjoyable time vacationing in Kentucky the week of July 8. Much of the time was spent relaxing and just enjoying being together. Our busy schedules don't always allow for a lot of together time. As you guessed, Michelle wants to fill you in on the details. It was definitely *hot* though. Being in the mountains helped some.

Gregg has been doing great with his lawns. The dry, hot weather, though, has slowed down his business—which he doesn't like. I told him he ought to offer a lawn-watering service as well! He and Jenny have set April 20 as their wedding date and already have it on the church calendar. So I guess it's official. I'm happy for them.

Michelle worked for my aunt yesterday—washing walls and polishing furniture—and made $75 toward her insurance payment for the year. She was happy and has only $60 more to go to have her insurance paid for the next year. She's helping my mom today with some things at her house. Tomorrow or Friday, she and I are going to take the day to play and enjoy each other.

Well, the outdoors is calling to me. It's beautiful today and not too hot yet, so I'm going to go for a walk in the neighborhood. There's nothing like a good walk to start the day out right and have some time alone with the Lord. I know Ginger will be a willing partner! At noon, I'm going to meet some friends for lunch to celebrate a birthday. I think I told you that four of us gals get together when one of us has a birthday and celebrate it. Glad it's not me that's another year older! However, I'm beginning to show the effects of aging—I have to get bifocals! Oh well, at least I'll be able to read better and not have to keep taking my glasses off to read some things.

Write soon.

Love,
Erin

*****

August 7, 1995
Dear Erin,

I'm deeply sorry I haven't written sooner. I've been too upset about some tests my mom was having this past week to write. I thought she would come and visit on the weekend but could not come because she did not have a ride. When I called her on Monday, I was relieved that her blood test results were good. She said that she will be down this Saturday with the Christian van that comes here once a month.

You are correct. I did say I was going to ask God's forgiveness. And like you stated in your letter, I was intending to wait until the last minutes of my life, which I was, so I didn't lie to you and Michelle on the phone when I said I was going to ask God for His forgiveness. And in my prayer I was going to say something like this: "God, as you know, I have doubts about your existence but—" No use lying, right, cause He would know if I still had doubts.

No, I am not playing games with God or am I afraid of being a Christian in prison. Like I've told you many times, I'll probably go to my grave with doubts about the existence of God and why

(Genesis). *I'm sorry,* but I'm being honest with you. *I wish I didn't have this doubt!*

Maybe I don't want to completely believe in God and go to heaven cause of my feelings (hate) toward myself. I can never forgive myself for what I've done with my life (what I've done in it), so how can I believe somebody else can forgive and love me? If you want to give up on me, I'll understand.

Yes, these people still have me on "lock down." They say it's for my protection, but that's bull. It's nothing but retaliation. These guys aren't going to do anything against me. If they were planning something, they certainly wouldn't be informing the prison officials. If you and I was planning on robbing a bank, we wouldn't inform the police of our plans, would we? That is what I wrote the warden. Some of the guys are upset though. Even though their lawyers have told them that my case is *not* going to hurt them like the media has been saying, there are some of these dummies who would rather believe their enemies, the GA Attorney General and prosecutors, rather than their own lawyers. My lawyers will sooner or later sue these people over this treatment.

Rob was planning on going to New Orleans to a death penalty protest rally this past weekend with some other Christians. But his boss wouldn't let him off as they have a deadline to finish painting a multi-million dollar house. He worked all seven days last week and his boss wants him to work all seven days this week too. My mom said that he looks worn out from working seven straight days in this heat.

Speaking of the heat, it has been more bearable since it's been cloudy and raining the past couple of days and only been in the high 80s, which is cool for down here. I will take any break from the heat we get!

Glad to hear you all had a good vacation in Kentucky. I am looking forward to Michelle's letter with all the details.

Good to hear Gregg's lawn business has been doing good. Have they decided where they are going to live after their marriage in April?

I know getting bifocals didn't make you happy. It is a sign we are getting old. ☹ I've been using bifocals for a year. It sure was an adjustment for me too since the lens in the glasses they furnish us with are so small. So, with the extra medicine I'm on and these small lens, I have to tilt my head a lot of times or I have part clear vision and part fuzzy.

When do you go back to work? I'm sure you can't wait. ☺

I'll let you go. Tell Michelle and everybody "hi." Thanks for caring and your prayers. Once again, I'm sorry!

Love,
Larry

*****

August 24, 1995
Dear Larry,

Were you beginning to wonder when I was going to get around to writing again? Today is the first chance I've had to sit down and write. As a matter of fact, I got up early so I could write before going to work today. Sorry it's been so long!

Speaking of work, I started back two days ago. Actually, I was ready to go back—believe it or not! The summer was starting to drag. It had been so hot and extremely muggy and humid for the last month or so that I could hardly get outside and enjoy the warm weather of summer and was truly sick of being cooped up inside! (I'm sure I don't have to tell you what that feels like!) This week has been very pleasant with the temperature in the low eighties—wouldn't you know it, just when I go back to work!

Thanks for responding to the comments from my last letter so honestly. I can understand where you're coming from and that you still have some doubts about God. I read the article on the prehistoric foot bones that you sent. I guess such an article does not prove to me that evolution is any truer. I think there is an extreme amount of guessing that goes on when bones are found as they were in Africa. Scientists want so much to prove evolution that their "theories" naturally will support it. I think the fact is that bones were discovered— but why couldn't they just as readily give the credit to God who was the creator of all living things?

Another question I have is, "Why would I want to give up on you?" I must admit that I was very disappointed (and as I reread my letter, I know that was easy to figure out). However, my feelings toward you have not changed. If God gave up on me every time I disappointed or hurt Him, I'd be in big trouble! So I'll still be praying for you in the same way. Your prayer to God was an honest one. You're right—you can't fool God. Keep praying that prayer and asking for His help to completely believe in Him.

Your feelings of hate toward yourself are a very powerful force in keeping you from believing that God can love and forgive you when you can't love and forgive yourself. Satan is working through those feelings to keep you from God. But remember that Satan is the "father of lies" (John 8:44b NCV). Romans 5:8, however, says, "But God shows his great love for us in this way: Christ died for us while we were still sinners" (NCV). As I've said before, God's love is not like man's love and forgiveness. He doesn't love us only when we've been good and love ourselves. He loves us just as we are—*without any conditions*. You're back on our church's prayer list each week, and many are still praying for and asking about you. My prayer is that your doubts will be settled soon and you can accept God's love into your life.

I read the article in the Atlanta paper about the inmate threats. It doesn't sound like you think that's the real reason you're on lockdown. If there is some truth to it and even one group has sent a threatening letter or is planning retribution, I would think you're much safer in lockdown. I'm sure it's got to be almost like being in solitary though. What do your attorneys have to say about the situation? Are you still in lockdown? If it is merely retaliation, is there any way that it can be proven? I can see your point that if the guys were planning on doing something that they wouldn't tell the warden—they'd keep it to themselves. Have you heard anything relative to when your case might be heard in the Supreme Court? Fill me in on what's happening.

Rob has really been working hard lately. I don't know how anyone can keep up a seven-day work schedule for very long—especially working outdoors in the oppressive heat. However, he is fortunate to have a job. What happened with him being able to visit you after the shoe incident?

Now for news from the home front. Michelle goes back to school on Monday, and Gregg starts back on Tuesday next week. I don't think either one is truly looking forward to going back. Michelle couldn't get a course to replace the physiology course that accidentally got put on her schedule, so she's going to be a teacher's assistant to two of her former teachers and is excited about that. As an assistant, she'll grade papers (which she loves to do), run copies, and do any other things they ask her to. It will be treated as one of her elective classes, so she will get credit and a grade. She will be an assistant for the math teacher the first semester and the English teacher the second semester.

Gregg so far hasn't been successful in getting more than the two classes he originally enrolled for back in the spring. The one management class he really needs is still full. So he'll be going just two days a week—on Tuesdays and Thursdays. He's not happy that he has a three-hour wait between classes, but we told him it would give him a lot of good study time. I don't think he totally agrees! You asked about where Gregg and Jenny will live after their marriage. I imagine they will live in an apartment.

A week from tomorrow, September 1, Pennfield is putting together an alumni band that will perform at the halftime show at the first football game. I'm seriously thinking about being a part of the band. Michelle's friend dropped out of band this year and is letting me use her clarinet. I think it will be fun. I need to find the time now to practice the music. All of the alumni band will be wearing matching sweatshirts and will perform one or two songs with the current high school band. We have to be at the school at five the day of the performance to practice marching. About four years ago, I was in the alumni band and thoroughly enjoyed it since it brought back memories of my high school days. Having Michelle in the high school band will be special too. I'll let you know how it goes.

I got my bifocals about a week ago and am doing quite well with them. The first couple of days, I got a headache from the strain of adjusting. However, now I've almost forgot I have them. When I glance off to the side, things sometimes look a little fuzzy, but other than that, they are working well. It's nice to not have to keep taking my glasses off to read smaller print. Since I have the blended lenses, no one can even tell they're bifocals—now isn't that vain! I would imagine it would be much more difficult adjusting to bifocals with the smaller lenses that you have.

Since it is almost 9 a.m. and I need to get to work, I'll be signing off. I'll be looking forward, however, to hearing from you again real soon. We care about you and are praying for you.

Love,
Erin

*****

September 4, 1995
Dear Erin,

Thank you for the beautiful birthday cards from you and Michelle! I got them a few days before my birthday.

It sure meant a lot to me that Mom and my older brother Tom visited me yesterday on my birthday. I was really hoping my younger brother, Steve, and Rob would visit me too. However, Steve surprised me with a visit last weekend. He said he'd be back yesterday too, so it hurt me that he didn't come. I also got a surprise "over-night express mail" envelope with a birthday card and letter from my sister! She said she had been planning to surprise me on my birthday by visiting me but their car had to be put in the shop two days before their planned trip.

I wrote the deputy warden who removed Rob from my visiting list and asked her to reinstate him or approve a "special visit" so he could visit me with the rest of my family on my birthday. I explained that there wasn't any "sinister motive" behind why my brother and I tried on each other's shoes. I pointed out that just like I inadvertently violated the "rules and regulations,' the deputy warden did too. I quoted from the "Visiting Rooms" section of the regulation manual that any time someone is removed from our visiting list they have to notify that person and the inmate. Cause of her failure to do that, my brother came to visit me one weekend with the Christian van and, after being informed he was barred from visiting me, he had to walk a mile to the truck stop to use the phone. The other people that came in the van were already inside the prison. Friday, when I hadn't received a reply from her, I asked my counselor to call her. He did and informed me that she said she didn't receive my letter. What a joke!

I just tried to call my sister, and the guard said I couldn't since all cell blocks were on a "special" lock at 9 p.m. My call would've went to 9:02. I asked the guard why he didn't let me make it at 8:45 p.m. like I requested. He said I didn't remind him at 8:45. I told him it's on the phone call request form. He said it was my job to remind him. I then countered by asking why it states for us to put the time we want to call on the "phone call request" form. When I didn't get any action, I requested to talk to the sergeant and informed him about what happened. I also pointed out a couple of weeks ago that they were letting me take my shower at 9 p.m. But I couldn't make my call since it would run two minutes past 9. Just another example of them messing with me.

Oh yeah! Two weeks ago the warden stopped at my cell. He informed me that he's never going to remove me from this "lock down." I asked him his reason and also why he moved me to G-4. More BS. So I'm going to be doing the rest of my time "locked down" 23 hours 50 minutes a day. My thanks for living and trying to help other people. My lawyer wrote the warden about the way I'm being treated. He sent me a copy of it. Just a waste of paper. These lawyers don't really care how we're treated. They just care that we don't die so they can win their case.

Anyways, I've decided to accept the way I'm being punished. I do not want to rescind my case from the Supreme Court docket since the bad ruling from the 11th Circuit Court of Appeals made on my case also affects all other cases. It's only right I let the case go forward so the U.S. Supreme Court can remove the Appeals Court's ruling from the books.

We've lost our cable TV for good. The governor ordered the boss man of all Georgia's prisons to remove them from all of the prisons. I won't be around, but remember I predicted it. In a few years from now, prisons across the nation will be "burning" (riots). The fad is now to make all prisons harsher. Alabama even has inmates "busting rocks." The prisons' wardens don't give us TV, recreation, and other things cause they like us. They do it to control and pacify us. If we don't have any privileges or reason to obey the rules, why should we? I also believe it is going to backfire in the states with life without parole. If a guy knows he has no hope of ever being released, he doesn't have much reason not to cause trouble in prison, does he?

On a different note, I've seen those blended lenses. I don't think you were vain for wanting that kind of bifocal.

I had an evangelist come visit me about a week and a half ago. When he saw me on TV, he wrote and asked if he could come visit me. Of course, I asked him about evolution vs. creation. His answer wasn't helpful to me, sad.

Well, I'll let you go. I want to write Michelle while in this "writing mood." ☺ So y'all take care! Thank you for caring and your prayers!

Love,
Larry

Think About It: Self-Forgiveness

Have you ever been in a mental boxing match with yourself? You continually think about something you have done or not done in your past that you are ashamed of or that has hurt another? With each mental round of rehearsing your wrong(s), do you get even more beat up? Perhaps you have even been down for the 10-count often and struggle more each time to get back up and on your feet to continue the match. Why? Because you cannot give up the unforgiveness or self-contempt you are wearing like a cape around your mind and heart. You remove the cape momentarily when you begin a new match but quickly adorn it again when the match is over. Are you getting tired of being in this "fight" with yourself that you feel you will never win? Be encouraged, for there is hope!

To forgive is an action word that means "to pardon an offense or an offender."[57] When one finds it hard to forgive, the unforgiving offense is like a "painful video [that] plays inside your head that you cannot erase . . . from your mental hard drive. It's even worse when the person starring in this video replay, over and over again, is you."[58]

One of Larry's issues was the inability to forgive himself for taking the lives of three people. Because he constantly replayed that video in his head for over ten years, the result was self-hatred and the feeling that he was undeserving of anyone's love—especially God's love. In his mind, murder was an unforgivable act, and he deserved to psychologically punish himself.

What about you? Are you walking around with a negative mental video playing over and over in your mind? What is your unforgivable deed? A failed marriage? Hate you carry around in your heart toward someone? An abortion and the life that was sacrificed? Premeditated or accidental murder? Abuse you inflicted on someone? Is it _____ (you fill in the blank)? Chances are, it is an action you have regretted or words spoken in anger that you have carried with you a *very* long time that is causing great grief and weighing you down in guilt.

Would it surprise you that the lack of self-forgiveness is "a form of pride? Whenever you hold yourself to a higher set of standards than you impose for others, your pride is involved."[59] When you forgive others for offenses against you but feel you do not deserve forgiveness when you wrong someone, you are in essence convincing yourself that you are superior, wiser than others, should have "known better," and should have acted differently. Proverbs 16:18 says, "Pride leads to destruction; a proud attitude brings ruin" (NCV). Does this describe you? Is pride getting in the way of allowing you to forgive yourself?

What are the different ways this "pride" can manifest itself in the lives of those who refuse to forgive themselves? Lack of self-forgiveness can hurt one in the following ways:

- You keep reliving what you've done
- You let it affect your decisions

- You feel paralyzed by your past
- You verbally abuse yourself, quietly in the recesses of your own heart
- You make yourself feel unworthy
- You are afraid to take healthy risks
- You spiral into despair
- You don't try to make things better because you don't think you deserve to make things better
- You struggle to forgive others
- You struggle to trust yourself[60]

Can you identify yourself in any of the descriptions given above? Is this really how you want to live the rest of your life?

If you are a Christian, the unwillingness to forgive yourself is a form of unbelief. Christ died on the cross to provide forgiveness for all sin. All who believe in Christ and request His forgiveness have the assurance of Psalm 103:12 that states, "He has taken our sins away from us as far as the east is from the west" (NCV). In Jeremiah 31:4, further encouragement is given in these words, "He remembers our sins no more" (KJV). Unlike humans, when God forgives, He also forgets.

If God has forgiven you, why do you have the need to hang on to the sins He no longer remembers? When you do, it is a form of telling Him that you do not believe His all-encompassing forgiveness includes you. Always remember that you are not God nor are you perfect. You *will* make mistakes and have regrets; in other words, you will be "human." With that being the case, why not lower your self-forgiveness standard and give to Him the heavy burden you have needlessly been carrying. He encourages you to do just that in Matthew 11:28: "Come to me, all of you who are tired and have heavy loads, and I will give you rest" (NCV). Are you craving some rest from the burden you have been carrying? It is yours for the asking!

If you are not a Christian, the first step to self-forgiveness is to acknowledge God is real and loves you and Jesus died on the cross to provide forgiveness for your past and future sins and then rose from the dead three days later. No fancy prayer is needed—just one straight from your heart admitting to Him that you want Him to be part of your life and need His forgiveness. He waits with open arms to accept *all* who come to Him. As you have learned throughout this book, His love is unconditional. Do you need to take this step to change the direction of your life? Will you?

Larry's desire when he requested a stay of execution in the chapter was to try to give back to society by donating an organ to the detective who arrested him so that he could at last do something useful with his life. Even though he could not restore the lives of the three people he killed, he wanted to make a difference in the life of another who was "on death row" because of his need for a kidney. He was putting into action a concept I recently read about that anyone who is harboring unforgiveness toward themselves might remember—"The reality is that you cannot change what has happened. You cannot restore lives to where they were before the event. However, you can make a difference in the lives of others. You can give back some of what you have taken away by finding a different place to invest your time and compassion."[61] Is it time to turn your negative feelings into some positive thoughts and actions to help you heal?

In the same article was this following quote that also bears remembering:

> Life is full of choices and every choice we make will either take us in a positive, life-giving direction or rob us of the opportunity to be a life-giving individual. Forgiving ourselves does not let us off the hook, it does not justify what we have done, and it is not a sign of weakness. Forgiveness is a choice that takes courage and strength, and it gives us the opportunity to become an overcomer rather than remaining a victim of our own scorn.[62]

What choice will you make? Are you willing to take off those boxing gloves, throw them into the ring, and walk in another direction?

Chapter 16

October 2, 1995
Dear Larry,

I can't believe it is October already! Sorry it's been so long. Your letter came at an extremely busy time. However, I've finally gotten things under control again, so hopefully, it won't take me so long to write next time.

How glad I was to hear that your mom and Tom got to visit you on your birthday and that Steve surprised you with a visit the weekend before! Then getting the surprise letter and card from your sister must have made your birthday special. Have you heard any more from the deputy warden on your request to have Rob's visiting rights restored? Too bad he could not have visited you on your birthday.

The semester has been a busy one for me. Fortunately, one of my classes was cancelled since I have some training to do for two new word processing classes that were added to the schedule. When classes started, I had only trained for the first class, so I've spent my spare time during the last couple of weeks training for the second part of the course and finally finished that last weekend. What a relief to have it done!

Michelle has been very busy with school and band. Last week she had eight tests. By Friday, she was relieved to have the week end! She also has a book to read for English that she did not get to choose so has had a hard time getting started on it. Marching band rehearsal is every Monday evening from seven to nine. In the next two weeks, the band will be competing against other bands from Michigan in a couple of marching festivals. If they perform like they have at the football games this season, they should for sure get a #1 rating!

Speaking of bands, I marched with the alumni band on September 1. What fun! We practiced a couple of hours before the football game and then performed the entire halftime show. Would you believe we even learned a dance routine to one of the songs in that amount of time? I felt a lot of pressure to not goof up but still enjoyed the experience. The crowd gave us lots of applause—especially after the dance routine. I was glad I participated. My back, however, bothered me for a few days afterward. It was worth it though.

Gregg and Jenny celebrated their third anniversary of dating last week. They are now planning on an April 20 wedding. It was a thrill for me to see Jenny being baptized on October 1 since she has been a Christian for two years now. Gregg says that she hates going under water so that could be why it took longer. She did survive, though, and had a huge smile on her face after her baptism! It was a joy to see!

Have you heard when the Supreme Court will be hearing your case? You certainly have a case worth fighting for. It saddens me, however, to think of you being on "lockdown" all the time. It appears the warden is trying to punish you since he told you he will never take you off lockdown. I'm sure you'd like to know the truth behind it too. How are you handling it?

This summer I read a very good book about Psalm 23 that was written by a man who was a shepherd in Africa for many years. He presents an excellent picture of God's love and character. I know you are still having difficulty believing in God, but perhaps reading the book will give you a perspective of Him that you haven't had before. Since I feel you could benefit from reading it and the book is small, I will be sending it to you by chapters so I can include it in my letters and not have to send it via the chaplain. The first two chapters are enclosed. Let me know what you think of it.

It is almost time for choir practice, so I better be signing off. Plus, I had to type this letter on Gregg's computer in his room and his guinea pigs do not smell very good today! As a matter of fact, I'm getting a headache! Write again soon. I still think of you and pray for you often.

Love,
Erin

*****

October 17, 1995
Dear Erin,

Sorry I haven't written sooner. I started writing the excuses in two other letters but after reading what I wrote realized how lame they were.

In a letter from my lawyer last week, I found out that my case will be heard by the U. S. Supreme Court at 10 a.m. on December 4.

Boy, these people sure upset me at times. As you will recall, I wrote the deputy warden a week before my birthday requesting she reinstate Rob to my visiting list or at least approve a "special visit" on my birthday. When she made her weekly round in G-4 with the warden and other officials, I stopped her and informed her that Rob didn't receive a letter and because of that came the following week to visit and was not allowed into the prison. She told me the letter must have gotten lost in our postal system. She said she has had letters get lost too. The warden was returning so she left with him.

A couple of weeks later, I wrote her again and gave the letter to my counselor to deliver to her office so she couldn't say she didn't receive my letter again. I informed her what was in my previous "lost" letter. Since my birthday had passed, I just asked her to reinstate Rob and pointed out how. like me, she inadvertently violated the (same) rules too by not sending Rob and me a letter informing us of his removal from my visiting list.

The following week I stopped her again. I told her that I didn't even receive my letter and that it is hard to believe both letters were lost. That got her a little mad—my insinuation that she was lying. I asked her how long Rob is barred for. She said it was too soon to reinstate him and besides it's up to the warden. The next

Wednesday during my talk with the psychologist, I lost my temper while explaining this stuff regarding Rob. I said if it wasn't for losing my visits with my family (being in the hole) that I would've grabbed the deputy warden's hair when she was at my cell and tried to pull her head through my bars. But I accept the way they are treating me cause that's how much my family visits mean to me. But when my execution is scheduled next year, I am going to knock that "bit--" out. Won't lose my family visits then as I'm not going to have any.

After cooling off, I realized what I did. Threatening a staff member is a very serious charge. I asked the doctor what she was going to do. She said she had to warn the deputy warden but would re-word it so I didn't really threaten her. She would tell her that I was upset with the way I was being treated and to use caution (she shouldn't be around when the execution is scheduled). The doctor is an ex-60s hippie; she's cool. When I got back to my cell, it sure upset me to know I still had that "coldness" in me. I hadn't had it since I killed those people. I know how much pain and remorse I have so I thought I had lost that "coldness." Another big reason why I have to die, cause I don't want to ever hurt anybody, animal and insect, again. Since I see I am capable of doing it, *I have to die.*

Anyways, I wrote the warden and told him how *much my family visits mean to me.* That is the only reason why I'm behaving. I also pointed out how I don't think it's fair or legal to be punished more than what I would have received in disciplinary court for the violation I committed (maximum loss of visiting privilege I could've lost is 90 days). So, I asked him to reinstate Rob to my visiting list. Last Friday during his round, he stopped at my cell and informed me that he had received my letter. He was going to reinstate Rob to my visiting list on November 1. Then he walked away.

Yesterday while making his rounds he stopped at my cell again. He called over the deputy warden and asked her if she had written the letters so Larry's brother can start visiting after November 1. She replied she had. He then said to me, "A couple of my guards messed up. Your brother got away. Next time I'll have him arrested." He then walked away. The deputy warden then said real harshly, "And your brother better not violate any rule!" She then walked away. Boy, did I get mad!

I was told by a staff member that they had received a tip that Rob's tennis shoes had drugs in them. That the sergeant messed up and was criticized for not confiscating the shoes so they could've been searched for drugs. So, by the warden's remarks, he believed the shoes did have drugs in them. You can believe I'll stop him during his next round. Going to ask him why does he continue to believe these "snitch" letters. That's why I'm on "lock down" cause some of these guys supposedly wrote letters saying what they're going to do to me. Now he receives another that my brother had drugs in the tennis shoes, and he believed that too. I'm also going to tell him that since he believes these letters he keeps on receiving on me that I'll get everybody in G-4 to write one saying they have no animosity toward me so believe them and let me off this lock down. I bet he won't believe these letters cause they aren't something bad toward me.

Well, what's your opinion on the O. J. Simpson verdict? I'm glad it exposed to the public how the police will lie. *But it's sure not fair that he got away with killing two people cause he's rich*! No doubt in my mind that he did it. I believe he'll lose in the civil suits the victims' families have filed against him as their lawyers have to prove to a jury that the evidence shows he more than likely did it (preponderance of evidence).

Oh yeah, in the lawyer's letter last week, when he informed me of the date my case is going before the U. S. Supreme Court, he asked me if Mom wanted to attend. I asked her last Sunday and told her that she could really enjoy herself—take a tour of the White House and the monuments besides watching the U. S. Supreme Court in session. The lawyers would take her with them, so expenses would be paid by them, a little vacation. She agreed it sure would be something, but she can't go cause of her foot. She's limping badly now and is hoping that when she goes on Medicare next month they'll pay for the operation she needs.

Too bad that DC is so far from you all. I know you and Michelle would find it all interesting. I'm going to ask the lawyer if his firm would pay for you two's expenses to go. They are one of the biggest law firms in DC so you know they sure can afford the cost. If they'll pay for it, would you want to go? I think it would be very educational for Michelle to see Congress and the Supreme Court in session. Heck, no harm in asking the lawyers to do this, all they can say is no, right?

Continue sending me the chapters from the book *A Shepherd Looks at Psalm 23* by Phillip Keller. I'm up to something. You'll be finding that out soon. My eyes are sure getting a workout lately. In addition to spending about six hours a day reading newspapers, I also read books and write letters.

We got a new guy in G-4 a couple days ago. He's 21 now. When he was 19, he stabbed his parents and young sister to death. He was a college student when he did it, never used drugs or alcohol, was on the high school football team before he went to college, and was a volunteer helping poor and elderly people. You figure it out. I sure can't, sad. His grandparents, who are Christians, asked the jury not to sentence him to death. So, I thought he had a little hope then of getting "life with no parole," but I wasn't surprised when the jury sentenced him to death.

Would you please send away for the entire series of "Search the Bible" messages by Pastor L. E. Tucker for me? It has 32 sermons for $5. I recently read one and liked it. I'm very interested in reading some of the sermon topics. When I get done with all 32 sermons, I'll send them to you. The address is The Quiet Hour, P. O. Box 3000, Redlands, CA 92373-1500.

I cannot remember if I told you that we are now getting sandwiches. It is unreal how bad my memory is at times. Glad I won't get old. Since I'm so absent-minded now, I know I sure would be one senile old man!

That's sure great that Jenny was baptized and is a Christian! I know that meant a lot to y'all too. I think an April wedding next year makes more sense than the November wedding this year they were thinking about.

Well, I'll let you go. Tell Michelle and everybody hi. I have some articles and pictures I'm going to send her. Thanks for caring and for your prayers.

Love,
Larry

*****

October 25, 1995
Dear Larry,

What great news that Rob gets to come visit again! Someone must have it in for you to keep sending letters to the warden. You certainly stuck up for yourself though. I know how important your family visits are to you. Only another week before Rob can come visit! You must be looking forward to seeing him again.

It sounds like you have some pretty strong feelings about the deputy warden. Since you thought those "cold" feelings weren't there anymore, I can understand why you were surprised and alarmed when they popped up again. It was probably pure anger that made you feel like you did because she was depriving you of something very important to you plus you saw her as lying to you. It was good that you had a chance to talk with your psychologist about your feelings. I'm glad you like her and feel you can talk to her. We all need someone we can talk with about our feelings. Did she do as she said and not get you into trouble?

There's someone else who can understand your feelings also, Larry. I'm sure you probably know by now whom I'm referring to. God knows *exactly* how and why you felt as you did. Despite your temporary urge to do harm to the deputy warden, God still loves you and can see value in you—even if you don't feel you're worthy. If you will surrender your will and life to Him, He can help you deal with those feelings and even take them completely away. I hope you are still praying and contemplating all that you know about God and His love for you. Don't give up—ask Him to continue to work in your heart to show you that He's real and to change your attitude toward Him and yourself.

It's too bad that your mom isn't able to make the trip to Washington DC, especially since it would have been free. I do know, however, that there is a lot of walking to get anywhere in Washington DC since we visited there about five years ago on one of our vacations. We spent three days there and were really tired from all the walking we had to do. You asked if Michelle and I would consider going if the attorneys would pay our expenses. I know that Michelle would not be able to go because of school and since she'll be going there in April with her band. I would not want to go by myself because I don't think it's good to travel alone. It would be a really unique experience to see the Supreme Court in session—one that most people never get. Because it would be your case that they would be hearing, it would be even more special. We feel very honored that you would think of us. Wouldn't someone else from your family like to go? I was wondering if just the attorneys would go or if you actually get to be there also.

Enclosed are the next few chapters from the book on Psalm 23. You've got me wondering what you're up to! What's your opinion about what you've read so far?

How sad that a twenty-one-year-old is now in your cell block. I can't imagine killing one's parents and sister, can you? He certainly seemed to have everything going for him, didn't he? I don't think we probably can figure it out without seeing into his mind. It does make one wonder why he did it though.

I have something that I've been thinking about. Maybe you can give me some insight on it. Which do you think is worse—being on death row for a limited number of years or life in prison without parole for the rest of your life? Neither option is desirable. It seems that a person's misery would be greater to be given a life sentence without parole. I'd like your perspective on this issue.

I knew when I heard the verdict on O. J. Simpson what you'd think. I agree that it looks like he probably killed his wife and her friend. The incredible number of lies told during the trial are what, I feel, got him a not guilty verdict. Only he knows if he did it, and he'll have to live with that the rest of his life. I know that it's not fair that he got off if he was truly guilty just because he was rich. Everyone should get equal treatment under the law—regardless of how rich or poor they are.

I'd be glad to send for the sermons for you by Pastor L .E. Tucker. Since I am not sure they would be considered a book by the prison, I'll have them sent to me and then see that you get them. I'll send for them tomorrow. (Sorry that I didn't do it earlier, but when I was rereading your letter, I remembered that I needed to do it. Guess you are not the only one with memory problems, huh? ☺)

No, you didn't tell me about the sandwiches that you are getting now! Is this a new policy? Fill me in on the details. Bet you're happy since you don't really like the food that well. Speaking of food, it is goodie box time again in December. Would you give us a quick run-down of what is allowable so that we don't send things that get taken out? If I remember correctly, the goodies have to be in clear packages so the contents can be seen. Tell us what you're hungry for, and we'll do our best to send those things. Let us know soon, though, so we can send the box out right after the first of December.

Halloween is just around the corner. Our church is planning a big outreach program for primarily our local teens on October 28 called Fright Night VI. Halloween is billed as being Satan's holiday, but our church feels that every day of the year belongs to the Lord—including Halloween. So this is our version of Halloween, and our purpose is to introduce teens to Christ. The evening begins with a program that has a lot of fun skits and some scary things planned and ends with a presentation of the gospel. After the program, the teens get transported north of town to a Fright Night trail that is always fun and scary for them. There are no ghosts, witches, goblins, etc., used to scare. Since there were over 600 teenagers who attended last year—our whole auditorium was full—this year, the event is being moved to a larger facility. The hope is to have at least 800. Michelle is selling tickets to the event at Pennfield High School and is putting invitations to it on every locker in the school. The kids at her school say that our church's Fright Night is the place to be! Dave, Gregg, and Jenny will all be helping on the trail. My mom and I are driving the teens to the trail after they arrive. Our youth pastor said that some groups are coming from as far away as Chicago. I love being a part of Fright Night!

The four-letter "S" word finally hit us last Friday. Yes—*snow*! (I really don't even like to say the word!) We woke up on Saturday to a snow-covered ground and really cold, windy weather. A lot of leaves have fallen since then as it's been quite cold and windy for the last few days. This morning, it was twenty-seven degrees when we got up, but the high today should be around fifty. Tomorrow, it's supposed to rain again and be in the thirties. Winter coat time is here! I had an *extremely* hard time taking that winter coat off the hanger and putting it on. It certainly felt good though when I walked outside!

I've shared all the news for now. In addition to the several news-papers you've been reading, now you have another "book" to read too! I will be looking forward to another letter from you. Sure hope the Supreme Court decision goes in your favor! Take care.

Love,
Erin

*****

November 9, 1995

Dear Erin,

Hope this letter finds you all well!

It was Mom's birthday on the 4th, and she had already informed me that she'd be here that day. Then this was the first time in over three months Rob could visit me so he was looking forward to coming too. When I didn't receive a visit, I knew some-thing was wrong. I got to call her today and found out that she was sick over the weekend. Rob did not come because he lost his driv-er's license last week during a "check point" and did not have any insurance. The police gave him a ticket and confiscated his license until he proves that he has insurance. It was disappointing to not get to see either of them.

The Fright Night program sure is a nice program your church planned for October 28. You've never mentioned it to me before. If Michelle still has an invitation to it left that she put on every locker at school (a very good idea), tell her to send me one. I'd like to read it. Make sure you tell me how it went. I'll tell Michelle to give me her report on it too. ☺

Well, I have some good and bad news for you all. First, the good news: *I now believe there is a Son of God, Jesus Christ!* That He died on the cross and was resurrected. What changed my belief? I didn't realize until reading a book that out of the twelve apostles, eleven died martyrs' deaths on the basis of two things: the resurrection of Christ and also their belief in Him as the Son of God. They were tortured and flogged, plus they finally faced death by some of the cruelest methods then known. Would they suffer and die like this for lies? No way!

If a few people commit a crime, one will always crack and confess when the "heat is on them." He'll also tell the names of the people who were with him during the crime. I've not only seen friends tell on each other, but I've seen family members tell on each other to save themselves (make a deal for no or lesser charges). There is no way all eleven of these men would accept being tortured and killed. One or more of them would've stopped their torture or saved themselves from being killed by confessing what they've been preaching about Jesus (He's the Son of God, His resurrection, His teachings, the miracles He performed, and so on) was lies.

Then Jesus' brother, James, didn't believe Jesus was the Son of God when Jesus was alive. So what happened to him that made him become a believer? He became one of the leaders of the Jerusalem church, wrote a book, the epistle of James, later was recognized as an apostle, and he also died a martyr's death by stoning. Again, what happened to James that changed him? "Then He appeared to James" (I Corinthians 15:7 NASB) is the only plausible explanation.

And what about Saul? What changed him so drastically from what he was, a non-believer in Christianity, violently hostile to the Christian faith? It is what happened to him on his journey near Damascus. "And last of all . . . He appeared to me also." (I Corinthians 15:8 NASB)

I could go on and on about the evidence in the book that made me a believer. However, I still have a major problem, the bad news. Cause of how much I hate myself and can't forgive myself, I still feel

I don't deserve God's (or anybody's) love and forgiveness. I feel I still deserve to go to hell.

I've taken a big step in the right direction. Hopefully before I die I can say I not only believe but I accept Jesus as my Savior. I now read my daily devotion, other religious material, and the Bible *every day*!

I'll probably be receiving a letter from you any day. I'll be writing again soon. Take care! Thanks for caring and for your prayers.

Love,
Larry

*****

November 15, 1995
Dear Larry,

I got your *wonderful* letter yesterday! I agree that you have taken a *very big* step toward becoming a Christian. Just being able to believe in Christ and His death and resurrection will help make the next steps possible. I know you have not convinced yourself that you are worthy of God's forgiveness and still feel you deserve to go to hell. I'll be praying that God will continue to work in your heart to show you why it's not necessary to continue to punish yourself for what you have done.

I've done a lot of thinking trying to relate your situation to a similar situation in the Bible so that perhaps you can see the connection between yourself and the *real* Bible character. Since you mentioned Saul (later renamed Paul) in your letter, let's focus on him. Here are the facts about him that are recorded in Acts beginning in Chapter 7:

- He was a powerful Jewish leader whose goal was to wreak havoc on the Christian church.
- He consented to the stoning and death of Stephen, a Christian. He played a big role in a premeditated murder.

- In Acts 26:20, he admits that he personally arrested many, many Christians and had them put to death.

The next few verses recount his dramatic conversion. I would encourage you to read the book of Acts and think about the following questions:

- What kind of attitude do you think Saul had when he was murdering the Christians?
- Do you think he was remorseful at all? I don't think so since he was on his way to Damascus to carry out more of his murderous plans and, I think, felt good about it! You have a true remorse and sorrow for what you did.
- How many more murders would he have had to his credit if God hadn't stopped him in his tracks? You admit to killing only three people—Saul was responsible for killing many, many more!
- Why didn't God put him on His "blacklist" because of his past instead of choosing to use him for future ministry?
- If you could interview Saul, what do you think he might tell you he *deserved* after thinking back on how cruel and evil he was before God got ahold of him? Do you think he could very well have thought, as you do, that hell is where he *deserved* to go?
- What thoughts must have been going through Saul's mind when he was struck down and blinded by God on the road to Damascus? My guess is that he may have thought God was zapping him for his murderous thoughts and actions, that he had just gotten *busted*!

In a court of his peers, he *should* very justly have been punished and received the death penalty. It is a good thing God and not man decided his destiny. But notice God's attitude toward Saul—He had compassion on him. God's response could have been real anger since he was murdering Christians—He had the power to take his life if He wanted to for what he had done. And Saul would have deserved it!

Why did God show compassion instead of revenge on him? The answer is found in Isaiah 55:8 that says, "The Lord says, 'My thoughts are not like your thoughts. Your ways are not like my ways'" (NCV). God knew Saul was acting under Satan's influence and could see right through to Saul's motives and knew his thoughts—which I'm sure were *not* good at that moment. He also had the ability to see his *real heart* and how He could use Saul's leadership abilities for His eternal purposes. So in an action that must have *totally* surprised Saul, God gave him forgiveness instead and decided to redirect his life in the right direction—serving Him. In other words, He showed Saul *mercy*, which I have explained to you in previous letters.

I suspect that having been in prison for a majority of your life, *many* people—jury, victims' families, prison personnel, etc.—have told you over and over again that you deserve death, that what you've done is unforgiveable. You have also gotten into the habit of telling yourself that so much that you firmly believe it. In 2 Samuel 24:14, David said, "I am in great trouble. Let the *Lord* punish us, because the *Lord* is very merciful. Don't let my punishment come from human beings" (NCV). Man judges much more harshly than God and is definitely incapable of forgiveness.

Unforgiving man is being controlled by Satan, who is the one that is *making* you believe that you deserve to go to hell—and he's doing a bang-up job at it! I'm going to be praying that God will work in your heart to help you realize that He doesn't think you deserve hell any more than He felt Saul deserved hell. He loves *you* just as much as He loved Saul—whether you can believe it or not. He's worked greatly in your life to help you believe in Him. Now, ask Him to help you get past this hurdle too. He will.

Sometimes, I've wondered if one of the reasons you want to donate your organs is so you can have more "worth" in God's eyes and the eyes of society. It may work for society, but it doesn't matter to God. He loves you just as you are. My mom sometimes says, "God loves us—warts and all." Being able to save lives through donating your organs would be very nice, but please don't think that is the only thing that would make God consider you worthy to be a Christian. You are just as worthy as anyone else. You just need His help to realize this truth and to forgive yourself. I've discovered that we humans are usually harshest on ourselves.

You asked for the highlights of Fright Night. I am still on a high from the evening! Before the event even started, God performed the following two miracles:

- As ticket sales progressed, we realized that there were going to be more than 600 teens who planned on coming—closer to 800. Since our church sanctuary could not seat that many, our youth pastor called the local auditorium that could seat over 1,000 to see if it was available on October 28, but it was already booked. He was told that if the group cancelled, which would be unlikely, our church could use it. The next day, he got a call that the group had cancelled, and it was ours to use!

- Because our Fright Night trail was outside, our prayer was for no rain that night and some clouds to make the trail spookier. Rain started on Wednesday and kept up until midmorning on Saturday and never rained again during the day. Of course, we were all happy about the rain stopping. We did not realize what a miracle it was until the out-of-town groups started arriving. All of them reported rain until they hit our city—and the groups were coming from all directions. It seems our city was the one dry spot that night. We knew then that God had answered our prayers so the *1,000* teens and sponsors who came could enjoy the event. Michelle guessed that about 90% of her school was there. *After* the event was over, the rain came—further proof that God is still in the miracle business today.

The program started with a couple of fun skits that the teens really liked. One of the skits was an audience participation. Anyone who had won a prize—actually caught a candy bar that was thrown randomly out into the crowd—were the actors. They didn't know what was coming up in the skit but just had to do what the narrator told them to as he told a story about Prudence Pureheart, her hero, and the villain. One guy had to play a dog, one of the girls was a cat, a couple of gals were chairs and a table, and a guy played the mother—complete with a wig. They were all good sports about doing the corny actions they had to perform, and the teens in the audience all had many good laughs. I will let Michelle tell you about the other skit in her letter.

After the skits, the program took on a more serious side. Our college-age teens acted out a song by a Christian recording artist titled "The Champion" that depicted a battle between Jesus and Satan that took place after Jesus had been without food for forty days. Satan tried three times to tempt Him to sin (see Matthew 4:1–11). Of course, Jesus resisted all three of those temptations—which made Satan angry. Finally, Satan thought he had defeated Jesus when He died on the cross. Jesus was depicted as being "out" (like in a boxing match) and the referee (God) began the 10-count. When the count got to about 5 or 6, Jesus began moving (to depict his resurrection from the dead on Easter). By the 9 count, Jesus was on his feet and was being declared the winner of the fight. In the end, Satan was shown bowing to Jesus—as he ultimately will—and admitting defeat. It was very dramatic and touched the hearts of a lot of those who were there.

The skit was followed up by the testimony of a man from our church who has battled cancer for several years and came very close to dying when he had a bone marrow transplant. He told the teens about how he came to realize his need for God in his life and how God had sustained and helped him deal through his cancer journey. When the youth pastor explained to the teens how to become a Christian and have their sins forgiven, ninety indicated that they had prayed the prayer to become a Christian! (The way we knew the exact number was from the cards that they turned in as they were leaving that indicated any decisions they had made.) Michelle had an opportunity to talk to two girls afterward who had asked God for forgiveness and made the decision to become Christians. Needless to say, we were all very happy!

After the program, we had the job of transporting the teens to the two identical Fright Night trails that were in the woods. I don't know exactly all that was on the trail since I didn't go through it myself—I know, I'm a chicken! I do know that at one point, they had to crawl over a Plexiglas area that had live rats and a rubber snake in it. (Jenny supplied the rats from the pet store she works at.) That grossed a lot of kids out. They also had tunnels they had to crawl through where people were hiding to reach out and touch or scare them. Dave's job was to stay hidden, crunch some leaves, and then snap a picture of the kids. Their expressions were priceless! I am enclosing a few pictures that I thought you might enjoy. My mom and I transported groups to the Fright Night trail from eight thirty to around eleven and enjoyed hearing the reactions to the trail. Overall, the teacher in me would give the event an A+!

Last Friday, my mom, Michelle, and I spent the night in Grand Rapids and planned to Christmas shop there on Saturday. The weather was so snowy on Saturday that we headed back home and shopped here instead! It was still fun to get away though. We had a good time, and I finished my Christmas shopping. Next on our list is to shop for your goodie box!

Say hi to your mom for me when she comes to visit. Has Rob gotten to come visit yet? Hope to hear from you again real soon.

Love,
Erin

*****

November 21, 1995
Dear Erin,

I just received your letter today. Thanks!

It sounds like things went well and everybody had fun at Fright Night. Also, sure glad it stopped raining, that would've ruined the evening. I got a smile out of looking at some of the expressions on their faces when Dave took their pictures. So glad you sent me some of them so I could feel I had a little part in the evening.

Rob still hasn't visited me cause he has no picture ID that he needs to visit me. I went through a lot getting him reinstated to my visiting list and he loses his driver's license a couple of days before I got him reinstated. Bad luck. Hopefully, he has one by now so he can visit me over the 4-day weekend this week as we won't be allowed any mail service, no lunches, no outside yard, etc.

I do have some good news. They finally let me off this "lock down" last Thursday! ☺ Yesterday was the first time in close to five months I could go outside and play basketball and volleyball with the other guys. Boy, am I sore! It was a long night too cause I couldn't sleep good with my muscles so sore. But it's sure good to have this extra freedom again!

No, I won't be allowed to go to DC for the Supreme Court hearing. When they hear a case, it's just the lawyers for both sides giving their arguments. Each side has 30 minutes for their arguments and questions and answers from the justices. This is done in *all* cases before the U.S. Supreme Court. You asked if some of my family members would like to go. Yes, they would. When I informed the lawyers that Mom couldn't go and asked if any of my other family members or you and Michelle could go, I never received a reply, sad.

Glad to hear you're enjoying the snow. ☺ (Hint) My Christmas present to you and Michelle is indirectly related to snow and cold. Have fun figuring it out. ☺

To save money, they quit giving us cooked meals for lunches. They give us sandwiches now. It's sure alright with me! They can't mess up sandwiches like they do when they over or under cook our meals. Some days we get one sandwich and some days two. Plus we are getting a lot more fruit with the sandwiches. So, instead of eating one of their meals a week, I'm eating at least one meal a day (except weekend and holidays when we don't get lunches).

Regarding a Christmas box this year, thank you for the offer again. ☺ Cause of two incidents last year, I'm surprised they are allowing us to receive boxes this year. One guy tried to slip a hack saw blade and another some "weed" (pot) in their Christmas boxes. The following is what they are allowing us this year: 4 cakes (I like angel food and pound cakes), peanuts, 2 packages of candy that is individually wrapped and not in foil, 2 packages of M&Ms, and cookies (I like oatmeal, Oreos, and sugar-coated ones). A few years ago they were a lot more liberal and we were allowed to receive meat, cheese, donuts, etc. We are allowed to receive boxes from December 1-24.

Saw myself on Atlanta's TV news last week. They showed a tape of me from my last court hearing and reported how my case is now scheduled for December 4 in front of the U.S. Supreme Court. Also reported was that the victims' families are appealing their denial of being allowed to witness my execution.

Y'all got your Christmas shopping done already, hey? No waiting for the last minute for y'all I see. But then knowing how women like to shop, I'm sure y'all will find another reason to go shopping. ☺

Well, I'll close. Hope you all have a nice "Turkey Day." (The turkey sure won't! ☺) Also thanks for caring and your prayers.

Love,
Larry

*****

November 28, 1995
Dear Larry,

I discovered that I forgot to enclose the remaining chapters of the Psalm 23 book that I've been sending you and wanted to get them to you. I also thought of a PS to my letter of the fifteenth that I wanted you to have. Have you ever gotten a PS over two weeks later?

This is the PS. As I was driving home from class last night, I was thinking of you and how I could explain the concept of mercy in a way that you could better understand. One word in a definition of mercy grabbed my attention—clemency. One definition of clemency is "a merciful, kind, or lenient act, especially toward an offender or enemy."[63]

Let's suppose the governor of Georgia sees an article about you, or in some way, your case is brought to his attention. For a reason no one can understand, he decides to grant you clemency—just because he feels like it. His written pardon for your crime is sent to the prison's warden, who takes the necessary steps to arrange for your immediate release. You are totally shocked at this turn of events and cannot understand how it could have happened. As the warden and guard come to release you, how would you react, after you got over the shock? Would you refuse to leave your cell and tell them you don't deserve the governor's clemency? Would you choose to remain on death row and take the punishment coming to you—the electric chair? If I were in your shoes, I certainly wouldn't do that, as I'm sure no other death-row prisoner wouldn't do! If it were me, I would accept the "gift" from the governor and be happy he gave it to me—whether I deserved it or not.

Larry, God is like this governor. He's offering you clemency from all your sins and crimes for which you feel you don't deserve forgiveness. Even though you can't understand why He would possibly want to do such a thing and find it unbelievable, the fact is that He offers it to you—with no strings attached—and no parole to be served. It's yours just for the taking. He's waiting to unlock the "prison door" of your heart and offer you unconditional forgiveness and peace from your self-hatred. Do you—or me or anyone—*deserve* what God is offering us? No! Do we have to *feel* like we deserve it in order to accept it? Does a prisoner have to feel he deserves clemency when he knows he committed the crimes he's in prison for? No! Does it make his pardon any less real? No! The governor won't force you to take the pardon, but you'd be foolish not to. Right? Please think about this and ask God to help you accept His offer of clemency He provided through Jesus Christ's death and resurrection—whether you feel like you deserve it or not.

What good news that you're out of lockdown! What made the warden change his mind? He said that he was never going to let you out. I'm sure you really appreciate the extra freedom that gives you. Does everyone seem to treat you okay? Are your muscles getting back in shape now so you don't hurt as much after your yard time?

Just a week from now will be your Supreme Court hearing. Let me know as soon as you can how it turns out. I am certain it should be in our papers here. I will be looking for it.

Michelle and her band will be marching in the Christmas parade tomorrow night so they have to go out and march this morning! Right now, it is only eighteen degrees and snowing. She jokingly asked me to break her foot this morning so she wouldn't have to go out and march in the cold. I'm sure she'll be just fine once she gets out as long as she dresses warm enough.

Would you believe that my Christmas presents are just about all wrapped thanks to my mom and Michelle helping me for four hours last Saturday? All that's left to wrap are Gregg and Michelle's gifts, which Dave will help me with when it gets closer to Christmas. Of course, your goodie box is high priority right now too! We love shopping for you! It should be in the mail by the first of the week.

This will be our last Christmas with Gregg living at home. If I think about it too much, I could get sad. It sure has been on my mind a lot the last few days though. I told him I would like an early Christmas present that only he could give me this year—to help us decorate the Christmas tree. He hasn't helped in quite a few years because he and Michelle would usually not get along, and then Dave would have to get on them. He said that he didn't have very good memories when it came to putting up the tree. I told him that's why he needs to do it this year so he could leave home with a positive memory. I think he's going to give me this gift. You can believe I'll be putting out the word that everyone had better get along! Having Gregg there helping us will be by far my best Christmas gift this year!

You sure know how to get Michelle and me going, don't you? What a hint you gave about your gift to us! Guess we'll just have to wait and see!

I've been reading another book by Phillip Yancy titled *The Jesus I Never Knew* that is very good. It helps one to look at Jesus in a little different light than normal and to see more into His true personality. There is one chapter in particular I want you to read, so I photocopied it and am also enclosing it. Please read it and think about what it says. Maybe you've never really looked at Jesus in quite the way He's shown either.

Have to go now since it's time for breakfast. Take care. Please think about what I shared with you about clemency and about the chapters of the books I sent.

Love,
Erin

*****

December 5, 1995
Dear Erin,

Well, I received the *big* box of *goodies* yesterday. There was many other boxes on the cart for other men. Your box was twice the size of any box! ☺ The angel food cake didn't last long. I sure thank you. It really meant a lot to me!

If only I can overcome my problem so I can accept the fact that you and others really do care for me. Another example of how badly I think of myself and can't accept the fact that people do care for me. I don't let people hug me—not even my mom. Sad, isn't it? That's how badly I think of myself and why it's so hard for me to accept and believe God (or anybody) loves and will forgive me.

I'll tell you that my Supreme Court hearing sure got plenty of media coverage down here. One Atlanta TV station went "live" to Washington, DC to get the report of the hearing from a reporter. Myself, I'm just glad it will soon be over so this so-called life will end. I'm really looking forward to that! I was planning on sending you the article out of today's paper. However, my lawyer is going to make copies of it, so I'll send it in my next letter. Was there any coverage in Battle Creek?

I will be mailing your and Michelle's presents out next week. Hope you won't open it until y'all open the rest of your presents. I sure wish I could've done more for you two. I paid a guy $20 to do that verse you sent me. When I was moved out of G-2, he was about half finished with it. Now here it is several months later and no "verse." That was going to be my Christmas present for you. So, it looks like he's not going to send it to me. Sad. I continue to help these guys but yet they keep "stabbing me in my back." I sure don't understand it. I could understand it if I was treating them bad. It would be pay back. Pitiful.

You asked if my muscles were doing better now. The second time I went outside I played basketball. Here it is a week later, and I'm still on muscle relaxer pills. You would've laughed (if it wasn't so painful, I would've too) watching me get out of bed last week. I'd roll off my bed to the floor. Couldn't bend my back to get off my bed like normal. Boy, was I hurting! Glad to say that it's a little sore but *a lot* better. Getting old is the problem.

If you don't mind, would you photocopy the rest of the book *The Jesus I Never Knew*? If it is easier, you could send me the book. The chapter you sent makes me want to read more.

I don't watch much TV any more, except when sports is on. I do also love to watch "America's Funniest Home Videos." Some of the ones of little kids and animals sure bring a smile to my face. I don't care for the "corny" host though. Oh yeah, something else about TV and how "sorry (pitiful)" most of these inmates are down here. (The majority of these death-row inmates couldn't survive in Michigan prisons.) Our cable was back on last week. So this inmate wrote the warden and told him it was on. Our cable was then shut back off. It was nice for the two days it was on to see commercial-free movies and sports.

I'm hoping Mom will visit this weekend. I didn't have any visitors this past weekend. Rob had to go to court yesterday. Hope I receive a letter tomorrow on what happened.

Well, I'll close for now as I'm so sleepy. I missed my afternoon sleep cause of the lawyer's visit. Tell Michelle I'll be writing her by Sunday night. Sorry this letter is messier than normal. You all take care!

Love,
Larry

Think About It: Anger

A bully. A gossiper. A rageaholic. A physical abuser. A terrorist. An obsessive person. A sex offender. An overly critical person. A murderer. A substance abuser. A deeply depressed person. What do all of these people have in common?

Did you guess it? One word that drives all of the types of people mentioned above is *anger*. Did you see yourself in the list of anger-driven people above? Were you surprised? Anger is "a strong feeling of displeasure and belligerence aroused by a wrong."[64] The wrong can be either real or perceived. Anger can be good when handled appropriately but destructive when handled in an unhealthy manner. Unfortunately, many have not learned to deal with anger correctly.

Unhealthy anger is normally expressed through aggressive, passive/aggressive, or suppressed behavior. *Aggressive anger* is the easiest type to spot since it involves an overt action. With aggressive anger, the victim suffers physically at the hands of the aggressor—through loss of life or violation or abuse of the body in some way. Remorse may follow the act but is not always the case.

Sometimes, an angry person is very intentional in plans to harm another, and the crime is planned well in advance. In the case of a mass murderer, serial killer, or sex offender, actions are intentional and very often stem from some type of abuse suffered in life that was never dealt with emotionally. Instead of taking the anger out on the abuser, however, innocent victims suffer. In the last several years, there have been many mass shootings in the United States, with many of them being at schools. Some of the murderers have been former students who were bullied and decided to get their revenge at the expense of innocent victims.

In other instances, the anger may cause an impulsive action. In Larry's case, his *impulsive* anger resulted in murder. He did not go to the victims' house with the intent to murder them but to talk to them about his overdue gambling debt. Because the conversation got out of control and he felt threatened by their attitudes and/or actions, his temper became violent. The end result was that three lives were sacrificed.

Do you have a short fuse like Larry? Could it lead you to act in ways you regret later? Recently, a rageaholic acted in a way that killed the occupants in another vehicle. Could being cut off in traffic or an action of another driver light your short fuse and land you in prison like it most likely will for this driver? There is a reason for your anger. Are you willing to get help to discover why before it is too late?

Passive/aggressive anger is not as easily identified but has the intention of harming another through more emotionally targeted actions. I can remember an instance as a young teen when my dad asked me to scratch his back. I was upset with him at the time, and it was the last thing I wanted to do. Being a "people pleaser," I did as asked. Instead of a nice soothing back scratch, however, he ended up with torn skin where my nails went too deep and drew blood because of my anger. I did not get punished since my dad must not have realized I had done it on purpose, but I was also never asked to scratch his back again either. Afterward, I felt bad about my aggressive action that were the result of my pent-up emotions.

The overly critical person also falls into this category. The criticism may or may not be deserved. It may even be given in a "joking" or sarcastic way, but the underlying intent is to be hurtful so the victim "pays" for the real or perceived wrong. On one occasion in my son's teen years, we were both being very critical of each other, and I could not understand why. After describing what was happening to my counselor, her immediate response was, "You are both angry with each other. You need to sit down and get your anger toward each other out in the open." That very night, Gregg and I had that conversation, which brought healing to our relationship. Our attitudes toward each other dramatically changed. We had to occasionally revisit that conversation in the future but at least knew the cause of our critical spirits.

Silence can also be used by a passive/aggressive person as an emotional punishment for its victim. I grew up in a home where my parents would use this tactic with each other. Instead of talking to each other when there was an issue, there was silence—sometimes for long periods. The greatest drawback with this type of behavior is that the "victim" may or may not know there is an unmet expectation or problem for which he/she is being "punished." What the perpetrator also does not realize is that the silence hurts others in the household (especially children) who are not the intended victim(s) and teaches by example that this is "normal" behavior to handle conflict. When I was dating Dave and I had an "issue" with him, I thought silence was the way to handle it. Thankfully, he was patient and quickly communicated to me that this was not the way to handle problems, and eventually, I learned to be more open and communicative. Without communication, little can be solved.

Suppressors fall into the last category of angry people. I was a classic example of a suppressor. Children growing up in homes where passive/aggressive behavior is practiced can be prime candidates to become suppressors. As I mentioned in an earlier "Think About It," I became a people pleaser who wanted to avoid conflict at any cost. Instead of my anger being directed outward, it is directed inward and kept suppressed. I became very adept at giving the outward impression that I was happy and had it all together and truly did not realize there was underlying anger. The end result of the suppressed anger for me was depression. The cost of being a suppressor can be great. If angry feelings are held in long enough, an unexpected "volcanic-like" explosion can even erupt (and will not be a pretty sight) that will take your victim totally by surprise. Are you a suppressor? Learning to communicate feelings is extremely important if you are to avoid the emotional consequences.

How should one deal with unhealthy anger? The ideal way to handle anger is in an assertive, nonharmful manner. The following are a few suggestions for resolving anger issues in a healthy way:

- Deal with your anger as soon as possible. The advice given in Ephesians 4:26 is the Biblical way to deal with anger— "When you are angry, do not sin, and be sure to stop being angry before the end of the day" (NCV). The longer the anger is kept inside and allowed to simmer, the more apt one is to express it in an unhealthy manner.
- Go to the person who has wronged you in private after you have had a chance to calm down. Words spoken in anger

tend to also anger the second party. When both people are angry, neither is capable of thinking straight.

- Use more "I" or "me" language rather than "you" language to avoid putting the other person on the defensive. Try to calmly talk to the person in terms of how the incident affected *you* rather than blaming him/her without giving any room for a rebuttal or apology. Be willing to listen to the other side of the story. In other words, seek to understand. Each of us tends to see things through different lenses because of life experiences. What you perceived may not be at all what the other person intended.

- Be willing to extend forgiveness to the person who wronged you—whether they are deceased or living—using the following process:

  o If the person is deceased and you want to get rid of your anger, write the person a letter in which you in honesty, with no holds barred, lay out everything that angered you and how his/her actions made you feel. It could be one major issue or a multitude of issues or hurts. Although you will not be able to send the letter, you will have had a chance to get your emotions out in the open and express them, which can be healing for you. Even if the person is still living, I encourage you to go through this process. However, do *not* send the letter to the person! The letter is for your own sake and healing.

  o Once you have written the letter, ask the Lord to help you forgive that person, as hard as it may be, because you want to be out of the prison your anger has kept you in.

  o Next, take a marker or pen and write in big letters over the front of the letter the word *forgiven*. Then to symbolize the release of the anger, which has been slowly eating you up inside, burn the letter. Does this mean you will never think about it again? No. But you can remember your decision to forgive and move on.

o   If the offender is still alive, think about making contact with him/her, and in a nonoffensive manner, offer forgiveness without blame. The offender may not even be aware of the hurt you have carried inside for so long. You will know if you can safely go to your offender.

Let me walk you through a tough situation that I had with a former boss when I was teaching to show you how I handled it using the above steps. My department chair called a two-person meeting (instead of a department meeting, which would have been the best idea) to discuss changes that were going to dramatically change how many of our classes were taught and increase (in our lab classes, actually triple) the number of hours we would be spending in the classroom. As soon as he detected any resistance to his plan, he went into his "steamroller" mode and made threats of eliminating our program if the faculty did not comply. His steamroller attitude and threats made me *extremely* angry. Rather than getting into an argument with him, I left the meeting to calm down.

After calming down and thinking overnight how to approach him, I decided that I should take up the actual program changes with other staff members, our union, and dean. I could, however, approach him about what I had control over—the unprofessional way I was treated in the meeting. When we met in private the next day, I told him that I was not there to discuss program changes but to discuss how I wanted to be treated as a professional that I was in future encounters. He admitted that he goes into steamroller mode when he senses resistance and that it kicked in. Our meeting ended on a positive note. Eventually, there was a compromise made on the proposal for program changes and hours worked.

In another encounter with this individual, he made comments to my office mate and me that were extremely hurtful—that we were not worth what we were being paid. (I might add that the issue was not just about his comment about our worth but that the integrity of our program, which we had worked very hard to build, was going to be greatly affected by the proposed program changes.) Both of us left feeling extremely angry. My anger took much longer to get over. I actually had to go have another private talk with him about being worth what I was being paid and also about how I wanted to be treated. We ended the meeting agreeing to disagree on the worth issue; however, it diffused some of the anger.

How angry was I? I could hardly stand the sight of him but had to walk by his office every day. My office mate and I made up our private nicknames for him. Neither of us had the enjoyment we once had to work the jobs we loved. It began eating me up inside. I finally wrote the letter bearing all my feelings toward the person—but one I never sent. It was, however, a good emotional outlet. To truly begin the forgiveness process, I then had to give up the nickname I had created. Finally, I had to start thinking of him in a different light—to see him as a lonely man who did not know the Lord and for some reason felt the need to control through threats and demeaning comments. As I tried to understand him, the anger began to subside. It has taken some time, but I finally feel that I have forgiven him. Will I ever forget how he made me feel? Probably not. However, I no longer feel the anger toward him that I did. I had to forgive him for my sake since anger can eat one up on the inside.

Have you ever said you have forgiven someone but thoughts of the offense keep popping back into your mind? Do you wonder if you have truly forgiven the person? It is hard to completely forget what was done against us. The following is a five-step litmus test, however, to help you see if you have truly forgiven someone:

1. *When the first thought you have about them is not the injury they caused in your life.* You should be able to have normal thoughts about the person occasionally. Remember, you are dropping the right to get even; the grudge you held against them.

2. *Ask yourself: Would you help them if you knew they were in trouble and you had the ability?* Most likely this is someone you once cared about . . . perhaps even loved. You would have assisted them if they needed help. While I'm not suggesting you would subject yourself to abuse or further harm, that you are obligated to help them, or even that

you should, but would you in your heart want to see them prosper or see them come to harm?

3. *Can you think positive thoughts about this person?* Again, you've likely been on positive terms with this person or in a close enough relationship for them to injure you to this extreme. Is there anything good you can come up with about them? If not, have you really forgiven them?

4. *Do you still think of getting even with the person?* There may be consequences that need to come for this person and you may have to see them through to protect others, but does your heart want to hurt them? If so, would you call this forgiveness?

5. *When you have stopped looking for them to fail.* If you have truly forgiven someone, then just like you would for anyone else, you would want them to succeed or at least do better in life. Forgiveness means you've stopped keeping a record of the person's wrongs.[65]

What about you? Are you dealing with anger issues? Are you tired of being held captive by them? If so, determine which type of anger issue(s) you have and make a conscious decision to work on forgiveness and healing. If you are unable to do so without help, seek out a professional counselor. You will never regret letting go of the "monster" within you.

Chapter 17

December 26, 1995

Dear Larry,

Christmas is now history, but it was a good one. It was our last one with Gregg at home. Believe me, I enjoyed every moment with him! The Tuesday before Christmas, he and I went shopping for Jenny's gifts from him and had an enjoyable lunch together.

I got my Christmas wish from Gregg! Not only did he help us decorate the tree, but also he spent all of Christmas Eve at home. After a pizza supper and opening a few gifts, we played a new game that Ginger gave the kids. Gregg and Dave were a team, and Michelle and I were a team. After the guys won the first three times, Michelle and I got the hang of the game and won the next four—much to our delight!

You would have smiled to watch Ginger help open gifts. We think she enjoyed tossing the Christmas paper and ribbons around as much as her several gifts—pig ears, a new stuffed animal, and a Koosh ball. Ginger keeps us laughing when she grabs the soft extensions on her ball and swings it ferociously back and forth hitting herself in the head. Later, we had our Christmas devotions and traditional birthday celebration for Jesus.

Christmas Day was busy but enjoyable. Jenny, my mom, and Dave's parents came for dinner. Afterward, we watched an updated version of *Miracle on 34th Street*. After Gregg and Jenny went to her grandma's for a couple of hours, they returned, and we played games until around 9:30 p.m. Sure was tired when I went to bed last night! It was a great day, though, with memories I will long hold in my heart.

Your Christmas presents for Michelle and me arrived on Friday, the twenty-second! How nice! The scarves, gloves, and hats will sure keep us warm this winter. Thanks for thinking of us. They're extra special since they came from you, and each time we wear them, we will think of you. Tell whoever made them that he did an excellent job! As soon as Michelle saw the package, she had to know what was in it. You probably guessed that we wouldn't be able to wait until Christmas Day! Sorry we didn't wait to open your gift to us!

I'm close to finishing the book *The Jesus I Never Knew*. I'll send the book to the chaplain and have him give it to you to read first. I think you'll enjoy it. Philip Yancey has a unique way of viewing Jesus that makes one think.

Sounds like you've been savoring your goodie box. What things did you like the best after the angel food cake that you gobbled right up? We wish we could do more for you during the year and are thrilled to get a chance in December to send you the goodie box. If there wasn't a weight limitation, we'd have added a few more things. It was hard to stop buying!

I'm glad that you feel you can share some of your inner feelings with me as it helps me to understand better where you're coming from and how you feel deep down. Since I've always had loving parents and others who have cared for me, it is hard to imagine feeling that no one truly cares about me. I think I can somewhat understand why you would feel like that though. Having spent a majority of your life in a prison environment, the likelihood is that you haven't been treated very humanely by anyone and probably been talked to and treated like you were no good. After hearing it so many times, you would naturally start to believe it. Please know, however, that there are many people who care for you.

As I've said before, the Lord has given Michelle and me a special love for you. There are people at Calvary who ask about you all the time and pray daily for you because they care about you and haven't even had the chance to meet you. God—above everyone else—loves you deeply. He is waiting to give you one of the best hugs you could ever imagine. My prediction is that you are going to experience that hug one day. (I *know* it's going to happen—I just don't know when.)

But God is working in your life, and I don't think it'll be much longer before you surrender to His love.

You mentioned that you don't let people hug you—not even your mom. I agree that it is sad. Hugs from people I care about are what keep me going. The thing I have missed most since my dad died is his many hugs. When he hugged you, you knew you had been hugged! I've dreamed of my dad several times since he died. In just about every dream, I end up getting a hug from him. (The Lord is certainly being good to me—He knows what I need and provides it!) It helps keep my dad real to me. As I read what you wrote, my first thought was that if I ever get the chance to visit you in prison, I'd want a hug. Hopefully, God will change your heart so that would be possible.

You mentioned that you watch *America's Funniest Home Videos*, but you don't care much for the corny host. When I read your comment, I had to laugh because that is *exactly* how Dave and I feel about him too! It was hard to understand why one of the inmates would tell the warden that the cable TV was back on since he ended up getting "punished" when it was turned back off too. He must have been very unpopular with the other inmates.

Michelle wants me to watch *Little House on the Prairie* with her, so I am signing off for now. Remember that you are loved!

Love,
Erin

*****

January 1, 1996
Dear Erin,

Happy New Year! I tried to call you last night at 8:45 to see what was wrong as I hadn't heard from you in a while. I thought you all would be home by then from the evening church service. I know it sure would've surprised you and Michelle, hey? However, the guard said nobody was home. I bet you all was out to celebrate New Year's. Then that afternoon I got your letter. It sure was a big relief nothing was wrong! I couldn't call back today cause our phone calls don't roll over to the next month.

It was good to hear you all had a nice Christmas and that you got your special gift from Gregg! Mom and my youngest brother visited me on the 24th. That was my best gift. She was supposed to have visited me over the three-day New Year's weekend, but didn't. Nobody did. Sure hope nothing is wrong! She will be able to visit me only one more time before she has her foot surgery on January 8. After she has the operation, she won't be able to visit me for over a month. ☹

I'm glad you all liked your presents! I know you won't be wearing your hat too much (don't want to mess up your hair ☺). I thought you might wear it, though, when y'all went sledding, skiing, or ice skating. I loved going sledding when I was younger.

As I mentioned in my last letter, you were supposed to have received that "verse" gift that the inmate in G-2 was half finished with when I left that cell block. Now that I'm not in the same cell block with him, I see he has no plans to give it to me or give me back my money. So, *sadly* to say, if we get a lawyer visit on the same day (all lawyers, paralegal, and pastoral visits are in the same room), I will start a fight with him and end up back in the "hole." It's the principle of it. I as a convict can't let him or anybody "take" something from me. Plus the way I look at it, he took $20 from Mom since it came from her monthly check.

Another *sad* example of the "convict principle." Doing 30 days in the "hole" now won't be as bad cause of the sandwiches we get Monday through Friday. The last time I did 30 days was so hard cause I'd go days without eating a meal cause of what they served. Of course, I'll lose my family visits too while in the "hole" but Mom won't be able to visit me after the 8th for over a month anyways.

In 197? (I forgot the year), I was up for parole in Michigan and was being released in a couple weeks. While I was playing cards on Christmas Day, another inmate came up and "sucker punched" me. I had to be taken to a public hospital to have about 100 stitches put in my face (my glasses shattered in my face). Since I was the victim of an assault, I wasn't given a disciplinary report, so my parole outdate wasn't in jeopardy. A *normal* person would've just "let it go" and went home a couple weeks later. But my convict breeding wouldn't let that happen. I got a knife (couldn't fight him with all the stitches in my face) and went looking for him. When I found him, he saw the knife and took off running. As I ran after him, he tripped and fell. I jumped on top of him and stabbed him a couple times in his chest. Would've killed him if one of his friends didn't knock me off him. So, instead of going home in a couple weeks, I was in the "hole" with a new charge, "Assault with the Intent to Commit Murder," which carries a sentence up to and including "life" in prison.

My trial had started and the jury already picked when my lawyer informed me during the recess after picking the jury that the victim and his friend was refusing to testify. Even though I was no longer at the same prison, my friends had informed them if they testified they was going to have more trouble. So the DA offered a plea bargain. I took it and was given one year, which ended up being a nine or ten-month sentence. So, you know some more of my *ugly past. Why it's so hard to forgive myself, cause of what I am.* I'm sorry!

I agree with you, the Lord is being good to you. He knows how much your dad meant to you and how special his hugs were to you. It's no coincidence when your dad comes back to you in your dreams that he always ends up hugging you. That sure is something. To me, more proof there is a God.

I've been "back sliding" the past couple weeks. Also when I do these sins, it does bother me afterward. Satan just won't let go of me, pitiful. One of my New Year's resolutions is to read the Bible *every day.* Plus to accept Jesus as my Savior. I know you'll pray that these resolutions will not be forsaken. But I know I can't be a convict (my convict principle) and be a Christian, so the war within myself continues.

I have to close as I hear the guards making their last round to pick up mail. Tell Michelle and everybody "hi." You all take care!

Love,
Larry

*****

January 9, 1996

Dear Larry,

Boy, was I *disappointed* that we weren't home to get your phone call on New Year's Eve! And you're right—we sure would have been surprised. It would have been the perfect way to end the year! Michelle and I hope it works out that you can call again sometime.

Dave and I went with another couple out to eat and then to Gull Lake Bible Conference for a concert that started at 8:30 p.m. and were gone until around 11 p.m. If I had any idea you were going to call, I would have changed plans and been home. Michelle was with my mom. Gregg and Jenny were home all evening since Gregg ended up getting a bad case of the flu on New Year's Eve. He didn't remember getting a call that night when I asked him about it. Do you suppose the guard may have called the wrong number?

I'm sorry that there was so much time between letters that you thought something was wrong. Things got really hectic at the end of the semester for me. Then with Christmas thrown in also, it was hard to find the time to write. I'll try to be more prompt so you don't have to wonder.

I'm glad the holidays are over. They were fun but way too busy. By New Year's Eve Day, I had really *had* it. Everyone thought I was their waitress, and I was getting no help. When I gave them the shocking news that I would not be cooking on New Year's Day, I think everyone took the hint because I started getting more help. The pizza was delicious on New Year's—especially since I didn't have to fix it! Michelle and I spent New Year's afternoon watching part 1 of *Scarlett*, the sequel to *Gone with the Wind*. I felt like a queen just kicking back and relaxing most of the day. The next day, Michelle and I indulged again and watched the three-hour part 2. Since I had read the book, it was fun to see it on video even though it wasn't exactly like the book.

Please don't get in trouble that will send you back to the "hole" over the crocheted verse picture that I didn't get. I'd feel *really* bad if you did. Enclosed is a $20 money order to help make up for your loss. Would you please consider the case closed? I understand about it being the principle of the matter that bothers you. But you'll end up a double loser if you fight him! And it still won't solve the problem.

In your last letter, you stated that you had been backsliding for the last couple of weeks and that these sins bother you. I was actually happy to read those words. If you had backslidden and didn't feel bad at all, I would question whether God was still working in your life. The fact that you are bothered is proof that God is at work making you feel the way you do! Just keep talking to God regularly and ask Him to help you through the struggles you are having about others and Him caring for you and to keep melting your heart so you can accept His love and forgiveness. Remember God will forgive you even if you can't forgive yourself.

What great New Year's resolutions—to read your Bible every day and to accept Jesus as your Savior! I'll be praying that you'll be able to keep them. If you reverse the order and accept Jesus first, reading your Bible will probably come easier because you'll have Him to encourage and prompt you to do so.

You commented that you can't be a convict and be a Christian too. Please read the enclosed devotional entitled "He Wants the Site." The point it makes is that when Christ comes into a life, He builds a new life for the person. That message is also found in 2 Corinthians 5:17: "When someone becomes a Christian, he becomes a brand new person inside. He is not the same anymore. A new life has begun!" (TLB). In your case, you will still be in prison and still be a convict in society's eyes; however, you will definitely change on the inside. God can take away your "convict principle" and help you think differently. I'm sure you think it is impossible to ever think differently than you do now, but with God's help, it is possible (*"For with God, all things are possible,"* Matthew 19:26b NCV). However, you won't know what I'm saying until *after* you accept Christ. So actually, God doesn't care what you are now or how bad you are (or think you are) because He has other plans for you anyway. With His help, you can think, act, and react in a different mode even though the convict principle seems so inbred in you. Tell me what you think after you read the devotional.

Many people in the Bible were radically changed after Jesus "touched" their lives. Luke 7:36–50 describes a sinful woman who was in sad shape. She needed Jesus's help to change from her sinful ways. From the moment Jesus touched her life and forgave her of her sins, she was a dramatically changed woman. Her gratefulness to Jesus for his forgiveness and love for her led her to bring a jar of expensive perfume and wash his feet with it. The men who were with Jesus still saw her as her former sinful self and asked Him how He could allow her to touch Him. Notice Jesus's response in verse 47: "I tell you that her many sins are forgiven, so she showed great love. But the person who is forgiven only a little will love only a little." (NCV)

Even though Jesus had already forgiven her, He said out loud that she was forgiven for the benefit of those men who were in the room questioning Him. But remember that Jesus Himself freely said that her sins were *many*. But that didn't stop Him from loving and forgiving her. What this means to me is that those who may feel they least deserve God's forgiveness are usually the ones who love Him most after their conversion because of their deep gratitude for the way He has changed their lives.

Also, read the story of the prodigal (wayward) son in Luke 15:11–32. Put yourself in the place of that son who ran away, squandered his inheritance, and committed all kinds of sin. He didn't feel he was worthy to be forgiven by his father. But notice his father's reaction when he saw him coming down the road to home! He ran to him, hugged him, and threw a big party in his honor to show that he still loved him. It didn't matter to the father whether his son deserved forgiveness or not. God feels the same about you as that father felt about his remorseful son.

Did you get the book *The Jesus I Never Knew*? If so, have you had a chance to read any of it yet? Let me know what you think about it, and think about what I have shared with you.

Have you heard how your mom is doing after her surgery? I'm sure it will be hard to be off her foot for a few weeks. Does she have someone to help her out during that time? It'll probably be a long month for you and her without a visit. I'm glad she and Steve got to visit on the twenty-fourth since it was so close to Christmas.

I'm going cross-country skiing tomorrow, so I'll be wearing the hat you sent. I don't have to worry about messing up my hair since it will be after work, and I get my hair done the next morning! Aren't I vain!

Did I tell you that Dave and I are going to Hawaii for nine nights in May for our twenty-fifth anniversary? We have our reservations all made! I wish we didn't have to wait four months to use them. We're staying three nights on each of the major islands. By May, I'm sure I'll be ready to get away as soon as the semester ends.

Well, guess I'll have to go for now since Dave is waiting to use the computer. I'll be praying that you experience Jesus's special touch in your life real soon also. Why? Because I care about you!

Goodbye for now!

Love,
Erin

*****

January 23, 1996
Dear Erin,

Sorry I haven't written in a while. I've become so lazy. I even got all my hair cut off last week so I don't have to comb it any more. (I wasn't anyways.) Just don't feel like doing much.

While playing basketball a couple weeks ago, I jumped up for the ball and came down on another guy's foot and badly injured my left ankle. My foot looked like I had an elephant foot. ☺ It is still swollen and hurts but is getting better. The red and purple-like bruises are just about gone. Even my toes had turned purple. I know why athletes say they would rather break the bone than strain it like this. The doctor said I won't be able to get any outdoor exercise for at least a month. ☹

By now you should've received the crocheted "verse" of Jeremiah 29:11. I wrote about it in my last letter, and to my surprise the guy sent it over a couple of days later. I won't have to go to the "hole" for 30 days now. ☺ I am sending your $20 back. I had a feeling you'd send it to me to try to prevent me from fighting the guy. So now you will have your gift and your $20 back. I couldn't keep your money as the "verse" was a gift from me. I did not think it would take so long when I asked you to send your favorite verse to me. I hope you like it. You have to put something behind it to make the writing stand out. Some of these guys said to use black velvet. Just think that guy made it out of thread!

I received the book, *The Jesus I Never Knew*. Thanks. Since I've been laid up, I'm almost finished reading it. I like the author's style of writing and haven't had any problems comprehending it. Plus it has brought me closer to Jesus. Chapter 7, "Message: A Sermon of Offense" gave me hope. The chapter was all about Jesus's Sermon on the Mount. The author's interpretation of it is the way I've always interpreted it. My hope came when I read, "Blessed are the poor in spirit, for theirs is the kingdom of heaven." (Matthew 5:3 KJV) Of course, I might be interpreting that wrong. I sure hope not.

During the last few days, Georgia has had some Michigan weather. These southerners "freak out" when they receive a little snow and cold weather. The East coast sure got hit hard. How is the weather in Michigan?

Mom's January 8 foot surgery was postponed until the 16th but got postponed again cause she was too weak. Since she was planning on visiting me during the recent three-day weekend and didn't come, I knew something was wrong. When I called, she told me that she was in the hospital where they gave her IV fluids for her dehydration caused by the flu. She said she would try to visit this past weekend but could not make it. Rob, however, got his driver's license back after paying the court's $510 fine. It sure was nice to see him again as it was the first time in over six months.

Well, our man, the representative in the GA's legislature who was suppose to introduce a bill to change our method of execution so we could donate our organs, did it. What a joke though. I don't know where he got it, but his method of execution so we could donate is the guillotine. My lawyer informed me today that the legislature voted "no." I told him I feel like I was tricked into signing my appeal papers cause of this issue as it wasn't given much of an effort. I also feel that people who are on the "organ waiting list" should've been able to testify on the issue. It could've really helped to see real and hurting people who probably will die cause of the shortage of organs. Plus the "cold statistics" should've been presented on how many people on the waiting list will die before their name comes up for an organ. Sad.

Would you go see a newly released movie *Dead Man Walking*? It's a true story about a death-row inmate and a nun who tries to convert the inmate. All the reviews I've read said it's a very powerful movie and expect to cry. Cause of the context of the movie, I think you shouldn't go by yourself but take Dave or Gregg with you. I know the violence in it will upset you, but this is reality. I will understand, however, if you don't think you can go.

So you and Dave are going to Hawaii in May for your 25th anniversary, huh? Not too many marriages make it that long anymore! You all should have a very good time being in that beautiful place. It will definitely be warmer than Michigan! You will need the time away to relax after getting through Gregg and Jenny's wedding. ☺

I want to write Michelle so I'll let you go. Boy, I sure got a smile out of the pictures she sent from Christmas. Enclosed is a recent picture of Mom and my brother Rob. I would like to have it back in your next letter.

Love,
Larry

*****

February 3, 1996
Dear Larry,

It's early Saturday morning, and I am the only one up. I've got a Christian radio station playing in the background and have this special time to think and write you. It's a perfect day to be inside with a cup of hot tea and a blanket wrapped around me since the thermometer is reading -14! Brrrr! I may just hibernate today!

Have you heard from your mom? Has she had her foot surgery yet? If so, hopefully, she made it safely through it and is feeling much better by now. I can imagine how good it was to see Rob again after such a long time! Has he gotten a chance to visit again?

I absolutely *love* my crocheted verse! I haven't had a chance yet to find black velvet backing for it. I want to frame it and hang it in a special spot where I can see it often *since it speaks to my heart.* Dave said that he may be able to make a frame. You will never know how much it means to me! It amazes me how someone can crochet such an intricate pattern and have it come out so good. Most of all, I am glad it came so you won't be going to the "hole" over it!

I'm glad *The Jesus I Never Knew* book has brought you closer to Jesus and given you hope. One of my prayers for you has been for you to experience hope. I'm sure you haven't misinterpreted the message from the "Sermon on the Mount"—especially the verse about the "poor in spirit." I can understand how you feel about getting to help some people if you are allowed to donate your organs so that you can feel better about yourself and feel you've made a difference in others' lives. Just remember that God doesn't require it in order to forgive you. His love is given unconditionally with no strings attached. It's so exciting to see my prayers being answered! I strongly feel that before long you're going to take the final step to accept God's forgiveness and surrender your life to Him.

What a bummer that you sprained your ankle playing basket-ball and have to be off it for at least a month and miss your outdoor time that you enjoy so much. I am happy, however, that it appears to be starting to heal. You will definitely have plenty of time to read and write.

It's incredible that your representative would offer the guillotine as a method of execution so that death-row inmates would be allowed to donate their organs! That sounds like a Middle Ages method of execution and just as barbaric as the electric chair. No wonder it didn't pass in the legislature.

What a nice picture of your mom and Rob! Thanks for sending it to me. I have not seen either of them in a long time. I am sending it back as you asked. I know it must be one of your favorite pictures.

I am sorry to tell you that I will not be able to go see the *Dead Man Walking* movie because I do not feel I can handle it emotionally.

Seeing someone being mistreated in any way is hard for me to watch. I leave the room if a prison movie is on TV. My heart hurts enough to know you will be dying before long. You said that you would understand if I could not go.

It is only two and a half months now until Gregg and Jenny's wedding. I have been keeping busy getting the guest list for our side of the family put together and thinking about lots of other details. Uppermost in my mind is how hard it will be when Gregg moves out. I know it will be quite an adjustment for me that I am not looking forward to going through. Every parent has to experience children leaving home, but it does not mean we have to *like* it. The good thing is that they will be living close by.

I thought you might like the enclosed page of cartoons out of one of my magazines. They made Michelle and me laugh. A laugh a day is good for the soul!

Well, everyone's up now, and it's time to get breakfast, so guess I better go. Write again soon! And keep praying!

Love,
Erin

*****

February 11, 1996
Dear Erin,

Hope this letter finds you all well. I'm not. I'm writing this from the "hole." Got into a fight, went to Disciplinary Court, and was given 30 days. ☹ I think I lost control cause I was frustrated that I didn't get a visit over the weekend. I realize Mom can't visit regularly because of her poor health. No excuse for my three brothers though. It really hurts me when I don't receive a visit. They mean so much to me! Plus we aren't going to be able to have many more cause I don't have much longer to live.

I called Mom the night before I began my 30 days, and she cried when I informed her I would be going to the "hole," which made me cry. Plus I found out she was going into the hospital the following morning. When I had a lawyer visit, he informed me that the surgery went as well as expected. She has to use a walker and crutches for over a month. That will sure be hard on her too. Pitiful.

I'm kinda glad I'm here in the "hole." I was getting behind in my letter writing and not reading the Bible like I should have. So now I'll be able to do both. While in my regular cell, I was reading two newspapers a day, watching TV, playing cards—worldly things. (The devil had control.) But now I can't do any of the above things. *God has made me time to read the Bible and other religious material.* So, I'm not upset for being over here like I was last time. I sneaked in with my legal material (which we are allowed to bring with us) your last letter. I got to bring my Bible but not any other religious material, so please send me some more because I know we were allowed to have them last time I was here. I've already written the chaplain to send me some things to read too.

A friend from a Michigan prison wrote me and told me that another woman guard was killed in one of Michigan's prisons, *sad.* I do not understand why the state has women work in maximum security prisons. It's the same as if you have them working on "death row." Since Michigan is a not a death sentence state, the maximum sentence for murder is "life." Those with life sentences (murderers, rapists, etc.) are kept in the maximum security section of the prison. These men have nothing to lose by raping and/or killing a woman guard, as they know with their "life" sentence they aren't ever getting released from prison anyways. Women should work in medium and minimum security prisons. The inmates there don't have much time left to serve before being released so are more than likely not going to hurt a female guard. If they do, they will lose their upcoming freedom.

I was in the maximum security prison in Marquette, Michigan, when they hired their first two female guards. One could've been accepted to pose in Playboy. The other one looked like she was a former beauty queen. I couldn't believe it. Cause of the job I had, I ended up a few times being alone with one of them. Lucky for her I wasn't one of the many rapists and murderers they had there!

On the flip side, do you remember that there was a string of rapes and murders over two years in the late 1960s that took place in the college town of Ypsilanti, Michigan? John Norman Collins was eventually arrested and convicted of being the "Co-Ed Killer" and sentenced to life in prison. He turned out to be a young, good-looking college kid. I did years with him in Marquette. He still swears that he's "innocent." I kind of believed him since they convicted him on "circumstantial evidence." He deeply loved his mother, was always helping other inmates, showed no trace of any violence or never argued. But the day those two female guards started working I knew he was "guilty." We were eating together at the table when he saw one of them. I couldn't believe how the expression on his face and eyes changed while looking at her. Like I said, it left me with no doubt he was guilty.

Mom has been writing long letters. ☺ She is laid up too so writing is no problem for her. So far the foot is coming along. She goes back to the doctor to have it examined this week. She is now trying to quit smoking. She said when she woke up in the recovery room after her foot surgery that she was close to death and it scared her. So she prayed to Jesus and also decided to stop smoking. ☺ Every time she writes, she brags on how many days she's been without a cigarette. I sure pray to Jesus asking Him to become a bigger part of her life and give her strength to quit smoking. As for me, my foot is better but the swelling around the ankle bone hasn't gone completely down.

Well, I've rambled on long enough. But I passed a lot of time. ☺ Would you believe I've written 38 letters so far? I think I might reach 100 before I am out of the "hole." Tell Michelle and everyone I said "hi." You are all in my prayers! Thanks for caring.

Love,
Larry

*****

February 13, 1996
Dear Erin,

I know that I just wrote you two days ago. Do not think that you have to write me right back since I know your schedule. I have more free time than you. ☺

You won't believe what just happened! A guard just opened my door. He had with him the *Beautiful Picture* and *Valentine's Day Card*. He gave me both and told me to sign the "Rejection Form" since I couldn't have the picture and could have my mother pick it up when she visits again. I have that Beautiful Picture in my hands. I see it's only on cardboard. So I tell him, "I can understand why I can't have it here in the "hole" but why not when I get out. It's only made of cardboard." He takes it from me and looks on the back and sides of it. He told me to sign the Rejection Form, which I did *slowly*. He then circles on the form the space that tells what to do with the rejected item the word "destroyed." Before I could say anything, *he gave it back to me*! I said to him, I know I can't have it in the "hole" and will keep it hid, but when I get back to my cell, I want to display it." He said, "OK." and left. So the prison officials will think it was destroyed but instead it will be *displayed in my cell so everybody can see it!*

After he left, I sat down. Really looked at it. Read the poem. And cried. (No kidding!) It means so much to me, what it represents to me that Jesus will be hugging me like that real soon! I spotted Jesus' head and hands as well as a dove in the clouds at my first glance of it. There is a rainbow that stretches from one end of his hand to the other hand too. I think it seems more realistic cause this picture was painted (even though it is a copy) by hands. Sure wish I could take it up to the visitor room to show my visitors.

When I die, my mom will have it. I'll write some words on the back of it. To comfort her, telling her don't be sad cause I'm gone. I left all this pain and suffering and now I'm here in heaven waiting on you. That's not the exact words, but it will be close. So again, out of my heart, I sure thank you and Michelle! It's so beautiful and means so much to me!

Thanks also for the article by Billy Graham, "The Reason We Have Hope." I really enjoyed it! I'm sending it to Mom too. The other article, "A Doctor Meets the Great Physician," amazed me at how God literally changes completely a person's life. I wish it would've happened to me many years ago. I realize it's still not too late for me but look at all the pain and grief I caused others and myself which wouldn't have happened if I had God in my life many years ago, sad.

I remember my grandma telling me all about heaven when I was a kid. After we talked for a while, she asked did I want to go to church with her on Sunday. Being filled with what she had just told me, I couldn't wait. Come Sunday when she called Mom to see if I was ready for church, I begged my way out of it. The devil had me under his control again.

I've finished reading in the Old Testament about Moses and Sampson. Reading about David's life now. I am glad I have my Bible here.

Well, I'll close. Y'all take care. Thanks so much for caring and your prayers. You are in my prayers too!

Love,
Larry

*****

February 18, 1996
Dear Larry,

I was surprised to get two letters from you so close together! You've really been keeping that pen moving lately—thirty-eight letters! I bet you will hit a hundred by the time you get out. I have to say, however, that I think I have been rubbing off on you—your letters are getting to be more like the "books" I have written to you in the past! ☺ Doesn't your hand start to bother you after writing so much? It makes my thumb ache to even think about writing that many letters! But I agree with you that it does help to pass the time. Plus, it is always nice to hear from you!

You do not know how happy I am that the guard allowed you to have the picture that I sent you for Valentine's Day. I was holding my breath after I learned that you were in the hole and was afraid you might not be able to have it. I saw that picture quite a long time ago at our Christian bookstore, but it was framed—and I knew you could not have that. Just recently, I found the picture version only and knew that you needed to have it. I was right since it touched your heart so much! I am praising Jesus for sending that particular guard to deliver your mail that day. Your deep expression of appreciation touched my heart deeply!

You remarked that "God has made me time to read the Bible and other religious material" and that "the devil had control" when you were in your regular cell. Then when you looked at the picture of Jesus hugging the man as He welcomes him into heaven, you commented, "Jesus will be hugging me like that real soon." Those remarks are ones that a Christian would make. Have you—perhaps subconsciously in your heart—made the decision to come over to Christ's side? If so, be sure you settle that issue with Christ and make it official and final. Realizing you feel God has His hand in your being in the hole and that you were not as upset this time shows me that you are maturing in your faith. I know you must be really lonely, but God can use this uninterrupted time of Bible reading and prayer to allow you to get to know Him better. He can make some dramatic changes in your thinking and will continue working in you. The prayer you prayed almost two years ago for Him to show you that He is real is being answered.

It was interesting what you wrote about the serial killer who you were in jail with in Marquette. So many times, it seems like the most unlikely person turns out to be the killer. After you observed him when a female guard was hired, I'm sure you could tell what he was really like. I also cannot understand why females would want to be guards—especially in male prisons. I could understand it more in an all-female prison. Everyone, however, has his/her own ideas about what profession to pursue. I would not choose to be a prison guard though.

You must be enjoying those long letters from your mom! I am glad she came through her surgery okay. She must have had a pretty rough time immediately after the surgery to have been near death. Such an experience does make one think about Jesus and want to get one's life straightened out. Quitting smoking will be a big step for her. I'll be praying along with you for her. Tell her that I'd be glad to send her some Christian literature if she'd like it.

Jenny and Gregg are on their way back right now from Grand Rapids with their new wire fox terrier puppy. They are leaning toward naming it Thunder or Lightning. Since they plan on having two, the dogs' names would go together—Thunder and Lightning. It'll be interesting to see how Ginger reacts since the puppy will be at our house a majority of the time. Jenny's dad will allow it to be at their house for no longer than two weeks and only when she is there. Michelle thinks Ginger will feel like her nose has been cut off! Gregg had hoped he would be moved into an apartment by the time the two-week period was up so he could take care of the puppy, but it doesn't look like that will be happening until a little later since they don't have a prospective place to live yet.

Michelle had today off school so we went out to lunch at the mall after I got home. We finished lunch off at the Dairy Queen and got a fattening dessert! Actually, mine was no fat and no cholesterol since I got yogurt. Can't gain any weight before the wedding!

Speaking of the wedding, which is now only two months away, I found a cream color, ankle-length, Victorian-style dress the other day that I really like and thought would look appropriate for the mother of the groom. Since the bridesmaids are wearing ankle-length dresses, I thought it would fit in good. I'll send you some snapshots from the wedding so you can get a better idea of what it is like. The bridesmaids are wearing hunter green. Next week, I'm taking a day off work to go dress shopping with my mom to help her find something. It'll be good to have a day off.

Well, Dave just pulled in the driveway from work, so I need to be signing off. Write again soon. And thanks for remembering all of us in your prayers. Things have been quite hectic with wedding plans!

Love,
Erin

*****

February 25, 1996
Dear Erin,

So Gregg and Jenny are getting a puppy, huh? And it will be at your house most of the time? I agree with Michelle that Ginger may be jealous of this intruder on her turf. Did they name the puppy Thunder or Lightning? How is the potty training going? Be sure to send me some pictures. I love dogs!

Did your mom find a dress for the wedding? Your dress sounds beautiful. You know that I will expect lots of pictures from the wedding. Sure wish I could be there. How are you holding up emotionally with it getting closer to the wedding?

You asked if I had come over to Christ's side in your last letter. I have had lots of time to think about your question. I would have to answer "Yes." As they would say in Star Wars, I came over from the "dark" side. I didn't want to tell you or anybody that I've accepted Jesus Christ as my Savior until I could say it comes from 100% of my heart. Otherwise, God will know my words are not 100% true. I don't like hypocrites (I know that's a sin), and I don't want to be one.

Every time I sneak a look at the picture of Jesus you sent, I can feel that I am going to have Jesus welcoming me to heaven like the man in the picture. I'm sure when I get back to my regular cell and display it, I'll have offers to buy it. No amount of money can buy it! Besides how much it means to me, I told you of my plans for it after I'm gone. Mom will have it with my personal message on the back of it. When she dies, another family member will have it. I assure you it will be in our family for many years, hopefully forever. You and Michelle are the ones who helped the most in saving me and stuck with me when I was being a "doubting Thomas." I'll give you two a big hug when we meet in heaven. ☺ ☺ I will still need your prayers to live like a Christian in the time I have left.

Thanks for the puzzles that you and Michelle have sent me to do while in the "hole." I bought some onion skin paper and carbon paper to make copies of some of them. When I go to the shower on Tuesday, Thursday, and Saturday, I slide the puzzles under other guy's doors. It gives them something to pass time, plus I pass time making copies. I am going to pass around the Billy Graham articles you sent to me too so others can read them.

I look forward to every letter I get, especially when I am in the "hole." My mom has not written to me so much in a long time. Since she is laid up, she now has plenty of time. I sure will be looking forward to her next visit! She is healing good after her surgery, which is a relief to me since I worry so much about her.

Would you believe that I have written so many letters that I am going to have to declare "bankruptcy"? If you do not hear from me for a while, it will be because I have run out of stamps.

I need to close now since mail will be picked up very soon and I want you to have the answer to your question you asked about me being a Christian! You all take care. Thanks again for your prayers and for never giving up on me.

Love,
Larry

Think About It: Surrender

Have you ever fought a tough battle that seemed impossible to win? An addiction? Anger? Low self-esteem? Compulsive lying? Hatred? Abuse? Suicidal thoughts? Feeling unlovable? Is your battle not listed? What is it?

No one is immune to fighting life's battles. It is not uncommon to feel that you are fighting them all on your own. When the "enemy's" attacks are relentless and the battle is hard and exhausting, do you wish for a battle partner, someone to "cover your back" and help you defeat the enemy? It is possible for that to happen, but first, you must decide if it is time to pick up and wave your "white flag of surrender."

Surrender is most commonly used as a verb denoting some action one needs to take. The action necessary is "to yield (something) to the possession or power of another."[66] For many, surrendering is extremely hard. Why? If I were to guess, it is because of pride and the idea that no one else is going to control their lives. If you fall into this category, let me ask, "How is it working for you?"

From Larry's letters, it was evident that being in control of his own life certainly did not work well for him. Instead, it brought him a lot of mental anguish and physical pain. For most of his life, he lost his personal freedom through incarceration. He admits to being controlled by Satan. Until he waved the "white flag of surrender," he lived a life without hope. He did, however, gradually take on the challenge of searching for God despite his spirit of unbelief and the notion that he was too bad to ever be forgiven even if such a God existed. His search, however, was rewarded with an assurance that there *is* a God who truly loved him and wanted to forgive him. Christ had already won Larry's battles against Satan when He died on the cross. Finally, he laid down his "weapon" of denial that kept forgiveness always out of his reach.

My personal journey to know the Lord was *much* different than Larry's. Even though I did not grow up in a Christian home the first ten years of my life, I had opportunities to go to a weekly children's Bible club in my neighborhood and to vacation bible school every summer. During those times, I heard many Bible stories, memorized Scripture verses, and, most importantly, learned about Jesus and His death on the cross for my sins. A bus from a local church picked my brother and me up on Sunday mornings and took us to Sunday school and church, where we further learned truths from the Bible.

Until I was ten years old, I knew all the stories and what one needed to do to go to heaven but had never made it personal. I knew, however, that I definitely did *not* want to go to hell. Because of my fear of going to hell, I wanted to be sure I asked Jesus to be my Savior but did not know what age one had to be to make that commitment. I did not know then that as soon as an individual understands the need for salvation, God holds him/her accountable as to whether His gift is accepted. I had been told the age of accountability was around ten or eleven. Because I have never been a risk-taker, I invited Jesus into my life right after I turned ten. At that time, my parents had started going to the church where they were married. When the pastor gave the invitation to come forward and become a Christian, I could not get down the aisle fast enough. The emotion I remember the most was "relief" that I would be going to heaven and can remember feeling like a big burden had been lifted from me. I felt so good inside and was very happy. I had the good fortune to grow up in the church and to eventually have Christian parents who loved and encouraged me.

What opposite ends of the spectrum Larry and I experienced as we grew up! Your life journey may have put you somewhere in the middle of the spectrum. Life experiences will be as unique as each individual. Even though we are each unique, we all, however, have one thing in common—our need to make the decision to whom we will commit our lives to, Christ or Satan. Christ, as our Creator, loves each of us equally—*regardless* of our background—and *wants* us to choose Him so He can shower on us the same love, mercy, and grace He gave Larry. He will not, however, *force* Himself on anyone but gives us a free will to accept or reject Him. Since you have read this book, you now *know* what is required to become one of Christ's children and will be held accountable for the decision you make.

What about you? Have you made the *most important* decision of your life yet? If not, did Larry's journey give you some hope? Are you ready to change your life direction and follow after Christ? If so, *surrender* is necessary. After reading about Larry's struggles, are you ready to surrender or at least think more about it? What does surrender require?

> *S*top believing Satan's lies.
> *U*nderstand your sin does not have to forever define you.
> *R*elease the excuses that are holding you back.
> *R*ealize Jesus died to forgive all your sins.
> *E*nd your struggle to live life "your way."
> *N*ever tell yourself you are a hopeless case.
> *D*etermine to believe John 3:16 is the truth and accept that it includes you.
> *E*nter into the salvation and peace only Jesus provides.
> *R*est in the arms of God's love and the hope of a future home in heaven.*

If you could sit across the table from Larry and have a face-to-face discussion after he has experienced heaven, what do you think he might say to you? Do you think he would tell you that surrender was the best decision he ever made? Just one look at his face would, I believe, be all the answer you would need to those questions!

*Many Scripture verses were mentioned throughout the book about salvation that comes through surrender. If you do not have a personal relationship with Christ, go to the topical Scripture verse appendix at the end of the book and read the salvation verses listed. If you make the decision to surrender but are not sure how to pray, the sample prayer below would be sufficient.

> *Dear Jesus, I know I have done wrong things that You call sin. I am sorry and ask Your forgiveness for all that I have done in the past. I believe you are God's Son and died a very horrible death on the cross to pay for my sins so that I can have a home in heaven when I die. I also believe that You rose from the dead and are now in heaven waiting for me. Please accept me as Your son (daughter) and help me to live the rest of my life for You. Thank you for loving me so much to die for me.*

Note from the Author

Have you ever heard of someone's conversion to Christianity (especially a prisoner's) and wondered if it was real and if there would be a change in that person's life? I have. Keep reading to learn if Larry's conversion was sincere, how he handled his newfound faith, and if he experienced the peace he was seeking.

Chapter 18

March 3, 1996

Dear Larry,

As I write this letter, you should now be out of the hole! ☺☺

To hear you say that you will be going to heaven really thrilled my heart! That is the *best* gift I'll *ever* receive from you! I liked your comment comparing you with "doubting Thomas." Yes, I agree. It does sound like you. I'm just *so* happy and relieved, though, that you, like doubting Thomas, didn't let your doubts stand in your way of accepting Christ. You and Thomas should have a good long talk when you get to heaven. And I *will* be waiting for that big hug when *we* meet in heaven.

Your comments about the picture meaning so much to you and your future plans for it touched my heart. How wonderful if it could stay in the family as a memory of you and a reminder that your family can choose heaven too. When I shared your initial comments from February 13 with Dave, would you believe he was so touched that he had tears in his eyes—as did I when I read them. I *know* the Lord prodded me to send that picture to you and then worked out all the details so you were allowed to have it! When our hearts are touched in that way by a picture, it is clearly the Lord speaking to us.

Would you do me a favor? After you greet your grandpa and grandma (and Jesus, of course), would you find my dad and give him a big hug for me and tell him how much I love him? He went so fast, and I was so choked up when he started having his heart problems that I couldn't get the words out—all I could do was hold and hug him. He knew I loved him, but I always wished had been able to tell him one last time.

Enclosed are a couple of pictures of Lightning. They named him correctly—he's sure active! It's almost worse than having a toddler around because he has to be watched so closely. (He loves to relieve himself on the carpet!) At first, Ginger was scared of the puppy but now just tolerates him. However, since he is such an "in your face" dog, her patience wears thin—as does mine. Gregg wasn't around yesterday, so I put him in his cage so Ginger and I could "relax" for a bit before I left to teach my night class. However, I had to listen to him whine for over two hours! He loves to chew and follows us around trying to bite at our feet and clothes. Today, when he disappeared for a while, he had chewed the cover of a new book that I was reading and had left laying on the floor. Ginger never did things like that. I have to remember to put everything up! We have him at our house a majority of the time. Oh well, I guess we'll survive. Thanks for listening to me vent (as if you had a choice!). He really is cute—when someone else is taking care of him!

Gregg and Jenny put in an application for a one-bedroom apartment that will be available on March 18, accepts pets, and is only about five minutes away from us. However, they have to pay $10 more a month for having a dog. Gregg is hoping that they'll only have to be in this apartment for about six months. I think they'll be there longer. I'm skeptical how Lightning is going to do in an apartment because when he's left alone and hears anyone around, he starts whining and barking. The neighbors probably won't like that for too long. For Gregg and Jenny's sake, I hope he outgrows this phase.

Michelle is excited to start track on Monday. She's stayed after school to run several days the last two weeks in order to get somewhat in shape. She ran two and a half miles on Wednesday! She had auditions for chairs in band again, and she and another gal tied for first chair. The other gal gets to sit in first-chair position though since the band director said that she had a better mark on tone. Michelle is okay with the decision and is glad to have first chair back.

I trust the enclosed *Far Side* cartoon will give you a smile and that the inspirational card will be an encouragement. You said that when you are in a regular cell, Satan makes it hard for you by providing so many distractions. At times when you feel he is trying to overwhelm you, read this card and call upon Jesus for strength to resist him.

By now, you should have had a visit from your mother. After being over a month since you saw her, I imagine you had a lot to catch up on. I am happy that her foot is doing better.

So you are close to declaring "bankruptcy" after writing so many letters, huh? In the next day or two, I'm going to send you a money order to help buy some stamps and to treat yourself to some goodies.

Michelle said, "Hi," and that she'll write again as soon as she finds time. Her class is the first graduating class that has to take proficiency exams in English, math, and science in order to get a state-endorsed diploma. They give them in the eleventh grade—probably so they can have another chance if they don't pass. The next two weeks is devoted to only the English portion of the exam.

Since I need to grade some papers and update the wedding guest list, I will close for now. It's hard to believe the wedding is only seven weeks away! I'm getting more used to the idea, though, as time passes!

Take care. Keep reading your Bible and praying. Write again soon! We will definitely keep praying for you!

Love,
Erin

*****

March 17, 1996
Dear Erin,

It was sure good talking to you and Michelle. Now you know how badly I talk. Just wish I could've expressed myself better, sorry.

Let me explain what I was trying to tell you about the Apostle Paul's epistles when we talked. After I finished reading the gospels while in the "hole," I started on Paul's letters. But I was having trouble understanding them in the King James Version of the Bible and gave up. I prayed that God would allow me to be able to understand Paul's words better. Then I received an article from a friend about the reading difficulty of the different Bible translations—the KJV is written at a 12th grade level. That article prompted me to remember the chaplain sent me a *New Life Study Testament*. When I started reading it, I was happy that it was in a style of writing I'm having no difficulty comprehending. ☺ So God answered my prayer!! Wouldn't you agree? I finished reading all of Paul's epistles that day!

Would you do something for me? I'd like you to help me write my final statement. I can't express myself well, you can. ☺ I'll be writing different thoughts and words I'd like to state, but I need an organizer to put them together. It would take me many pages of words to express it in my own words (because I ramble). You will be able to make it a lot shorter, clearer, and more meaningful. This means a lot to me cause it will be aired and printed. I'd like to touch some people's hearts so hopefully they'll change their wrong beliefs about capital punishment and what a *real Christian* is.

I got out of the "hole" on Friday, February 23. Mom visited me on Sunday. It was *so* good to see her! She brought me one of her egg sandwiches that I love by hiding it in her bra. ☺

I received a message on the 14th to call my lawyer. No doubt in my mind it was to inform me of the US Supreme Court's ruling since that's how I'll get the news first. However, it wasn't that news. He informed me to watch the evening news cause there would be a story about a person who sent a letter to the Parole and Pardon Board back in June when I was scheduled to die supporting my desire to donate my organs. He stated that he would like my kidneys as both of his are in bad shape. If he doesn't receive a kidney soon, he'll die. He's on a dialysis machine now. He didn't want the publicity, so his lawyer kept his name anonymous. When their effort to get the State to allow me to donate a kidney before my execution failed, they decided to go public. Their interview will be on the evening news.

I watched it. What makes it even more unusual and why the media picked it up too is that the man who wants my kidney *helped put me here on death row*. He's a former (retired) chief of detectives with 30 years of being a police officer. During the early news broadcast, his lawyer stated how the Attorney General's office just informed him that I wouldn't be allowed to donate my kidney, no explanation given. The former detective went into details of his condition and how he couldn't understand why they wouldn't allow me to donate my kidney. He risked his life and served the State for 30 years, and now the State won't help him. They then showed some tapes of me.

Well, after the story was on TV, calls from the public started coming in. The 11 p.m. news had an explanation from the Department of Corrections. They stated I was too "dangerous" to be taken to a hospital to have the surgery. Makes sense to the public. Of course, they didn't mention how GA's Department of Correction has a prison hospital where all our surgeries are performed. I was taken there once. So I could have the surgery there with no threat to the public. But, like I just stated, they didn't mention that.

The following day the Associated Press published a short article with this statement: "Larry Lonchar, 44, plans to ask the court to allow him to donate a kidney to Melvin Ferguson, the 60-year-old retired chief of detectives who helped tie Lonchar to a 1986 triple slaying."[67] Mr. Ferguson said he didn't realize this would get national attention and again went into his feelings on trying to understand why the State won't help him. The State Department of Corrections spokesman was also interviewed and stated how they weren't going to change their decision. "Larry will not be allowed to donate his kidney."[68]

Well, today I received two letters from my lawyer—one was a copy of a letter he sent to GA's Attorney General and the other was a copy of a letter from Dr. Jack Kevorkian stating how he couldn't understand the State's decision and why. Dr. Kevorkian said that an option would be to over anesthetize the inmate, which would kill him, and then harvest the organs when he was officially declared brain dead. That makes sense to me. While watching the evening news, there it was again. They interviewed the detective again, read part of Dr. Kevorkian's letter, and showed the tape of me again too.

My lawyer informed me that *Dateline* wants to do a story on it too. Since they can't interview me in person, they will be in my lawyer's office when I call. That way they can do the interview over the phone. I'm going to discuss this with the prison officials first. I don't want to do it unless they say it's ok, which they probably won't. As I don't want to risk losing my telephone privilege. My monthly calls mean too much to me to lose.

In going through my papers, I found a letter I wrote to the warden in September about organ donation. I thought you would like to read it.

Thank you for the $20. I'm using it to put some weight back on. ☺

Today was yard day. I've told you how deer graze and play in the big field behind the prison. Well, now we have turkeys out there. Last week and today there were at least 30 of them. I sure enjoyed watching them all. I believe a "scout" found this safe area and called all of his relatives to come live here. ☺ My ankle is still swollen after two plus months, so the doctor ordered some x-rays of it. When I go to the yard, I can't play any kind of ball. I just enjoy the fresh air and now the turkeys and deer.

Well, I'll let you go. Sorry for all of the scratch outs. I'm sure struggling with words tonight. Thanks for your caring and your prayers. You all are in my prayers!

Love,
Larry

*****

Dear Warden Thomas,

I'm sure you are well aware of the dire need of organs. Two thousand plus people *die* in just our country each year who were on the "organ waiting list" cause of the shortage of organs. You and Commissioner Ault could *save lives* by allowing me (us) to donate kidneys, bone marrow, blood, and other body items.

Inmate Dobbs was allowed to donate one of his kidneys to his mother a couple years ago. Since I haven't had the opportunity to discuss this with Inmate Dobbs, I've no knowledge where the surgery was performed. I assume it was performed at GA's prison hospital, but the fact is, *it was performed.*

If the surgery wasn't performed at the prison hospital, all future surgery would. That would eliminate the security concern. Also, I'm sure the "Organ Procurement and Transplantation Network" would assist this program (reimbursement of expenses, doctors to perform the surgery, etc.).

I know from the letters I've received that there are men, women, and children out there who face death and *would gladly accept* what I (us) have to offer. Also, not only would this program *save lives*, it would set a precedent, which I'm sure other states would follow (*more lives saved*).

Thank you for your time.

Larry G. Lonchar EF209811 G-4-90
cc: Governor Zell Miller

*****

March 27, 1996
Dear Larry,

What a thrill it was for us to get your call! I thought you expressed yourself very well during our conversation. We were probably all just a bit "nervous" since we rarely get to talk. Your voice reminded me of my dad's side of the family, accent and all. The only problem with the call is that the fifteen minutes went by entirely too fast! I could have talked much longer—but then I like to talk too. I sure hope we get that opportunity again.

I read your letter to the warden and thought you expressed yourself very well. Mentioning possible help from the Organ Procurement and Transplantation Network was very good because their help would remove the cost argument the prison might give. Obviously, however, the minds of the prison officials are very closed on the issue.

You asked in your last letter if I would help you write your final statement. I'd consider it an honor! Just send me your written thoughts that you want expressed, and I'll do my best to help you get them in final form. Let's both pray that the Lord will lead you in what to say that can touch some hearts in a special way and reveal your thoughts about what a real Christian is. You have a great opportunity to impact many lives by what you write—maybe this is how God intends to use you to do something very special with your life and to make an impact on society.

As I was thinking about you today and praying for you, I thought back to the Larry I first started writing three years ago. You are not the same person you were then! I can very clearly see how Christ has been working in your life over the last two years especially. And I praise Him for it! I personally consider it a miracle. Do you? Remember how you said in a few of your letters that you would believe if only you could see a miracle? I certainly have seen one in the great transformation that's taken place in your life!

I've thought of the perfect place to hang the crocheted verse that you sent me—in the upstairs hallway next to my bedroom. Every time I walk upstairs, I'll be able to see it. Now, I just have to find a decent way to frame it. Since Dave is quite handy and enjoys little carpentry projects, he said that he can make me a special frame.

Gregg is now all settled in the apartment. Jenny will move in after the wedding but has been spending her spare time there putting her touches on it. I enjoyed getting to help him move. However, that evening when it was time to leave, I felt a big punch hit my heart that broke a piece of it off! I wanted to grab him and take him back home with me. It just did not seem real that he now had his own place and would never live at our home again. Although I kept a smile on my face when I said good night, inside, my heart was crying. When I got in the car, the tears started flowing. I am *gradually* getting used to him not living with us. The crying spells are less frequent. It helps that Gregg and I have been able to have lunch together at least once a week during the last few weeks, which I have thoroughly enjoyed. We'll probably be able to keep doing that at least until his lawn business starts up after Easter. Then, I know he'll be kept quite busy. I'm hoping that occasionally in the summer I may get to see him by himself every once in a while when Jenny is working. My mother thinks he'll be around quite a bit. We'll see.

The wedding is getting closer—only three weeks away. I think I'm going to do okay emotionally—but still keep praying for me. The church is having a shower for Jenny on April 2. I'm having a hard time not buying too much for them to get started. I got them a big electric griddle for the church shower. Her family is also having a shower. That gave me an excuse to pick up some things for their bathroom medicine cabinet that would cost a lot if they had to go out and buy them. Before I knew it, I had spent $40! My mom told me I had better stay out of stores until after the wedding. I agree!

Since it is almost time for me to go meet my mother to go walking, I need to sign off. I will be looking forward to hearing from you again real soon. And as always, I'm praying for you.

Love,
Erin

*****

April 1, 1996
Dear Erin,

I got the results back from the x-rays of my back and ankle. For the past two weeks I've been taking seven pills three times a day for them. It's sure making me sleep, which is why I'm late in writing this letter. Now I am back to my 1-1/2 anti-depressant pills a day. My back muscles still aren't normal but I can live without taking more pills for it.

I hope the pain in your heart has healed some. I know it hurt when Gregg moved out. Hey, you want me to pray that you won't cry through their wedding ceremony? Why worry or feel bad about that. It's normal. I know things are going to start getting hectic and more tense as the wedding day approaches. So, don't worry about writing me. I sure will understand.

I'm sure you know by now that the U.S. Supreme Court issued their ruling yesterday on allowing me to appeal my case based on the 22 counts of errors in my arrest and conviction and my claim that electrocution is cruel and unusual punishment. I asked for a legal opinion on each of the 22 counts with the hope of delaying my execution long enough to have the legislature change the method of execution so I can possibly donate my organs. Unfortunately, it means that I have to live longer, but it will be worth it if I can make a difference by being an organ donor.

Two lawyers called me when it came over their fax machine. One is visiting me today and bringing me a copy of the 14-page ruling. It is all over the news down here. There was a big article in the paper about the hearing. Another article regarding the victim's daughter, which sure hurt me, was also in the paper. It's so hard for me to believe God or anybody can love and forgive me when I get reminded (like that article) of how much pain I've caused her and others. Sad! Boy I bet there will be some hateful letters about me to the newspaper's "Letters to the Editors" after those articles.

Well, in case you didn't notice by my return address, I'm back in the "hole." The warden on Tuesday morning brought a tour of high school kids through G-4. To me, it's being disrespectful to us. Like we are a zoo. We're the animals in the cages and they are the tourists who come stare at us. So, I said, "Y'all forgot to throw us peanuts." (Like they do at a zoo.) The warden didn't like that. He told me to be quiet, which of course I didn't. I said. "I'm just being honest. Y'all come in here and look at us like animals in cages, so y'all should bring some peanuts for us." I expressed my feelings and always will. So he ordered me moved to the bad cell in the "hole" and charged me with insubordination. If it wasn't the warden involved, I wouldn't even be here until after I went to disciplinary court.

Since I haven't gone to disciplinary court yet, I'm allowed my property. ☺ So, I have my "goodies" and other property. Of course, there's no TV or yard call. Instead of a bed, I have a slab of cement. But with my property, it's not bad. Once I go to disciplinary court and get my sentence, then they'll take all my "goodies" and other property. One thing they won't be able to take from me is my ruling from the Supreme Court that I have not even read yet. I will also get to keep my Bible and pen, paper, and stamps. I'll also write my thoughts for my final statement. Going to re-read the New Testament and use quotes from it to support my feelings and belief.

I sure hope you have a nice Easter! This Easter will mean more to me cause I now believe Jesus did die and was resurrected. I remember when I was young how much I looked forward to Easter but for not the right reason (for the Easter egg hunt and the jelly beans). ☺

Well, I will let you go. Tell Michelle I'll be writing her next week. Help pass some time after they take my property. Plus I'll update you on what's going on with me. A lawyer is suppose to visit me tomorrow. Thanks for caring and your prayers!

Love,
Larry

*****

April 13, 1996
Dear Larry,

I know it's not after the wedding like I said it would be before I wrote again, but I had a few minutes, so I thought I would write a shorter letter.

I didn't notice until you mentioned it in your letter that you were in the hole again. Will it be for thirty days again—just for talking back to the warden? That seems like overkill. I can understand how you felt, though, about having people come through on "tour." I was really surprised that they would bring high school students through as I was under the impression that no one under eighteen was allowed into the prison. Is that true? I was wondering if we would have a chance to visit if Michelle would have been able to visit too since she's only seventeen? Have you had your disciplinary hearing yet? Will they reduce your thirty days by the time you've already been in the hole?

Just a week from today, we'll be watching Gregg and Jenny get married! I wish you could be there with us. You were right that it wouldn't probably do much good to pray for me to not cry as it is normal. I think I'll do okay if I get past the songs. Music always touches my heart. Jenny will be a nice daughter-in-law and seems to be fitting well into the family. I am happy that she has included me in so many plans for the wedding. It has made me feel closer to her.

Gregg and Jenny now also have a boxer puppy named Thunder. The person they bought Thunder from is going to keep him during their honeymoon. We get to keep Lightning. Aren't we so *very* lucky? I would not want two puppies at once to housebreak!

Michelle had her first track meet on Wednesday and ran in the 100-meter sprint and the 400- and 800-meter relays. She placed second in the 100-meter and first in the 800-meter relay. Both the boys and girls teams from her school won the meet.

Well, I said this was going to be short so I'm going to close. We'll be taking lots of pictures of the wedding and will send some to you.

Love,
Erin

*****

April 24, 1996
Dear Erin,

I hope by the time you get this letter that you are getting recuperated from the wedding. I know it was beautiful. Thank you for wishing I could be there. Did you cry? (You know I had to ask!) I'm sure looking forward to the pictures. Yes, I can understand how much it meant to you for Jenny to include you in many plans for the wedding. Also, it sure was great to read, "Jenny will be a nice daughter-in-law and seems to be fitting well into the family."

Boy, do Gregg and Jenny have their hands full with two puppies, especially when they aren't potty trained. Since puppies like to chew, they will have some things chewed up too. I agree that I would not want two puppies at the same time.

I got released from the "hole" on Saturday, the 20th. I received the maximum sentence, 14 days for the charge. But I did six days waiting to go to court on it. That's a total of 20 days I'll have done for expressing my opinion. I don't like it when I feel somebody is being disrespectful to me. I read in the New Testament that God does not respect one person more than another. Even though I know what

I'm in prison for, I'm still a human being and expect to be treated like one. But the majority of the employees here don't consider us human beings. At least in Michigan prisons, the employees did. The majority of staff here would not even be hired in a Michigan prison. They don't want guards with bad attitudes and disrespectful thinking about the inmates. As it just leads to trouble since the inmates won't accept it there like these inmates do down here.

Not only did I have to stay in the "hole" longer than normal, but when I got out they put me in the worse cell in G-House as there is a bulletin board that blocks any air from coming into this cell. If they leave me here permanently, it will be suffocating when the temperatures get really warm this summer. Plus they only gave me a mattress, no sheets, blankets, pillow, clothes, and so on. The only clothes I have is the pants and shirt I had on when they took me to the "hole." I borrowed a sweatshirt off another guy. Been sleeping in my clothes and sweatshirt. It's been chilly in here at night (40s). On top of that, I have been going through withdrawal from my anti-depressant medication. My prescription expired four days ago. Tonight they finally started it back. More games they are playing with me since being released.

Yes, people under 18 are allowed to visit us. There isn't an age requirement. But when a person under 18 visits, she/he must be with a person who is over 18. So Michelle could visit.

I recently read an article from "Insight for Living" by Charles Swindoll that said Jesus will tug at the hidden cords of our heart. I know He has done that with me. It really bothers me, though, when I know I "backslide" from him when I do something impulsively. It reminds me that the demon spirit that is inside of me still controls me at times. Do you believe we can be possessed by demon spirits? I do after reading a pamphlet on it by a Christian author, Gordon Lindsey, who wrote an entire series on the origin of demons. If you can find it, would you get me the one titled, "The Scarlet Sin"? It's about the demon of murder. I want to see if I can relate to it. Thanks!

The guard just said it's 3 a.m. I better wrap this up. Got to wash up and read my Bible before I go to sleep. So, I doubt if I'll go to sleep before 4 a.m. Tell everyone I said "hi" and thanks for caring and your prayers. You all are in my prayers.

Love,
Larry

*****

April 29, 1996
Dear Larry,

If you could see me now, I have a *big* smile on my face! The wedding is over, our week of dog sitting has come to an end(!), a busy week at work is over, and I finally have a day to myself to spend as I want to. It's great!

Gregg's friends had a bachelor party for him on Friday night after the rehearsal dinner. Of course, it was all clean fun. They had his arms duct taped to his sides, and two bowling balls were chained to his legs and a big sign on him read, "Help I've lost my mind and tomorrow I lose my freedom." He was then escorted to a grocery store and given a list of "wedding survival kit" items he had to actually ask people to get off the shelf for him. Gregg never really told me what was on the list—and probably never will. Someone said that they saw Gregg and his friends later eating at Denny's, and Gregg still had his sign on. They got him home about 2:30 a.m. I have no doubt they all had fun. I'm sure it will be an evening Gregg won't soon forget. However, he should have expected almost everything that happened since he's been in on planning several bachelor parties himself!

I know you're curious about the wedding. It was absolutely beautiful! (But then I may be a little prejudiced!) Jenny was absolutely gorgeous, and Gregg looked very handsome. Everything went off as planned. Approximately 250 guests attended the wedding and reception—it was one of the larger weddings our church has had. Gregg and Jenny both seemed very relaxed through the whole wedding and acted like they totally enjoyed themselves. And a miracle happened—I didn't cry! Bet you're surprised, aren't you? When I first saw Gregg in his tux just before the wedding and gave him a hug,

I came close but didn't break down—I knew I had to have pictures taken in about five minutes, so that helped. I sure didn't want to mess up my makeup! ☺

During the wedding, I was so happy for them because I knew that they were both happy and were looking forward to being married. It actually was a *fun* day. It was good that I had already heard the songs at the rehearsal, so I was prepared for them—that saved some tears too. Even when they took off for their honeymoon, I was happy and prayed all week that they would have a good, relaxing time—which they did. I'm sending you a few pictures so you can get some idea of what the wedding was like. I was exhausted the next day, though, and came very close to falling asleep in church—Michelle had to nudge me one time! In the afternoon, I got to take a nap and then relaxed the rest of the day.

The newlyweds went to Gatlinburg, Tennessee, stayed at a cabin in the mountains for their honeymoon, and returned home on Thursday afternoon. Last night, Jenny's parents, my mom, and Dave and I watched them open their wedding gifts that had been brought to our house after the wedding. It was fun being able to see what they got. It took all of us to load the gifts up and take them back to the apartment afterward. Today (the twenty-seventh) is Jenny's twenty-first birthday, so we celebrated it last night after the gifts were opened. Her dad bought her a cake and took the day off work so he could be there for the gift opening and to celebrate her birthday. I really like her parents. It seems like we've known them for a long time and should all get along well.

What an *extremely* challenging week we had dog sitting with Lightning—Gregg and Jenny's wire fox terror, I mean terrier! I have never seen such a dog in my life! When Dave and Michelle brought him to our house after the wedding, they had to give him a complete bath after being in his cage for a majority of the day. When I got up on Sunday morning, it took me twenty minutes to clean up his cage and him. Normally, dogs do not want to go to the bathroom in their bed, or if they do, it's in one spot. This dog doesn't care where he goes—and then jumps around in it! I was ready to take him to a kennel and board him for a week after less than a day. Michelle was having a fit about it, so I relented and let him stay here. We thought the cage was the issue so decided to keep him in our downstairs bathroom since we are planning on getting new carpet soon. It did not make any difference—every morning was the same story. Because he jumped around so much, all of the papers we put down were pushed aside and his poop was ground into the carpet! That day, I went out and bought some cheap plastic drop cloths to put under the papers so I could just roll up the mess and throw it away. That worked much better.

In addition, Lightning went nuts when cooped up and kept jumping up against the door trying to get out. I had some blankets for him to lay on and left a toy for him to chew on, but that didn't help. Most of the night, he would be okay but would start his whining, barking, and jumping around 4 to 5 a.m. every day. When let out of the bathroom, he would act better but just had no control over his bladder. We would put him outdoors, see him go to the bathroom, and let him in; and five minutes later, he would be peeing on the floor—and not just in one spot. He streak peed—kept walking while peeing. Lightning was the perfect name for him. It was a *terrible* week! You can see why I'm smiling today, can't you? It's okay for him to visit, but I sure don't want to take care of him again until he's housebroken!

I watched *Dateline* last Friday night. Gregg happened to have TV on Wednesday night and heard that you would be interviewed on Friday, so we taped it since it was airing during the rehearsal dinner. I thought it was a positive view on organ donation. The only negative was the prison commissioner. But then I know he has a negative attitude about you anyway from what you've told me. I felt the reporter was really questioning why he was trying to prohibit you from donating your kidney and even cited cases of other death-row inmates who had been able to donate an organ. The prison commissioner didn't have a good explanation to give other than he thought you were trying to play a trick on the retired police detective. The detective, however, said that he was an adult and would deal with that possibility if it came up but that he didn't think it would. *Dateline* seemed to be on your side. What kind of impression did you get from hearing about the show from others? Sure was too bad you didn't get a chance to watch it.

You asked me if I believe a person can be possessed by demon spirits. Since there are stories in the New Testament about people who had demon spirits inside of them, I know it is possible (see Acts 8:7, Luke 4:31–37, and Luke 8:26–36). In all instances, it took an encounter with Jesus for the demons to flee. I think people who are involved in the occult—fortune-telling, witchcraft, Satan worship, etc.—are prime targets for demon spirits to take up residence in their bodies. My feeling is that Satan is in control of *any* person who has not personally asked Christ for forgiveness of sin and accepted His gift of salvation. While Satan may be in control, however, the person is not necessarily demon-possessed like the people mentioned in the Bible.

(By the way, the series of articles by Gordon Lindsay are out of print, so I could not order them.)

When a person accepts Christ as personal Savior, however, Christ, in the form of the Holy Spirit, moves into his/her body and becomes a *helper* to resist Satan's attacks and to live the Christian life. Satan or his demons are not allowed to enter into a body that Christ controls, nor would he want to since Christ is his archenemy. Therefore, I do not believe that Christians can be demon-possessed.

That doesn't mean, however, that Christians never slip once in a while and fall back into ways that are considered sinful. That is our sin nature trying to surface again. But Christ forgives us for these "slips"—just as He will now forgive you if you "backslide" and do something impulsive. Sure, you will feel bad about your slips, but Christ's love for you is unconditional and does not change at those times. I know how it is to do or say things that I'm sorry for afterward and have even wondered at times how Christ could still love me after I've disappointed Him. At those times, however, He often assures me of His love by "speaking" through a devotional, a Scripture passage, a song, or a sermon. He always knows how to reach to the very center of our hearts to "speak" to us.

It encouraged my heart to read that you needed to read your Bible before you went to bed, even though it was 3 a.m. Actually, you convicted me. It seems with my busy schedule that I haven't had the time to spend in Bible reading and prayer lately that I would like. I've really missed that time too! See how God works?

Has your mom gotten to visit yet? I hope she's feeling better. She has certainly had a rough time physically. I'll continue praying for her.

Keep reading your Bible, praying, and letting God work in your life. He loves you and so do we.

Love,
Erin

*****

May 9, 1996
Dear Erin,

Sorry I haven't written sooner. I've been waiting on Mom to send the wedding pictures back to me so I can return them to you. Thanks for sharing them with me!

The bride and groom sure made a beautiful couple. Besides Jenny's wedding gown, I think (Mom agreed too) that your dress was the prettiest. Mom and I also agreed that you was the second most beautiful lady at the wedding. ☺ Good to hear you didn't mess up your makeup by crying! Mom and I also really loved the way Michelle had her hair done in a heart-shaped braid and with the flowers in it. It was a pretty big wedding for close to 250 people being there. Sure wish I could see the video of it. Better yet, wish I could've been there! I have prayed that their marriage lasts. Now days, it's rare. Another sign of how bad the world has become.

Boy, Gregg's bachelor party sounded like fun. I know having two bowling balls chained to his legs and wearing that sign in the store sure got him some laughs from people in the store. That's sure a good one!

It sounds like something is wrong with Lightning for him to act like that. Have they asked the vet about his behavior? Sounds like you won't be volunteering to dog sit their dogs whenever they go on a vacation. ☺

Thanks for sharing with me your views on the *Dateline* show. I am sad to hear that you watched it cause I heard they went into detail about the crime. The 911 tape even makes me cry. Mom said the show really had her so upset that even with her sleeping pills she couldn't go to sleep. Sure hurts me! My dad, who attended my trial, said the survivor told some lies. He testified at my trial that it wasn't me who he saw come back in and kill Ms. Sweat. However, on the show he told the reporter that he saw me do it. I also heard the prison commissioner really talked bad about me and told many lies. That is probably why he refused *Dateline's* request to interview me so I couldn't defend myself and point out the lies. This man has been commissioner for a couple months. So, how does he have an opinion on me? I'm going to get a transcript of the show. I then will write them with my response. They sometimes do follow-up stories.

Thanks also for sending me the book *And the Angels Were Silent* by Max Lucado. I read it in one day and enjoyed it, easy reading. Maybe it was cause of the large print? ☺ I sure love reading everything about Jesus! Another inmate is reading it now. Others will also read it. ☺

I sure wish you a happy Mother's Day! I'll call Mom Sunday. Sure hurts me I'm not out there with her! Pitiful. When I called her after being released from the "hole," her voice was clear and strong. However, she had just been released from the hospital six days before. Her doctor said if she continues smoking she won't live to see 1997.

How is Michelle's track season going and Gregg's lawn business?

Almost time for your vacation to Hawaii. I know you're looking forward to that. Hope the weather is nice the whole time you two are there. Be sure to take some pictures to send me.

I'm going to close so I can lay down.

Love,
Larry

*****

May 13, 1996

Dear Larry,

Today is another day that I have a big smile on my face as I write you. It's our last day of classes! All my grades are done and ready to be turned in tomorrow. ☺

I had a nice Mother's Day last Sunday. After church and dinner with family, I got to relax and take a much-needed nap! Did you get to call your mom last weekend? How's she doing?

How are *you* doing? Have you gotten your clothes, sheets, pillow, etc., back yet? Every time you get out of the "hole," it seems your punishment continues. I do not totally understand prison politics but wonder if that happens to everyone or just to you since the prison staff is upset about your appeals. It seems that being in the "hole" would be punishment enough.

I found a black frame kit for the crocheted verse you sent me; and Dave is going to mount, frame, and put glass over it to protect it from the dust. I can hardly wait to get it on the wall!

When I was at our Christian bookstore, I found the enclosed name card with your name on it. I decided to buy it because I felt it was so appropriate. Larry means *victorious*, and that's exactly what I feel you are and can be as a new Christian.

Michelle had a home track meet today and competed in four races—the 400-meter individual and the 400-, 800-, and 1-mile relays. She was not real up for it since the season is starting to drag right now and her shin splints are quite bad. Once the meet began, her adrenaline started flowing, and she perked up. After her three relay teams placed first and she placed first in her individual event, she was very happy! Those wins will help her through her last track meet and regionals that are coming up. She is excited that she earned a school letter in track this year.

Gregg is getting very busy right now with his lawn business. He's picked up quite a few more lawns this year and some spring cleanup jobs. He has about twenty-eight regular mowing customers this year and is growing his business.

We leave for Hawaii on Monday, May 20! I picked up our tickets last Friday, so now the trip seems more real! I can hardly wait!

Michelle still says that it's not fair that she has to go to school while we're off having such a good time in a much warmer climate. She's only kidding, of course! She and my mom will have a good time. I'll send you a postcard from Hawaii.

I'm looking for a letter from you any day now. Take care and keep looking to Christ for strength to endure.

Love,
Erin

Think About It: Organ Donation

Larry's deepest desire, which was denied, was to be an organ donor. Why? It was the one way he could give back to others and "redeem" what he felt was a wasted life. In contrast to the grief he caused by taking lives, others could experience life-giving joy by his sacrifice. Have you ever thought about becoming an organ donor? Are you already a registered organ donor? As an organ donor, you have the potential to help save lives like Larry wished to do.

According to the most recent Organ Procurement and Transplantation Network statistics, 115,017 people are in need of an organ transplant with one person being added to the national list every ten minutes. On the average, ninety-two transplants are performed daily. One organ donor has the capability of saving eight lives. There are over 75,000 people on the active waiting list whose lives depend more each day on getting a transplant. Did you know that the average wait time is five to seven years?[69] There is a severe shortage of donors in our country.

One can be a living donor. A parent, child, sibling, other family member, spouse, or even a complete stranger who has a compatible blood type and is a match can be considered. The following organs can be donated from a live donor: one kidney, a segment of the liver, the lobe of a lung, or a portion or the pancreas and intestine.[70] A lady from my church donated one of her kidneys to a close friend to extend her life. At the time, I thought, *What a kind, selfless person she is to make that sacrifice for her friend. I am not sure I could do that.* I greatly admired her.

The other type of organ donor can be a deceased donor. There are eight organs that can be donated—the liver, heart, two lungs, two kidneys, pancreas, and small intestine. In addition to organs, tissues—skin, corneas, bone tissue, including tendons and cartilage, heart valves, and blood vessels—can also be donated to improve the quality of life for many ill people. One organ donor can potentially impact the lives of fifty-eight people.[71] Added to the list in the last ten years have been the hands and face, which are typically more like tissue grafts. Whether or not you qualify as a donor depends on your physical condition and the condition of your organs, not your age.[72]

One hesitation that I personally had about being an organ donor was whether or not I would receive the same quality of medical and nursing care if I was near death as someone who was not a potential donor. After doing some research, I was reassured by finding this answer to my question,

> The quality of your care will not change, regardless of your decision. Organ and tissue recovery takes place after all efforts to save your life have been exhausted and death has been declared. The doctors involved in saving your life are entirely different from the medical team involved in recovering organs and tissues.[73]

Another determining factor is that the donor must officially be declared brain dead by the medical staff.

> Brain death is an established medical and legal diagnosis of death. It occurs in patients who have suffered a severe injury to the brain as a result of trauma or some other medical cause. As a result of the injury, the brain swells and obstructs its own blood supply. Without blood flow, all brain

tissue dies. Brain death is the most common circumstance under which patients donate organs, because while they have been declared dead the mechanical support has maintained blood flow to the organs. This occurs only in the hospital, typically in an intensive care setting.[74]

I recently decided to become an organ donor in honor of Larry's fight to donate his organs. The Bible says to "love your neighbor as yourself" (Matthew 22:39 NCV). To me, giving life or sight to another would help fulfill this commandment. If I or one of my family members needed an organ transplant, I would certainly hope that someone would unselfishly give of themselves to play that life-giving role for me or them.

If you have thought about being a donor but need more information to make an informed decision, visit one or two of the following sites:

- www.organdonor.gov
- www.donorrecovery.org
- The Organ Procurement and Transplant Network (https://optn.transplant.hrsa.gov) where you can actually register to be a donor
- Your local Secretary of State's office where you can add the designation to your driver's license

Would you be surprised to learn that "95% of U.S. adults support organ donation but only 54% actually sign up to be donors?"[75] Have you considered organ donation but never pursued making it official? Will you help provide life for another individual? Your selfless sacrifice could give hope to those needing transplants and to their families. It is, however, a very personal decision that only you can make.

Chapter 19

June 4, 1996

Dear Erin,

Hope your Hawaii vacation was fun. I received the post card. Boy, it's sure beautiful there. How hot did it get there? It's been in the 90's the last two weeks here—set all kinds of Georgia records for this early in the summer.

Thanks for the pretty name card. I have it right next to my picture, "When I Come Home to Heaven." ☺ It will stay in our family too. Thanks also for believing I can be victorious.

Michelle finished her track season on a high. For her to have shin splints real bad again this year, the training must be wrong. Hope her shins start feeling better now that the season is over. I'm sure she will write me about how her team did overall.

Boy, Gregg's lawn business sure is growing. Maybe a future business there for him. He can hire some other workers and keep the business growing.

I received a transcript of the *Dateline* show. Boy, was some lies told. But the prison commissioner still was made to look bad.

The Olympics are only a month away and preparation for them is daily news down here. One worker died ☹ while putting up the lights at one of the new stadiums. Turned out the design was in error. Wasn't built strong enough to hold the lights. They've had some other problems too but overall it's on schedule. Atlanta will be an extremely busy place soon.

Well to the news which you won't like, why I saved it for last. I started the process last week of waiving my habeas corpus appeal with the Supreme Court. This time once the court grants me this, even if I wanted to change my mind and stop it like before, I won't be allowed to. I will die. I wish I could express myself better so I could help you understand this is the best for me. Wish we wasn't so far away so we could visit. I might be able to explain it all to you that way, but then I'm not articulate either.

I didn't dismiss the lawsuit on the organs but dropped all other counts. But I'm pretty sure we won't win anyways, which is so sad. They just won't allow me (us) to do this cause they know what the majority of the public's opinion is of us and don't want to do anything that will change its perspective of us.

I should be hearing from the Attorney General this week. I'll keep you updated. I'm sorry!!! Don't be sad, cause of you and Michelle (a couple other people too), I'll be going to a better place, heaven. ☺☺ But you two are the ones who helped the most in saving me. I'll give you two a big hug when we meet in heaven. ☺

Well, I'll let you go. You all take care. Thanks for praying for me. You are all in my prayers.

Love,
Larry

*****

June 10, 1996
Dear Larry,

Seems like such a long time since I've written you! We had a *wonderful* time for the nine days we were in Hawaii! The best part was getting away from all the home and work responsibilities and relaxing. Dave and I having the time by ourselves was also nice. The weather was great—temps were in the mid to high eighties with just a brief rain shower. All of our hotels were located on the beach real close to the Pacific Ocean. We always had a nice view from our room and didn't have to walk far to be at the ocean. We spent three days each on Oahu, Kauai, and Maui.

Our favorite island was Kauai because of its beauty, less hectic pace, and lack of commercialism. Every morning, however, we were awakened by screeching peacocks that lived on the hotel property. For as beautiful as they are, they sure make a terrible sound. The highlight was a helicopter tour of the island since so much of it is inaccessible by car. I enjoyed the first half of the trip but was airsick the last half since the pilot kept going up and down so many times to show us the valleys. Dave was in picture-taking heaven!

Of course, Pearl Harbor was the highlight on Oahu. At Pearl Harbor, we saw a 30-minute video on what happened when the Japanese attacked Pearl Harbor and then were taken by boat out to the USS Arizona that was hit and sunk within seven minutes after the attack. There were over 1,700 men on that ship. Because it sunk so fast, no one was rescued. I didn't realize that they were still all entombed inside the Arizona.

Maui was a cross between Oahu and Kauai. It was definitely more commercialized but still had a semirelaxed pace. I enjoyed our hotel there the best as it was the closest to the ocean, and our room had a gorgeous ocean view. Since there was no air conditioning, we left the 12-foot sliding door open all the time so could always hear the ocean. I *loved* hearing the ocean all night. We experienced our first luau/pig roast there too and got to sample some of the native food and entertainment. We would go back in a heartbeat!

Yesterday was Gregg's twenty-second birthday! He should not be getting so old. I've decided that he and Michelle can age, but I'm going to put myself on "hold" for a while! Too bad my body isn't cooperating.

My crocheted verse is all framed and hung! Having the black satin behind it makes it easy to read. I *love* it! You'll never know how much it means to me! Thank you for having it made for me. I will send a picture of it to you soon.

So sorry to hear the temps are already in the nineties. You must be terribly hot being in the bad cell. If only I could package up some air conditioning and send it to you!

Saturday was a hard day for me after I got your letter. Talk about having mixed emotions! I am so happy that you are now a Christian but yet sad to know that I'll be losing you soon. You've become one of my best friends. I'm so thankful the Lord brought you into my life and urged me to write you the first time over three years ago. You're one of the few people that really cares and that I can freely express my feelings to. I'll miss that. I do understand why you want to waive your appeals since life on death row must be truly awful and the organ donation possibility looks pretty slim. I'll wait to hear further from you after you hear from the attorney general's office. By the way, could you explain to me more about a habeas corpus appeal so I can better understand the process?

Are you still planning on having me help you edit your final statement? I am waiting for your thoughts and have plenty of time right now.

I too wish we lived closer because I would love to visit you. I've started praying that if it is the Lord's will for us to get to visit, He'll work it out. Right now, it doesn't seem like it will happen with all that's going on this summer. July is pretty free, but I don't think that it would be wise to come during the Olympic weeks with all the traffic and thousands of people. Would you be able to add Michelle's, Dave's, and my name to your visitor list just in case an opportunity to visit might open up at the last minute? You just never know how the Lord might work! Is there special paperwork we would need to fill out to get to visit? Please don't get your hopes up too much because, as I said, it doesn't look real hopeful right now. But I don't want to completely close the door to that possibility. The Lord has worked out seemingly impossible odds before.

Michelle has a lot to tell you, so you will be hearing from her soon now that school is out. We'll both be continuing to pray for you, but now, we pray in a different way since you're a Christian. Remember that the Holy Spirit resides within you and is there to give you wisdom, comfort, and the ability to stand against any attacks Satan may try to send your way—and I'm sure he's planning on doing that. You belong to Christ and nothing can ever change that fact. Read John 10:28–29 for assurance of this fact.

Love,
Erin

*****

July 16, 1996
Dear Erin,

I am sitting here and enjoying the breeze that's blowing in. It's been cloudy and raining off and on so the temperature has been in the high 80s and low 90s. But the weatherman is saying it's over with and going back to the upper 90s. Last week during our morning yard call, it was cloudy with a nice breeze. I laid down on the cement and slept the whole three hours!

I am glad my attorneys were able to put pressure on the warden to get me moved out of that awful cell with no air flow. I also got my sheets, clothes, etc. back. Yeah, I wish you could package up some air conditioning and send it to me. Remember in the old movies how the convict got his file in by having it baked into a cake? Wonder if these people would notice if you bake a big cake and put a window air conditioner in it? ☺

You asked for an explanation of what habeas corpus means. A habeas corpus is a legal appeal process that all inmates have available at both the state and federal levels if they feel their constitutional rights have been violated in any way. My habeas corpus appeal contained 22 counts that I wanted a legal decision on from the Supreme Court and also requested a new trial or resentencing. One claim I made is that electrocution is cruel and unusual punishment in hopes of getting the method of execution changed so that I can donate my organs. By including the other counts, I felt I would have a longer time for that to possibly happen. Since I have never filed a federal appeal, the Supreme Court accepted my appeal.

On June 12, the federal judge had a "status" hearing on my case. I wasn't present. He agreed to give my lawyer a chance to come visit me and try to convince me to withdraw my "Motion to Dismiss My Habeas Corpus." If I wouldn't, he would have me in his court on June 21 to rule on it, and the lawyers knew he would have to rule in my favor. The next day my lawyer from the Georgia Resource Center and an attorney from New Orleans came to visit (*beg* would be a better word) me to sign the affidavit they had and give them until November. If I would, the New Orleans attorney agreed to take over the lawsuit on the organ issue and said he thought this federal judge might rule for us. So, they stated how not only would I be helping Mr. Ferguson but every death row inmate in the USA whose state has the "chair" for their method of execution. Well, cause of what I've learned from the Bible, I signed it. When I talked with him on the phone, I told him that I wanted all other issues on the petition dismissed that could get my conviction and death sentence reversed. So the judge will only decide if the "chair" is unconstitutional. That would mean I will still be executed.

A couple weeks later, I got an "overnight delivery" package from my attorney. In it he wrote a 12-page personal letter and also sent the habeas corpus petition he had just filed. He expressed why he couldn't file the petition with only the one claim which would be sending me to my death this year if the judge denied the one claim. He told me that he was confident that because of the errors made in my case that were presented in my original habeas corpus appeal that my conviction and/or death sentence might be reversed. Knowing him, it didn't surprise me that he didn't stick to our agreement since he is totally against capital punishment. So now I have to dismiss *completely* my habeas corpus petition. *It's sure sad.* I stayed alive, have to suffer through another summer so I could help Ferguson who needs an organ and inmates by getting rid of the "chair," and didn't succeed on any of them.

Have you been watching much of the Olympics? The heat has been hard on the athletes—the heat index was 110° the other day. The rain over the weekend has kept the temperature down to the low 90s.

I will find out for you what has to happen for you all to visit me. A visit sure would be good but it is probably doubtful that it can happen before the court rules and I am executed. One of the very nice things about our visits here is that they are referred to as "contact" visits. We do not have to visit using a phone with a piece of glass separating us from our visitors. My mom and brothers get to come inside a special cell in the visitor's area and we can sit close and talk the entire time.

I'm hoping to call you all this month when the right guard is working. You are my best friend. I feel I can share everything with you. Michelle is good for me too since she makes me smile when I get her newsy letters, jokes, and puzzles.

Tell Michelle I am waiting on my mom to send me the track and honors night pictures back. When I get them, I will write her and return them with the letter.

Well, I'll let you go. You all take care!

Love,
Larry

*****

July 27, 1996
Dear Larry,

Once again, it has taken me a while to write. We took a few days and went up north and relaxed by the lake—even though some of the time it was sweatshirt and jeans weather. One day we rented a pontoon boat, and Dave fished. I enjoyed reading and listening to the waves. Do you think we are water lovers?

How you must have enjoyed the cooler weather and breeze you had for a few days! I know how it feels to have the fresh breeze blowing in your face. That three-hour sleep you had in the exercise yard must have been very peaceful and relaxing since you have told me you don't sleep very well at all with the heat and humidity. Our temperatures have been in the seventies and eighties, very nice!

I had to laugh at your idea of baking an air conditioner inside a cake. It would have to be a mighty huge cake! I *think* the guards may get a little suspicious.

Thanks for sharing the attorney's long letter with me. It appears that he really cares about you. I did not realize you had known each other so long. It would be hard knowing that a friend would die quicker by him filing the paper, so I can understand his viewpoint. I also understand your side too—that he wasn't truthful to you. Have you heard anything more since you sent your letter to the court?

We've spent many hours watching the Olympics this week. Gymnastics has been our main interest. Did you see the women's gymnastics team finals in the middle of the week? I felt so bad for Kerri Strug when she injured her foot. What determination, though, to perform that second vault with an injured foot! She won the event for the Americans! Michelle is most looking forward to the track events, which started last night.

I couldn't believe when I heard the news this morning that there had been a bombing in the downtown Atlanta area that killed two and injured over a hundred. How sad! Whoever made the bomb must be sick. It sure won't make the United States look good in the eyes of the other countries. I'm just glad that it didn't happen where the Olympians or other people were actually staying.

I've run out of news, so I'll be closing. I will be expecting a letter from you soon.

Love
Erin

*****

August 8, 1996
Dear Erin,

How good it was to talk with you two last night! During our call, you mentioned that Michelle had her senior pictures taken and you and Dave celebrated your 25th wedding anniversary. Congratulations to both of you once again on your anniversary. I am looking forward to seeing Michelle's proofs. She sure is growing up! She was only in eighth grade when we started writing. And now she is officially a senior. Hard to believe.

I think Dave and you do like spending time around water! Tell Dave that I loved fishing when I was younger. My brothers and I would get up early and ride our bikes two miles to the lake, rent a boat for a dollar, and by noon would have caught over 100 fish. Then we would take a swim and return home before it got too hot. Boy, a swim would feel good right now!

The Olympics is now over. I watched and enjoyed them a lot. Yes, I watched the women win the gold medal in the gymnastics. Kerri Strug will probably be the greatest moment (happy one) of the Olympics! Sad to say, though, these Olympics will now be remembered for the bomb. The person will be caught soon and will end up here or on a federal death row. Our world sure is getting sicker, sad.

My mom and Tom came to visit me last weekend. It sure was good seeing them since they had not been able to visit for a while. Tom has had a bad summer cold that started in his head and moved to his chest. He still did not feel or look good on Sunday.

While playing basketball last week, I had words with another inmate. It's common here during the summer when playing on the cement that makes it seem much hotter than it is (over 100° every time we are out there) for us to lose control (words) a lot. Anyways, this guy sure wanted to fight. I surprised myself and would not fight him. I am sure I looked bad with some of the other inmates for not fighting. It wasn't that I was scared. No doubt I would've won, but I let it go. I even broke my personal glasses lens to use as a weapon— part of my Michigan prison way of life. But this time I thought of what the Bible has taught me and let the matter go. It even surprised me, but it also made me feel good to know I have changed. ☺ No more personal glasses though. ☹ I know that God is working in my life!

I'll be starting on my "last statement" any day. So you'll be hearing from me soon for your assistance. I sent a letter to dismiss my habeas corpus appeal so will probably go to court sometime next week.

What a surprise to get the new Bible that you sent me! I have never seen one that has devotionals for each chapter. I love the way Max Lucado writes and the New Century Version is so easy to understand. I'll read the pages from my new Bible tonight. I prefer doing my Bible reading at night cause it's real quiet then.

Well, I'll let you go since it is almost mail pick up time. Tell everybody "hi" for me. Thanks for caring and your prayers! You all take care.

Love,
Larry

*****

August 20, 1996
Dear Larry,

Michelle and I certainly enjoyed our call with you too! As always, however, the time just went too fast.

After our talk, I called Ms. Partain this morning as you suggested. She was very nice to me and said that you would need to send me the necessary paperwork for a special visit. I asked her if it was likely that she would approve a visit by Michelle, Dave, and me; and she said that she didn't see why not if everything checked out okay. She does want proof that we are relatives, so I told her that I would send a copy of my birth certificate to show that I had the same last name as your mom. Your mom will also have to send you a copy of her birth certificate. After the forms and birth certificates are received, a background check has to be done before permission for a visit can be granted—which I can understand. I'm sure we should all pass! I prayed before I called for a positive response. One hurdle has been jumped over anyway!

What concerns me is the amount of time all of this will take since you mentioned in our call that your court date is September 7, which is not that far away. I'm not sure we'll have official approval in time to make the airline reservations—which I don't feel I can make until we have definite approval since they are nonrefundable. Another complication is that Michelle cannot go until October 26 because of band and school obligations. All of us will have to pray that the Lord will intervene to speed up the approval process if it's

His will we come. I have to confess, however, that patience is not one of my strong points; and I'm really having a hard time with having to wait—so also pray the Lord will teach me patience in all of this. My biggest issue is the uncertainty of whether everything will work out in time. I'm certain you have learned to have *lots* of patience through your dealings with our legal system!

A few minutes ago, I read the two legal documents you sent describing electrocution and why it should be banned. To be honest, my stomach feels sick right now. I always thought electrocution would be much quicker—almost instantaneous. It *is* a cruel and unusual punishment! I can't bear the thought of you going through that! Are you *sure* you don't want to continue with your fight to get the method changed and be able to donate your organs?

What a joy for me when I read about your basketball incident. I *knew* God was changing you—and that was proof. You must have felt so good to see God's control at work in your life! Too bad about your glasses though. Do you have any glasses at all now to use? Can you get the one lens replaced?

Thanks for the Serenity Prayer card that you sent and for writing that you feel it fits you now—another proof that God is at work in your life. It must be evident to others around you too. You're getting an opportunity to serve God by being a witness to Him right where you are. I'll keep praying for God's continued working in your life. By the way, that prayer is one of my favorites—I have to keep reminding myself of its words though!

I want to get this to the post office so it can go out this afternoon. Hopefully, you'll get it tomorrow so you can request the special visit forms and get them sent to me. Would you let me know if you got it the next day or not? How I am hoping the Lord allows us to visit!

Love,
Erin

*****

August 30, 1996

Dear Larry,

Summer is officially over. I have started back to work, and Michelle is settling into her senior year.

Hope your birthday card arrives on time. We thought that by sending it out on Thursday, you should get it on Tuesday, your birthday. Were we right? How nice it would have been to celebrate the day with you.

As I mentioned in your card, we received the forms last Wednesday and got them filled out and notarized on Thursday. I hope everything is in order. Please let me know when you get them. I sent my birth certificate to establish the family relationship but did not notice any place on the form that asked for the relationship to be stated. Is that something you tell them? I want to put down exactly what relationship you tell them so they won't deny our coming in that day because of a "technicality." Has your mom sent her birth certificate to verify that we are cousins? We put down October 26 to visit since there was no way we could be sure of September 7. Keep praying that it works out. If not, as you said, we'll definitely get to see each other in heaven! There, we won't need anyone's special approval and permission. And there won't be any time constraints.

Be sure to fill us in on everything we need to know so that we do things right when we get to the prison. I would not want to do something wrong without realizing it is against the rules and get you in trouble. I asked if I could put down a couple of different dates in case October 26 would be too late, but Ms. Pertain said that I could only put one—and that it could be changed if need be. I'm not sure what the process to change is or how long it takes. She said that within forty-eight hours after she receives the forms from you, you should know whether the visit is approved. You then have to send us a copy of the approval. If it's other than October 26, then only Dave and I will come.

I'll be looking forward to getting the final visit approval and to hear from you after your court date. You are the Lord's child now so

He'll work out all the details and will be walking with you every step of the way. You know we'll be praying.

Love,
Erin

*****

September 3, 1996
Dear Erin,

I received today your beautiful birthday card! Also, thanks for the money. Sure was perfect timing to receive the birthday card right on my birthday. It made my day! I did not get a visit from family over the Labor Day weekend since they are in Florida with my sister.

Boy, school sure starts early up there now. I know the teachers (you) had to report earlier than the students. When I went to school, it started after Labor Day. I never had my birthday when school was in session.

When I took out your letter again, I found Michelle's picture. Boy, that's a beautiful picture! I sure love it! That's going to be the picture for the yearbook, right?

I will submit the special visit forms this week as soon as Mom sends me her birth certificate. I just have to give the papers to my counselor who will give them to Ms. Partain. We'll get the paperwork all processed down here and then have you make your plane reservations. You should have a month in advance to give the airlines so you can still get a discount. I would not want you to buy plane tickets that are non-refundable and then find out that you are not approved. If Michelle cannot come, I will understand.

If the visit gets arranged, don't worry. I'll tell you every little detail. Like you said, we sure don't want a technicality to prevent you from getting in after coming so far to see me.

My attorney, Clive, wasn't too happy with the judge's "order." He asked the judge to have me be sent down to the State Hospital so I could have a complete psychiatric evaluation instead of the judge's plan of sending a court-appointed psychiatrist here on the 11th for a two-hour talk with me. The court-appointed doctor was used by the State a couple years ago in my case. The lawyers know he's not impartial and gives the State the kind of psychiatric evaluation they want.

He sure was like that in my case too. For example, a couple years ago when he did his evaluation, he asked me did I kill those people. I stated I wasn't going to answer that as he was suppose to be evaluating me for my present competence, to determine if I'm competent to waive my appeals. When he testified in court, he stated that I told him I had killed those people. I almost fell out of my chair. He saw from the witness stand how agitated I became. During a recess, he walked over to me and asked what did he say that agitated me so much. I told him about his lie. He said he remembered now, I was right. So, when he returned to the witness stand, he informed the judge he was wrong on what he testified to earlier. But then he said, "But Lonchar didn't say he didn't kill them either!" What a joke, hey?

Another issue my lawyer argued was that I be removed from death row, that this environment is one of the reasons why I want to die to escape this place. So, I feel the hearing on the 12th isn't going to be short and simple like I thought.

They have one of us scheduled for execution on the 10th. He is the same one who was scheduled a few months ago but the U.S. Supreme Court stopped it to decide if the newly passed law that restricts our appeals was constitutional. I know him and his mother well. His mother is a real Christian too. She is a widow, and now she's going to lose her only child. But I know her faith will sure help her through it.

The time has slipped by on me. They'll be here any minute to pick this up so I got to close. Thanks for caring and your prayers. You all are in my thought and prayers!

Love,
Larry

*****

September 13, 1996

Dear Erin,

Did someone call you on the 12th to inform you of what happened in court? In case they didn't, I'll tell you what happened yesterday.

During the court hearing the psychiatrist who evaluated me on Thursday and I were put on the witness stand and asked questions by both sides (State and lawyers) and the judge. The Department of Corrections spokesman sure is not too likeable of a person. He stated now there are questions if I could even have been able to donate a kidney to Ferguson cause we wasn't tested to see if we "matched." Isn't that something? That is what we were trying to get them to do but they wouldn't allow it. He also stated I created this controversy for publicity. He was in that courtroom so he knows I just "signed my death certificate," so how could he say I'm doing this for publicity?

The judge made it real clear to me if he grants my wish to dismiss my appeal that I will die. Even if I wanted to change my mind and stop my execution, I won't be allowed to this time. He said he would issue his ruling in a short period of time. The lawyers admit he will grant my wish. I'm going to ask the lawyers if they are going to appeal the judge's ruling and also what their guess is on how long I have left so you guys will know. I didn't get a chance to ask them after the hearing since as soon as it ended the guards took me from the room.

A highlight of the day was the ride to court. I got to see the new Olympic stadium, the caldron, and other Olympic stuff. ☺ That caldron is small. Looking at it on TV a person would think it was large. It felt extremely good to be out of the prison for a few hours.

All day today the Atlanta TV station aired interviews after the hearing with my lawyer, the Department of Corrections spokesman, and Rick Smith, the survivor of this sad tragedy. Since cameras aren't allowed in federal court, an artist drew pictures of me in the courtroom.

I have to start writing my "Last Statement" this week. I've been putting it off cause of my laziness. Now that I know for sure I don't have long left, I have got to get on it. The following verse is what I'm going to put in my goodbye letters to tell people why they shouldn't be sad cause of my death: "To be absent from the body is to be present with the Lord" (2 Corinthians 5:8).

To answer a couple of your questions. Visiting hours are from 9 a.m. to 3 p.m. on Saturday. We won't have to submit any other forms if we change it from October 26th to an earlier date.

Well, I'll close. You'll be hearing from me soon I'm sure. You all take care!

Love,
Larry

*****

September 20, 1996
Dear Larry,

Since your hearing was on the twelfth, I decided to wait until after I heard back from you to write again. Your attorney gave me a brief call after the hearing, but I learned more of the detail from your letter.

From what you said in your letter, the judge definitely made it very clear that you would not get another chance to appeal your execution. What I read in a newspaper article you sent me greatly surprised me. "Camp even told Lonchar his current appeal contains 'substantial allegations . . . that could result in either your sentence or conviction being set aside.'"[76] Was his statement accurate? Does this mean that you may have been able to walk away a free man? How likely do you think that possibility would have been? Could you explain to me why you would not want to follow through with the appeal if your conviction could be overturned?

After all that has transpired, I feel, like you, that October 26 may be too late to visit. If we find out it is, I'd like to pursue coming earlier—although Michelle won't be able to join us because of marching band commitments. If we do get to come, though, will we get copies of the approved visitation forms to bring with us?

I'm glad you got your birthday card right on the day of your birthday! I was hoping you would. The picture I sent was not the one for the yearbook—that one will be a more formal close-up shot. We're expecting to get her pictures back any day and will send you some other poses. Michelle says "hi" and hopes you got her card, letter, and picture and that she will be hearing from you again.

Would you believe that I had another dream last night about you? In it, I got to come visit you. Although I know the details could never play out like I dreamed them, maybe it was yet another sign from the Lord that our visit will be a reality. In the dream, we just walked into the prison visitor area without ever going through any security. (Boy, I know that's inaccurate!) You'll really laugh when I tell you about the rest of it. There was a very high-end cafeteria there and small shops that you could shop in while visiting. When Dave and I got there, we looked around and found you sitting in the cafeteria waiting for us . . . and to have a good meal. I remember being happy that you were already there so we could visit. Didn't I tell you that you would laugh? My dreams are a big joke with my family who think they border on weird sometimes. Anyways, guess we'll have to see what happens.

My office partner said that for an extra $20 we can buy insurance that will allow us to change the date of our flight or cancel it entirely. I'm going to check that out when I make reservations. It might be best to wait until you hear something from the judge before making the reservations. On one airline, we are going to be able to come for a really reasonable rate even if we make the reservations a couple of days in advance of our flight and leave out of Detroit. If it's for us to come, the Lord will save two seats for us. Keep praying that it will work out—and it will if the Lord wants this visit to happen!

Gregg just stopped by to get his mail. We got to talking about his "boys," and I thought you would get a kick out of what we talked about. When either of them do something they shouldn't, Gregg and Jenny give them a "time out." They have to sit in a chair for a certain amount of time. The other day when he had both dogs here for the afternoon, they started digging in the backyard, and Dave was getting upset. So Gregg brought them in and made them sit on the couch until the football game he was watching was over. I'm amazed that they sat there. Isn't that funny? What amazes me is that even

Lightning can do it! It sounded like Lightning gets most of the time outs—but that really shouldn't be surprising, should it!

I can understand how one could put off writing a last statement. It's probably not all laziness, as you say. Once you start writing, the reality of everything will start to set in more. I would probably react just the same as you.

Second Corinthians 5:8 is a great verse to share in your goodbye letters! Writing your letters can be a wonderful opportunity to share your newfound faith in Christ. That verse will certainly let them know that you're a changed man since a year ago in June, you said that you were going to hell and deserved to! I'm still so thrilled and rejoicing over your salvation! Your changed life is very evident in your letters. I'm so happy that you'll be in heaven and thank God for His special touch in your life. The only word that I can use to describe the change is a miracle that only Christ could perform!

Love,
Erin

*****

September 27, 1996
Dear Erin,

It's unreal how lazy I've become. I haven't started on my "Last Statement" and have several letters to write—one to the victim's daughter, one to retired detective Ferguson, and one to Michelle and you. Please tell Michelle that I did get the birthday card she sent me. That was her polite way of telling me how I should've at least thanked her. ☺ That is why I'm getting off my lazy butt and writing her.

You asked if I have to send the visitation forms back when they're approved or is there some proof you get that it was approved. You won't need any documents. I'll receive a memo from Ms. Partain informing me if my request for a "special visit" with you all has been approved or disapproved. My mom sent me her birth certificate so proof of family relationship is now established. I will send you a copy of the memo she sends me. I thought I would have received the memo from her by now. I'll ask my counselor to "look into it" when we know positively that I'll be alive October 26th.

My lawyer was wrong when he informed me the judge would issue his ruling within a week since it was two weeks yesterday. If he doesn't issue it this week, I know I'll be alive for October 26 because my trial judge would have to wait until he receives the federal judge's ruling. Then he schedules the execution week for three weeks in advance. What I will do is call you since October begins a new month.

You asked me to explain further about when the judge stated how my appeal has "substantial allegations that could result in my sentence or conviction being set aside." I told you how Lawyer Smith had reneged on our agreement. He filed all 22 claims of errors instead of just the one claim (the "chair" being cruel and unusual punishment). That is what the judge was referring to when he made that statement.

The lawyers were 100% sure the judge would set aside my conviction and sentence. That means I'd be back at square #1—like I was just arrested. I would be returned to the county jail. The prosecutor would have to decide to retry me or release me. In some cases, when certain evidence has been ruled inadmissible by a higher court, a prosecutor won't retry the case. The defendant is then released or the prosecutor will offer a plea bargain. Then again, he can decide to seek the death penalty again. I'm pretty sure I wouldn't end up with the death sentence again. But I'd end up with a life sentence(s). I could've had a life sentence this time as I was offered a plea bargain. I turned it down.

Plus I don't want to put my victims' families through another trial. I've hurt them enough and don't want to re-open their wounds again. They want my life. It's the least I can do for them. I feel I owe them that. Most victims' families believe it will help in their healing. According to research done by the anti-death penalty people in which they interviewed the victims' families after the execution, it turns out it doesn't help most of the time. Even months and years afterward, a majority admitted the killer's death didn't help them like they thought it would.

The "riot squad" did a major shake down on us two days ago right after lunch. Boy, they were real petty too. A year ago I'm sure I would be in the "hole" now. But because of my religion, I didn't get mad. ☺ I had eaten one of the two sandwiches we had gotten and wrapped the other one to eat later. At 12:30 p.m., they shook us down. They took my sandwich. During our breakfast meal once every couple weeks, we get two small packages of jelly. I have a deal with a couple other guys for their jelly too. When there is a kind of meat in our sandwiches that I do not like, I remove it and make me a peanut butter and jelly sandwich. We can buy peanut butter off the store. Anyways, they even took my jellies. Here they give us jelly and sandwiches and then turn around and take them. Really petty, hey? Plus I had to box some of my Christian books up. Mom will have to pick them up when she visits. They said including my Bible, I'm only allowed seven books. There were several new books I had not read yet, but the rest was my books about Jesus which I like reading. Are you surprised that I held my temper? ☺ I am sure everyone else was surprised.

Got a smile reading about the "boys" and how they are given "timeouts." I feel it's good discipline. Better than being swatted which a lot of pet owners do when their pets have done something they shouldn't have.

Mom came to visit me today. Sure was good to see her. She told me that she had to have a biopsy done after her mammogram but it came back ok. I sure was relieved to hear that! Then she developed an infection that is related to her liver and is on an antibiotic for that but is starting to feel better. She sure is having her share of health issues. I worry about her.

While I am on a writing kick, I need to let you go and start on some of my other letters before I get lazy again. Sure hope we are visiting next month at this time! You all take care.

Love,
Larry

*****

377

October 4, 1996

Dear Larry,

Have you felt like you've been on an emotional roller coaster the last few weeks? I know I would feel that way if it were me. So much is "up in the air" for you right now as you await the judge's ruling to come through and a date to be set. We are being taught patience.

The letters you are writing to Mr. Ferguson and the victim's daughter especially will take some real thought. I have been praying that you will have the right words to express yourself to them.

I was already hopeful that we'd be able to visit on October 26. After getting your last letter, I feel even more so. In fact, it appears October 26 is the *only* date that we will be able to come. I've been praying for the Lord's will and specifically asked for Him to work it out so we could come on the twenty-sixth if He wanted us to visit. I feel that if I change the date, I would be trying to manipulate the details myself instead of letting Him take care of them. Do you understand what I mean? Michelle would not be able to come until after Thanksgiving if we waited, and I do not want to miss getting to visit you. So our visit is truly in the Lord's hands at this point, and He will have to arrange the details. So the judge will have to cooperate and wait longer to give his ruling (although he doesn't know it is actually out of his hands).

Thanks for explaining to me why you did not want to pursue a new trial. It would be very emotional for all involved—your family and the victims' families. The possibility of being released would probably be quite slim, and the alternative of life in prison is not one that you would want either. You are ready to be done with prison life and get to live your new life with Jesus outside of prison. In the time you have remaining, however, you can be used by Him.

It appears the "riot squad" was on a power trip when they came through. You're right—they were real petty. I couldn't believe they confiscated your jellies and saved sandwich! Sure can't see what harm food could do! It is sad you had to give up some of the books you had not read yet. But at least you got to keep your favorites. How nice it would have been if you could have given the books to some of the other guys. The squad probably supervised while you packed them up for shipment to your mom though. I am sure you would have let me know if your Welcome Home to Heaven picture had been confiscated! Guess you'll have to start collecting your jelly again. The peanut butter and jelly sandwiches must taste good when you don't like the meat on the sandwiches. Sure was a good move for you when they started giving sandwiches. I am *so proud* of the way you handled yourself during this incident—another proof that you are growing in your faith and changing!

On a lighter note, have I ever told you about Michelle and Ginger playing hide-and-seek? I have to hold Ginger until Michelle hides. Then, when she's ready, Ginger runs to find her. When she "sniffs" her out and barks, Michelle will come out. But until she barks, Michelle stays hidden. Ginger just loves to play the game! We all love watching them have fun together. None of our other poodles have ever learned to play hide-and-seek.

I've been thinking about how I can best correspond with you in the three or four weeks that we have left. The Lord has laid on my heart to be an encourager for you. So my letters may not be long, but I'm going to try to write a little something every few days and send you something to encourage you and remind you of the Lord's love for you. The devotional I'm sending today is from another of Max Lucado's books that I just started reading and is one I thought you could relate to. (You can tell that he's one of my favorite authors. He just has a way of getting to my heart!)

Keep "looking up" to the One who truly loves you and cares about you. Every day, I ask Him to help you feel His presence in your life and to wrap His loving arms around you if you're feeling down. I know He's been answering those prayers. I'll be looking forward to hearing from you again soon—by either letter or phone. The twenty-sixth will be here before we know it! As a matter of fact, if things continue to go as planned, we should be visiting face to face in just three weeks at this very time!

Love,
Erin

Think About It: Hope

What is your current greatest hope? A cancer-free life for you and your family? A long-needed vacation? A child? A husband or wife? Family harmony? Financial security? A job? Better health? An organ transplant? A true friend? A chance to make a difference in the world? A second chance to live your life differently? Is your hope not listed? Then, add it to the list.

Hope is defined as "to look forward to with desire and reasonable confidence or to believe, desire, or trust that something will happen."[77] Hope spurs one to keep going and pushing forward in life. Without hope, life can become depressing or without purpose.

There are actually two kinds of hope—worldly and spiritual. The majority of the hopes mentioned in the first paragraph are worldly ones. For some, that is the only type of hope known. With only worldly hope, one may feel he/she must be in complete charge of making "dreams" happen. For hopes that are out of one's control, then luck will determine if the hopes are realized. For most of Larry's life, this was his situation. No matter how hard he tried, he could not accomplish what he wanted in his own strength and power. He was a miserable person, living a miserable life, and without real hope. Have you ever felt like Larry at any time in your life? Perhaps you may even feel this way now. It is an exhausting way to live with many emotional roller coaster rides and deep disappointments. The end result can be depression and the desire to give up when your hopes go unfulfilled. Worldly hope is not *true* hope.

Do you currently live in the worldly hope realm? Do you wish you could be more confident that your hopes could have a better chance for being realized—especially that of getting a second chance to live your life differently or to make a real difference in the world? If so, then consider the second source of hope—spiritual hope. Spiritual hope is based on another part of the definition of the word, "a person or thing in which expectations are centered."[78] True hope is found in centering your hope in the person of Jesus Christ—as Larry eventually did. Look at some benefits of this type of hope from the verses on the next page.

> Blessed be the God and Father of our Lord Jesus Christ! According to His great mercy, He has caused us to be born again to a living hope through the resurrection of Jesus Christ from the dead. (1 Peter 1:3 NCV)
>
> May the God of hope fill you with all joy and peace as you trust in Him, so that you may overflow with hope by the power of the Holy Spirit. (Romans 15:13 NCV)
>
> "For I know the plans I have for you," declares the Lord, "plans to prosper you and not to harm you, plans to give you hope and a future." (Jeremiah 29:11 NCV)

Ponder the following quote: "If you belong to Christ, you are tethered to Christ."[79] Being tethered to someone depicts a *very* close relationship. If I am going to be tethered to someone, I would want it to be someone I can totally trust and depend upon. Christ is the only Someone that can meet these requirements. How does one become "tethered" to Christ? At the moment one gives one's life to Christ, He (in the form of the Holy Spirit) enters that person and establishes the only personal relationship that can give true hope. That hope is summarized in Romans 8:38–39:

> And I am convinced that nothing can ever separate us from God's love. Neither death nor life, neither angels nor demons, neither our fears for today nor our worries about tomorrow—not even the powers of hell can separate us from God's love. No power in the sky above or in the earth below—indeed, nothing in all creation will ever be able to separate us from the love of God that is revealed in Christ Jesus our Lord. (NLT)

Throughout this book, you have learned how to have that relationship. Do you?

Does it mean that Christians have all of their hopes realized? That they will never have cancer or other health issues, family problems, financial problems, disappointments, etc.? Absolutely not! However, they do have the assurance that no matter what happens, Christ is in control. Because the Holy Spirit resides within, Christians are never left to "do life" alone. Because Christ loves His children so much, He gives them what is best in the long term. Larry's greatest dream was to be able to donate his organs to save lives. That wish, however, was not granted to him during his lifetime. However, it is now being realized since his views on organ donation greatly affected me (and perhaps others) and led me to become an organ donor.

The *greatest* spiritual hope, however, comes at the time of death. Christ gives the hope of eternal life to all who accept Him as personal Savior. Christians know with a certainty, like Larry did, that a home in heaven waits for them after this life on earth ends. Though we or our loved ones naturally grieve over a death, we do not "grieve like the rest of mankind, who have no hope" (1 Thessalonians 4:13 NIV). Our hope is that we will see our Christian loved ones in heaven when our life on earth ends. This hope leads to joy and peace throughout our lifetimes.

What kind of hope do you currently depend on—earthly or spiritual? If Larry could have a personal conversation with you, he would urge you to choose the hope he eventually chose that is worth building your life upon.

Chapter 20

October 14, 1996

Dear Erin,

It sure was good to talk to you last Wednesday night. As you can tell, I'm not too articulate. So, during our visit, keep that in mind.

Speaking of the visit, it sure bothers me how much money it is costing you and Dave to come visit! ☺ I wanted to tell you on the phone when you told me the price of the tickets to forget the trip. I was afraid you would take it the wrong way, thinking I didn't want to visit with you two.

There is a Christian couple that lives by the prison who has cabins for out-of-state visitors that you two can stay in. That way you will save hotel money. They also will pick you up at the airport and bring you to and from the prison for our visit. They will then return you to the airport. It would also save you money from not having to rent a car. If you decide to stay there, I will have them call you. However, you may want to rent a car so you can drive around and see the sites in Atlanta. Mom sure wants you to stop by her place too! Enclosed with my letter are detailed directions and maps I drew on how to get to the cabins, the prison, and my mom's apartment.

You asked when we talked if I wanted you to bring my mom when you come. After thinking about it, I would prefer to visit with just you two. Then Mom and my brothers can visit me the next day, Sunday. The same people cannot visit both days. By then I'm sure the execution will be scheduled, so I'm sure they will want to visit. This way I'll have a visit Saturday and Sunday! ☺

Once you leave the visiting room, you cannot get back in. That is why there are vending machines that are available from 9 a.m. to 3 p.m. Visitors can buy sodas and snacks to get through lunch hunger if they stay that long. Once you arrive, it will be up to you how long you stay. But like I told you in an earlier letter, visiting ends at 3 p.m.

When you arrive at the prison and park, you two then walk to the prison entrance. Right across from the entrance there is a guard tower. You have to stop there and holler up to the guard who you are visiting. He'll check his list and then inform you to go into the entrance of the prison. You might have to mention that it is a "special visit." Tell them that you are my "cousin" and Dave is a "friend" like it states on the enclosed memo from Ms. Partain.

Only bring your purse, Dave, his wallet, and car keys. You two can wear your jewelry. You can wear a dress or pants, whatever is comfortable for sitting in. Dave has to wear pants (jeans, etc.). What I mean is that he can't wear shorts, only women can. Doesn't make sense, hey?

Once in the prison, you will put your purse, wallet, and car keys in a locker. Both of you will need to show them your picture ID (driver's license, etc.) when you sign in. Be sure to put "cousin" and "friend" on the sign-in sheet so it matches Ms. Partain's memo. Bring the enclosed memo in case they say their records don't have you two scheduled to visit. They are known to do that, just to mess with our visitors. The lady guards where you sign in are known to be rude to our visitors, too.

All you will be allowed to bring in the visiting room is change and one dollar bills, both for the vending machines. Be prepared to sit on some uncomfortable plastic chairs. Like I told you on the phone, there is no smoking allowed so you will not have to be concerned about your allergies to cigarette smoke. It's air conditioned too. ☺ Don't be nervous. I won't bite. ☺

Since it's my last days, I'm buying as many goodies as I can with the money I have. Might as well snack good my last days, hey?

Sure got a big smile reading about Michelle and Ginger's hide and seek game. Has Ginger ever failed to find Michelle? If so, I bet she starts to whine until she comes out.

Enclosed is a copy of a letter I sent retired detective Ferguson and his response. Sure wish I could have helped him out by donating my kidney to him.

Tell Michelle I am sorry I missed her when I called. I sure was looking forward to visiting with her too but understand why she cannot come. I'll see her in heaven. I should also get to call you on my last day and talk to her one last time.

It's now after 4:30 a.m. so I'll close. Thanks for caring and your prayers. I sure am looking forward to seeing you and Dave on the 26th!

Love,
Larry

Letter to Retired Detective Ferguson

October 1, 1996

Dear Mr. Ferguson,

Before I die, which will be soon, I just wanted to tell you that the Department of Corrections Commissioner was wrong. I would have given you one of my kidneys. He even lied when he stated on NBC *Dateline* that he knows me, that he has looked in my eyes. We have never met.

I have recently received a copy of a snitch letter that death row Inmate Spivey wrote regarding me. He stated I was just playing "games" with you. That I would not have given you my kidney and some other lies. Spivey has a habit of writing snitch letters and to prosecutors too. He informs them that Inmate So and So lived in his cell block while on death row and bragged and laughed to him about the murder(s) he committed. Spivey would then be used as a witness against the other inmate at his new trial. Because of his lies, he is in "protective custody." Why am I telling you all this? In case the Department of Corrections has or does send you a copy of Spivey's snitch letter to try to justify their compassionless refusal to allow me to donate a kidney to you.

Enclosed is a copy of an article that was in the American Bar Association Journal as well as my reply to the article. I'm sending you these because even though I wasn't allowed to give you one of my kidneys, I hope you will continue to be an advocate for this issue.

I reiterate, I would have given you not just one of my kidneys but both of them and my heart. I read of your heart problem too. You have earned the right to life. I feel I forfeited my right to life.

You are in my prayers. (Matthew 22:39-40—what I have recently learned from our God!)

Love,
Larry Lonchar

Response from Detective Ferguson

October 9, 1996
Dear Larry,

Thank you for your letter. I am glad that we are able to communicate one on one.

The DOC commissioner told NBC *Dateline* that he had never talked to me concerning the organ issue when I had in fact talked with him on the telephone on one occasion expressing my wish to have blood samples taken from you to be submitted for testing for transplant. He stated that he had no objection as long as the State Attorney General had no objections and would approve.

I have not received a snitch letter or copy from the death row inmate, Spivey, concerning you and I really don't expect to because the State has made no effort to accommodate me or show me any compassion concerning my plight or health.

I have read the article in the ABA Journal, and I totally agree with your letter of response. I never doubted that you would follow through and donate one of your kidneys to me. In fact, I trust you more than any of the State's spokespersons because they have been less than honorable concerning this matter. I find it very difficult to forgive them for their political position.

I certainly plan to continue to be an advocate for this issue; and, if everything goes as planned, we hope to have a bill before the Legislature this January.

Please continue to communicate any information or your feelings concerning this issue as your help and support is needed. Our joint efforts will lead to a window of opportunity for any prisoner in the future who desires to be an organ donor. It is my opinion that we have the voting public on our side; and in the future, I plan to run a state-wide survey to prove that you and I are right and the State is wrong.

I know that time is running out for you, and I wish I had the opportunity to see you to personally say "thanks," but I doubt seriously that the State would approve a visit.

I am very pleased to know that you have made peace with our maker.

Sincerely,
Melvin Ferguson

*****

October 18, 1996
Dear Larry,

Michelle was really bummed to miss your recent phone call. She said that she probably wouldn't get to talk to you again. I told her that she might have a chance if you are able to call us on your last day. (I hate to even say that.)

I'm glad you didn't tell us not to come when I talked with you on the phone. You know me pretty well. I would have thought you didn't really want us to come. Don't worry about the price of the tickets—we aren't. We always get away for a weekend in October—we're considering this our getaway. Only this year, we're going a little farther!

We already have our hotel reservations made so we will just keep those since it will be easy to find from the airport. We've never been to Atlanta before, so we will probably do a little exploring too.

I look forward to seeing the Olympic stadium and some of the other sites. We'll give your mom a call and get together with her while we're there. I was thinking she might like to go out to dinner with us as our guest. I'll call her and ask what she feels up to.

I so appreciate how specific you were in telling us what to expect when we get to the prison, what is acceptable dress, what items we can bring, and what denomination our money needs to be in. Certainly we can buy things from the vending machine for you too. I think you mentioned on weekends that you normally do not get a lunch. No way would we buy something and eat in front of you!

Boy, those directions you gave on how to get to your mom's apartment and the prison are great! I'll be taking them with me. I never expected maps! Sounds like everything is easy to find—which is good.

Thanks for sending the copy of your letter to Mr. Ferguson and his response. I didn't realize that some guy was writing snitch letters. That's probably part of the reason why the warden was talking like that about you. I can see why Inmate Spivey would be in protective custody since there are probably several inmates who are very ticked at him. You did a good job of expressing your honest desire to give Mr. Ferguson your kidney(s) and even heart. He sounded convinced of your sincerity. The reference to the verses in Matthew were a great testimony of your new faith!

I'm glad you don't bite! ☺ I guess I should tell you that we don't bite either! We'll probably be a little nervous until we finally get to visit. I don't understand your comment that you're not too articulate. I haven't noticed that when talking with you on the phone. I'm sure we'll find plenty to talk about. I don't know exactly what time we'll be there on Saturday, but it will be close to the beginning of visiting hours. Knowing me, I'll be awake real early and anxious to get there!

Use the money order that's enclosed to really treat yourself. Buy your favorite goodies, and think of us when you eat them. We won't get to send you a goodie box this Christmas, so we thought we'd just let you buy your favorite snacks now. So go ahead and splurge—you deserve it!

I asked Michelle if there had ever been a time when Ginger hasn't been able to find her when they were playing hide-and-seek. She said she didn't think so. Ginger has a really good sniffer! When she does find her, she keeps barking until Michelle comes out! You would love watching them together.

Just a few words of encouragement from Ephesians 1:11 to give you something to ponder. Do you know that you are considered a treasure to God? "Moreover, because of what Christ has done, we have become gifts to God that he delights in" (TLB). This verse makes me sure feel special to Him. Remember that He feels this way about you too!

It's getting late and has been a long day, so I'm going to end. I'll write a note the first of the week, but it might not reach you before our visit. See you Saturday!

Love,
Erin

*****

October 20, 1996
Dear Erin,

I'm hoping you receive this letter before you leave as I have an invitation from my mom and brother for you. When you get in town and are all settled, *call Mom.* Also, my oldest brother, Tom, wants you two, Mom, and Rob to come to his house for a cook-out. You'll sure like him. He's such a good man. I have enclosed their phone numbers.

I am so looking forward to our visit! I hope you two are talkers. ☺ I'm sure not one. With three of us, though, we should find enough to talk about.

Last week they put some new chairs in the visiting rooms. ☺ They are more comfortable than the old ones and have a little cushion on them, not much though. The old ones didn't have a cushion.

I sure am surprised that the "Execution Order" wasn't signed last week as the Attorney General was all over the media on the 10th saying how his office would be getting it signed in a day or two. I'm glad they didn't because I was worried that I would die on my mom's or Tom's birthdays at the beginning of November. If they sign it this week, which I'm sure they will, it will be after their birthdays.

Tell Michelle she will talk to me again. I am planning on calling your house on my "last day."

Well, I'll let you go. See you Saturday. ☺

Love,
Larry

*****

October 27, 1996
Dear Erin,

Hope you made it home alright! I can't tell you enough how much your two's visit meant to me! Thank you so much! It was 99% perfect, our visit. If Michelle could have come, it would have been 100%. Boy, you are attractive and young looking too! ☺ When I got back to my cell after our visit, I thought of a lot of things I wanted to talk about during our visit. We will have to talk about them in my next call or in heaven.

I would have ate more "goodies" out of the machine but you two had spent all that money on me already—plane tickets, hotel, car rental, and other expenses. Thank you for the $20 I received last week too! It came right on time. I'll sure be buying some goodies! You send me more money than my family!

Tom and Rob visited me today. I was surprised to see Tom with a beard. It makes him look older. Mom wasn't feeling good so she couldn't come. They told me how nice of a time you all had together. That sure made me happy too!

If you don't mind, tell me what Mom said when you gave her the book, *And the Angels Were Silent,* by Max Lucado. Like you worked on me to become a Christian, I'm working on her. ☺ I know in my heart that she isn't going to live much longer. I'm aware of her health problems. Her body is just about done in. Why I have to get her soul well. I can't fix her body.

Did you two do any sight-seeing?

Found out after our visit that the Supreme Court (GA) who heard some arguments on Wayne Feltner last week lifted the "stay" they had granted him last month. The judge then signed a new "execution order" the very next day. Here I could have had my "execution order" signed two weeks ago. I think God knows I'm not yet (close) ready, but I will be soon! I still have some letters to write. Plus He wanted us to have our visit first. ☺

I have to get my lazy butt going. Have to write my "Last Statement" which I sure need your help with. Plus some other letters that are important. I received Michelle's letter today. So, I'll write her and enclose it with this letter. My attorney comes tomorrow and I'll ask him to mail your letter to save me the postage.

I know you aren't looking forward to the cold and snow that will soon be upon you all. Don't fall this year!

Well, I'll let you go. Again, thank you so much for caring and your prayers!

Love,
Larry

*****

October 28, 1996
Dear Erin,

Today I received a call from my lawyer. We were talking about other things when she mentioned she had seen the attorney from New Orleans at their office during her lunch break. I told her I haven't heard from him in two weeks plus and probably won't again until he calls me to inform me that my "Execution Order" has been signed. She went quiet and told me to hang on for a second. A minute later, he came on the line. I asked him what he was doing in Atlanta. He said he was in town to come see me tomorrow after he received the news. I said "What news?" He then informed me my trial judge had signed the "Execution Order" Friday. Seems like I would have heard it before now.

On the news this evening, they said I'm scheduled for execution on November 13 at 2 p.m. and Wayne Feltner on November 14 at 7 p.m. I'm sure by the time you receive this you will already know. How about I call you the weekend of the 9th and 10th? Write and tell me what would be a good time to catch you all at home. Have it after 3 p.m. in case I have a visit, ok?

I am glad that we did not know about my execution date when you came for your visit since it would have put a damper on our time together. I am learning that the Lord's timing is good.

Let me close so I can get busy writing my other letters. If I do not get a chance to write again, we will definitely talk one or two more times. I know this news is probably hard for you. Just remember that I will be going to a better place.

Love,
Larry

*****

October 29, 1996
Dear Larry,

What a joy it was to visit with you on Saturday! I'm still thanking our God for working out all the details! It is a time that I will always treasure in my memories. Whether you realized it or not, you were truly a blessing to both Dave and me. I'm grateful I got to see firsthand how happy and positive you are about your circumstances. It is refreshing to see things through the eyes of a new Christian. God must surely be looking down on you with a big, satisfied smile on His face!

What a witness you are being at the prison and to other people that you are coming in contact with. Your changed life and attitudes must speak so loudly to others and make them know that something supernatural has happened to you—something that only Christ could reach down and do in a life! I'm sure those around you are baffled, and I can understand why the warden asked you, "What's *wrong* with you, Larry? You shouldn't be so happy. You are going to be dying soon." Only another Christian would be able to understand.

We had a safe flight back on Sunday. When we went to church that night, you wouldn't believe how many people at church asked about you! So many have been praying that we'd get to visit you and that all would go well. It was a thrill for Dave and me to share with them that it was a wonderful trip and what a blessing you were to us. We were being stopped by so many people that Pastor Spencer asked us to give a short report during the evening worship service.

It was extremely hard to come "down" after such a great weekend. Even on Monday, it was still hard to settle down. However, I came crashing down when my phone rang around 3:30 p.m. when Laura, one of your attorneys, called to tell me your execution date is set for November 13. I'm *extremely* glad the judge's order got in late Friday night so we didn't know about it on Saturday. I know that was also the Lord's working. Knowing a date certainly makes it so much more real—even though we knew it was coming soon. When I was crying and feeling bad, Dave told me that I need to look at it as your promotion day—when you finally get to go home. So that's what I'm going to do. Knowing how you feel about it makes it easier for me to view it in a more positive way. I know you're looking forward to getting out of prison since it's such a terrible life and that heaven will be such a paradise for you. I'm not going to be sad because I know you aren't! But I'm *sure* going to miss one of my best friends!

After our visit, I learned that you arranged for Tom to have us over to his house for dinner on Saturday night. That was very thoughtful of you. We enjoyed ourselves. It had been years since I had seen Rob, your mom, and Tom. He and Lindy made us feel right at home. I'm glad we had the opportunity to visit with them. Before I even got into the house, Tom told me what powerful letters I had written to you—and I wondered how he knew. Then, he told me that you had sent my letters to your mom and family. That was my surprise for the night—but a good one. Not only did I get to witness to you, but also to them.

Enclosed is another devotional by Max Lucado that is on the subject of death. I really liked the perspective that he gives and thought you may appreciate reading it. He sure makes death less threatening. I think that it's not death itself that so many fear, but the fear comes in not knowing exactly how they will die. Will it be cancer, stroke, heart attack, etc.? Death itself isn't painful—it's the circumstances that cause our death that are. But if we can only remember that no matter how death comes that Jesus is also right there with us as Christians, then death should not be feared. I know that this is how you are viewing it. I'm going to make it more of a practice to think this way too. We have to keep thinking about what is just on the other side of death—an eternity in heaven with Jesus! It just won't get any better! You'll probably be all settled in by the time I get there. I'll let you and my dad take me on a tour.

I told Michelle that you would call her with one of your two calls for November. She was happy to hear that because she so wants to talk to you again. She said that her Monday night band rehearsals are now over, so either Monday or Tuesday nights should be a good time to call.

I mentioned a song titled "The Old Rugged Cross Made the Difference"[80] to you on Saturday during our visit. I've enclosed the words so you could see the actual message of the song. Every time I've heard it lately, I think of you and how your life has been changed by God.

I'm continuing to pray for the Lord's strength for you and your family as you go through your last days. I'll also be remembering your mom, Tom, Rob, Tina, and Steve and pray that Christ will touch their hearts in the same way that He's touched yours. I will also be praying for guidance and motivation for you as you write your last letters and final statement.

Since it is suppertime, I need to sign off. Gregg is eating supper with us tonight since Jenny is working until ten. It'll be nice to visit with him and help get my mind off the phone call from Laura. Keep looking to Jesus for every decision you make and keep showing His love to those you are around. We love you.

Love,
Erin

*****

November 3, 1996

Dear Larry,

How good to get at least one more letter from you! I certainly understand if you cannot write again since there are many letters to be written as well as your final statement. If for some reason you do not get the final statement done for me to help you with it, I know the Lord will guide you in writing it. You only need ask Him for His help.

Thanks for the nice compliments about me in your last letter. I told Dave that you said I looked young. He said to tell you that's because I live with him—that he waits on me hand and foot! I told him I needed a good laugh! We always joke good naturedly with each other. I'm always teasing him about being older than me—like I did when we visited. He tells me he robbed the cradle. As you know, we started dating when I was in the tenth grade, and he had just graduated. He always takes teasing well and is equally good at dishing it out!

You asked what your mom said when I gave her the book. She seemed very appreciative. I told her that it was one that you had enjoyed and thought she might also like it. I put stars next to the chapters that I felt she would get the most out of—that talked more about salvation. I gave it to her in the car before we got to Tom's because she told me on the way that he was going to take her home that night. Originally, I was going to give it to her when we took her home. But the Lord had his hand even in that. We got lost on the way to Tom's and sat in a Wendy's parking lot for about a half hour—which gave me an opportunity to talk alone with her and give her the book. When we got to Tom's, she showed Rob and him what she had been given and twice during the evening commented about wanting to make sure her book left with her. I feel that she intends to read it and is pleased to have it. I also put a *Knowing God Personally* booklet in it that presents the plan of salvation. My mom said that she thinks your mom will be quite receptive to them both. We can only encourage her—Christ is the One who has to touch her heart. But we both know that He can certainly work in a person's heart! Our prayers on behalf of your mom are known to Christ. He wants her saved even more than we do.

I got a smile out of the way you said that you were "working on her like I worked on you to become a Christian." Your comment "I have to get her soul well" was touching. That's exactly what the Lord does, isn't it—He heals our soul! You're very perceptive. I love hearing the way you express yourself as a new Christian.

The Lord has laid a burden on my heart for your mom (as He has on yours) and for your brothers. I feel when the burden is there, it's for a reason. A burden on my heart for you in 1993 is what led me to write to you the very first time. I'm *so* glad I listened to the Lord and wrote, or I would have missed out on such a wonderful friendship with you. But most of all, you may have missed out on heaven!

Because of another burden placed on my heart, I have written a letter to your family and sent them a cassette tape with three songs for them to listen to. A copy of the letter is enclosed so you know what I wrote. I hope the tape and letter can bring them a small measure of comfort. Your mom should receive it by the end of the week. So if she and your brothers visit on Sunday, as I would hope they will, you can ask them about it if you feel led to. Maybe between the two of us, we can get the message of Christ's love to them. How I wish I could visit you again!

I know you are disappointed that you didn't get your desire to give back something to society by donating your organs. However, the Lord is still giving you an opportunity to give to others. You don't realize how much He is using you to speak to the hearts of others through your testimony. The verse you chose for your good-bye letters, 2 Corinthians 5:6, will be an additional testimony. Who knows how many you'll be able to reach just by what you say and write in the few days you have left and through your final statement. You won't know the total impact you had until you get to heaven. Actually, this gift you're giving is much better than donating an organ because it will have eternal results.

Since I will be talking with you a couple more times before the thirteenth, this will be my last formal letter. I will, however, send you some encouragement cards between now and then. So long for now my cousin, dear friend, and brother in the Lord!

Love you,
Erin

Letter to Larry's Family

November 2, 1996
Dear Elsie and Family,

I felt I needed to write you as you have all been on my mind so much during the last couple of weeks—but especially since I knew that a date has been set. I know how hard it is to lose someone you so dearly love since I've experienced it firsthand when my dad died about two and half years ago. That was a time of deep grief in my life. During that time, God taught me some important things that helped me deal with my grief, and I want to share some of them with you as a possible help for you as you grieve.

God often speaks to my heart through music. Over the last two years, three songs have especially meant a lot to me, and I wanted to share them with you. But before you listen to the tape, please read this letter first.

Larry has come to know the real meaning of these songs in the last six months since he's become a Christian. I'd like you to try to hear these songs through his ears and to try to see from his heart why they now have a very special meaning. I don't know how much of what I'm going to tell you that Larry's had an opportunity to share with you, but many changes have taken place within his heart and life during the last year. Perhaps you've noticed the gradual change and may have even wondered about it.

A year ago in November, Larry wrote telling me that he had some good news—that he now believed there was a God. This was a *major* breakthrough for him because up to that point, he didn't believe God existed. God spoke to his heart, however, through a book on the twelve disciples that someone sent him to read. Since that time, God has continued to work in his life. From the very first letters that I got from Larry beginning in 1993, he said that he envied those who were Christians and wished he could be a Christian but never would be able to because he didn't believe there was a God. The road has not been easy for him.

Once his belief in God came, however, he then struggled with the issue of forgiveness. He didn't believe God would want to forgive him for the things he had done throughout his life—but even more important, he didn't feel he could ever deserve God's love. He eventually realized that none of us *deserve* God's love and forgiveness—that's why Christ had to die. His death and resurrection purchased our forgiveness of sins, and He presented salvation to every man and woman as a gift—with no strings attached. Larry finally reached out and took the gift Christ was offering to him—and he's been a changed man ever since.

He now knows true peace—something that in 1993 he thought only death could bring to him. He told Dave and me when we visited that he's so grateful that his attempt at suicide and the two execution orders that ended in appeals didn't take his life because he would not have been ready to die. He gives God the credit for intervening and realized that death then would not have resulted in the peace he was so craving. Larry knows that only Christ can give true peace.

Larry told us that he's ready to go this time. Actually, he's longing to escape life on death row—which is really no life at all. You may be wondering why anyone would *want* to die. I could sense when we visited that you are struggling with his desire to die. I can understand why—you dearly love him and will miss him greatly. A part of you will be gone. Plus, the way he will be dying is so difficult to handle. I am really struggling with the method.

About two weeks ago, however, I put a tape on and heard a song titled "Sheltered in the Arms of God" that has helped me to deal a little better with the situation. Really listen to the words and know that because Larry is now a Christian, he will not be going through death alone. None of us can be there that day, but God will be. Actually, think of him as tenderly holding Larry in His arms and carrying him every inch of the way. He loves Larry even more than we possibly could and doesn't want him to suffer any more than he has to. I've been praying that God will insulate him that day and in His mercy take him quickly. The third line of the song says, "I'll have no fear in death since Jesus walks beside me."[81] Larry told me that he's not afraid. Why? Because he knows that what awaits him on the other side of the chair is so much better than the life he's had in prison.

In listening to the song, Dave said that it reminds him of the words of Psalm 23.

> The Lord is my Shepherd; I have everything that I need. He lets me rest in green pastures. He leads me to calm water. He gives me new strength. He leads me on paths that are right for the good of His name. Even if I walk through the very dark valley of death, I will not be afraid because you are with me. Your rod and your staff comfort me . . . Surely your goodness and love will be with me all my life and I will live in the house of the Lord (heaven) forever. (NCV)

In talking with Larry and reading his letters, these could very well have been his words.

The second song on the tape is titled "Finally Home."[82] This was the song that our pastor sang at our request at my dad's funeral, so it's very special to me. The words of the chorus especially touch my heart. It made losing my dad so much easier to take knowing that he was in heaven and knowing how thrilled he must be to see Jesus for the first time and to know that it was his new home—one he'd never have to leave. This is what Larry is looking forward to also.

Even though I knew my dad was in heaven, I still missed him terribly. And many days, I wished he could be around to talk to and hug. Then, several months after his death, I heard the third song that is on the tape—"If You Could See Me Now"[83]—that helped me change my mind about wishing him back. The chorus of the song talks about seeing him walking the streets of gold with no pain and being totally content—so happy that we would never wish him back to the life he had before. When I thought of how my dad's health had deteriorated and how hard it was for him to get around, I knew that he was so much better off in heaven with Jesus. If we can think of Larry as being happier than he's ever been and being finally free of prison and all the negative things that he has had to endure throughout his life, maybe it will help us in our grief.

I don't know what your reaction to my letter will be, but I'm praying that you will accept it with the spirit of love that it's being written in. My heart is aching for all of you. I'm sharing your grief because Larry is also special to me. I think he would like for you to know these things about his new life.

His greatest joy would be to have all of his family in heaven with him. I don't know your hearts—only God and you do. If you don't have a personal relationship with Christ that includes forgiveness of sins like Larry experienced, my prayer is that you will come to know Christ personally sometime soon. The booklet that I have enclosed, *Knowing God Personally*, will tell you how to have this relationship. It's so simple but so extremely important. Larry wants to be able to personally greet each of you with a hug in heaven. But knowing God personally is the only way that will be possible. For Christians, death is not goodbye because we have the hope of seeing our loved ones in heaven again someday soon.

Take care. Dave, Michelle, my mom, and I will all be praying for you. I'm only a phone call away if you would ever care to talk. I'm a good listener. Mom and I learned in the grief recovery class we took that *time*, *talk*, and *tears* are all necessary to the grief process and healing.

Love,
Erin

Final Call with Larry

November 13, 1996 at 6 p.m.

Operator	Will you accept a collect call from Larry Lonchar?
Erin	Yes . . . Hello!
Larry	Hi! I am glad it worked out that I could call y'all tonight.
Erin	I imagine this has been quite a day for you. What have you done with your time?
Larry	The day has actually gone by fast. I wrote my last letters to my family members and watched the news on TV relating to my execution.
Erin	Did you get your final statement written? If so, can you remember what you said? I would like to know and see if it gets reported accurately.
Larry	I actually have it here with me. "To the people of Georgia, Thank you for killing me. You thought you were punishing me, but you rewarded me by sending me to a better place—heaven."
Erin	It is simple and to the point. I am happy that it included that you are going to heaven! That is so much better than what your final statement would have been last time.
Larry	I also had my last meal not long ago.

Erin	What did you order?
Larry	I had strawberries, grapes, peaches, plums, and a vanilla shake—food I haven't had for a long time.
Erin	Has the chaplain been with you?
Larry	Yes, Chaplain Lavelle has been with me since 2 p.m. and will stay with me until the end. I don't know if I ever told you but I was part of a prayer and revival group that the Chaplain started in August. Will you do me a favor and call the Chaplain tomorrow to ask him how I handled the execution?
Erin	Yes, I will. I am so glad that he is there with you. Thanks for telling me you were part of the prayer group.
Larry	Is Michelle on the phone too?
Michelle	Yes, I am on the phone in my mom's bedroom.
Larry	You take good care of Ginger. I sure loved reading about her in your letters. Thanks for all of my jokes too. You gave me many smiles.
Michelle	I love jokes! I am happy they made you smile. I promise to take good care of Ginger. I know you encouraged my mom to let me have a dog. Thank you for that! I am going to miss you.
Larry	You'll get to see me and talk to me in heaven.

Michelle	Yes, I'll finally get to see you since I did not get to come visit! Will you give my grandpa a big hug from me and my mom when you see him?
Larry	You bet I will!
Erin (interrupts)	Channel 3 news is on right now and is airing the interview I did with a Christian reporter from there this afternoon. I wanted to make sure that everyone knew you were a Christian and a changed man. We are recording it so I can watch it later.
Larry	I have really made the news today! I thought your local news would carry the execution news.
Erin	A reporter from our local paper also interviewed me this afternoon. I was so upset that the paper had printed the old quote about you saying you would be going to hell. After crying about that, I contacted someone I knew at the newspaper to see how I could get in touch with the reporter to tell him it was no longer true. Because I was a family member, he jumped at the opportunity to interview me. I told the reporter before he came that I would not talk about your crimes but only how you have changed. He agreed and kept his promise.
Larry	Boy, you sure have been popular today. Thanks for doing those interviews and telling how I have changed.

Erin	Pastor Spencer is here right now to pray with us. Just a second, I want to ask him if he will sing a song to you that he sang at my dad's funeral—"Finally Home"—and then pray with you.
Pastor Spencer	Hi, Larry. How good to get to speak with you. Erin has asked me to sing a song and pray with you.
Pastor Spencer	Sings song "Finally Home."
Larry	Thanks. That beautiful song sure describes me in a short time! I am ready to meet Jesus.
Pastor Spencer	Let's have a short prayer. Father, what do we pray at a time like this? We thank you for loving Larry and for offering him so great a salvation. We thank you for cousin Erin writing and sharing her heart and Yours for Larry's soul. It is with absolute hope and confidence in You, the Resurrection and the Life, that we commit Larry to you with the assurance that we will one day see him again. Even now, bless Larry and his family. Thank you, God, in Jesus's matchless name, Amen!
Larry	Thank you again.
Pastor Spencer	Our church will be praying for you tonight at our 7 p.m. prayer meeting.
Larry	That will mean a lot to me.

Erin	I am so glad that you called while Pastor Spencer was here so you could hear the song. I absolutely love to hear him sing.
Larry	I need to tell you something. Tom and my attorney are trying to appeal my execution at seven. I will not agree to it though. I am ready to go.
Erin	Thanks for telling me. I know you are ready to go. I will be praying then that their appeal will be dismissed.
Larry	I also have a favor to ask. Will you keep in touch with my mom? She needs Jesus so she can join me in heaven.
Erin	I had already decided to keep in touch with her. I want her to be with us too. And you know that I do not give up easily once I set my mind to it!
Larry	Thank you! Yes, I know you do not give up easily! One other thing I want you to know before our time runs out. I have decided to donate my body to science for a couple of reasons, to save funeral expenses for my mom and so that the effects of execution on the body can be studied. It will be two years before my mom gets my ashes.
Erin	That is a very selfless thing to do. I am surprised it will take two years.

Larry	Well, the guard just told me I have to be wrapping up our conversation. I still have some calls to make to my family. Pray for them since tonight will be hard for them.
Erin	The time has just gone way too fast! I don't want to hang up or say goodbye (as voice catches).
Michelle	Goodbye, Larry. I love you! I will look forward to seeing you in heaven.
Larry	Goodbye, Michelle. Love you too.
Erin	(Trying to hold it together emotionally) I am not going to say goodbye but see you later since we'll get to see each other in heaven.
Larry	The guard said I have to hang up. Bye! Love you!
Erin	See you later! Love you!

Think About It: Peace

Have you ever been in a place similar to Larry—you want peace so badly but it alludes you? Nothing you try brings the tranquility, contentment, and calmness you are seeking. You may even wonder if there is such a thing in today's crazy, mixed-up world.

Larry thought only death could bring him the peace he was seeking a majority of his life. As much as he craved peace, he continually fought against the source of it. Why? He was being blinded by Satan to the truth that death would *not* be his solution. Without Jesus as his personal Savior, he would have discovered that his assumption was terribly wrong and would have been condemned to an eternity of torment—worse than the physical and mental torment he experienced in prison and on death row.

What Larry needed was to meet the only source of peace. Jesus told us in John 14:27 just before His return to heaven the following: "I am leaving you with a gift—peace of mind and heart. And the peace I give is a gift the world cannot give. So don't be troubled or afraid" (NCV). Even though Christ made the gift available, however, He also gave a condition for being able to receive it in Romans 5:1, "Since we have been made right with God by our faith, we have peace with God. This happened through our Lord Jesus Christ" (NCV). Larry discovered this secret to peace before his death—a personal relationship with Jesus—which radically changed his outlook and made his final days bearable and even happy.

Are you longing for peace like Larry finally experienced near the end of his life? Isaiah 26:3 gives the secret, "You [Jesus] will keep in perfect peace all who trust in you, all whose thoughts are fixed on you." Can you face death with the same peace that Larry did? It is only possible if you have personally met the peace giver and invited Him to be the Lord of your life like he did. Doing so is as simple as ABC:

- Admit Jesus is God's Son.
- Believe He came to earth, lived a sinless life, died for your sins, and rose again.
- Confess your sins and ask for His forgiveness.

Even for Christians, however, there will be hard times, times when worry can seem to steal our peace, times of sadness. At those times, Jesus encourages us to trust Him to see us through such situations and draw on the strength only He can give. Why should we trust Him? Because He knows the future and has promised, "I will never fail you. I will never abandon you" (Hebrews 13:5 NCV). He is the reason for our peace.

Have peace? Want peace? The decision is totally yours.

Epilogue

After our phone call and as 7 p.m. approached, I went to my bedroom, kneeled by my bed, and began praying—for Larry as he faced his execution and for his family members who I knew must be going through one of the most horrible nights of their lives.

While praying, my thoughts focused on how God must have felt the day His Son faced an excruciating death on a Roman cross to take upon Himself the sins of the entire world. Tears of grief must have been flowing from His eyes as they were from mine for my cousin. The main difference, however, is that Jesus had done no wrong deserving of execution. He faced death because of His great love for us and to purchase our ticket to heaven.

Because of the last-minute appeal from his brother and attorney, Larry was executed not at 7 p.m. but at 12:39 a.m. on Thursday, November 14. As he was strapped into the chair and the electrodes attached, it was reported that he was smiling. Larry's very last words were, "Father, forgive them for they know not what they do."[84] A couple of minutes later, he was gone from earth and present with his Savior!

As Larry requested, I called Chaplain Lavelle, who had been with him since 2 p.m. on November 13. In a conversation the two had during the day, Larry told him, "God was the one who stopped the other two executions. If I had died in either one of them, I would have been lost. I'm ready to go now, and I'm sure of going this time." There were times throughout the day when those around him were joking and trying to irritate him, but he handled the irritations well and remained calm. At one time, Larry commented, "Some people are just that way." The chaplain also said, "You couldn't ask for any-one to handle the situation better than Larry. The Lord was with him, and he was in peace all the way. He faced death with calm and the assurance of going to heaven. We prayed together before saying goodbye."

As I promised, I kept in touch with his mother. She gave me a copy of the letter that Larry wrote to his family on the back of his special "When I Come Home to Heaven" picture:

11-8-1996

To My Family:
"*Death* is nothing at all. I have only slipped away into the next room. I am I, and you are you. Whatever we were to each other that we still are. Call me by my old familiar name, speak to me in the easy way which you always used. Put no dif-ference in your tone, wear no forced air of solem-nity or sorrow. Laugh as we always laughed at the little jokes we enjoyed together. Let my name be ever the household word that it always was. Let it be spoken without effort, without the trace of a shadow on it. Life means all that it ever meant. It is the same as it ever was; there is unbroken conti-nuity. Why should I be out of mind because I am out of sight? I am waiting for you, for an interval, somewhere very near, just 'round the corner.

All is well."[85]

Don't be sad, as I'm now in heaven. I will be waiting for you all, so we can be together for eternity. ☺

Love,
Larry

Before his mother's death a few years later, she also accepted Christ as her personal Savior. Today, she and Larry are rejoicing together in heaven and enjoying their new lives with Jesus—the only true Source of peace.

Afterword

The purpose for writing this book was to demonstrate what God did for my cousin Larry in forgiving his sin and receiving him as a child of God. However, beyond that wonderful miracle, it's about what God did for me, the writer. It is also about what God can do for you, the reader! "Praise the Lord! Salvation and glory and power belong to our God" (Revelation 19:1b NLT).

Appendix of Scripture Verses by Topic

Anger	Matthew 11:25 Ephesians 4:26 Colossians 3:13
Attributes of God/Christ	Deuteronomy 29:29a Psalm 73:1 and 90:2 Isaiah 55:8 1 Samuel 16:7b Matthew 19:26B Mark 10:27 John 1:3 and 14:8–9 2 Corinthians 1:9 2 Thessalonians 1:6 2 Peter 3:9b
Creation	Genesis 1:1 Genesis 2:18
Divorce	Matthew 19:3–6,9 Ephesians 5:25
Domestic Violence Hotline	1-800-799-SAFE (7233)
Faith	Matthew 17:20 Hebrews 11:1
False prophets	Matthew 7:15 Mark 13:22 2 Peter 2:11

Forgiveness	Psalm 103:1–4, 8–13 Jeremiah 31:4 Matthew 11:28 2 Peter 3:9b 1 John 1:9
Grace	Ephesians 2:8–9
Grief	John 11:35 1 Thessalonians 4:13
Hate	Genesis 4:1–16 1 John 3:15
Heaven (Existence of)	Luke 23:43 John 14:2 Acts 7:55–56 2 Corinthians 5:8 Revelation 21:4, 10–11, and 21–25
Hell/Satan (Existence of)	Isaiah 14:12 Luke 16:23–24 John 8:10,44 2 Corinthians 4:3–4 1 Peter 5:8 1 John 3:10–12 Revelation 14:10–11 and 20:7–15
Holy Spirit	John 14:16–17, 26 Acts 4:8 and 31 Romans 5:5 and 8:16 1 Corinthians 3:16 Galatians 4:6
Hope	Jeremiah 29:11 Romans 5:5–10, 8:38–39, and 15:7,13 Hebrews 6:19 1 Thessalonians 4:13 1 Peter 1:3

Judging	Matthew 7:1–5 John 8:1–11 Romans 2:1–3 Ephesians 4:15
Judgment	Hebrews 9:27
Judgment seat of Christ	Romans 14:11 1 Corinthians 3:10–15
Great White Throne Judgment	2 Corinthians 5:10 Revelation 20:10–15
Mercy	Psalm 116:1–5 Luke 23:42–43 Ephesians 2:4–5 Titus 3:4–5a
Miracles	Exodus 14:10–29 2 Kings 5:1–14 Daniel 4 and 6 Matthew 8:23–27 Mark 4:35–41 Luke 7:1–10 Luke 8:22–25, 26–39, and 22:50–51 John 9:1–12 and 11:1–44
Peace	Isaiah 26:3 John 14:27 Romans 5:1
Promises	Matthew 11:28 John 10:28–29 and John 16:53 2 Corinthians 5:8 Hebrews 13:5
Pride	Proverbs 16:18
Salvation	Jeremiah 29:13 John 3:16, 14:6, 16:33 Acts 16:31 Romans 3:23, 5:8, 6:23, 10:9–13

	2 Corinthians 5:17 1 John 1:9,12 Revelation 3:20
Self-esteem	Psalm 139:13–18 Isaiah 49:16 Jeremiah 1:5a Zephaniah 3:17 Matthew 10:30 Romans 5:8 and 8:26b Ephesians 1:11 and 2:10 1 Peter 2:9
Strength	Philippians 4:13
Suicide National Prevention Hotline	1-800-273-8255
Trials	Isaiah 40:27–31 and 43:2 James 1:2–3

Notes

1. "Execution date scheduled for man with ties to B.C," *Battle Creek Enquirer* (Battle Creek, February 9, 1993), accessed January 19, 2017. http://www.newspapers.com/image/206412998.

2. "An Interview with Lonchar: 'Capital Punishment, it's the easy way out,'" *Atlanta Journal-Constitution* (Atlanta, February 25, 1993), F6.

3. Trace Christenson, "Lonchar: 'I wasted my life.'" *Battle Creek Enquirer* (Battle Creek, February 21, 1993), A1.

4. Eric Norton, "The Effects of Divorce on Children and Families." Columbia Center for Community Health Partnerships, http://www.columbiacchp.org/2009/04/effects-of-divorce-on-chidren-and.html.

5. National Coalition Against Domestic Violence, "Statistics." https://ncadv.org/statistics

6. State of George Supreme Court, "Lonchar v. The State.258 Ga. 447 (1988), 369 S.E.2d 749 45437 State of Georgia Supreme Court Record, dated July 29, 1988," Atlanta, Georgia, *Ravel Law*, 1988. https://www.ravellaw.com/opinions/268f207a0bf52132b2547419842ea337

7. Kerry Hendry, "Execution Planned Wednesday: Time running out for ex-B.C. man convicted of murder." *Battle Creek Enquirer* (Battle Creek, October 12, 1996), A1.

8. Death Penalty Information Center, "Size of Death Row by Year (1968-present)," accessed January 25, 2018, https://deathpenalty-info.org/death-row-inmates-state-and-size-death-row-year#year.

9. Bill Bright, "Would You Like to Know God Personally," Bright Media Foundation and Campus Crusade for Christ (Orlando, Florida, 2014), www.cru.org/us/en/how-to-know-god/would-you-like-to-know-god-personally.html.

10. Laura Mufson, et al., "Overcoming Depression: How Psychologists Help with Depressive Disorders," American Psychological Association (October 2016), accessed January 27, 2018, www.apa.org/helpcenter/depression.aspx.

11. "Facts and Statistics," Anxiety and Depression Association of America, accessed January 27, 2018, https://adaa.org/about-adaa/press-room/facts-statistics.

12. "The Facts," National Network of Depression Centers, accessed January 27, 2018, https://nndc.org/the-facts.

13. *Ibid.*

14. Hank Handegraff, "The Testimony of a Former Skeptic," Institute for Creation Research (April 1, 1990), http://www.icr.org/article/testimony-former-skeptic.

15. Kenneth Ham, "Were You There?" Institute for Creation Research (October 9, 1989), http://www.icr.org/article/670/88/.

16. *Ibid.*

17. *Ibid.*

18. *Ibid.*

19. Hank Handegraff, "The Testimony of a Former Skeptic," Institute for Creation Research (April 1, 1990), http://www.icr.org/article/testimony-former-skeptic.

20. *Ibid.*

21. www.dictionary.com

22. *Ibid.*

23. **Amée LaTour,** "8 Common Causes of Low Self Esteem: Taking Charge of Your Own Worth," Good Choices Good Life, Inc. (2014), www.goodchoicesgoodlife.org/choices-for-young-people/boosting-self-esteem.

24. Charles Swindoll, *Growing Strong in the Seasons of Life* (Portland: Multnomah Press, 1983, 1990; Zondervan, Reissue edition, August 29, 1994), page 380.

25. "Grief and Loss," Beyond Blue, Ltd. (2018), www.beyondblue. org.au/the-facts/grief-and-loss.

26. Lysa TerKeurst, "Why Isn't God Answering My Prayer," Proverbs 31 Ministries devotional (April 20, 2017), https:// proverbs31.org/read/devotions/full-post/2017/04/20/why-isnt-god-answering-my-prayer.

27. David Kessler and Elizabeth Kubler-Ross, "The Five Stages of Grief," adapted from *On Grief and Grieving: Finding the Meaning of Grief Through the Five Stages of Loss* (2014), https://grief.com/the-five-stages-of-grief.

28. *Ibid.*

29. Isaiah 14:12

30. Genesis 4:1–16

31. www.dictionary.com.

32. *Ibid.*

33. Exodus 14:10–29

34. Daniel 6

35. Daniel 4

36. John 11:1–44

37. Matthew 8:23–27, Mark 4:35–41, and Luke 8:22–25

38. Luke 8:26–39

39. 2 Kings 5:1–14

40. Luke 7:1–10

41. John 9:1–12

42. Luke 22:50–51

43. Mary Stevenson, "Footprints in the Sand," Only the Bible website (April 27, 2010), https://onlythebible.com/Poems/Footprints-in-the-Sand-Poem.html.

44. David Masci, "Five Facts about the Death Penalty," Pew Research Center (Washington DC, April 24, 2017), www.pewresearch. org/fact-tank/2017/04/24/5-facts-about-the-death-penalty/.

45. *Ibid.*

46. "How Much Does It Cost to Execute a Death Row Inmate?," Criminal Justice Degree Hub (2015), www.criminaljusticedegreehub.com/how-much-does-it-cost-to-execute-a-death-row-inmate.

47. "What Makes the Texas Death Penalty So Expensive?" Texas Coalition Against the Death Penalty (2010), http://tcadp.org/wp-content/uploads/2010/06/What-makes-the-Texas-death-penalty-so-expensive-print.pdf.

48. "An Interview with Lonchar: 'Capital Punishment, it's the easy way out,'" *The Atlanta Journal-Constitution,* (Atlanta, February 25, 1993), F6.

49. "Facts About the Death Penalty," Death Penalty Information Center (Washington DC), https://deathpenaltyinfo.org/documents/FactSheet.pdf.

50. Pam Levy, "One in 25 Executed in U.S. is Innocent, Study Claims," *Newsweek* (April 28, 2014), http://www.newsweek.com/one-25-executed-us-innocent-study-claims-248889.

51. David Masci, "Five Facts about the Death Penalty," Pew Research Center, (Washington DC, April 24, 2017), www.pewresearch.org/fact-tank/2017/04/24/5-facts-about-the-death-penalty/.

52. Matthew Schmalz, "Is the Death Penalty Un-Christian?," Religion News Service (April 28, 2017), https://religionnews.com/2017/04/28/is-the-death-penalty-un-christian.

53. Max Lucado, *He Chose the Nails* (Nashville: Word Publishing, 2000), p.54.

54. Leslie Sturm, *Mercy Tree* lyrics, www.christianpowerpraise.net/songs/Mercy_Tree__by__Lacey_Sturm.

55. www.dictionary.com.

56. Max Lucado, *Just Like Jesus* (Nashville: Word Publishing, 1998), p. 20.

57. www.dictionary.com.

58. Mark Merrill, "9 Tips for When You Can't Forgive Yourself," Mark Merrill website, www.markmerrill.com/9-tips-for-when-you-cant-forgive-yourself.

59. "Forgiving Yourself," All About God website, Colorado Springs, www.allaboutgod.com/forgiving-yourself.htm.

60. Mark Merrill, "9 Tips for When You Can't Forgive Yourself," Mark Merrill website, www.markmerrill.com/9-tips-for-when-you-cant-forgive-yourself.

61. "Forgiving Yourself," All About God website, Colorado Springs, www.allaboutgod.com/forgiving-yourself.htm.

62. *Ibid.*

63. William Morris, Editor, *The American Heritage Dictionary of the American Language: New College Edition* (Boston: Houghton-Mifflin Company, 1978).

64. www.dictionary.com.

65. Ron Edmondson, "5 Ways to Tell if You Have Forgiven Someone," iDisciple website (2017), www.idisciple.org/post/5-ways-to-tell-if-you-ve-forgiven-someone?rid=9168675.

66. *Ibid.*

67. Associated Press, "Lonchar wants to give kidney to detective," *Battle Creek Enquirer* (Battle Creek, March 15, 1996), 2A.

68. *Ibid.*

69. Organ Procurement and Transplantation Network (January 2018), www.optn.transplant.hrsa.gov.

70. Finger Lakes Donor Recovery Network, Rochester, www.donor-recovery.org/learn/frequently-asked-questions/#q3.

71. *Ibid.*

72. "What Can Be Donated," U.S. Department of Health and Human Services Administration, www.organdonor.gov/about/what.html.

73. *Ibid.*

74. *Ibid.*

75. "Organ Donor Statistics," U.S. Department of Health and Human Services Administration, www.organdonor.gov/statistics-stories/statistics.html.

76. Bill Rankin, "Lonchar again decides he wants to die," *The Atlanta Journal-Constitution* (Atlanta, September 13, 1996).

77. www.dictionary.com.

78. *Ibid.*

79. Shana Shutte, "Why Hope is a Sure Thing," Wisdom Hunters (December 5, 2017), https://www.wisdomhunters.com/why-hope-is-a-sure-thing/.

80. Bill and Gloria Gaither, "The Old Rugged Cross Made the Difference, Lyrics on Demand (1980), www.lyricsondemand.

com/g/gaithervocalbandlyrics/theoldruggedcrossmadethedifferencelyrics.html.

81. Joyce Reba (Dottie) Rambo, "Sheltered in the Arms of God," PeerMusic, Ltd (1969), www.azlyrics.com/lyrics/hillaryscott/shelteredinthearmsofgod.html.

82. L. E. Singer and Don Wyrtzen, "Finally Home" (Capitol CMG Publishing). For lyrics, go to www.digitalsongsandhymns.com/songs/3639.

83. Kim Noblitt and Roger Breland of Truth, "If You Could See Me Now" (2005). To hear the song and see the lyrics, go to www.youtube.com/watch?v=ivM1ytYswNA.

84. Elliott Minor, "Georgia Executes Larry Lonchar" (New York: *The Associated Press*, November 14, 1996).

85. Henry Scott-Holland, *Death is Nothing at All* (London, 1910). Written as part of a sermon, www.familyfriendpoems.com/poem/death-is-nothing-at-all-by-henry-scott-holland.

About the Author

Erin Taylor Daniels is a wife, the mother to two adult children, and the grandmother to a grandson who is her joy. She grew up in the Midwest and taught professionally at a community college. The passion for teaching also led her to teach children's Sunday school classes and many women's Bible studies. The Lord is the first love of her life, and she writes and serves to bring honor and glory to Him.